The Shame of Survival

URSULA MAHLENDORF

The Shame of Survival

Working Through a Nazi Childhood

THE PENNSYLVANIA STATE UNIVERSITY PRESS
UNIVERSITY PARK, PENNSYLVANIA

LIBRARY OF CONGRESS
CATALOGING-IN-PUBLICATION DATA

Mahlendorf, Ursula R.

The shame of survival : working through a Nazi childhood / Ursula Mahlendorf.

p.   cm.

Includes bibliographical references and index.

Summary: "An autobiographical account of the author's childhood and young adulthood
in Nazi Germany, the postwar occupation, and her eventual relocation to the West.
Contributes to current debates on history and memory, and on everyday and women's
history from a feminist, psychoanalytically informed perspective"
—Provided by publisher.

ISBN 978-0-271-03447-8 (cloth : alk. paper)

1. Mahlendorf, Ursula R.—Childhood and youth.

2. World War, 1939–1945—Personal narratives, German.

3. College teachers—California—Santa Barbara—Biography.

I. Title.

D811.5.M25165   2009

943.086092—dc22

[B]

2008034248

The Pennsylvania State University Press is a member of the
Association of American University Presses.

It is the policy of
The Pennsylvania State University Press
to use acid-free paper. This book is printed on Natures Manual, containing
50% post-consumer waste, and meets the minimum requirements of
American National Standard for Information Sciences—
Permanence of Paper for Printed Library Material,
ANSI Z39.48–1992.

Contents

Illustrations

Acknowledgments

Many people have had a role in my writing this book. First and foremost are the generations of undergraduate students I taught over a teaching career spanning more than forty years. They allowed me through their interest to study this period of German history and my own involvement in it. Over almost my entire adulthood, my close friends Jack Carleton, Alice Aspinwall, and Isabelle Greene cajoled me to write down what I had experienced during my first twenty years. The actual writing, however, would never have proceeded beyond the first few pages without the constant and enthusiastic encouragement of my first readers: in Santa Barbara, Muriel Zimmerman and David Sprecher; in San Diego, Gay Parnell; in Washington, D.C., Sharon Alperovitz. Each of them read the manuscript in its several versions and each responded to it in uniquely helpful ways. My "New Directions in Psychoanalysis" long-term writing group, Judith Stein, Sheila Resnik, Peter Shaft, and Michael Bieber, provided commentary and sustaining emotional support. My first three editors, Sara Lippincott, Leonard Tourney, and Kathie Hepler, taught me where I needed to cut and where to add. The manuscript would have lapsed in a last revision if Sandy Thatcher, director of Penn State Press, had not expressed his faith in its importance so unfailingly. Suzanne Wolk, copyeditor for the Press, gave the manuscript its final polish. My brother Hans-Joachim Mahlendorf was always available with a perspective different from mine on the events of our early years and with information on names of persons, streets, and localities. My niece, Annette Mahlendorf, redrew and lettered more clearly the maps of our town that my brother and I constructed. David Sprecher photographed my sculptures, as well as our maps. To all of them I owe thanks.

INTRODUCTION

There is first of all the obligation that we in Germany have—even if no one else any longer assumes it—to keep alive the memory of the suffering of those murdered by German hands, and to keep it alive quite openly and not just in our own minds. These dead justifiably have a claim on a weak anamnestic power of solidarity, which those born later can only practice in the medium of memory which is constantly renewed, often desperate, but at any rate alive and circulating.

—*Jürgen Habermas, "On the Public Use of History"*

Violent action is unclear to most of those who get caught up in it. Experience is fragmentary; cause and effect, why and how, are torn apart. Only sequence exists. First this then that. And afterwards, for those who survive, a lifetime of trying to understand.

—*Salman Rushdie,* Fury

Writing now, in Santa Barbara, California, I can hardly believe that the events and experiences of 1933 to 1952—my formative years and tragic, criminal years for my native country, Germany—took place more than sixty years ago, so vividly do they rise up in my mind. At age sixteen in 1945, I was already aware that my family's history and my experiences needed to be recorded. But it took the long years since then and the encouragement of many friends who know my story to muster the courage to write them down. Not that I feared running into feelings or remembering traumatic experiences that might surprise me. Rather, I was afraid of discovering who I might have become had the Nazi regime lasted.

Mine is a story of growing up in Nazi Germany in a small town of former Silesia, and of being trained in Nazi ideology and its practices. It tells how I experienced this training and how I unlearned Nazi ideology and attempted to undo its impact on my development. It is a story of ordinary lower-class and middle-class people living in an ordinary backwater of the 1930s to mid-1940s. I describe what it was like to grow up under leaders and among a people of whom some committed the crimes of the Holocaust and most stood by and made no attempt to stop the perpetrators. At this late stage of my life it seemed more important to me than ever to write about my childhood and adolescence as a member of the Hitler Youth, and about its aftermath, because so few personal accounts of involvement in Hitler Youth exist. Even fewer seem to understand the implications of such a childhood, or to attempt to formulate the obligations that arise from it.

I took part in the Jungmädel (young girls), the junior branch of the Hitler Jugend (Hitler Youth, or HJ), from age ten to fourteen, as most children in Germany did after it became obligatory in 1939. As an eleven-year-old, I attended yearlong leadership training, and for the last two years of Jungmädel was a squad leader. After graduation from grammar school at age fourteen, I went to a Nazi teachers' seminary for a number of months and belonged to the Bund Deutscher Mädchen (League of German Girls), the Hitler Youth for girls aged fourteen to eighteen. I always knew that I participated in Hitler Youth with greater enthusiasm than my classmates in the fifth to eighth grade. I now understand some of the reasons for this: my father, before he died in 1935, had become a member of the SS. After Father's death, Hitler gradually became an idealized substitute father for me. I championed Hitler's cause all the more as my mother showed her disapproval of my real father and of Hitler's party.

In writing this account I discovered, to my relief and surprise, that by the time I was thirteen or fourteen I had begun a rebellion against the conformity that the Hitler Youth demanded of us, even though I was unaware of what I was doing or feeling. From my first full encounter with the extent of Nazi crimes, revealed during the Nuremberg trials, I had some, if limited, understanding that I had been given the kind of indoctrination and training that could have enabled me to participate in the persecution of the enemies of Nazism. I certainly possessed the youthful enthusiasm and sustained some of the psychological trauma that can be exploited by unscrupulous leaders. And at the end of the war, I was frightened and confused enough to have sought emotional release through violence. But I was too young during the Nazi period to have participated in their crimes.

As a member of the cohort of Germans who spent their entire childhood under the Nazis and who became politically aware of the damage done by Nazism as an adult living abroad, I felt that as a teacher of German literature I had a special obligation to speak to my students about what we Germans had participated in and what happened to us. I had to tell them about the enthusiasms and the beliefs I held then, the disillusionment, anger, grief, shame, and remorse I experienced after German defeat, and the grief, guilt, and shame that haunt me still. During my forty years of university teaching, I searched German literary texts for the relationship between individual conscious and unconscious psychology and political ideology and power. I traced vestiges of everyday fascism in the contemporary world, and I investigated the historical roots of Nazism in German educational institutions and abusive child-rearing practices. I wrote on the psychology of Nazi women informers and on how German writers dealt with and continue to deal with their Nazi past.

From the late 1970s on, feminism provided me with a language to understand issues of class, race, ethnicity, and gender and made me conscious of the gender, ethnicity, and class imprints on my body and my early life. Feminism also confirmed what I knew intimately from personal experience: The personal is the political. Politics under Nazism invaded every sphere of life: every move could acquire political implications for girls and boys as it did for women and men. Both my teaching and my research gave me the larger factual, historical frame into which I could easily place my own experience, all the more so in that, from the age of about eight or nine, I was keenly aware of such political events as the pogrom of Kristallnacht in 1938 or the German army's march into Austria. The actual writing of this account proved to be an entirely new experience, however.

I first thought about writing an account of my Hitler Youth experience in 2001, when I taught a freshman seminar on growing up in Nazi Germany after a long interval of retirement. I was surprised that my undergraduates relied on the Internet for their information about Nazi Germany. Members of the Hitler Youth, both boys and girls, had become clichés, inane caricatures mouthing Nazi slogans, the boys trained in weapon use and the girls prepared to bear numerous offspring for the Führer. My students were not interested in the 1960s memoirs of Hitler Youth that I assigned, Melitta Maschmann's *Account Rendered* (1963) or Hans Peter Richter's *I Was There* (1962). Both accounts were too distanced, too defensive, or too focused on externals to allow my students to empathize with and understand the motivations of their writers. My students could not grasp how young people could be drawn into situations where they remained unaware of anyone except their own kind or unmoved by the suffering of fellow humans.

I thought that it was important for my students to identify with my age cohort, the Hitler Youth generation—boys and girls born between the mid-1920s and mid-1930s. I wanted my students to see this generation as humanly understandable despite spending their formative years under Nazi training, education, and indoctrination. It seemed to me important to show today's students, through an early life history like my own, how the right leaders in an ordinary small town could produce potential perpetrators. I wanted my students to be able to identify with this girl, with her personal situation in her family and her town, with her interests and her emotions, her motivations, her wishes and her goals, so that they would not, with the clarity of perfect hindsight, dismiss who she almost became with a facile "this would never happen to me."

Of that generation, a few were fortunate, either by remote location or by family tradition (Catholic, socialist, communist), to have participated only minimally in Hitler Youth or avoided it altogether. But the majority did participate, and most of us, boys and girls alike, participated with "heart and soul," as we used to say. At one time or other, many of us wanted to become, and some did become, leaders who wished to play a role in the future of our fatherland. While it may be uplifting to study the resisters, it is much more necessary to understand the perpetrators and bystanders, if we want to prevent the repetition of a regime like Hitler's.

Many of my early memories of persons, places, and moods are indelibly inscribed on my mind and body. With Primo Levi, I believe that survivors of traumatic events "are divided into two well-defined groups: those who repress their past *en bloc,* and those whose memory of the offense persists, as though carved in stone." Like him, I feel "as if at that time my mind had gone through a period of exalted perceptivity, during which not a detail was lost." But as I began to write and rewrite, I encountered numerous difficulties with writing a memoir of what I remember about growing up during the Nazi period. Though I vividly recalled my early family, my teachers, and my reading, and clearly remembered the HJ practices and its ideology, I realized that the memoirs of the period, the novels of Nazi childhood like Christa Wolf's *Patterns of Childhood* (1976), and historical research and documentation of Nazi crimes could not help but influence my understanding of my own recollections. Reading often stimulated me to recall forgotten or repressed detail. I tried to use primarily memories of experiences whose emotional impact on me as a child I could recall in clear, sensuous detail, associated with a specific person, environment, or occasion. So as to enliven the narrative, I transposed some episodes into dialogue. The persons, events, sequences, and relationships of this narrative are based on my recollection. Usually a situation would first come to mind in stark and vivid outline. As I wrote, more detail would emerge. In shaping the narrative, much of it had to be eliminated as irrelevant to my primary purpose. In a very few cases, for the sake of teachers or friends still living, I have omitted or altered names. Beyond the personal, and for the benefit of the English-speaking reader, I have provided, sometimes at the beginning of chapters and sometimes in their course, brief sketches of the relevant historical background so as to set my personal experience in the local as well as the wider historical, political, and social context of Germany from the 1920s to the 1950s.

As we have learned from Holocaust studies and memory research, the memories of participants, victims, and bystanders are often unreliable, particularly when the person who remembers has been traumatized or has strong feelings about the subject matter, as I certainly do. Social, educational, experiential background influences not only the perception of an event or person but also its processing into short-term and long-term memory. The potential for unreliability, distortion, and confabulation of embarrassing or incriminating memories is all the greater, and the temptation to hide, deny, or overlook experiences can be expected when social disapproval or shaming by an internal ego-ideal is at work.

Writing this memoir led me to a head-on conflict between memory and history. The same remembered event looked different in light of later historical research and changing perspective and my own later personal or social judgments. Over a lifetime, I have experienced many, sometimes radical, physical, emotional, and intellectual dislocations: from German Silesia to Polish Silesia, to the Federal Republic, to the United States; from enthusiasm for Hitler Youth, to ambivalence, to anger, to rejection, to condemnation, to remorse and shame; from nationalism, militarism, and ethnic phobia to internationalism, pacifism, multiculturalism; from Nazi to feminist, psychoanalytic, and liberal-democratic left-leaning positions. Each act of remembering from a different juncture in my personal life, from a new point of reference, brought different details of the experience into view and reshaped the remembered experience. Each act of remembering lifted previously unimportant or forgotten details from suppression, and revealed suddenly an aspect of the experience the full significance of which I had not appreciated at all. Full understanding came only years later. Often, for those of us who recall a Nazi childhood, the sudden emergence of a forgotten detail may turn a harmless idyll into a suggestive nightmare.

Let me give an example. From April 1944 to January 1945, during my fifteenth year, I attended a teachers' seminary for girls. Into the 1980s I vividly remembered several of my teachers and a few classmates. I knew that this seminary was different from the seminaries my grammar school teachers had attended. One went to those seminaries only after completing the *Abitur* (the high school comprehensive examination), whereas we could attend after grammar school or middle school. We had worn our HJ uniforms there, since we were fourteen years old and therefore belonged to the Bund Deutscher Mädchen (BDM). I did not believe that this membership played a large role in our lives other than continuing the kind of regimentation we had been used to from the Jungmädel (the young girls, ages ten to fourteen). It seemed a rather ordinary wartime boarding school with one extraordinarily good teacher. It was only in the late 1980s that I read that the seminary I attended was a Nazi response to wartime shortages of high school graduates and teachers. These seminaries were intended to train an ideologically reliable cadre of young teachers who could be used to teach the children of ethnic Germans and the Reich's Germans in the eastern territories annexed to the Reich after their conquest by our troops.

This knowledge cast my earlier memories in a different interpretive frame. I then recalled that the director of the school had indeed spoken to us of our mission to teach in the East, but I had failed to understand the import of this mission. With this new knowledge, I came to see the school and its teachers in a political light, and the subjects we studied and the strategies our teachers used took on new and different meanings. My favorite literature teacher's privileging of the humanistic Greco-Roman Western tradition over the Germanic tradition—both of which I remembered being represented in our textbook—cast her in the role of the opposition to the Nazi director, a BDM leader.

My memory, stimulated by the change of perspective, provided additional details about the looks and dress of the two women that begged to be understood politically.

My view and memories of the seminary deepened again in the late 1990s as I studied the opportunities the BDM and Nazi women's organizations provided for females through new leadership and career paths. I began to wonder about my awareness of the personal advantages that leadership and a Nazi career might have offered me. Remembering my burning social ambition, my desire for an education, my handling of the entrance examination to the seminary, I realized how ready I was—even at age fourteen—to use this new opportunity, no matter where it led. I understood for the first time that I had been much more implicated in the Nazi regime than I had known. Many times in my life I have been haunted by the feeling that I, like Kafka's land surveyor in *The Castle*, had been in the castle without knowing it.

The example I give is only one of many in which a seemingly harmless memory took on sinister meaning. The new meaning elicited further forgotten details, demanding a recasting of the experience. In my narrative I have tried to show the girl I was, with all her contradictions. In telling my story, I will sometimes interrupt and comment on what the experience meant to me at different stages of my life. But that girl still lives in me. She is part of my identity.

I started the actual writing of this account in 2004, after a former student of mine died of breast cancer. She had fully understood and promised to carry on my work on the sociopolitics of traumatic experience and its depth psychology. After her death, my research on the political and cultural consequences of child abuse in German-speaking countries bogged down. As a diversion from this complex and arduous academic undertaking, I wrote a few episodes of my early life, and it seemed as if I had opened a floodgate. The mourning for one friend led me to express my grief for the family and friends of my childhood. After that, it was easy to let memories come and to record them for a first draft of the memoir. As I wrote and rewrote, the narrative became increasingly an attempt to understand what I had failed to understand in my earlier teaching about my Hitler Youth experience, German culpability, and the Holocaust. Writing, structuring, and restructuring the narrative became another working through. The first episode that I wrote told of my disillusionment with my HJ leaders, their betrayal, my almost becoming a victim of a

Nazi suicide pact as Germany was defeated, and my survival. Pride at having survived was the first emotion elicited by my early story, and "Survivor" became the title of the first version. While writing a second version that included my family's history, I came to realize that each memory consisted of layers of different understandings of each detail of my experience. Each new and different layer moved me from a superficial knowledge of my part in the HJ to a deeper insight into my implication in Nazism.

These revelations produced in me ever deeper responses of shame. Shame that I had participated enthusiastically, shame that I, an adult liberal of the Left and a feminist, had failed for so long to understand the connection between the career the Nazis offered a girl like me and the institution's purpose, which might have made me into a perpetrator. Shame, finally, that in my pride at having survived the Nazi regime, I had appropriated the term *survivor* from the victims of the Holocaust, the potential perpetrator making herself into a victim as well.

With each new understanding and each new version of the memoir, the title changed: *Survivor; Work of Mourning; Dislocations;* and, finally, *The Shame of Survival: Working Through a Nazi Childhood.* I decided to keep this title to indicate that I feel shame about having survived the victims of the Holocaust whose only crime was that they were not Aryan and German but rather Polish, Roma and Sinti, communist, Jewish, Jehovah's Witness, or anti-Nazi, while I, the potential perpetrator, won the privilege of living. The second part of the title, *Working Through a Nazi Childhood,* is meant to suggest that I understand that this privilege carries an obligation to tell how a perpetrator is made, how she is reeducated, and how, like all workings through, the process remains open ended.

Having been a refugee, having been expelled from my hometown at age sixteen without any possessions, having emigrated as a university student to the United States with only a suitcase, I have no records of my early life, few pictures, and no diaries, journals, local newspaper clippings, or letters. As memories of my early childhood came crowding in—first events and then more and more details, particularly details about the places of my childhood—I found that I could reconstruct the floor plan of the house I lived in until age four, down to the staircases and hallways that I dreaded. I could visualize the streets of the town where I walked on my way to nursery school. I could draw maps of sections of the town we lived in till I was sixteen, including the houses, churches, and public buildings, both before and after their destruction during the last days of the war. My mind held an entire geography of childhood, and, to my surprise, my grief at the loss of the hometown of my early years turned into celebration.

I have included my sketches and outlines of that geography of my neighborhood and my town instead of the few pictures that others, like my brothers, have of the persons and places I grew up with. I have a few photographs of myself—a snapshot of my older brother and me at ages four and three. I also have two passport pictures, at age twelve and sixteen, respectively. But I have no visual record of some of the people who were most important to me as a child. I have therefore included photographs of sculptures through which I later attempted to re-create several of the people I loved and mourned.

As important as it was to me to note our continuous euphoria over the chain of initial German victories in World War II, it was equally important to record the breakdown of our family and the social order, and the degradation of social inhibitions during the last months of the war. I remembered the symptoms of the breakdown without understanding what they signified. At the time, I was confused by what I saw. My only intention was to hold on to what seemed stable to me: my Hitler Youth identity, my favorite teacher, and my goal of becoming a teacher. Writing about that period was wrenching. Through the process of writing, I realized that it took the actual betrayal by my Hitler Youth leaders, our flight from the Russians, my survival of a group suicide attempt, and my understanding of our total defeat to eradicate my belief in Nazi causes. As painful and traumatic as the loss of the war was for me, I understood only by writing that anger and disillusionment had begun to lead me to question myself and to reflect on my actions and convictions; that loss had strengthened me in my resolve to pursue an education.

The end of World War II, the Nuremberg trials, and postwar encounters with several political concentration camp survivors provided me with intellectual insight into the crimes of Nazism and German militarism. Intellectual insight is easy, as I was to learn. Like many Germans, I came to understand the full impact of what my country had done to German and European Jewry, as well as to all the countries it fought, only when I came to live abroad in the 1950s and when I met and became friends with men and women who had lost members of their families or who had themselves been harmed. During my entire life, sometimes on the most trivial occasions, I discovered in myself attitudes, unconscious biases, and emotional reactions that dated back to my Hitler Youth years. These had led a subterranean life, despite my conscious belief in democratic forms of governance and my commitment to account for Nazism and to counter its resurgence.

Having been an adolescent during the Russian occupation and Polish administration, during our eviction from Silesia and resettlement in West Germany, I looked at these experiences as challenges and at some of them even as adventures. Most of the autobiographical records of these experiences by German "victims" of the war, particularly those recorded and collected in the immediate postwar period, strike me as self-pitying and claim an innocence we did not possess—with the notable exception of the diary kept during the Russian invasion by "Anonyma," published in the United States as *A Woman in Berlin* (2005). I never regarded myself as a victim. Yet I rarely if ever spoke about this time of my life even to my friends, fearing that any remark about the Russian invasion and our eviction by the Polish militia might be misconstrued as a cry for sympathy, or as a desire for revenge or a demand for restitution. In their propaganda, the political Right in Germany, as well as some of the refugee organizations of the Federal Republic of Germany, exploited the impulse to seek revenge and compensation more than enough, and I did not want to add to their clamor. I could think of writing about these experiences only after anti-Nazi writers like W. G. Sebald in "Between History and Natural History: On the Literary Description of Total Destruction" (1982) and Günter Grass in *Crabwalk* (2002) had begun to discuss the suppression of the destruction of German cities and of civilian and refugee casualties. I understood and understand the bombings, the hardship of the invasion, and our eviction as the price we all paid for our hubris, for our conquests, for our inhumanity in seeking world domination. And I am glad that today's democratic Germany, for the most part, seems to have profited from the lesson of total defeat. I can recall these events in eastern Germany now because the borders that were set in 1945 are firmly established. Germany and Poland live as equal partners now within the framework of the European Union. The Allies had been right when they decreed at Potsdam that the border conflicts that had led to the war could be resolved only by separating the populations.

In writing about the immediate postwar years, it seemed imperative to put my personal striving for an education into the larger framework of the reeducation efforts of the Allied occupation, particularly the Americans, during the late 1940s, and into the context of the social legislation on behalf of refugees of the new Federal Republic in the early 1950s. These policies and institutional measures gave me and other young Germans opportunities for education, self-development, and careers in a democratic society that we would not have had otherwise. I pursued my quest for an education through the early 1950s, when I emigrated to the United States and found at the university an intellectual home that made my further development possible. This latest working through of my early life, by writing, is but one more foray into a past that is not dead.

Chapter One

MY FAMILY AND THE NAZIS, 1929–1936

SHORTLY BEFORE NOON ON OCTOBER 24, 1929—Black Thursday, the day the New York Stock Exchange crashed—I was born in the German province of Lower Silesia, in the city of Strehlen (now Strzelin, in southwestern Poland), the second child of my parents, Ernst Mahlendorf and his wife, Erna, née Gebel. My brother, Hans-Joachim (we called him Jochen), was a year older. The Mahlendorf family's fortunes, already on shaky ground since the German defeat in the Great War (as World War I was then called), declined precipitously in the last years of the Weimar Republic, in large part because of the worldwide economic crisis. In early 1933, with German businesses failing and more than seven million people unemployed, my family's plumbing installation business went bankrupt.

My father's family had moved to Strehlen from Eberswalde, near Berlin, just before the Great War, hoping to build up their business in eastern Germany, where many small communities were thriving thanks to the nation's increasing industrialization. Strehlen may have been a poor choice: A town of some ten thousand inhabitants about twenty miles south of Breslau (now Wroclaw), the Silesian capital, it was still too poor to sustain such a business. Its population, mostly tradesmen and laborers in the local granite quarries, still lived in houses with no electricity and minimal plumbing—and the war would slow the town's anticipated economic growth. War debt and the ensuing inflation ensured that Germany's economy would remain fragile; in this respect my family shared in the misfortune of many German middle-class citizens, who lost their savings, businesses, and positions and feared losing their prized middle-class standing as well.

As children, Jochen and I played with the inflated German currency our mother had kept, bills that acquainted us with numbers in the billions. How devastating the inflation was can be gleaned from looking at the conversion rate to the U.S. dollar. In 1914, just before the outbreak of war, an American dollar was worth four reichsmarks; by January 1922 the ratio was 1:191; by early 1923 it was 1:18,000; at the height of the inflation, in late 1923, it had become 1:4.2 trillion. Mother told of going on a day's excursion to the Eulengebirge in the Silesian mountains in the summer of 1923 carrying a rucksack full of billion-mark bills. By nightfall, half a rucksack would not buy her even a lemonade.

Moreover, as in any small town, Strehlen's middle class of merchants, shopkeepers, and professionals was slow to accept the Mahlendorf newcomers, who, after all, were competing in a limited market. Grandmother Mahlendorf sought to support her husband's failing business by cooking daily dinners for young professionals in her own home. My parents' marriage in 1927, though it brought the Mahlendorfs a small dowry and ties to an established Silesian family, could only postpone but not prevent the firm's collapse. My mother's family, the Gebels, of farming stock, had lost their investments in national bonds in the war's aftermath, and what savings were left had melted away in the inflation of 1921–23. Their remaining real estate was sold to finance Mother's dowry and ensure an inheritance for her two brothers.

After a short period of economic recovery in the mid-1920s, the crash of 1929 brought renewed losses and unemployment, along with civil unrest between parties of the extreme Left and extreme Right. German families on the political right usually blamed the hardships the German middle class suffered after the Great War, and the failure of the German financial/economic system (until Hitler's policies provided order, work, and prosperity), on the imposition of onerous reparations by the victorious Allies. Curiously, although my family identified with the German National People's Party (the right-wing, anti-democratic party that succeeded the German Conservative Party), the stories I remember hearing about the collapse of our family fortunes during the Weimar Republic stressed personal rather than national, economic, or political factors. According to my mother and her Gebel relatives, it was Mahlendorf extravagance and overreaching ambition that led to the firm's bankruptcy, while the loss of the Gebel fortune had resulted from my Gebel grandfather's illness and lack of business sense. His wife, my grandmother, whom we called Oma, had brought up their three children, and after he fell ill she had run the farm by herself. She and my grandfather eventually sold it and bought war bonds and a fine house in Strehlen with the proceeds; my grandfather died shortly afterward. When the Great War came, Oma's eldest son was drafted and went missing in Russia. With Germany's defeat, the bonds became worthless. Her son returned from Russia and she mortgaged her fine house to help him establish himself in business. His business failed, and she lost all her property except for a small pension and was forced to move into two rooms on Breslauer Street that did not even have electricity.

At the time of my birth, my mother and father, twenty-six and thirty-two, respectively, were living in a three-room apartment in my paternal grandparents' house on Bahnhofstrasse (Railroad Station Street), not far from the town center. My father and his younger brother Willi, both trained as mechanical engineers, worked in the family plumbing business, which Grandfather Mahlendorf ran from a smithy and shop on the ground floor. Mother resented having to help her mother-in-law cook dinner for the paying guests. My grandmother in turn, though she adored my brother as the family heir, found fault with Mother's every move, particularly her pregnancy so soon after Jochen's birth. My father absented himself as often as he could on business trips. As money got tighter and tighter in the deepening Depression, Mother got out of the house by going to work as a seamstress with Aunt Lene, her cousin and best friend.

I don't know how old I was when Mother told me that she had tried to abort me, devastated by her mother-in-law's disapproval and insistence that the family did not have the money to support another child so soon after the first one. But it seems to me that she repeated the story several times, and I always asked for it with the same impulse that makes you touch an aching tooth with your tongue, hoping that this time it will not hurt. I understood from the first that she had felt shamed by her in-laws, but only after puberty did I fully comprehend the sexual implications of that shame. For a woman to feel sexual desire was shameful. "I jumped from the table to lose the fetus," she told me. "I tried to loosen it by running, by bouncing up and down and by going for long bike rides; I swallowed quinine, but nothing helped—you would not leave." The memory typifies my conflicted relationship to my mother, an ambivalence that fueled my later rebellion against her, my wish to become as different from her as I could.

When I asked anxiously whether she loved me now, she assured me that "of course, after you were born I loved you just as much as I loved Jochen." Nevertheless, in all my relations with her during childhood and adolescence, I never forgot that I was the baby who was not wanted, who could not be aborted. When I was angry with her, I would say to myself in obstinate triumph, "I wouldn't leave. Serves you right!" When I felt neglected or overlooked, I would think, "I don't exist. I am the aborted baby."

The birth, a breech birth, was difficult; Mother was at home, alone, and assisted only by a midwife, who managed to save me from being strangled by the umbilical cord. Father returned from a business trip a day later and was immediately disappointed at the birth of a girl—or so Mother insisted, angry at his failure to come home sooner.

"You were big, and had no difficulty in taking my milk, like Jochen did," Mother would later tell me. "You were an easy baby—no colic or rashes. Jochen spent a lot of time with Grandmother Mahlendorf. She fed him soy milk and didn't think I took enough care of his rashes." Mother and I clung to each other for the first year of my life because Grandmother rejected us both. This closeness gave me a resilience I have come to count on.

Another story of hers concerned a game the adults played with me in those early days: I was apparently a very serious baby, and whenever family members or friends leaned over my crib to look at me, they would say, "Ulla, laugh a little." At that, my face would wrinkle up and I'd begin to cry, while the adults laughed uproariously. Many child-rearing practices I grew up with dated to eighteenth- and nineteenth-century theories about infants and children, and the adults of my childhood strike me in retrospect as singularly lacking in empathy. Adults and their affairs mattered, children did not; they were incidental. Adults claimed the choicest bits of food at table; children received the leftovers. Jochen and I hated the visits from our aunts. At the coffee hour, when the doughnuts we craved were served, we were not allowed to help ourselves until the aunts had finished. One particularly stout aunt could be counted on to polish off all the doughnuts. On one visit, as she reached for the last one, Jochen snatched it up and compounded his malfeasance by exclaiming, "No, you won't get *that!*" I don't remember the rest, but the incident became a family joke.

My brother and I drifted through the big house and were taken care of now by this, now by that adult. Jochen attached himself to Grandmother Mahlendorf and Aunt Lene; I sought shelter with Oma, my maternal grandmother, when she was around, and with several of the Mahlendorf servants when she was not. Like all children of households where the adults cannot give them enough attention, Jochen and I fought constantly, both verbally and physically. I gave as good as I got. But when other children attacked one of us, we made a common front. I stopped fighting with him—physically, at least—when I was eight, having realized that he had the upper hand in strength, but his claim that Papa Ernst (as we called our father) loved him best because he was a boy, and that I could never be as good as he was because I was only a girl, provoked me to intellectual competition.

I have clear visual memories of the house on Bahnhofstrasse. What I remember chiefly is an anxious dread of the dark stairway and the dim hallway that led to our rooms, past the stained-glass doors to my grandparents' part of the house. Once I'm in our kitchen, the feeling gets lighter. What happens there is familiar: Mother bathing me in a tub on the table, wrapping me in the white bath towel with pale green and red stripes. Or I am in my crib by the window in the bedroom, looking through the bars, ill, hot, and uncomfortable. The rooms in my grandparents' part of the house are bigger than ours and so is the furniture, particularly the kitchen table, with its wide shelf underneath for large copper pots, my place for hiding from the adults. The adjoining dining room has an even bigger table, for the paying dinner guests, with a gleaming white tablecloth. I know I am not welcome there. I am too loud, I cry too much, I fight with Jochen.

A different story was told to me in my late teens by Lotte T., one of the young professionals at Grandmother Mahlendorf's dinner table, later my leader in the Hitler Youth, and still later, in the first years after the war, my tutor in mathematics and English. When I told her that as a child I had felt unaccepted by the family, she contradicted me. "You were very much part of that family," she said. "You and your brother always played with us in the dining room. Once when I said that I had no family, you, age three, eyes large with worry, broke into our conversation with 'No family? No grandma? No grandpa? No Mama? No Papa? No Oma? No Jochen? Nobody at all? Nobody at all?' We all laughed, and you were 'Nobody at All' [*Kein nuscht und kein garnuscht*] from then on!" Of these early days, however, I remember spaces and moods far more clearly than people (except Jochen). Grandmother Mahlendorf is there as a forbidding, scolding presence in a white apron, more sensed than seen; Grandfather Mahlendorf, taciturn, distant, looms high above us. My mother and father don't appear at all in these very early memories.

Almost all the remembered scenes in the house are about my being in trouble. Jochen and I play with Father's old trains up in the attic. We aren't allowed to, because we might break the locomotive, but I find the set and so we do. When this is discovered, I am sent to our apartment because I have been bad. There is my brother's birthday: We have a party in the big dining room, and a small round side table is covered with presents. I envy Jochen the big red ball he gets; it's huge and shiny. I get a bar of chocolate. Furiously jealous, I hit Jochen over the head with it. He bawls, and I am sent away to our apartment.

Another scene is of Santa Claus's arrival in Grandmother's kitchen. We are three and four. We stand before him; he towers over us in red coat and long white beard. He has a knapsack; from its bottom dangle a pair of socks and tennis shoes. That is the bad child he is taking away, we don't know where — somewhere terrible, to a land where birds peck out your eyes. He booms, "Have you been good? Can you sing 'O Tannenbaum' for me?" "Yes," we say, and sing for him. I feel Jochen's hand trembling in mine. "It's not Santa Claus, it's Uncle Bruno," I shout, having recognized his voice, and I run up to the man in red and white and pull off his cotton beard. Then, frightened, I dive under the kitchen table. The memory stops there.

These brief scenes are fragments arising from the matrix of uneasiness and apprehension that was my early childhood. It seemed to me that almost anything could make adults angry. I wanted to please, but I never did. I was happier outside the house. There was a big unpaved dirt side yard, a sandbox, and space to run around; interesting machinery and trucks for Grandfather's business were parked in back. I still sense myself in my small, compact body. How sturdy it felt, playing in the sandbox with the neighbor kids. But I liked best being in town, out on the streets. I'm told that I started running away almost as soon as I could walk. The big iron gate that separated the yard from the street often stood open, because trucks and horse-drawn carts had to get to my grandfather's smithy. The gate gave onto tree-lined Bahnhofstrasse, with its tall, late nineteenth-century apartment houses. A block away was the railroad station; in the other direction, Bahnhofstrasse ended at the intersection of Münsterberger and Nimpscher streets. You could take a shortcut to Münsterberger Street through Kleine Bahnhof Strasse (Little Railroad Station Street), but you had to be careful not to walk on the left side of the street, because the greengrocer's St. Bernard might come out and bark at you, and you never knew — he might bite. The right side of Kleine Bahnhof Strasse bordered on a park where there were benches, a lawn, and a round flowerbed.

Jochen and me at ages four and three

The St. Bernard would not cross the street, so you were safe on the right side. The store window of the greengrocer's shone with bananas, pineapples, and oranges, and bins with apples overflowed out onto the sidewalk. If Papa Ernst or Oma came along, it was safe to stare through the glass at the costly fruit within. Papa Ernst would sometimes go in to buy fruit, and the grocer might even give me a mandarin orange. At the corner of Münsterberger and Bahnhofstrasse and right next to the park was a three-story house where Aunt Lene lived. The family visited her often because Mother worked with her, and every time we went there, her disapproving eyes, her pursed mouth, a cutting word, would make me spill my cocoa.

In the early 1930s the struggles between the political Right (Nazis and German Nationals) and Left (socialists and communists) spread from the larger cities into our small town. One fall day in 1932, Uncle Willi and I, about age three, were approaching Aunt Lene's house when we saw, in front of the pub on Münsterberger Street, a crowd of quarry workers. Down Nimpscher Street toward Münsterberger marched a troop of Nazi SA (Sturm Abteilung) men in their mustard-colored uniforms. Shots were exchanged, and Uncle Willi pulled me into Aunt Lene's entryway. It still seems to me that I hear the whistle of bullets. Here, in front of that house, across from the pub, was my introduction to political violence. The quarry workers, who were communists and socialists, fought the Stahlhelm (Steel Helmets, a group still loyal to the Kaiser) or the Nazi Party in the streets and at rallies. Before 1933 both my father and Uncle Willi belonged to the Stahlhelm, but I don't know whether they ever participated in any of the brawls. I do know that they voted for the Nazi Party from the early 1930s on; like other members of the impoverished German middle class, they feared a communist takeover and a loss of social status.

I know that they sang in the church choir, too, because on some Sunday mornings I was allowed to sit up in the choir gallery of St. Michael's Reformed Lutheran Church. Grandfather Mahlendorf, though, was apolitical; being an atheist, he never went to church, and on Sundays he would go for walks in the woods. Sometimes, as I got older, he would take me along. "Listen to the trees' sermon," he admonished when I chattered too much. Stores with large display windows beckoned on Münsterberger Street on the way to the center of town, but I remember only the bakery and confectioners, the tropical fruit store, the ice-cream parlor in the arcade at the corner of City Hall Square, and the large toy store on the square with an electric train in the window at Christmastime. Imposing baroque merchant houses lined City Hall Square, testifying to the town's past as a trading post when Silesia was part of the Austro-Hungarian Empire and Strehlen was an important stop on the route from Breslau to Prague and to Krakow in Polish Upper Silesia.

Crossing City Hall Square with Papa Ernst always made me proud, because the policeman at the corner would lift his cap to greet him. If Jochen and I were alone, on the way to nursery school, we liked to cross the full width of the square, past City Hall, with the tallest tower in town, to Grosse Kirchstrasse (Great Church Street). We anxiously tried to avoid the policeman on these occasions, because Papa Ernst had said that we should never cross the busy and dangerous square but instead walk along its west and south sides to reach Grosse Kirchstrasse, from which, down a block, you entered the alley leading to the Protestant nursery school. Right across from the alley loomed the great church itself—St. Michael's, covered in ivy, a late Gothic church that dated back to the time before the Reformation but now was properly Lutheran.

The town population was mostly Protestant but had a substantial Catholic minority—along with a tiny Jewish minority of about 0.8 percent (the Silesian average), most of whom belonged to the middle class. Protestant children like Jochen and me considered the Catholic neighborhoods—their church, convent, and hospital on the south side of town—off limits. Despite the Nazi school reform in 1937, when I was seven, which abolished denominational schools and prided itself on bringing together children of different religions and classes, I never had Catholic friends, nor did I know any Catholic families. Prejudice toward Catholics was firmly rooted among us Protestants. As far as we were concerned, Catholics were lower class, dishonest, lazy, and dirty. I would change my mind about Catholics when we were thrown together during the last days of World War II and during the postwar Russian occupation, finding them to be much the same as my coreligionists—and often more communicative and compassionate.

I thrived at nursery school. There were two classrooms and a big chestnut-shaded yard with a huge sandbox and a covered deck for rainy days. Each classroom housed a different group of children and had its own teacher. We attended Monday through Friday from nine in the morning till four in the afternoon and Saturdays from nine to noon. I started when I was hardly toilet trained, at about age two, when Mother began working in Aunt Lene's dressmaking business to make ends meet.

Jochen hated nursery school, and when he was sick or refused to go, I went by myself. In the mornings I felt fine about this since it was light, but during the winter months it was dark when school let out at four. Parents waited at the school's gate on the alley, but nobody came for me unless Oma was able to do so. Through the alley and along Grosse Kirchstrasse to City Hall Square, I stuck, mostly unnoticed, to a group of adults and children who were walking my way. From then on, I was on my own. I don't remember ever talking to anyone on these homeward walks, but I admired some of the other children from afar—Gretl, who was popular with everybody, and Bertl, whose cropped blond woolly hair surrounded her face like a halo. My friends were the Riedel boys—Peter, a year older than I, and Manfred, who was my age and my favorite sandbox playmate. Their parents owned a locksmith business and knew my parents. The boys came to school by themselves, too, but they lived just around the corner, in the opposite direction.

Aunt Martha, a deaconess at St. Michael's and a tall, bony woman, was the head teacher. Aunt Magda, older and comfortably corpulent, had charge of the younger children. Both women were unmarried and belonged to a Protestant order; they lived in a convent on Mill Street. We called them Sister Martha and Sister Magda when we were older, but for us little kids they were Aunt Martha and Aunt Magda. Aunt Magda loved to laugh, hugged us frequently, and read stories to us—most of them New Testament tales about the Christ child and others about children so good I despaired of even trying to be like them. I loved being read to; we would sit on the floor in a circle around Aunt Magda, who was enthroned on a majestic wooden chair. I liked it even better when she helped us weave colored strips of construction paper or fold sheets of the stuff into birds, ships, and planes. Real airplanes were still a rarity then, and when one flew across the bit of sky visible from the play yard we'd rush outside to watch it. I can still feel the glow of pride when I finished making a paper plane myself and showed it off with an "I made this!" The satisfaction of producing a tangible object has stayed with me, and I still feel it as strongly now after completing a sculpture as I did at age four making a paper airplane.

In the winter and spring of 1933, the vague unease I had sensed at home turned into definite unhappiness and a series of domestic catastrophes. Mother cried often, the adults' expressions were set and hard, and no one paid attention to my brother and me. In quick succession Grandmother Mahlendorf died of a blood clot that lodged in her brain, my grandfather's firm finally went under, and the family sold most of the furniture. There was a forlorn, anxious, ominous feeling about coming home from nursery school to an empty house, with all the doors open. I would call, no answer; I would look through darkening rooms, but no one was there.

I later learned from my mother that of all the family troubles of those years, Grandmother Mahlendorf's sudden death hit her hardest. She felt profoundly guilty about having hated her so much. Father now joined the ranks of the many unemployed in town, and for the noon meal we went to the public soup kitchen and brought home potato soup in milk cans. I went there several times with Oma, who had taken Grandmother Mahlendorf's place in the family. The adults quarreled about going to the soup kitchen. Father did not want us to go there or eat the meals, because he found it humiliating. Oma was a realist and knew that children had to be fed.

At Oma's two-room apartment on Breslauer Street, about five blocks from our house on Bahnhofstrasse, I was welcome. I loved going there and staying overnight, even though the apartment house she lived in was gloomy and smelly and its residents were so poor that they had no electricity. At night, you went to bed with a candle, and that was scary, because I was frightened of fire. I would not fall asleep until Oma blew out the candle, and even then I lay awake, afraid that it hadn't really been extinguished. And yet I felt safer with her snoring loudly in the bed next to mine than I did anywhere else.

My fear of fire started just about that time. Did it reflect the adults' distress? Did I first experience it when our Christmas tree caught fire? Whenever I saw an open flame, be it ever so small, panic would seize me. I would feel a bolt of lightning tear through my bowels, pain shoot through my chest. I would double over, almost paralyzed; all I could do was scream. The weeks before Christmas were purgatory for me, because open candles were everywhere— on the advent wreath at nursery school, in store and apartment windows, and finally on Christmas trees. I loved the smell of the Christmas greens and the wax candles—but I hated the flames. Torchlight parades went through town throughout 1933, celebrating Hitler's rise to the German chancellorship, his birthday, and his continuing political victories. All the windows in town were illuminated with candles. Again and again, marchers bearing torches paraded through the streets, singing and shouting. If I knew ahead of time that there was going to be a march, I could hide, and I did.

Everyone soon became sick of my histrionics, and Sister Martha attempted to cure me of the panic by what now would be called behavior modification. Every day I was made to come closer to the iron stove at the nursery. Every step closer to the stove earned me a candy. At one step away from the stove, Aunt Magda took my hand, opened the grate with her other hand and helped me stay in place looking at the flames. Next, without her help, I had to look into the flames for one second. I was "cured" when I could stare into the fire without trembling while Sister Martha counted to ten. That's how I learned to count to ten—and to control my body. I still felt the fear, but I knew enough not to show it—I did not want to risk losing the candy.

To cure the fear itself, I took matters into my own hands—literally. Big wooden matches with orange tips were kept in a drawer next to our kitchen stove. Matches were off limits; we were not even to open the drawer. I got a handful of them and slid on my belly under the large sofa in Papa Ernst's office. I struck one of them on the floor, held it between index finger and thumb, and blew it out when my fingers began to feel the heat. I had just lit a second one when I heard Oma's shout, felt my legs jerked so violently that I landed at her feet, match in hand, singeing my fingers. In her terror, she struck me; later, she apologized for hitting me and said that I was better off being afraid of fire than playing with it. My fire phobia would be extinguished altogether a few years later, by fear of the war.

Of the adults in this early period of my life, I remember my own parents the least. Most of the memories come from stories told to me by Mother and various relatives, and these stories paint Papa and Mama as people without much thought of anything but having fun. As young parents during the late 1920s to mid-1930s, both of them attempted to avoid their ever-worsening personal situation and responsibilities by singing, dancing, acting in amateur theatricals, partying with their friends, and playing skat, a card game something like bridge. They both had good reasons for indulging in the high life. My father had been ill with kidney disease since the age of twelve (which kept him out of World War I). He must have known that he would die young, and live to the fullest he did. Mother lost her own father when she was twelve; she had been his favorite child and she never forgave him for dying. She escaped anger and grief in frenetic activity, retaining the attitude of an adolescent till her death at eighty-four.

She was fun to be with, in an adolescent way; she loved to dress up and sing in her lively soprano. I must have been four or five when our nursery school went to a performance of a play staged (as most of these amateur productions were) at the Imperial Eagle Hotel. Suddenly Mama emerged from a side door at stage right. At first I didn't recognize her. She was dressed in a little black maid's dress with white ruffled apron and she danced across the stage with a broom. Then she stopped midstage, leaned on a table, and began to sing:

> Die Zigeuner sind lustig,
> Die Zigeuner sind froh.
> Sie verkaufen ihre Betten
> Und schlafen auf Stroh.
>
> Gypsies are merry,
> Gypsies are carefree.
> They sell their beds
> And sleep on straw.

How beautiful she was, with her petite figure, short red-brown hair, and shining emerald eyes, and how lightly and gracefully she moved! This was and was not my mother. I envied this elegant stranger, could never be as beautiful as she was. The gypsy song still typifies one side of her for me. Yet there was another side! She had a fearful temper and if provoked, one glance of her icy green eyes and her threatening silence would slice right through me. She preferred, however, to rule us children by manipulation, such as promises that she might or might not keep. She read voraciously, and not only light fare. When at age sixty-three she visited me in the United States, she learned to read English when she had finished the German books in our university library. A year later she tackled Henry James's *Golden Bowl* and read it with understanding.

Father could take up any instrument and play it; he loved to accompany folk singing on the accordion or the piano. He lived for his clubs—the musical groups (a men's choir of twelve, a mixed choir, the church choir), the Freemasons, and the Stahlhelm. A born storyteller and jokester, he was the life of every party. He and Mother had met through the church choir and soon belonged to the same skat circle.

In 1932, just before his mother's death and the other family disasters, my father—together with other members of the Stahlhelm—became a member of the Nazi Party. He was offered membership in the SA, the Storm Troopers, but disliking and ridiculing the SA uniforms ("shit-colored," in popular parlance) and the members' lower-class standing, my father, with his friend Bruno and his brother Willi, applied to join the SS, the Schutzstaffel (Protective Squadron), instead. In town, the SS were considered an elite middle-class group, and their black uniforms appealed to his sense of elegance. Though he was neither athletic nor tall enough to meet the ss requirement of five feet nine inches, he was accepted. The unthinking and class-ridden mindset of my father and his friends might have been less disastrous had they not lived in the Weimar Republic, a fledgling democracy that needed a thoughtful electorate committed to democratic processes, political responsibility, and social justice. All through my childhood I was proud of Father's having been an early member of the party and not like the opportunists who joined in droves after Hitler's takeover in 1933.

I do not know how actively my father participated in ss activities (apart from the torchlight parading and attendance at meetings) or even how much of its racist ideology he shared. Nor, for that matter, do I remember ever seeing him in the coveted black ss uniform. At any rate, the participation of all three men was short: Bruno died in a car accident in 1934; Father was bedridden on and off with kidney disease from 1934 on and died after a kidney operation in September 1935; and Uncle Willi, unable to find suitable work as an engineer in Germany, emigrated to Kenya just before Father's death.

When I discovered—at age seventeen, during the Nuremberg trials—what role the ss had played in the establishment and running of the concentration camps and the German police state, I began questioning my mother about my father's membership in the ss and his knowledge of its function. As usual during such questioning on my part, her answers remained general and evasive. She asserted that in 1933–34 neither of them knew much of anything about the organization's function but that my father began to feel uneasy about the town troop: "Er war immer weniger mit ihren Aktionen einverstanden" (He agreed less and less with their actions). Over the years Jochen and I would continue to question her about what they knew, in those early days, about their involvement in Nazism. It was always awkward: I was bothered by what I thought were evasions, but fearing her punitive silences I did not press her. She told us little except that by 1934 Father no longer went to the ss meetings because of his illness, that he disapproved of the town troop's "political" activities, and that he probably would have resigned from the troop had he lived. She saw herself as apolitical during those years and never joined the Nazi Party or any of its women's groups. Being the sole breadwinner for three small children after her husband's death, she said, she had neither the time nor the energy to do so.

Jochen and I agreed, late in life, that we were glad that Father had died when he did. But even then we did not dare speak of what we dreaded—particularly after we had read the historian Christopher Browning's *Ordinary Men* (1992). What shocked us was the culpability of the Reserve Police Battalion 101 on the eastern front in the early 1940s. These family men, nonparty members—ordinary men—shot thousands of Jewish women, children, and old people at close range, whom they had first forced to dig the ditches into which they would fall. Battalion members were given the option not to participate; they were not forced to kill. Yet they did, for days on end. They were not "a few bad apples." There were more than a hundred such battalions, thousands of such men. Might our father have become one of them?

The revelations during the Nuremberg trials of the incarceration and gassing of millions of Germany's Jewish citizens, the "reprisals" against the populations of countries occupied during the war, the torture and shooting of those the Nazis defined as alien, degenerate, not "Aryan," did not entirely come as a surprise to me. I despised the adults who claimed they had known nothing about what was happening. Even though I did not understand their greater significance at the time, I could remember "incidents" in town, from at least 1936 on (my first year in grade school) that should certainly have told an adult the score: the deportation of communist quarry workers; Kristallnacht and the temporary incarceration of prominent Jewish townsmen in Buchenwald concentration camp; boycotts, closings, and expropriation of Jewish stores; the disappearance of the town's Jewish citizens, including our dentist, my brother's friends, and one of my classmates. During the war I overheard a customer of Mother's remark that our troops shot innocent villagers by the score in German-occupied Poland if partisans in the neighborhood had attacked them. From my early teens on, I heard adults speak of neighbors reporting neighbors, friends betraying each other, Germans profiting from the expropriation of the wealth of Jewish fellow citizens—yet whenever I learned, as an adult, of one or another specific crime, I felt revulsion, horror, guilt, and dread. Dread because I was never sure that, had I been older, or had the regime lasted longer than it did, I might not have betrayed a friend, reported a neighbor, killed when ordered to kill.

I have often thought that I saw much of what adults refused to see because, as a child, I felt no responsibility for these events. The refusal of Oskar, Günter Grass's protagonist in *The Tin Drum,* to grow older than three during the Nazi period made immediate sense to me when I first read the book. Oskar's clear-eyed perspective, which takes in what the adults will not see, was for me more than a literary device. It was a perspective possible for members of my generation, the Hitler Youth generation that experienced Nazism as children and young teenagers. We did not feel responsible then, but now we feel the weight of responsibility for what we saw and lived through. Many of us swore to ourselves as young adults that we would oppose racism and fascism wherever we encountered them. Many of us are haunted by the specter of what we might have done had we been adults. With experience abroad, increasing age, and growing emotional understanding of the incurable pain, heartbreak, and damage our countrymen inflicted, my mourning over this, our history, has grown stronger and stronger. No amount of conscious knowledge that you cannot be responsible for what you experience as a child, no attempt at dismantling this guilt, erases the shame and the grief.

Late in 1934 my family sold the big house on Bahnhofstrasse and we moved to the Baronie, a large apartment building across town. I arrived at the Baronie for the first time after nursery school let out. My way home from nursery school would now be much shorter, just down to the end of Grosse Kirchstrasse at the corner of Promenade Street. On that first day, Manfred Riedel, my sandbox friend, and I walked together the short distance to the Imperial Eagle Hotel, as his family lived down where Promenade Street ended at Woiselwitz Street. Our new apartment house looked imposing to me, three stories high, with a second-story balcony, arched windows, and a tower in back with its peak rising above the roofline.

Hesitantly I entered through a huge double-winged door into an expansive hallway with three red-tiled steps leading up to a landing. A wide staircase to the right went up to the second floor, while the hall led back to what I had been told was the door of our apartment, on the right under the staircase. Arriving at the door, I looked to the left, where three wide steps led down to the landlord's kitchen, its door open to the hallway. I banged on our apartment door and tried to open it, and a kindly voice came from the kitchen.

"You must be Ulla," a large, gray-haired woman in a white smock said, inspecting me with friendly brown eyes. "Your family went back to your old apartment for a bit. Why don't you wait here until they return?" I stepped down into the kitchen, feeling shy and awkward. A girl my age was sitting

Eisenberg's

Baronie

The Baronie from memory, drawing by author

there: brown braids, brown eyes, a square face, a pretty, dark red dress. "This is Elli," the white-smocked woman said. "Her family lives up on the third floor. And I am Frau Gurn."

This kitchen, where the children of the Baronie gathered, would become my place of comfort when no one was at home, when Mother was busy, or when I felt unwanted there. For the next ten years the Baronie, its gardens, stables, barns and sheds, and its hospitable landlords, the Gurns, offered us children security, a stable living community, and a large playground and fascinating gardens to explore. Looking back, this semirural, idyllic setting and its people provided an almost nineteenth-century counterworld of ordinary comfort and peace to the unstable twentieth-century Nazi world. Into this space of safety, Father's and Oma's deaths, Mother's struggles to feed us, and my preoccupation with Hitler Youth came to intrude more and more.

Herr Gurn, a taciturn Great War invalid whose right leg up to the thigh had been amputated, dominated the first floor of the Baronie with the thump of his ill-fitting wooden prosthesis, its leather knee joint with its steel fittings creaking and clanging as he inched along. A tall, gaunt man, his face drawn by pain lines, he kept his distance from the tenants. Occasionally, when we children were all too rambunctious, he called us to order with a stern voice. He ran the beer and lemonade bottling plant and its distribution business from the shed attached to the Baronie. He did not object when his wife rewarded us with his lemonade if we helped her cut beans or shell peas for canning.

Frau Gurn, with a ready smile and a comfortable demeanor, took care of maintaining good relations with the tenants of the apartment house. She was a superb storyteller and delighted in ghost stories, like the one about the headless prisoner in the basement, and loved to tell them in a hoarse whisper, so that the hairs on the back of my neck rose. The apartment house was built on the foundations of what had been the local baron's castle (hence its name). The foundations and the rusted iron bars of a prison enclosure were still visible in parts of the basement. There was even a windowless subbasement, so deep underground that during the war we would use it as an air-raid shelter. Its darkest corner sported a walled-off archway. In Frau Gurn's tales, a secret passage ran from that archway all the way up to Rummelsberg Castle in the woods five miles from town. Through this passage the baron had escaped from the Prussian troops of Frederick the Great to the Austrian side, which held Rummelsberg Castle during the Silesian wars of the eighteenth century. In other versions of the tale, the baron escaped by jumping from the Baronie tower, which reached two whole stories above the roof. Its three lower stories, once ammunition-storage and gunnery rooms, now served as kitchens for three of the building's apartments. The tower room on the fourth floor, right under the roof, had been converted into a guest room, with its large windows opening to all four quarters of the compass. All through my childhood I daydreamed about this room becoming mine when I grew up, when the war ended, when. . . . The tower's peaked top story served as a dovecote, and when we climbed up there to help Frau Gurn catch some doves for a noodle soup, the view took my breath away.

At any rate, the baron jumped to escape the Prussians, sometimes from the second, sometimes from the third, sometimes from the fourth floor of the tower. He always broke an ankle or a leg, and he always escaped the Prussians in spite of it. After my brother Jochen broke his arm and was taken screaming to the doctor, I remember wondering how much it had hurt the baron to run on a broken leg all the way to the Rummelsberg, five miles away.

I wonder now why Frau Gurn presented the baron's escape from the Prussians as admirable and gloried in his tricking them by using the secret passage or jumping from the tower. After all, at the time even we children had absorbed enough German Nationalist indoctrination to favor the Prussians over the Austrians. Yet here we all were, cheering the baron, identifying with his pain, delighted that he had escaped our side! All through my childhood, the Silesian wars of the eighteenth century between Frederick the Great and Maria Theresa of Austria, which ended with Silesia becoming Prussian, fascinated me—partly because of Frau Gurn's stories but also because the house we lived in had made this history into an almost contemporary event. I needed only to go into the cellar and see the iron bars of the former dungeon, and the arch to the secret passage, to enter that history.

Next to the Gurns' garden, behind a row of mock orange bushes, Frau Gurn had set up a white wooden bench, some wooden folding chairs, and a table. In this arbor she shelled peas, cut up beans or cucumbers, and cleaned strawberries, currants, and gooseberries for canning. She invited us to help, and we were happy to do so, as we could eat as much of the fruit as we wanted. Even better was the reward of lemonade on hot July and August evenings. But best of all were her stories. While winter stories in her kitchen—when we picked feathers for featherbeds—were about ghosts, wars, and giants, her summer stories were about her own adventures, almost being swept away by a spring flood in the mountains or fleeing with her husband from their village in Polish Upper Silesia after the Great War in a hail of bullets. Her descriptions of the suddenly rising floodwaters of mountain creeks dominated my nightmares for years, yet I would not have stayed away for anything from those summer evenings, when the honeyed fragrance of the linden trees on Promenade Street drifted over to us as dusk turned to night.

More children lived down the street and came to play with us, as we had lots of space to jump rope and play hide-and-seek, hopscotch, and catch. A large, unpaved, sandy front yard, where Herr Gurn parked his beer trucks, separated the Baronie from Promenade Street. This avenue, paved with local granite blocks and planted with a wide canopy of linden trees, was part of the old town wall and good for spinning tops. Across the street towered a four-story brick school we called "Red School"—a Catholic primary school and the first of three adjacent schools, each with a large, chestnut-lined schoolyard that fronted on Promenade Street. After school hours, these schoolyards served as an immense playground for the children of the neighborhood. The farthest school was Stone School, the Protestant primary school, with a small triangular park that separated the schoolyard from Promenade Street. At its farthest extension, Promenade Street itself became a park that still contained sections of the old town wall.

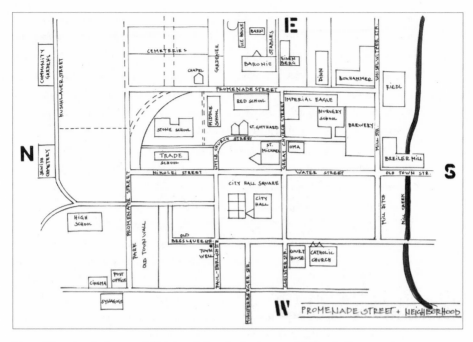

Map of Promenade Street neighborhood, drawing by Annette Mahlendorf

To the left of the Baronie was a stonemason's stone yard and house. To its right were the Gurn gardens, a plant nursery, and the house of the town's undertaker and nurseryman. To the right of the undertaker's house, a small fieldstone chapel served three adjoining cemeteries. The Baronie had a large backyard, with stables for horses, several barns, an icehouse, a sandpit, a flower garden, a vegetable garden, and an orchard. A stone wall separated all this from the fields of the farmers on Woiselwitz Street. We children were free to roam through the yards, the gardens, and the cemeteries. The huge horse chestnut trees in the schoolyards and cemeteries provided us with maybugs in spring and chestnuts in fall. We collected the maybugs and kept them in cigar boxes filled with leaves, with air holes punched through the lids. Frau Gurn bought some from us to feed to the chickens, and a ragman gave us some pennies for sacks of chestnuts. I saved my pennies and used them at the semiannual fairs on City Hall Square, where you could see Siamese twins in the peepshows, buy sweets, and ride the carousel.

After we had moved to the Baronie, going to nursery school became much easier. The Riedel boys waited for me at the Imperial Eagle and we'd run together. Jochen was in first grade now, at Stone School, down the street from the Baronie. He was beginning to read, and I envied him for this. I tried, mostly in vain, to get him to read to me. Because I wanted to read so badly, I began to hang on to any printed material I could find. As I was coming home one afternoon from nursery school, a man handed me a magazine, which I took eagerly and pressed close to my chest. A big boy came running up and reached for my magazine and tried to wrest it away. I held on and howled. I would not let go. Oma came running toward me as the boy tore most of the magazine out of my hands and ran off. Only part of the cover was left. I clung to Oma crying, not understanding the meaning of her angry mutterings about giving political propaganda to kindergarteners.

One of my favorite places was the railroad station, where you could watch the trains come and go. On some evenings Father would take Jochen and me up to the Nimpscher Street bridge to watch the red and green lights twinkling along the railroad tracks below and the distant gas lanterns illuminating the platforms. Walking home through the darkness, we imagined traveling to Breslau and even on to Berlin. In late 1934 Uncle Willi took a room in a house right next to the station, thus providing me with another reason for my peregrinations up to the bridge and then down to the station. Unlike the other adults in the family, Willi had played with us and paid us a lot of attention ever since I could remember. He taught me how to swim in the municipal pool and took us sledding on the Marienberg course. Together on a sled with him, we'd fly down the "big kids' course," and the town bullies would stand aside. He could be counted on to bring us little presents when he traveled. I particularly treasured a matchbox car, which I always kept in my skirt pocket.

One day in 1935, when I rang his doorbell, there was no answer. Since nobody was home, I watched the trains from his front yard. I came back the next day and the next. No one was home. Finally his landlady answered his bell from an upstairs window. "Go away! Hasn't anyone told you that your uncle moved away?"

I clutched my matchbox car. "No, he didn't!" He would have told us, I thought. She must be wrong. But the window upstairs closed and that was the end of it. I found out a few years later that Uncle Willi had sold all his and Grandfather Mahlendorf's remaining assets to buy himself a ticket for Kenya and had left town without telling anyone. I felt his desertion more directly and painfully than I would my father's death, a few months later.

For a brief period after the move to the Baronie, life returned to normal. Father found work with the city administration, and every morning he left wearing a suit and carrying a briefcase. But during the winter of 1934–35 he fell ill and stayed in bed for days. Before Jochen and I were put into our cots, we crawled under the covers with him and he told us stories. We wanted to tell him stories, too, and out-shouted each other trying to get him to listen. "My story! Me, me!" He would point to the alarm clock. "Ulla, wait, let me have five minutes of silence," he would say. I would look at the clock for what seemed ages and then begin my story again. "No, you must watch the big hand. When it moves from where it is now to the ten, that will be five minutes." I would watch the big hand, and it would not move at all for what seemed an eternity. I would begin again. "I'll give you a penny if you can be quiet till the big hand is on ten!" he would say. But I never could.

That summer he went back to work. Grandfather Mahlendorf, who had left to work in a copper smithy in Neisse, visited for the strawberry season. As we walked to the community garden where Grandfather had planted strawberries a few years back, we joked with Father about Mother's big belly.

"Why is she so fat?" Father would tease.

"She ate too many strawberries!" Jochen and I would shout in unison.

Shortly after Grandfather had returned to Neisse, I woke up in the middle of the night as Father carried me to his office from the bedroom we shared with our parents and put me down on the sofa, where Jochen was already curled up. I whispered to him, "What's going on?" but fell asleep before I heard his answer. At daybreak I woke to hear a baby cry and rushed to the bedroom door, where Father was standing. He picked me up. "You have a baby brother," he announced.

"What's his name?" Jochen asked, coming up behind me.

"You children can help us choose one," Father answered. We spent the next few days talking about names for the baby. I don't remember which name our parents favored, but Jochen and I wanted him named Werner, after the baker's son on City Hall Square, whom we both admired because his father gave us an *Amerikaner,* a large cookie with black and white icing, every time we went shopping for bread.

Jochen and I had no idea how ill Father was, because he had gone back to work and our apartment was filled with his voice, his laughter, his piano and accordion playing, his friends. Mother chided him about taking it easy and keeping to the diet the family physician had prescribed. On the days when he felt better, he went out to the pub in the Imperial Eagle for a beer and devilled eggs, both of which his doctor had forbidden. When he came home from these expeditions, they would quarrel. He would laugh at her worrying and take either Jochen or me for a walk and an ice cream at the Marienberg, a hilltop café in the park at the south end of town. One day, after I came home from kindergarten, Father was gone. Mother explained, "Doctor Brücke sent him to Landeck spa. He'll have to keep to his diet there and he'll gain strength for his kidney operation."

"Is he going to be very sick again?" I asked anxiously.

"He is going to be well again, after the operation," she said.

On his return from the spa, Mother, Jochen, and I met him at the railroad station and took him home by way of Promenade Street through the park, jumping around him, glad that he was back with us. He was laughing and happy, telling us of the friends he had made while he was away. I don't remember when he went into the hospital to have the diseased kidney removed. The operation was successful, but three days later uremia set in. The remaining kidney failed to take over the function of the removed kidney; it too was diseased. Nor do I remember when we were told that he had died. I have only a vague recollection of Mother coming home from a visit to the hospital wearing a hat with a black veil. "I didn't believe he would die," Mother told me much later. "He was so alive. He loved life."

I don't remember much of the funeral except that huge, impressive, uniformed ss men carried his coffin. And I clearly remember the party afterward. Coffee and cakes were served on the dining room table, extended by several leaves for the occasion and covered with Mother's damask linen. I could not understand why some of the guests seemed so ordinary and so cheerful, even laughing occasionally, while Mother and Oma were serious and sometimes crying. When our aunts and uncles left, they promised us they would visit soon. The following Christmas Eve they overwhelmed us with presents, but we never saw any of them again. For weeks Jochen and I held funerals, for dolls, for any dead animal we could find. Jochen was the preacher who gave the sermon; I was the relatives who lamented and wept. "Your father has gone to heaven," our Sunday school teacher said, but none of the adults in the family ever talked to us about his death. I overheard them say that we did not understand what had happened. Their concern seemed chiefly directed at Jochen. "A boy needs his father," they said. "A father is not as important for a girl."

Father's death left Mother unprepared, without material resources or provisions for herself and us children, such as an insurance payment or a pension. Grandfather Mahlendorf was in Neisse, Uncle Willi in Kenya. Only Oma and

Mother's bachelor brother, Kurt, were left to help. Oma moved in with us, taking over our care and sharing her pension with us. Uncle Kurt brought us potatoes, bread, all kinds of produce, and eggs from the farm he managed for a widow some ten miles from town. Mother took a course in dressmaking, got the needed trade-union certification, and opened up a dressmaking business in our living room. She also rented out Father's office in the apartment on a part-time basis, first to the local ss troop and shortly after to a local hunters' organization. Since their secretary held office hours for only two days a week, Mother was allowed to keep her piano in the room, and a sofa for taking naps on the other five days of the week.

I kept up my walks to the station to watch the trains. By now Hitler had outlawed opposing political parties, and one day in 1936 or 1937—I was in first or second grade—I found a number of my classmates and their mothers thronging a small park next to the station and pressing up against the fence that separated the park from the station platforms. They were quarry families whose fathers were communists. They were desperately poor and dirty; the quarry children had lice, and they were rough. Fräulein Schäfer, my grade-school teacher, had mocked Herta, a pale, timid quarry kid in my class, when she didn't bring a dime for the school excursion. "Your father had enough money to get drunk on Saturday," she said, and Herta's head sank down on the desk, her face flushed with shame.

Keeping my distance, I moved closer to the fence, until I could see that the mothers and children were watching a freight train being loaded. Policemen were pushing men into the wagons. The women wept and screamed at the policemen. The children stared, ashen faced, and the babies in strollers screamed with their mothers. No one would tell me what was going on. I was terrified and ran off, forgetting that my father was dead, glad that I had not seen him among the men being loaded into the wagons. I rushed home and told Mother what I had seen, but, busy with a customer, she paid no attention. The terror stayed with me for days. I don't recall who told me that these men were troublemakers and communists, that they had been taken to a camp to learn not to cause trouble, and that they would eventually come back. After that, no one ever talked about the deportation. A few of the fathers of my classmates, including Herta's, did return a few years later, only to be sent to the front after the war broke out in 1939. The station now became for me a dangerous place where terrible things could happen. I stopped going there, my curiosity about trains and travel gone for good.

Chapter Two

A SMALL QUARRY TOWN, 1936–1938

SO AS TO BETTER UNDERSTAND THE CHANGES that Hitler's assumption of power brought to everyday life in Germany, let us backtrack to the political and civil order that preceded his regime—the ill-fated Weimar Republic (1919–33)—and look briefly at the events that brought him to power. From early in my life, teachers as well as members of my family spoke about the changes from Weimar to Hitler—politics dominated family get-togethers—and I came to see them through their eyes. While my grandparents' generation looked back with undisguised yearning to the days of the Kaiser, my teachers and parents welcomed the transformation the Nazis wrought from a democratic civil order to authoritarian rule. It was largely accomplished by the time I had any awareness of the society outside my immediate family, yet I remember my family's and teachers' reactions to several events and sometimes my own perplexity or fear about what I did not understand.

From its very beginning, after Germany's defeat in World War I, the Weimar citizenry—at least those from the political center to the Right, like my family—believed in the so-called *Dolchstosslegende,* "the stab in the back" administered to the German army by the home front—that is, by communists, socialists, and Jews. New and untested in democratic process, the Weimar Republic was thus burdened by unpopularity as well as by the massive war debt.

It was a presidential parliamentary democracy much like that of England or France. Its *Reichspräsident* was a figurehead and was charged with appointing

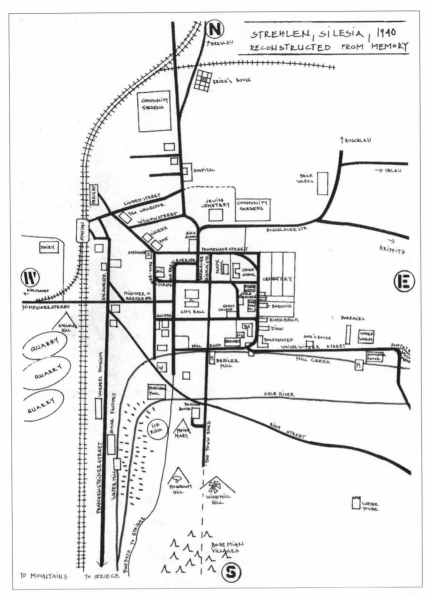

Strehlen map, reconstructed from memory by Ursula and Jochen Mahlendorf, drawing by Annette Mahlendorf

as chancellor the leader of a party (or coalition) that could muster a two-thirds majority in national elections for the Reichstag (parliament). The chancellor headed the executive branch of government, consisting of a largely conservative civil service that administered the judiciary and the public school system as well as the entire civil administration of the state, from the foreign service down to local town and village administrations. The president did have one potentially disastrous power—the right to invoke an emergency law in political situations that threatened the republic. This power was bestowed by the infamous article 48 of the Weimar constitution, by which the president could suspend the constitution temporarily. The republic's first president, Friedrich Ebert, a Social Democrat, held the office from 1919 to 1925 and used this power only to stabilize the democracy. But the potential for abuse of the presidential prerogatives increased when the widely trusted general Paul von Hindenburg—a member of the Prussian rural nobility still loyal to the former emperor—was elected president in 1925. Though he was in his eighties and in ill health by 1932, the political Right ran him again for the presidency and he was reelected. He played a fatal role in the failure of the republic.

In the economic and political crises that accompanied the Great Depression, Hindenburg repeatedly suspended the constitution and made the civil service and the army directly responsible not to the constitution but to him, as president of the Reich. In effect, from 1930 on Hindenburg governed by emergency law. When he died in 1934, Hitler, who had been appointed chancellor in 1933 and had consolidated his power within a year, became head of state. From then until 1945, the army, all ministries, and their public employees (including all our local officials, our local police, our teachers, and, most damaging to the judiciary, all judges) took their oath of office directly from Hitler. The presidential power, exercised through article 48, put an end to all democratic governance at both the national and the local levels.

Another factor leading to the failure of the Weimar Republic was simply the great number of contending political parties. Its governing coalitions became increasingly unstable. Hitler's Nazi Party remained a fringe party through most of the Weimar period, until the massive unemployment resulting from the Depression drove most of the working class to the Communist Party, on the fringe Left. Rising anger over tax increases, salary cuts for the large civil service, business bankruptcies, and farming failures moved the lower middle class and middle class from the conservative center into Hitler's party, or at least far to the Right. The political clashes between Right and Left, of which my hometown saw quite a few, the street fighting between their paramilitary groups in urban centers, led these disaffected citizens, fearful of a communist takeover, to call for a "strong man" to enforce order. As a consequence, Hitler's party increased its seats in the Reichstag from a mere dozen out of 491 seats in 1928 to 107 out of 577 only two years later, and to 230 seats out of 608 in July 1932. My parents, their friends, and at least half the people in our town rejoiced when Hindenburg appointed Hitler chancellor in January 1933 in the expectation that he and the Nazis would bring order and stability.

Thus Hitler came to power by presidential appointment. At least twice between 1931 and 1933 Hitler had been offered a role in democratic governance in a coalition of right-wing parties. It was during another political crisis, in January 1933, that Hindenburg called on Hitler to assume the chancellorship. Because of the burning of the Reichstag in February 1933—perpetrated by the Nazis and attributed by them to a communist—Hindenburg once again invoked article 48 "for the protection of the people and the state." This suspension of the constitution and its bill of rights gave Hitler the cover to complete his takeover, to outlaw the parties of the Left, shut down their presses, and arrest many communist and socialist leaders, including their local representatives.

The elections of March 1933, despite ss and sa intimidation, did not give the Nazis a majority, but they formed a coalition with the German Nationalists, giving them 51 percent of the seats in the Reichstag, which confirmed Hitler as chancellor for four years. With the "Enabling Law" the Reichstag gave Hitler the right to make and apply laws without the consent of Parliament, thus giving him dictatorial powers. In our town in the March election, the Nazis won 50 percent of the vote and from then on dominated our lives.

By July 1933 all other political parties had been dissolved "voluntarily" or outlawed. When Hindenburg died in August 1934, Hitler abolished the title and office of *Reichspräsident* and replaced it with the title and office of *Führer und Reichskanzler*. All through the Nazi years, the fiction of legality was maintained through ever more restrictive administrative statutes and regulations.

The Nazi takeover and Hitler's consolidation of political power after January 1933 affected our town profoundly. Since the Nazi Party held a small majority in our town from March 1933 on, Nazification came quickly. From 1933 to 1935, local, regional, and provincial administrators belonging to parties other than the Nazi Party—even those of the political Right—were dismissed in the *Gleichschaltung* (the consolidation, under the Nazi banner, of all trade and professional organizations, conservative parties, and social institutions) and replaced by Nazi Party members. These new officials operated under the principles of Nazi leadership—that is, without either local elections or citizen advice or consent. During the Weimar period our town had had an elected town council, on which two of Father's friends represented the growing Nazi Party. Social Democrats and even a few communists had served the interests of the town's blue-collar workers. With the banning of socialists and communists, these councilors lost their mandate, their parties disappeared from local elections, and the town council was dissolved. From 1933 to 1937, communists and socialists and their leaders were sent to so-called reeducation camps.

The entire civil service, including the schools and the courts, was integrated into Nazi professional and civil-servant organizations. Formerly apolitical trade and professional institutions became Nazi organizations, with Nazis appointed as leaders. All of my grammar school teachers belonged to the National Socialist teacher organization.

The local economy picked up with Hitler's autobahn project and other building programs. Unemployment in our town disappeared quickly. The local quarries reemployed the quarry workers of the Great Depression and the building industry began to revive, as unemployed trades- and workmen found work constructing new four- to six-family apartment houses out on Frankensteiner Street close to the quarries, and as a housing settlement of small two-family houses went up out on Breslauer Street. All through my early school years, as I wandered the outskirts of town with classmates, we scampered through the building sites of apartment buildings and small one- and two-family houses. I envied my cousin, whose father, newly employed by the town administration, bought one of these for his family.

Strict censorship replaced freedom of the press. The town's daily newspaper even "absorbed" a local conservative, anti-Semitic weekly and presented a unified front as dictated from Berlin by the newly created Ministry of Public Enlightenment and Propaganda. The expulsion of Jews and political opponents in cultural, academic, and professional circles met with no organized or public opposition from us. Only an end to imports of "luxury foods"—butter, coffee, cocoa, and tropical fruits—in 1936, in order to finance the production of weapons, created a popular stir. "Cannons instead of butter!" the minister of propaganda, Joseph Goebbels, proclaimed. Oma and Mother grumbled about the lack of butter and coffee, and we children missed the oranges and sweets.

The obligatory two-year military service established in 1936 and the compulsory six-month Arbeitsdienst (Labor Service) emptied the town of young male civilians. To accommodate the increase in all forms of national service, the academic program of the nation's high schools was shortened by a year. Because of the Nazis' anti-intellectual and antifeminist stance, university enrollments were cut, and those for women were reduced by two-thirds from their Weimar levels. In 1936 the Hitler Youth for boys ages ten to eighteen was given official status as an educational institution, and in 1939 it became compulsory for boys and girls alike. As a result of these measures, our town—like many towns all over Germany—was overrun with uniformed soldiers and Arbeitsdienst members on leave and with uniformed Hitler Youth marching in the streets.

At the Nuremberg party rally of September 1933, Hitler had announced sterilization laws aimed at persons afflicted with or institutionalized for hereditary illnesses, which included not only all severe physical malformations but also mental illnesses, epilepsy, and "feeblemindedness," and even criminality and vagrancy. Several institutionalized children of family friends were sterilized as a result of these measures—or killed following the euthanasia measures of the 1930s. At age six or seven, I was horrified and frightened when the adults did not protest that the exotically beautiful, nubile daughter of Mother's friend Else, said to be Mongoloid, disappeared to a "special institution for such people" and shortly thereafter "died of pneumonia." "She had no judgment. She was beginning to throw herself at Papa's journeymen. How could we control her at home?" Else had complained to Mother. The colorfully dressed gypsies of my earliest childhood, who had camped on the outskirts of town in their dark green wagons, disappeared—into concentration camps, as I found out much later.

At the 1935 Nuremberg rally, Hitler announced the Nuremberg laws directed against German Jews, banning marriage between Jews and so-called Aryans, criminalizing extramarital relationships with Jews, and forbidding the employment of Aryan women under age forty-five in Jewish households—a measure that forced the town's Jewish minority to dismiss its domestic help. Jewish stores in town were boycotted. The names of public places and streets were changed from those honoring Weimar politicians, Jewish writers, and Jewish Nobel Prize winners to those of Nazi functionaries. Strehlen's Lindenstrasse became Adolf Hitlerstrasse. Paul Ehrlichstrasse—named after the town's only famous son (1854–1915), a Nobel laureate in medicine and a member of Strehlen's Jewish minority—became Horst Wesselstrasse, after the Nazi thug murdered by communists in Berlin in 1930.

The town, including my family, cheered the 1935 return of the Saarland to Germany after a plebiscite. Though fearful of the risk of war, we also celebrated the German troops' reclamation of the industries of the Ruhr and the Rhineland. Indoctrination by family and school was such that even as an eight-year-old I believed in the betrayal of our soldiers at the front by the communists at home—the *Dolchstosslegende* that was said to have brought about Germany's defeat and the emperor's abdication. I learned early that democracy meant chaos and unemployment, while Hitler and his party had brought order, work, and prosperity—even while Mother spoke of the good times she had had during the Weimar days.

Just before he died, Papa had bought a radio for the family. He put up a triangular board at shoulder height in a corner of the living room, close to the kitchen door. All through my childhood this simple receiver provided us with news and music, and allowed us to participate in national celebrations. A photograph of the Führer framed in black strips of wood hung to its left. His harsh, gravelly voice, with its rolling *rrr*s, cutting rasp, and clipped syllables, still sounds in my ears. Even more insistently I hear the thousands of voices crying out rhythmically, "Sieg Heil, Sieg Heil," in a frenzy over the Olympics, over the return of the Saarland, over the Rhineland and Sudetenland invasions. Seas of flags appeared at windows all along Grosse Kirchstrasse, City Hall Square, and the entire center of town when, in the spring of 1938, Hitler annexed Austria and the Sudeten, the German-settled parts of the former Czechoslovakia. Over our three-station living room radio, I listened to the applauding crowds and thrilled to the announcement of Hitler's seizure of what we considered German territories by right. I was intoxicated by the jubilation of the "freed populations," by the adulation of the crowds at party rallies. Via the radio, I became an avid consumer of Nazi propaganda.

On the whole, however, the political victory of Nazism benefited my family very little. It is likely that my father had obtained his position in county administration in late 1934 because he was a party member. But because of his illness his term was brief. My family's connections with the party and the ss disappeared after his death in September 1935. Mother did not seek any relationship with the party and managed our family at a level of genteel poverty, with the assistance of Oma and Uncle Kurt.

This was my town and its political climate as I started primary school after Easter 1936, still wearing mourning for Father's death six months earlier. I had not wanted to leave kindergarten; I missed its comforting friendliness. The first grade struck me as huge and confusing. I knew none of the children. Mother came with me on my first day. We went along Promenade Street, past Red School and the lycée, now a middle school, my mother had attended, to Stone School, a huge, forbidding granite building that looked like a castle. Mother left after Fräulein Schäfer, the teacher, entered the classroom ("I have a customer at ten and I must get back to work"). A number of other mothers stood along the wall of the classroom, holding on to the *Schultüte*, a brightly colored cornucopia filled with candies that many well-off children received as a reward after their first day of school. Several children giggled. "Quiet!" Fräulein Schäfer commanded. "Come up front. I'll teach you to pay attention!" With that she administered several strokes of her cane on the outstretched palm of a boy who hadn't stopped giggling fast enough to suit her.

Many of the girls in class wore dresses that were not as nice as mine. I shrank from my bench mate, whose uncombed hair meant, I thought, that she had lice. She and a number of other children were dirty, their faces unwashed, their hands grimy. I soon learned that these were quarry children. When school let out, waiting parents were there to take photographs of their first-graders. On my way home, glad to be free again, I followed Manfred, whom I had not noticed earlier on the other side of the classroom. We ran along the low walls of the schools to get home, balancing and jumping up and down. His mother walked on the sidewalk beside us, holding a large *Schultüte*. When we parted, Frau Riedel reached into it and handed me a fistful of candy.

I felt ambivalent about the quarry children. The quarry families lived in barracks at the edges of town. Family lore depicted them as rowdies, as children of communists and criminals. I feared their rough talk and their even rougher play at recess. The bigger kids pushed us small first- and second-graders around. One of the bullies tripped me so that I fell down the stairs and broke my arm. Since I was wearing black after my father's death, they teased me: "Hey, you, you don't have a father."

How did they know? "I sure do!" I shot back. "I do, too! But you don't!" The joke on them and me, of course, was that many of them had lost their fathers, too—not to death but to prison or deportation.

Like the other middle-class children in my class, I avoided them, yet when Fräulein Schäfer harassed the quarry kids and the other children giggled, I felt uneasy and ashamed—about what, I did not know. As Mother's dressmaking business barely kept us above water, not having money for school excursions was a reality for me, too. With my one black dress soon soiled and tattered,

I felt poor, just like the quarry children. Oma had to buy my shoes—sturdy shoes without frills or bows like the black lacquered shoes I wanted. On one occasion a poorly dressed woman was sitting next to us in the store, trying on shoes. We overheard her decide against a pair of fine shoes as too expensive. "How much money can you afford to spend?" Oma asked her. Finding out that an additional ten marks were all that was required, she gave the woman the necessary sum. I was stuck with the sturdy shoes. "We are fortunate," Oma explained when I complained. "You need to be helpful when you're fortunate."

The following year, 1937, Hitler abolished the old primary school system. Instead of separating children by grade and religious affiliation, which he held to be detrimental to national unity, he created boys' and girls' schools. Nazi indoctrination henceforth would proceed along gender lines—military discipline for boys and domestic discipline for girls. For me the change meant a shorter walk—right across the street, to Red School—and it spelled the end of my friendship with Manfred. Now I would be walking home with the girls, with Hanne Knorrek and Rita Boxhammer, who lived in an apartment house at the corner of Promenade and Woiselwitz streets. We kept our distance from the quarry children.

My aunts overflowed with advice and admonishment whenever they visited: "If you don't [obey, help, love] your Mother, you'll end up in the barracks," or "you'll be sent to the orphanage." The quarry families lived in barracks, of course, and by my second year of school I understood the disgrace of living like them all too well. I could not escape knowing that I was not all that different from the quarry kids, and that I had better make friends with them.

And so I did. As we played ball during recess, a big girl joined us. She had flaming red hair, about which the boys often teased her, and her name was Agatha. It surprises me that I still remember her name, as I have forgotten most of the others. It seemed to me a splendid name, like that of an important film star whose pictures we admired in the displays of Krause's Cinema, across from the synagogue (which became the home of the motorized SA after November 1938). Agatha had freckles all over, ran faster than any of us, and always caught the ball in dodgeball. She threw the soft rubber ball so fiercely that it knocked you to the ground even if you caught it. I admired Agatha from a distance, and after I had been sneaking around her for a few weeks, she adopted me—that is, she allowed me to tag along after her. Her family lived in the barracks at the end of Woiselwitz Street. As we walked there one afternoon, I pointed to a villa in an overgrown flower garden on Woiselwitz Street. "Mama lived there when she was little," I bragged. "No, she didn't. I don't believe it!" Agatha snorted. Mother's family had indeed owned that house in the 1920s, but I did not want to contradict the magnificent Agatha.

The barracks at the end of Woiselwitz Street were bordered by a weed-infested meadow, the municipal waterworks, and the "River" Ohle, a creek that became a torrent every spring and fall and flooded the neighborhood, including the barracks. Right across from the barracks sat the redbrick town slaughterhouse, a ghoulish building from whose high, iron-barred windows came the cries of frightened cows and pigs. Dirty children with runny noses played on the crumbling asphalt that surrounded the barracks. Agatha had me wait outside while she went in to get a ball for us to play catch with. Close up, the barracks were not that bad, I decided. The long wooden one-story structure was covered with tarpaper; the windows, patched in a few places with plywood, were large, and some had lace curtains, like ours; there were four doors on each side of the building, leading to eight one-room flats. I never went inside, but after I started playing with Agatha, the barracks lost their threat. The orphanage never did.

I do not know which of my friends set me up—was it Agatha or one of the boys who lived in the Woiselwitz barracks? At any rate, they taught me a rhyme and dared me to sing it aloud in our front yard. One day, riding around in Oma's little wagon, pushing myself with one foot and steering in a circle, I sang out what I had been taught, over and over again: "Lulu das Negerweib reisst sich die Haare aus dem Unterleib" (Lulu the blackamoor tears out the hair of her pussy). Passersby stared at me, and the more outraged they looked, the louder I sang. I particularly remember the scandalized scowl on the face of the teacher who lived upstairs. No one stopped me until Oma summoned me inside from the bedroom window. "Just don't sing that song again, Ulla," she said sternly and rather sadly. "The kids taught you something you don't yet understand." A few years later, when I understood the sexual connotations of the song, I was fearfully embarrassed whenever I said hello to the teacher from upstairs. The racial slur did not occur to me until the 1960s.

The quarries were ever present. The high-pitched quarry siren called workers four times a day, at 7:00 in the morning to begin work, at noon for lunch break, at 1:00 for the end of lunch break, at 6:00 for evening break. A higher-pitched siren sounded at 4:00 in the afternoon, warning of the explosions as blocks of granite for the next day's work were dynamited off the rock face. The entire town could regulate its day by the sirens and the four o'clock explosions.

The town's streets were safe to play on, since cars and trucks were a rarity. Only right after 6:00 P.M., when columns of quarry workers raced home on their bikes along Grosse Kirchstrasse and took a right turn onto Promenade Street and a left at Woiselwitz Street did we scurry to the sidewalks, watching until they had passed. On Saturdays the quarries let out at noon, but you could not predict when the bikers would come. Some rode by right away; others dawdled by later, having gone to the pubs on Münsterberger or Breslauer streets. On some evenings we would see a whole troop of bikers coming down Grosse Kirchstrasse, bawling a song I recognized years later as the Internationale. Their bikes swayed from side to side as they made the right turn onto Promenade Street. On winter evenings when the roadway was iced over, some skidded and fell on top of each other, much to the delight of us children.

My first-grade bench mate Helga's father worked in the quarries. Helga lived behind a pub on Breslauer Street, in the courtyard of what decades before must have been a farmyard and its outbuildings. The stables and barns had been converted into small apartments and were inhabited by workers at the cigar factory and the quarries. We often played catch and jumped rope in the courtyard with the kids who lived there. Their mothers watched from the windows and called to one another across the yard. Once, two of them rushed outdoors screaming. They beat at each other, their arms flailing, until the taller woman got hold of the other's hair and jerked her forward, pulling out a handful. The smaller woman reached up into the other's face and scratched her, shrieking and tearing at her blouse. I stood rooted to the spot, terrified. I had never seen adults fight. Neighbors rushed out to separate them and the two hurled curses at each other, using a vocabulary I was unfamiliar with. I don't remember ever going back into the yard.

One day Agatha took me to pick snowdrops on the mill meadows. Snowdrops were protected flowers, Agatha told me, but the *Polente* (copper), if he caught us, would not punish us as long as we hadn't torn out any of the bulbs — he would only make us throw away the flowers. I was impressed that Agatha called policemen "coppers." I refused to imagine what "punish" could mean.

We passed the barracks and the waterworks and then took a footpath, wet and slippery with puddles from the winter snow, along the creek bed. Weeping willows grew on both sides of the creek, their branches, covered with silky catkins, hanging down into the slow-moving black-green water. Later, when I learned how witches were tested in the Middle Ages, this creek became the water into which they were thrown to find out whether they were telling the truth. I saw the witch in my mind's eye, surrounded by her wide skirts. She floated along, watched over by children, who gazed at her slow, dark progression. Later still, after I discovered Shakespeare, it was Ophelia I watched.

When the path went by the watermill, we hid from the miller's geese, which, if they saw or heard us, would announce our presence with loud hisses and squawks, protecting the mill yard just as the Romans' geese had protected the Forum. The miller, who owned the meadows beyond, did not like our picking snowdrops there. A short distance after the mill, a smaller creek blocked our way. Agatha jumped over it lightly, but my attempt fell short and I slipped down the steep bank into the water, clinging to my basket and the old pair of scissors I needed for the expedition.

Ahead was the meadow, white with flowers. We rushed forward. My wet feet did not matter, because the meadow was partly flooded anyway. The snowdrops grew wild, their stalks strong, their leaves voluptuous, their white bells ample, particularly near the willows on the higher banks of the creek. They were thinner and smaller in the meadow, where they had to contend with leftover patches of snow and repeated flooding. It was easy to fill our baskets, but we had to get home quickly to put the flowers in water so they would not wilt. I began to dread the walk home. How was I going to get across that creek without losing my flowers? Was the miller going to catch us? Were we going to meet a copper? This time I jumped the creek, basket and all. We snuck past the mill and ran triumphantly up the path that led to Woiselwitz Street.

"Stop! What do you have in your baskets?" boomed a voice behind us. I froze. Agatha dashed off and disappeared behind the waterworks. The policeman was on a bike and so did not pursue her but concentrated on me.

"Snowdrops," I answered, with an ease that astonished me. "Please, please, let me keep them. They're for my father. He's sick in the hospital." I cast my eyes down, as if in apology for having done something terrible.

"Run along," he said, "but don't let me catch you again!"

I felt ashamed for having lied to him. All through those years, I was ashamed about my lying and pretending about one thing or another to some adult or other. And the snowdrop lie had been pathetic. The snowdrops were neither for my father nor for his grave; rather, I had planned to give them to Frau Neumann, the owner of the convenience store next to the Boxhammers' smithy, who always gave me licorice whenever I brought her flowers from Oma's garden.

In fall and winter, when school let out at noon, I would dawdle on my circuitous way home. On some afternoons I stopped in at the shoemaker's at the corner of Promenade and Woiselwitz and watched how he stitched a leather seam or soled a shoe. I also liked the Riedels' locksmith shop opposite, where Manfred's father welded iron gates, fences, and locks. Sometimes Manfred talked his father into making us tin soldiers by pouring hot liquid lead into iron forms. But most fascinating was Boxhammers' smithy, at the beginning of Woiselwitz Street. Shuddering, I scanned the open forge with its bellows as Herr Boxhammer took a red-hot horseshoe from the coals with long tongs. While the farmer held up the horse's hoof, Herr Boxhammer, after having dipped the shoe briefly into a bucket of water, pressed it onto the hoof. The stench of singed horn made me gasp. I could not understand why the horse did not mind the burning or the nails.

The greatest pleasure was going to the stationery shop on Grosse Kirchstrasse. The tiny dark-haired lady who tended it watched patiently as I slowly patrolled the shelves, deciding what to spend my dime on. A new copybook? No. A blue diary? Colored paper? Crepe paper? A sheet of paper dolls? I took in the dry, fresh smell of paper in deep breaths and asked the price of this and that. I had earned a penny here, a penny there, doing chores for the neighbors, like carrying the Müllers' dachshund upstairs or fetching milk for Frau Eisenberg, the stonemason's wife, next door. I came to know what the tradespeople working in our neighborhood did and what the shops in town sold and for how much.

In summer after school, the neighborhood kids would play until dusk settled. In one of our games we drew a large circle in the dirt and took turns flinging down our opened pocketknives onto another child's marked-out pie-shaped territory. We called this aggressive exercise "Countries." Its aim was to carve out a part of someone else's country and annex it to yours. The game would end only when one of us owned all the territory. We did not know we were playing a war game that our own country was beginning to wage in earnest, or that our choice of countries reflected the opinions of the adults in our lives. Most of us wanted to be Germany (for me, England or France would do, as I had heard Uncle Willi and Father speak with admiration of English engineering and Mother of French elegance). None of us wanted to be Poland or Russia.

By now Oma and Mother were worried about war. "The last war was bad enough," Oma muttered. "I don't think I can take another one." Frau Gurn, our landlady, was more specific about what war meant. She told of the fighting she had experienced during the Great War in what was now Poland, about Herr Gurn's losing his leg from an exploding grenade, about their flight from Polish Upper Silesia in 1919 after Germany lost the war, when the Upper Silesian mines were ceded to Poland. "And now that they have planes," she added, "they'll bomb us, set our house on fire with firebombs."

I was terrified of the bombs, imagining them to fall like hail. I just wanted the adults to stop talking about war. Then one day I thought of a way out. The Führer would order a big roof to be built over the country, a roof made of steel. Then the fire bombs would just slip off the sides and not burn us. I was affronted by the laughter when I told Mother and Oma my solution to the bombing problem.

Oma, who lived with us now, seemed very old to me—dressed as she always was all in black, in a long cotton skirt, blouse, and apron—but she was only in her early sixties. She was thin and beginning to stoop; her face was brown and wrinkled, her hair white. She lost her temper easily, which was doubtless due to cancer of the liver, of which she would die in 1938. Having to take care of three small children was no easy task, and Oma was most impatient with Jochen. She indulged me because, as she repeatedly said, "Everybody in the family caters to Jochen. Ulla is my girl."

Oma had grown up the daughter of a well-off farming family who took pride in having been free landowners before the freeing of the serfs in 1807. Her mother died in childbirth when Oma was twelve, and Oma and her sisters had to take over the household and raise the younger siblings. Her eldest sister married first and received a large dowry; she, too, died in childbirth the following year, and her young widower asked the next-oldest sister, Ida, to marry him and care for his motherless infant. Oma, the third of the sisters, was glad she was already engaged to her future husband, another farmer, so that she did not qualify as a replacement. She would sometimes tell me of her struggles to run the farm when her husband fell ill. Her family history became part of my own through her stories, and I felt a particular kinship with, and pride in, these hardworking, down-to-earth people.

Oma liked to visit her many relatives in the country, and sometimes I'd go with her. We usually went to the country in the mornings. While Oma talked with Aunt Wally, a gaunt, gray-haired woman who had a farm in Jeline, some eight miles away, and was a widow like Oma, I played in the garden or visited with the farmhands' children. I was fascinated by the rooms the farmworkers lived in—the artificial flowers and the plush pictures of saints in the kitchen, the vivid green and blue paint on the walls. I found it odd that some of the smaller children scratched the painted plaster off the walls and sucked it like candy. I understood later that they must have suffered from calcium deficiency. These families were very poor; their children wore torn and dirty clothes, seldom washed, smelled bad, and had eczema on their hands and faces. They spoke Silesian dialect; one of the girls was lame, probably from an untreated hip condition. Unlike the quarry children, they were not threatening—most probably because I belonged to the owner's house and so enjoyed a kind of protected status.

I admired Aunt Wally's old nineteenth-century two-story house, with its large windows, central hallway, and massive staircase leading up to the second floor. I loved its smell, a pungent aroma of stale bread emanating from the unventilated pantry next to the dining room. One side of the hallway served as a winter garden, where coffee and cake were served in the afternoons to the family and the guests who happened to visit. Nothing could have driven me away from these gatherings. The adults talked of the upcoming harvest, how the wheat was about ready to be cut, what damage the last hail had done, what insurance they had against rain or hailstorms, what crop yielded the best income. After coffee, I would accompany them as they inspected the farmyard and the fields. I learned what crops they planted and how they tested the season's wheat by rubbing the ears of grain between thumb and index finger. Before supper I was allowed to help feed the pigs, always afraid that the fat sow would attack one of her litter, squealing and squiggling to reach the trough. A farmhand would drive Oma and me in a horse-drawn coach to the Grossburg station after supper, through the dusk, kerosene lamps flickering, wheels rumbling over the cobblestones. I nestled against Oma in the gathering darkness and usually had to be wakened once we arrived at the station.

Back in Strehlen, I loved going to the community gardens with Oma, one close to the Jewish cemetery, the other a mile away, through cornfields and past the hospital on the cobblestone Breslauer Street. While she weeded and watered, I tried to help, but I would soon tire of it and go play with the children in the neighboring gardens. I did like helping with the harvesting, picking strawberries, gooseberries, and currants. We also had fruit trees, and she allowed me to harvest the summer apples, because they were within easy reach.

But she picked the Anjou pears herself, placing them carefully in a basket lined with cotton towels. We could eat all the apples and fruit she harvested, but once, when she caught Jochen and me handing the Anjou pears out the bedroom window to the neighbor children, she flew at us like an avenging white-haired angel. The Anjou pears were for her alone.

From spring to fall, she grew flowers. In late spring the dark purple lilacs spread their fragrance; profusions of pink and ruby-red peonies bloomed at Whitsuntide. Bright red gladiolas lined the fence in June. Purple and white dahlias and red-and-white-flecked Sweet Williams dominated in July and August; white, yellow, and rust-colored chrysanthemums lasted till the first snow in late October. When we left the garden in the evening, we would take along a bunch of flowers for the apartment. We put the apples and cabbages that Oma had harvested into her wooden hand wagon; sometimes, when it was late and I was tired, she let me lie down on a sack on top of them and pulled me home, the wagon's steel-rimmed wheels rattling over the cobblestones. I would gaze up at the stars and sing

> Wer hat die schönsten Schäfchen?
> Die hat der goldne Mond,
> Der hinter jenen Bäumen
> Am Himmel oben wohnt.
>
> Who has the finest little sheep?
> It is the moon,
> The golden moon,
> Which lives up in the heavens.

I have never felt as content as when I was being pulled along in Oma's wagon, inhaling the sweet smell of the apples mixed with the astringent fragrance of asters, singing softly, half asleep.

Every Easter in Silesia, children up to the age of ten went *Schmagoostern.* I don't know the origin of this custom or its name (aside from the last two syllables, which denote Easter in the Silesian dialect), but it seems to be a remnant of a pagan fertility rite. We would bend fresh willow branches into the shape of a small carpet beater, bound with colored ribbons. Flowers and branches of fresh greens were woven into the head of the beater. When I tried to make my first *Schmagooster,* the ribbons would not hold the bent branches together. "I can't do it!" I cried. Oma, who had supplied the flowers and helped us gather the willow branches from the bank of Mill Creek, exclaimed, "Well, Mr. Can't died a long time ago, so you'll have to learn to do it yourself." From then on, whenever I protested about not being able to do something, Oma or Mother would invoke the death of Mr. Can't.

Dressed in our Sunday best, we would visit the houses of friends of the family. We started at baker Moses' shop, shook our *Schmagooster* sticks up and down, tapped Aunt Gretl, the baker's sister-in-law, with them and cried, *"Schmagoostern!"* We were allowed to shout this and "beat" the adult until we were given a sweet or a cookie as a kind of ransom. Next we went to Aunt Klara, who lived on Horst Wessel Street. Oma could not get used to the new name and would tell me about Paul Ehrlich—that he had won the Nobel Prize in 1908 for inventing a cure for cancer and that he was Jewish. I didn't understand what that meant. Aunt Klara was our favorite when we went *Schmagoostern*. She always exclaimed, "Don't you look pretty in your new Easter dress!" and had a whole bag of candies ready for us. Next we went to the Preuss sisters, my parents' skat partners, who lived in one of the new apartment houses built for town officials. After 1935 we were told not to bother the Preuss sisters— they were Jewish.

Oma was not particularly religious, but occasionally she would take me along to St. Gotthardt's, a little Romanesque church a block from the Baronie. Watching her during the service, I felt that she wasn't really listening, that she was relaxing. Closing her eyes to think, to feel? When she sang the hymns, tears rolled down her cheeks. Did she know that she was already ill with cancer? I felt comfortable being with her. I loved her, as she held my hand or rested her palm on my head.

On Christmas Eve, all of us except Oma, who always stayed home to cook a special Silesian meal, would go to the early evening Christmas service at St. Michael's. The church, filled with people, sparkled with advent wreaths, and there was always a tall Christmas tree in the nave. Jochen and I would climb up to the choir loft, he to watch the organist and I to watch the entrance of the children's procession, each child bearing a candle and singing, "O come, all ye children, ye men and ye women." (Besides, up in the loft I was safe from all the candles below.) We would walk home through the clear, frosty, starry night, snow crunching under our feet. At home, the kitchen greeted us with the fragrance of *Pfefferkuchen,* dark beer, and sausages, the main ingredients of Oma's special Christmas Eve dinner, but we had to wait for Aunt Lene and her mother to arrive before we could sit down to eat. Aunt Lene, short and stocky with close-set eyes, was Jochen's favorite aunt and my childhood nemesis, in whose disapproving presence I turned into a clumsy oaf. Her sharp "Don't drop that, be careful!" generally had the opposite effect, but I tolerated her on Christmas Eve because she could be counted on to bring me a book as a Christmas present. After the meal, which we ate at the kitchen table, the adults disappeared into the living room. When they called us in with a little bell, we rushed through the door and stopped before reaching the table with the lighted tree. We were not allowed to touch the presents displayed beneath until we had sung "Silent Night."

It was in needlework class, when I was eight, that I first heard that Oma was very ill. I had already made a potholder for her out of white yarn, decorated with a red border. The teacher's sample had looked beautiful to me, but mine, with its uneven loops and crooked rows of dirty dishrag hue, struck me as an object I wanted to hide. Oma had accepted it gladly, however, rewarding me with a rare hug and promising to use it daily. My new project was to be an onion net for her. She always complained that onions stored in the cupboard sprouted and rotted, and that she had wanted to buy a net to hang them up so that the air could keep them dry. Fräulein Schäfer readily agreed that an onion net was a good idea. I worked on it feverishly and was almost finished when Oma went to the hospital. When I visited her before the operation, I told her I would have a wonderful present for her when she came home. For several days after the operation I was told she was too ill for me to see her. One day I went anyway and stood outside the door to her room until the nurses shooed me away. The next morning, Jochen and I were standing by our bedroom window looking out at the front yard. As Mother approached, once again dressed in a black hat and veil, Jochen said, "She is crying. Oma must have died."

"No! You can't see through the veil if she is crying!" I exclaimed. The realization came only slowly that Oma was dead, that I had lost her, that we would never again go to the gardens, that she would never bring me home again at night while the steel-rimmed wheels of her wagon rattled over the cobblestones. I don't remember the funeral, but even as I write this, I am crying.

Oma was a gruff person by the time she moved in with us—sometimes impatient with her young grandchildren. For all that, I loved her more than anyone then. She never complained. She was not bitter—sad and depressed, yes, but not beaten down by her misfortunes. When I asked how she had died, Mother said, "She was tired. She knew she was dying, but she said she didn't

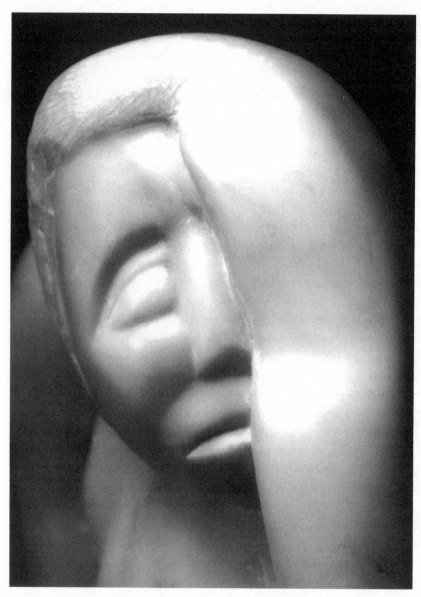

Oma, marble sculpture, 1985, by author

mind. But she would have liked to see you grown up." Only as an adult would I fully realize how strong and resilient her love and nurturing had made me—how much of a model of self-reliance she had been.

Slowly I realized how much I had lost with Oma's death. Since I could not go with her to the community gardens, I was at a loss about what to do after school. Mother enrolled me in an after-school program for preteens run by the Nazi Party that met in barracks at the western edge of town, next to a sports field. I felt totally lost there, as I did not know any of the children. I resented the "shit-brown" uniform we had to wear. I never got to know the unfriendly women who ran the program, and I was not at all interested in their structured games, inane coloring books, and boring stories about poor children grateful for Winterhilfe food distribution—since 1933, "winter help" SA men and Hitler Youth had been rattling their collection cans at every street corner in town. Most clearly I remember walking home from the program at dusk, as the stars were beginning to come out. It was chilly, the streets were deserted, the gas streetlamps were flickering, and I felt a sense of hopelessness and forlornness I have rarely felt since. Mother began chiding me for walking hunched over, head down, dragging my feet. I tried to straighten up, but most of the time I just did not care.

I was happiest when I could disappear into a book. I took books like *The Adventures of Rolf Torring* to school with me and read them under the desktop. Back home, I quickly disappeared into the bedroom we all shared, slouched down on its hard sofa, and continued reading. There was an unlimited number of adventure books about intrepid detectives, or explorers who roamed through Asia, Africa, South America, fighting robbers and outlaws, huge boas, jaguars, and tigers. They crawled through caves and sewers to find lost treasures and arms caches; they were thanked by maharajas and kings. They were better than English, American, French, or Spanish detectives and explorers. They were German and proud of it, colonizers and conquerors, spies for the Kaiser, friends of the Boers. I learned my nationalist sentiments and my world geography from these penny novels—geography I had to unlearn in postwar high school and later, when I traveled. Everything was exotic and alien. Best of all, when an eighty- or ninety-page adventure ended, I could delve into another one.

I began having nightmares populated by the wild animals of these stories. A tiger would jump from behind one of the headstones in the Eisenbergs' stone yard and bury his claws in my mother's shoulder. I was terrified that she would die, the only adult left to me. She died in every one of my dreams during this period—of illness, run over by trains, swallowed by giant snakes, drowned in a raging flood. I woke up sweating and crying and could not get back to sleep. She was often gone at night, usually to play skat or visit friends. My brothers slept peacefully, but I saw her dead and took up another book and read till either she returned or dawn broke. Then I would get a few hours of sleep before being wakened for school. And there I read on, read and read, never minding what Fräulein Schäfer spewed forth up front at her desk.

I was neither a particularly good nor a particularly bad student. I read too much to pay attention in class. I was too nervous and daydreamed too much to be able to do chains of sums in my head. Fräulein Schäfer made us all stand up and then gave us a problem: "3 plus 4, times 2, minus 10, equals?" The pupil who said the right sum first could sit down. I was always the last student standing. On the other hand, I was good at reading aloud, and even better at writing stories. Not that I wrote the stories down. I made them up as I read them, dramatically, from my copybook. Since Fräulein Schäfer was near-sighted and never checked on my writing, I got away with my deceit. Except once. We had a substitute teacher who had been told that our homework was to write a story. She asked for volunteers to read theirs, and as usual I volunteered. When I got through "reading," she exclaimed, "Well done! Now just let me check the spelling!" The class giggled as I went up to her desk with my copybook, since they had long since caught on to my stratagem. The rest is a blur. I only know that from then on I wrote the stories down, and they weren't half as lively.

I came to resent Uncle Kurt's regular Sunday visits after Oma's death, because my younger brother, Werner, and I were left behind at the Baronie, while he and Mother went to the movies and Jochen visited Aunt Lene, where the two of us were not wanted. I remember the long, dull Sunday afternoons in the front yard with Werner as he sat on a truck-trailer coupling, gripped an imaginary steering wheel, and pretended to drive the truck, or dreamily pushed a soccer ball through the dust of the front yard while I waited for the street's other children to return from their Sunday afternoon walks with their families.

I despised the interminable Sunday afternoons, feeling excluded from what I observed as normal family life.

On his ninth birthday Jochen got a bicycle; Mother and Aunt Lene had had my father's bike refurbished for him. I brimmed with jealousy and protest.

Boy soccer player, oil-based clay sculpture, 1993, by author

"Why always him! Why does he get a bike? What about me?" I plagued Aunt Lene, Uncle Kurt, and Mother until Uncle Kurt relented and gave Mother twenty marks to buy me a secondhand women's bike. Exploring on bikes with Jochen and Manfred became my favorite activity, next to reading. I learned to handle the bike in no time, though I could barely reach the pedals when I was sitting on the seat. I wobbled along, standing on the pedals for balance. I loved the speed, the wind in my hair, the maneuvers necessary to avoid rocks on the footpath while we raced down the steep incline of Rummelsberg. The world opened up for us as we explored the villages around Strehlen and the quarries, reservoirs, woods, and meadows for miles around. We oriented ourselves on these tours through the countryside by Zopten Mountain's pair of hazy blue peaks in the west. I luxuriated in my newfound freedom from the narrow confines of Promenade Street. No more boring, empty Sunday afternoons! I nudged Werner to go play with dirty Paulchen, his friend down the street, and took off.

We played at being reporters hunting down a criminal, or spies who traveled on secret missions along the back alleys of Singapore and Bombay, like Rolf Torring. Since we were required to be in school only until noon, at home for the noon meal, and back home after dark, we often strayed far from the Baronie. Only once, when, on an October afternoon in 1938, Jochen and I decided to visit Grandfather Mahlendorf in Neisse, sixty kilometers away, did we overestimate our energy and underestimate the distance. We were only a little more than halfway there when it got dark and started to drizzle. We arrived, wet and exhausted, at Grandfather's apartment around ten o'clock that night. Mother had telephoned him a few hours earlier: "They came in for a second when I was busy with a customer and said they wanted to go see you. I yelled after them to stop but they were gone!"

Because of Father's death and Mother's marginal income from dressmaking after 1935, our small family lost whatever social class standing it had had earlier. Oma's death took away what stability and connection with the larger family had been mine. My shame over our poverty led me to understand myself as a lower-class child. This conviction grew over the next few years and threw me into a conflict. I remember vividly being torn between my identification with and sympathy for such quarry kids as Agatha and Helga, even while I burned with desire to emulate my middle-class schoolmates. Yet what strikes me even more forcibly now, in looking back on the mid-1930s, is the juxtaposition between my ordinary, even idyllic and secure childhood in this small town and the fate of its Jewish and socialist and communist populations. While we lived our narrow daily lives, they were harassed, sent to prison, and forced to leave town. My mother, Oma, my relatives, Mother's customers surely talked about their Jewish friends and acquaintances, even if not about the working class. Yet I do not remember a single word about the harassment, the deportations, or the exodus. Even when we, the German Aryan population, were harassed and finally evicted from town by the Polish militia in 1946, nobody mentioned the parallel.

Chapter Three

KRISTALLNACHT AND THE BEGINNING OF
WORLD WAR II, 1938–1940

UP UNTIL KRISTALLNACHT (CRYSTAL NIGHT) in November 1938, I had no clear
conception of who or what Jews were, or even any curiosity about them. I
did not know that Kaiser's health food store or the other stores in the center
of town were Jewish stores. Like the Catholics, whom we Protestants considered outsiders and whose church and cemetery I had never entered, Jews
for me were another mysterious religious group. They had their own house
of worship, the synagogue across from the post office, and their own cemetery out on Kuschlauer Street, both of which I remember as off limits and
with feelings of awe. The infamous caricatures of Jews in *Der Stürmer*, the ss
paper, must have held no fascination for me, because I have no recollection of
them, though *Der Stürmer* was on display in special caged display cases on several streets. Though a classmate, our dentist, Dr. Gerstel, and several family
friends and acquaintances were Jewish, I wasn't aware of it.

Until the mid-1930s our town did have a visible and prominent Jewish
middle class of merchants and professional men. At least four or five Jewish-
owned stores were located right on City Hall Square, and several building
material businesses, a brick factory, and the town-owned quarries were owned
or leased by Jewish families. About twenty Jewish families had settled in town
in the course of the nineteenth century and paid for the right to become citizens as proclaimed in the Prussian Emancipation Declaration of 1812. By 1887,
when many families had lived in town for more than three generations and

the congregation numbered about ninety members, they had a synagogue built. But the congregation did not grow substantially in the course of the early twentieth century, and they never employed a rabbi; they used a cantor for high holidays and bar mitzvahs. As Jews had grown more prosperous with the acquisition of full civil rights in Prussia in 1870 and availed themselves of the education available to them as a consequence, Strehlen's Christian middle class of the 1890s responded to the competition of Jewish merchants and professionals with at times flagrant anti-Semitism. An example was their Anti-Semite Club.

I was shocked, when I looked into the history of the Strehlen Jewish community, to discover that what Hitler planned as the ultimate goal of his anti-Jewish policies had already appeared as a primitive and grotesque inscription on an 1893 beer stein of this local Anti-Semite Club. The beer stein documents the members of the club, respectable citizens all, among them a court preacher, two physicians, a nobleman, and several business owners, and outlines their organization's charges against Jews and their goal of ridding society of Jews. Miniature pictures and verse on this stein include the same denunciations the Nazis were to make forty years later, slurs about Jewish business practices in dealing with Aryan farmers and craftsmen that were all too familiar to me from my indoctrination in the Hitler Youth:

> Dieser Pflug wär nicht so schwer,
> Wenn Aron, Jonas, Hirschfeld nicht wär.

> This plow would not be so heavy
> If Aaron, Jonas, Hirschfeld were not weighing it down.

Another miniature, with a picture of a smith being handed a presumably usurious promissory note, declares:

> Das Handwerk schafft um kargen Lohn,
> Den Segen rafft sich der Cohn.

> This craftsman toils for scant pay,
> But Cohn carries off all the profit.

Still another sinister medallion of sayings and pictures on the stein passes a sentence based on these charges of exploitation and usury, a judgment that presages the "solution to the Jewish problem" my townsmen brought about in the course of the 1930s. In this miniature, the Jews are expelled by a bat-swinging German. They pass by a "German House" with the sign "Jews are not allowed" and follow a sign that says "to Jerusalem," while a group of Germans "celebrate happily to be rid of their Jews."

Despite the anti-Semitism the Jewish community encountered, many of their members attempted to integrate themselves into the town. During the empire and the Weimar Republic several Jewish businessmen proved their good citizenship by sitting on town councils and commissions and participating in national celebrations; others took up such typically German nationalist activities as staffing the voluntary fire brigade and leading the local athletics club for men. Several Jewish physicians and dentists served the town faithfully and therefore received its respect. Several prominent Jewish professionals, businessmen, and factory owners demonstrated their gratitude and loyalty and remembered the local poor in their wills, among them "our" Nobel Prize winner in medicine, Paul Ehrlich, the town's only claim to fame. During the Great Depression, so as to prevent rickets and alleviate infant and childhood calcium deficiency, a Jewish landowner had milk distributed to needy families. The milk distribution store on Convent Street existed as late as 1935, when I went with Oma to fetch milk for my infant brother. As the Nazi threat increased during the Weimar Republic years, a Jewish citizen founded a local subsidiary of the national organization Black, Red, Gold—an organization named after the colors of the Weimar flag—and pledged to defend the endangered Weimar constitution and the rights it guaranteed. Tragically and ironically, local anti-Semitic prejudice, Nazi propaganda, and Christian envy and greed won out, when in 1933 the organization dissolved and its Aryan members joined the sa and the ss.

From 1933 on, the Jewish stores in town as well as local Jewish physicians became subject to public boycotts, suffered the increasing unfriendliness of our citizenry, and were harassed by the sa and ss. Over the next few years signs appeared on Jewish stores in town, reading: ACHTUNG, VOLKSGENOSSEN! KAUFT NICHT BEI JUDEN! (Attention, citizens! Do not buy in Jewish stores!). I remember the reproof Oma received from a man at the door to Kaiser's health food store when she went in. We both were particularly sad about the closing of this, our favorite store. Oma bought garlic pills for her digestion at Kaiser's. Its polished wooden shelves with their gleaming boxes contained spices and herbs whose fragrance enticed us to linger. Its friendly owner always handed me deliciously tickling eucalyptus candy that, as Oma said, was good for you and healthy.

By 1938 the owners of most of the Jewish businesses around City Hall Square had sold them at vastly reduced rates to Aryan businessmen and left for overseas, to Palestine, the United States, China, Australia, and South America. Ironically, like many German Jews, most of them still felt themselves such loyal Germans that they traveled overseas on German-owned ships. Only a very few middle-class Jewish families remained in town.

What happened on our local stage was repeated on the national scene. Harassment by the SS and SA and boycotts of Jewish-owned businesses had alarmed many of Germany's half a million Jews even before Hitler proclaimed the Nuremberg laws of 1935. The public burning of books at the country's major universities in May 1933 was only the most conspicuous sign of the persecution of everything Jewish—indeed, of everything communist, socialist, or politically suspect as well. Everything that the political Right thought decadent, Jewish, international, un-German—including works of psychoanalysis, modernism, expressionism, and Dadaism—was condemned. The press and the book trade (publishers, book dealers, and the many small private lending libraries) were "Aryanized"—that is, their owners were dispossessed and their stock was cleared of anything the Nazis objected to. Within a few months in 1933, Germany lost most of its cultural and artistic elite.

Those Jews who understood the Nazi threat early, who had connections abroad and were mobile or wealthy enough, left the country. Liberal and leftist artists and intellectuals (Jewish or not) like Arnold Schönberg, Alfred Döblin, Thomas and Heinrich Mann, Bertolt Brecht, and Lion Feuchtwanger were in immediate danger because of their open opposition to Nazi culture and politics, and many left soon after Hitler's assumption of the chancellorship and the burning of the Reichstag. Hoping that the Nazi regime would last only a few weeks, most sought temporary refuge in nearby Austria, Switzerland, Czechoslovakia, the Scandinavian countries, or France. Jewish academics and scientists—among them Albert Einstein, Hannah Arendt, Theodor Adorno, and Max Horkheimer—were dismissed or driven from their university positions in the summer of 1933; in time, many would find positions in the United States. Some 60,000 German Jews left Germany in 1933–34; they were soon joined by ordinary middle-class Jewish citizens of all political persuasions like many of my hometown. The number of Jewish émigrés in 1935 was approximately 20,000; in 1936, 25,000; in 1937, 23,000; in 1938, almost 40,000. When Hitler's troops annexed Austria, with a Jewish population of 207,000, another wave of emigration followed. By 1941, when the infamous "final solution" was under way and emigration had slowed to a trickle, some 270,000 German Jewish refugees had left for whatever country they could get affidavits to.

From the beginning of the Nazi regime, the minister of Volksaufklärung (public enlightenment) und Propaganda, Joseph Goebbels, had spread his poisonous anti-Semitism in speeches carried in the press and over the radio. The government imposed one restrictive regulation after another on its Jewish citizens. They were refused police protection, could not inherit land, and could be arrested without cause and held without due process. It became illegal for Jews to use public baths, swimming pools, parks, public buildings. They were dismissed from the civil service and from university positions (all German institutions of higher learning were public), nor could they study there; they were excluded from the Reichskulturkammer, the public cultural organization to which artists, writers, composers, orchestra conductors, musicians, actors, and journalists had to belong to be able to create, publish, perform, exhibit. By 1938 Jewish children had been dismissed from public grade schools. When the war began, the property of Jews who had not left was confiscated, and they were moved to special *Judenhäuser* (Jewish houses) in working-class districts— that is, to newly established ghettoes. After the Polish campaign, of course, they would be sent to concentration camps and worked to death or gassed.

Christian Strehlen had remained largely unaware of the Nazi campaign against Weimar and Jewish culture during the run-up to the war, if only because most townspeople were avid nationalists and few had either the education or the inclination to participate in cultural and intellectual life beyond reading the German classics and occasional attendance at the theater or opera in Breslau, the provincial capital. I would learn the full dimensions of this culture war only after I began to study German literature in the United States, at Brown University, in 1953, where I encountered the works of Jewish and other exiled writers—Franz Kafka, Thomas Mann, Else Lasker-Schüler, Gertrud Kolmar. I came to love and admire the literature, art, and culture of expressionism and Weimar Germany—and to be appalled that most German intellectuals and the educated German middle class of the 1930s and '40s had disowned, persecuted or allowed to be persecuted, killed or allowed to be killed the best minds among them. As a scholar and lover of German literature, music, and art, I cannot forgive the German intellectual "elite" (not all of whom were Nazis) for their betrayal of their Jewish fellow citizens, and with that their betrayal of the Western tradition of the Enlightenment in which they had been raised. Though I have come to understand many of the reasons for their moral failure, it still angers me—particularly when contemporary German official publications, without referring to that infamous history, claim as their own the intellectuals and artists Germany disowned under Nazism.

During the Berlin Olympics of 1936, when many foreigners visited Germany, the Nazis temporarily scaled back their public displays of anti-Semitism, only to resume persecution more aggressively by 1938. On November 9 of that year, they used the murder of a Nazi diplomat by an exiled Jewish student in Paris as a pretext for staging a supposedly spontaneous pogrom: Kristallnacht. In towns and cities large and small all over Germany, ss and sa men burned synagogues, smashed the windows of Jewish-owned stores and businesses, looted and demolished their contents, and attacked and imprisoned Jewish citizens. No one living in Germany at the time can claim that they heard nothing of Kristallnacht. At nine years old I saw and heard what happened in our town and was terrified by it, though I failed to understand its full significance.

It was late at night, and I was still awake, when I heard screaming and crashing, splintering glass. Mother was not home and I was afraid. Even so, I rushed to the bedroom window and opened it to find out what the shouts and commotion were all about. The gas lamp at the corner of Grosse Kirchstrasse and Promenade Street flickered as usual. Jochen and I stood at the window, looking out across Promenade Street. We saw people running up Grosse Kirchstrasse toward City Hall Square, heard cries and what sounded like gunshots in the distance, and more shattering of glass. The sky above the buildings in the direction of City Hall Square turned red. Herr Gurn limped across the Baronie's front yard, out to the street. "I cannot see anything," he called to his wife. "It's coming from City Hall Square, or beyond." And he hobbled out of sight. The far-off commotion continued. We stood and shivered in the November night air. Finally, after what seemed hours, Mother came down Grosse Kirchstrasse, accompanied by Herr Gurn. They stood and talked at the front door, where Frau Gurn was waiting. The distant noise diminished.

"What happened, Mama?" we called down to her.

"They broke down the Gerstels' door, bashed in their windows, threw their mattresses, the dentist chair, all his papers down to the street. The Gerstels and their kids were out in their nightshirts; they took Doctor Gerstel away."

"Who did? Why? What did Doctor Gerstel do?"

Mother shot me a glance that silenced me. It was the same glance I would receive from her a few years later when I began asking questions about sex. "Don't ask," it said. "Don't ever dare to ask that again."

Next morning, before school, I ran the four long blocks up to Münsterberg Street where the Gerstels lived. The gray morning street was still littered; papers were strewn about. Their iron front gate hung crooked from one upper hinge. The windows were broken, and the street and sidewalk were covered with glass shards. A blind on a second-story window flapped in the morning breeze. A few townspeople went by—silently. Children gathered and stared; some picked up papers. When I got to school, all the children were talking excitedly as we lined up to go to our classrooms. I saw that Eva's seat, next to Ilse, was empty.

"Where is Eva?" I asked Fräulein Schäfer.

She banged down the top of her desk, a sign that she was angry and that we were to be quiet at once. She shot me the same glance that Mother had the night before. But I was not to be shut up as easily as that. "I went by the Gerstels' house," I continued. "Their windows were bashed in. Mother said the Gerstel kids were out in the street, everything was all lit up, there were a lot of torches. They caught the measles from me and Jochen, and you are not supposed to look into the light when you have the measles. You'll go blind!"

"That is enough, sit down," was all the reply I got. "The Gerstels and Eva's parents are going abroad," said Fräulein Schäfer, and, turning to Ilse, added, "Eva will not be back."

For days I worried about the Gerstel kids having the measles and being exposed to daylight, having to travel on a ship and going blind. They were friends of Jochen's and had caught the measles from us; it was our fault if they went blind. How could adults be so stupid as to let them go about in daylight when they had the measles?

During a conversation years later, Jochen remembered different details about Kristallnacht. "I don't recall what happened at the Gerstels'," he said. "But I was friends with the Stargardter boys, in whose house Aunt Lene had her apartment. Before Kristallnacht, we used to race our bikes in their yard. Afterward, the street was littered with paper and glass. Their father's safe was emptied of its contents and its door was broken off, and it lay out on Frankensteiner Street. The boys looked out of the second-story bedroom window. I motioned to them to come down and play, but they weren't allowed to."

"Do you remember that the synagogue burned down?" I asked him.

"That's what I remembered, and I thought I saw the blackened bricks of the building the next day," he answered. "But then a few years ago, I read that the mayor prevented the fire—that the synagogue was looted and the sanctuary desecrated but the building was not burned down."

"I saw that the sky was red," I countered. "I've been thinking all along that it was from the burning synagogue. But come to think of it, the motorized Storm Troopers used the building as a meeting place sometime afterward. So it must have survived Kristallnacht."

Jochen remembered Storm Troopers coming out of the building with their motorbikes, too. "Motorbikes parked in the sanctuary!" he said angrily. "Maybe the horizon seemed red to us because we were frightened," he added after an embarrassed silence, "or maybe the SA and the SS surrounded the synagogue carrying torches."

The discrepancies in our memories only point up how violent and confusing Kristallnacht was to us—and how quickly life under the Nazis erased the terrible event, and the Jewish community, from our minds.

Mother would later claim to have no recollection at all of that night. Did she feel so helpless and guilty that she blocked it out? "What happened to the Preuss sisters, Mother?" I asked her on one occasion in the early 1950s.

"Grete's sister committed suicide," came the answer. "And Grete had an affair with Uncle Bruno just before he died, in 1934. His wife threatened to report us to the SS if we stayed friendly with the Preuss sisters. And that's why we asked Grete to stop coming to the skat evenings for a while. We lost touch with her after that."

Afraid she might snap at me, I did not follow up on this evasion. My skepticism was confirmed when I talked to Jochen about it after Mother's death. He too had asked about the Preuss sisters and had received a somewhat different answer about the affair and its consequences. "Bruno's wife threatened to report Grete Preuss to the SS," she told him. "We didn't want her to get into trouble, and that's why we didn't see her again." Jochen and I both remembered another story of Mother's about a different period in her relationship with Grete Preuss. Mother encountered Grete again on Windmill Hill, way out of town, in the summer of 1939, just before the war broke out. They walked and talked together until they reached the edge of town. Then Grete said, "Let me go ahead and you wait. You don't want to be seen with me. I don't want you to get into trouble."

Years later, long after I learned that what I heard that night was called Kristallnacht, I began to reconstruct with Jochen what happened that night to many of Strehlen's Jews. I learned that, unlike in other German cities and towns, ours no longer had Jewish stores to vandalize and destroy because all Jewish-owned stores had closed by 1938. Therefore on Kristallnacht ss and sa men in civilian dress vandalized the synagogue, a number of private residences, and the offices of several prominent Jewish professionals and businessowners. The attackers belonged to out-of-town troops, while our local ss vandalized Jewish property in neighboring municipalities so as to remain anonymous. Dr. Gerstel and Herr Stargardter had stayed in town because they thought themselves safe, as the early Nuremberg laws excluded decorated Great War veterans from persecution. Both men believed their standing as war veterans gave them security and that their professions as dentist and owner of a building materials company made them indispensable. For several months after the attack, both men, as well as all Jewish men remaining in town, were sent to concentration camp Buchenwald near Weimar, while their wives sold their properties in forced sales and negotiated for exit permits, payments of an exit tax, visas, and for the release of their men. Both families barely managed to emigrate abroad before the onset of the war.

Another merchant family, the Jacobs, was not as fortunate. They were German patriots and could not imagine taking anything but a German ship. At the beginning of the war, in September 1939, their ship turned around on the high seas. Having sold all their possessions before departure, they returned to Strehlen and lived in poverty until, in 1941, they reported to Breslau to be sent to Theresienstadt camp. No one knows where they or the other Jews who had remained in town, like my parents' friend Grete Preuss, died. During the 1930s and 1940s, did Mother ever think about the families who were driven out, many of whom she must have known as their customer?

Gradually, after Kristallnacht, I forgot Eva and the Gerstel children. The Preuss sisters, too, left my life almost without a trace. I forgot about Kristallnacht, about what I had heard and seen. Jews disappeared from my experience as living people and became an abstraction. There may well have been some Jewish people who stayed in Strehlen after Kristallnacht, but I don't recall ever seeing a person wearing a yellow star after this became obligatory in 1941. The only person I knew who was close to anyone Jewish was the son of Dr. Hahn, whom I became aware of toward the end of the war. Dr. Hahn, who continued to serve a small private practice of loyal patients, had been half Jewish.

Designated as a quarter Jew, his son was allowed to attend high school but not to join the Hitler Youth. I wondered what he felt about being an outsider.

After Kristallnacht I would learn a new definition of the word "Jewish": it meant dishonest and deceitful. Goebbels, on the radio, spoke of Jews as untrustworthy, as people who took advantage of German good-heartedness in business dealings, as perpetrators of an international conspiracy against Germany. At the time, most of this made no sense to me, but gradually it sank in. Later, after I had joined the Jungmädel and we learned that Jews were subhuman, fat, smelled bad, and were cowards, I did not associate Eva or the Gerstels and their children or the Preuss sisters with being Jewish. I would remember all of them, and the events of Kristallnacht, in a flash of recognition in May 1945 when, somewhere on a refugee-clogged road in Sudeten Czechoslovakia, disoriented with fear, I encountered a group of emaciated, bald, rag-covered figures. "They are Jews," someone said, adding that they had been newly freed from a nearby concentration camp.

After the Nazi period, when I began to understand where anti-Semitism had led us Germans, I, like many of my generation, found it difficult to ever use the German word *Jude.* Its toxic Nazi connotations seemed bearable only in compounds like *Judenverfolgung,* persecution of Jews, the word that clarified one's position on and recognized our responsibility for the Holocaust. The euphemism that gained popular favor during the Kohl area of the conservative Christian Democrats, "unsere jüdischen Mitbürger" or even "unsere jüdischen Brüder und Schwestern" (our Jewish fellow citizens or our Jewish brothers and sisters), I found nauseatingly hypocritical. That was exactly what German Jews had not been to us. I was grateful that the Federal Republic of Germany paid reparations to the state of Israel; and that it, though often in a belated, grudging, and cruelly bureaucratic manner, compensated survivors and refugees from Nazism for their homes, their loss of health, profession, income, and education. When, in 1970, Chancellor Brandt fell to his knees at the memorial of the victims of the Warsaw ghetto uprising, I felt that with this spontaneous gesture he expressed for all Germans the contrition and grief with which we need to honor the Jewish dead.

Ever since Oma's death and the loss of her help with the household and finances, Mother's struggle to feed and care for the three of us had increased. She sought to lighten her load by asking her relatives to take us in during the longer breaks from school. Once rationing started, in 1939, our country visits would leave her and my younger brother, Werner, the full use of the rationing cards. Consequently, she warned me early that summer that I would have to spend the coming vacation with her cousin Helene Schulte in Zülzendorf, a village about thirty kilometers from home. Mother had tried to send me to other relatives in the country the previous summer, when Jochen had been sent to stay with Uncle Kurt. I had protested in vain, was sent anyway, misbehaved, fell ill, and was sent back home early, having created so much turmoil in that household that Mother decided I was still too young to spend six weeks by myself with relatives I scarcely knew.

I would be fed better at Aunt Helene's than at home, she said. That was true enough. Breakfast and supper at our house usually consisted of bread and marmalade or evil-tasting margarine. Dinners were monotonous. Most days we had *Eintopf,* a casserole of potatoes and various vegetables boiled in bouillon and thickened with flour. On Saturday, when the fifteen-year-old household help had her day off, we got a dime each to get a wiener or some herring. Mother cooked on Sundays, and then a half-pound roast for the four of us produced more delicious smells than substance. But she always made plenty of potato dumplings and cabbage, so we looked forward to the Sunday meal. "This year," she cajoled, "you are almost grown up, so I am sure you'll be more responsible and help me save expenses."

In fact, I *had* been saving expenses by getting a free meal—every Friday since Oma died—with two elderly ladies who owned the dress and fabric shop where Mother bought her dressmaking supplies. Initially I had hated going there, because the two old ladies made me wash up in the kitchen before allowing me into their dining room. But I began to like the well-cooked meals their housekeeper provided; since Oma's death, the succession of girls who watched over my younger brother had produced unspeakably bad meals. Besides serving tasty and varied fare, the two old ladies owned children's books and novels and soon allowed me to stay and read them after our noon dinner. Anyone could win my favorable opinion by providing reading material and, better still, allowing me to talk to them about what I read. Maybe at the Schultes' house they also had books. With this thought I tried to console myself.

Mother came with me on my first trip to Zülzendorf. It was an hour's train ride with one change, from the national rail lines to a small local line. When we arrived at the Zülzendorf station, there was no carriage waiting for us. We walked the mile down to the estate that Uncle Richard Schulte, Aunt

Helene's husband, managed for an absentee nobleman. The Schultes lived in the nobleman's residence, a large and comfortable country house with an adjoining park, from which now and then resounded the shrieks and calls of half a dozen peacocks.

From the very beginning Aunt Helene made it clear, by the way she spoke to Mother, that she saw us as poor relations on whom she was bestowing her favor. I disliked her from the minute I heard her speak the kind of High German that Silesians use who aspire to upper-class status. An imposing, heavy woman, she towered over my petite mother. The two cousins had been competitors in their late teens and Mother, better looking than Aunt Helene, had lorded it over her. Aunt Helene was now apparently paying her back.

I accompanied Mother to the train station, feeling downcast and afraid and trying not to cry, so as not to worry her. "I'll write as soon as I get home," she promised. I was fearfully homesick and lonely for the next week. Mother did not write, and I was terrified that something had happened to her. Was she ill? Had she had an accident?

On my second evening at the Schultes', Aunt Helene led me into the hall that connected the kitchen with the dining room. "It'll be your job to clean this hall every evening," she told me. "Put the chairs on the table, roll up the runners, and take them out to the back porch. In the morning, bring back the runners and take down the chairs." I did just as I was told, but Aunt Helene was never satisfied. The chairs were heavy wooden peasant furniture, in high fashion during the Nazis' infatuation with German peasant styles. Their high backs, in solid, gray-painted oak, featured cut-out hearts surrounded by a wreath of painted flowers: daisies, red poppies, and blue cornflowers. The wreaths continued along the racks of the sideboard, which held lead plates embossed with coats of arms. A heavy, wreath-decorated chest completed the set. I could hardly lift the chairs, and the dark red runners left a coat of dust on my forearms. I came to hate the furniture, the style, the entire hall.

I could not sleep, and if I did fall asleep my old nightmares returned. I slept in one of the guest rooms up in the attic. The room at the other end of the long corridor was for Selma, the household help, and Herta, who was my aunt's apprentice in a program for "future farmwives." The estate's secretary had her room halfway down the hall. I hardly spoke to anyone at all during the first week and spent hours hiding out in the park with the peacocks, emerging only when called for meals. One night as I lay in bed, I looked up at the ceiling and saw a huge spider; then suddenly more spiders crawled up the walls and met on the ceiling over my bed. I jumped out of bed, raced to the door and down the corridor, screaming hysterically, "Spiders!! Spiders all over everything!! Spiders!!" I fell against the secretary's door, even as the door at the end of the hall opened. Herta, a tall, brown-haired sixteen-year-old, reached me first and put her arms around me. I was shaking with sobs. "Spiders!" was all I could say. Herta pushed me into the secretary's room, sat me down on the bed, and stayed with me while the secretary went to my room to check on what had frightened me.

With both women talking to me gently, I gradually calmed down. When I had recovered, the secretary said, "I found only one spider. Come and look. It's all right. Maybe you had a nightmare, but it's all right, we are right here."

"Why don't you come and sleep in my room," Herta said when she saw my hesitation. "Selma is gone for the night and her bed is free. We'll get your bedding and you'll sleep with me. We can go see if there are more spiders in the morning."

I worried about Uncle Richard and Aunt Helene being upset with me for having made a fuss—or, worse, laughing at me for being afraid of a spider. Both women promised they would not tell on me. From that day on, Herta became my friend and confidante. She comforted me about Mother's not writing. ("You know, don't you, how busy she is. She probably thinks you are having a good time!") I talked to Herta about home, about not liking Aunt Helene much (Herta didn't like her much either), about loving to read.

Herta knew of an old bookcase filled with books in the attic and told me where to look. Now that I had something to read, I was no longer afraid to stay in my room at night. I was supposed to turn out my lights by ten at the latest. I took the small table lamp under the covers and read as long as I pleased—*Robinson Crusoe, The Prince and the Pauper, David Copperfield*. These were books of a quality entirely new to me, and I read them over and over again, identifying with their lost and abandoned characters.

One Sunday afternoon in the middle of my visit, everyone who worked for the Schultes, including Herta and Selma, was ordered to come help bring in the hay. A thunderstorm was threatening, and the hay had to be brought into the barn before it hit. As Uncle Richard was leaving for the fields with his buggy, he caught sight of me. "Hey, Ulla," he called to me, "come along, we need all hands."

"It's Sunday," I protested. "I'm in my Sunday dress. I can't go."

"Yes, you can. Everyone is needed. The hay has to get into the barn."

I had a full-blown temper tantrum as he lifted me into the buggy. Still sniffling, I was handed up onto the hay wagon and told to stamp down the hay as it was forked up by the farmhands and stacked by Herta and Selma. We had finished three wagonloads by the time the rain started and had the fourth in the barn by the time the storm became fierce. From that day on, Uncle Richard made me help in the fields at least a few hours every day, but I remained outraged—angry and resentful at having to work like an ordinary field hand.

On the day I was to leave for home, Uncle Richard called me into his office. The secretary handed me a time sheet she had filled out for me and asked me to check it. I was astounded, as I had not expected to be clocked or paid. I had worked some fifty hours over the three weeks; at eighty pennies per hour, my wages amounted to forty marks, more money than I had ever seen, let alone possessed.

"You buy yourself what you want with it," Uncle Richard said, "and mind you, buy what you want! You worked hard for it."

Heartily embarrassed at having been so disagreeable, and pleased by the money (and even more by the recognition), I learned an important lesson that day: I could work and earn my keep. I could become independent. The depression that had made me languid, interested only in escaping into books, lifted. I would buy a new winter coat and, yes, a book—the first book I'd ever bought for myself! Maybe *David Copperfield,* which I had not been able to finish for a second time that summer and had had to abandon. I was actually sad to leave—particularly to say goodbye to Herta, who promised she would be there next summer.

It was late August when I left for home. The train was overcrowded when it arrived on the platform at Zülzendorf, half an hour late. People were talking about Hitler's ultimatum to Poland. Although the Polish border was only about seventy miles from Zülzendorf, I had had no access to any source of news and had heard nothing about what the radio described as attacks by Poles on ethnic Germans in Posnia, the Polish territory bordering Silesia on the east. Similar news the year before about Czech attacks on ethnic Germans had prepared German citizens before the German army marched into the Sudetenland.

On September 1, in the early morning hours, German troops would attack Poland along its entire border. This time, Hitler would overreach. His ostensible reason for the attack was his demand for free passage through the Polish corridor (Posnia) to the harbor city of Danzig on the Baltic Sea. England and France would declare war on Germany a few days later. Poland would be overrun by German troops in a few weeks.

"There is going to be a war," an old man said to his neighbor on the platform at Zülzendorf. "It's just like 1914. It's the right time, too—August, just like 1914."

"It's not like that at all," another man said. "Nobody is shouting for war. Look at the people!" It was true, nobody was shouting "Sieg Heil!" as they had when Austria and the Sudetenland joined the Reich. The crowd on the platform was anxious, as impatient to get home as I was, their faces grim, lined with worry.

At Kamenz, where I had to change trains, the crowds were even larger. The public address system announced that the train to Breslau was late. When it got dark and there was still no announcement about when the train would arrive, I went to the waiting room. It too was crowded—noisy and filled with smoke. Sandwiches were all sold out, so my money was not good for anything. I worried that I might lose it—that someone would steal my suitcase if I needed to go to the restroom and left it outside because the restroom floor was dirty and wet with urine. The train came in at about midnight, overcrowded, of course. A column of us pressed in at the compartment door, and a man lifted my suitcase up to the baggage net as I was pushed farther into the compartment to where I could hardly see it. The train lurched forward, pressing us all against one another. I was smaller than the adults, whose bulk towered over me, and I could hardly breathe. Maddeningly, the train stopped for an endless stretch of time at each of the four stations before Strehlen. When we arrived there at last, someone hauled me over the crowd and out the door, and someone else threw my suitcase after me. Everything was okay!

It was past two o'clock in the morning. The station was filled with anxious people, but I did not recognize anyone I knew. No one was there to meet me, since the train was hours late, and I lugged my suitcase home alone. It was no more than a ten-minute walk, but I was hungry, and the way seemed endless. The Baronie's front door would be locked, I knew, so I stopped in the front yard below our bedroom window and pelted it with pebbles. After a long while, Mother heard me. "Thank God, you're here," she called from the window. "We left the front door open. Just turn the key when you are in."

She was sound asleep by the time I got to the bedroom, and so was Werner. Jochen was apparently still at Uncle Kurt's.

When I woke up the next morning, Mother was already at work at her dressmaking in the living room. By now she had two apprentices: Trudi, a dark-haired, freckled, boisterous seventeen-year-old, and Ida, a sandy-haired pale hunchback with a snickering laugh. Trudi, who had quickly become a member of the family, talked about her date the night before and how she was looking forward to her vacation, coming up the next day.

"Aunt Lene, Werner, and I are leaving for Charlottenbrunn tomorrow," Mother informed me. "Jochen is staying at Uncle Kurt's for another week. I have asked Aunt Friede in Segen to take you for a week. You can walk to school from Segen; it's only a kilometer. Werner and I will take you out there tonight." I knew protest was in vain, but I tried it anyway: "Why can't I ever go with you? You always take the boys, never me."

I sulked for the rest of the day and at dusk walked the kilometer with them to the farming hamlet of Segen and Aunt Friede's, pushing my all too familiar suitcase in Werner's old baby buggy.

Two nights later I was roused from sleep by distant thunder—though I am still not sure whether I imagined it, anxious as I was. Was it a thunderstorm? The thunder did not seem to be coming any closer. There was no lightning. Strange shadows were thrown on the bedroom wall by the dim streetlight below my window. Sometimes a faint *rat-a-tat-tat* seemed to follow the thunder. I was afraid to leave my bed. There was no other sound in the house or in the night outside. I lay awake as the distant thunder continued, it seemed to me, for ages. Suddenly it was morning. The sun shone through my window, and I knew it was later than usual. The thundering had stopped, but the downstairs echoed with voices and the clatter of dishes. No one had awakened me to go to school. I jumped into my clothes and rushed down to the kitchen. The downstairs hallway was crowded with soldiers, and so were the kitchen and the yard. Aunt Friede was making them coffee.

"WAR!" the radio blared, and a choir began singing "Deutschland, Deutschland, über Alles." I could hardly contain my trembling.

"You'll be okay," said a soldier who saw my tears beginning.

"I won't be," I thought. "Where are Mother and Werner? How will they get home, now that it's war?"

My Uncle Friedemann was sitting on the kitchen sofa, very still, gray faced, his lips twitching. I had usually been afraid of him, because he never spoke and sometimes acted crazy; he had been buried alive in a trench during the Great War. Now I felt a kinship with him; he was obviously as scared as I was.

"There won't be any school today," Aunt Friede said. "The front is close, and we have to take care of the reserves. So why don't you help me with making sandwiches for the soldiers?"

My fear left as she kept me busy all day. Mother telephoned late that evening and talked to Aunt Friede. She and Werner had come home safely after a horrendous train journey. I was to return the next day.

After that first day of the war, the adults assured me that there was little reason to be afraid. The radio told us that the front had moved away from the Silesian border, into Poland, and after a week the German troops marched triumphantly into Warsaw. I vividly remember one of the few newsreels I saw in the fall of 1939. Usually I did not have money to go to the movies, as Jochen and I did not receive allowances. But I was rich for a few weeks from the summer's work, so I could afford it. I have forgotten what the feature was, but the newsreel that preceded it has stayed with me. Marching music played as the camera zoomed in on a crowd of Polish refugees who were caught on the open road as the German army overtook them. Women, teenagers, children, and old men clutching their possessions—a birdcage, a doll, a rabbit. Some lugged suitcases, others pulled small wagons. Farmers urged their slow-moving cattle along and tugged at the bridles of their limping horses. Their faces pale with exhaustion, their eyes wide with terror, their clothes disheveled, these haggard people trudged along, out of sync with the newsreel's brisk march music. The voice of an announcer repeated over and over again a snatch of verse that, I later learned, dated from the Thirty Years' War: "God smote them into the dust, / both men and horses, men and wagons."

There in the darkened movie house, I understood clearly, as a shudder went down my spine, what it meant to be defeated. In 1945, during the Russian invasion, as I stumbled along that country road in Czechoslovakia with a similar crowd of refugees, that same image appeared in my mind's eye, as the announcer's words of six years earlier resounded in my head over and over and over again. But for us that fall, life went on as it had before the outbreak of war. We were glad that the war against Poland was over, that everything would return to normal.

More important for me in late 1939 and early 1940, another, personal campaign had begun and came to occupy my life: my struggle to obtain a higher education. Although by 1939 Germany's public schools up to the eighth grade were free of charge, all schools of higher education—middle schools, high schools, universities, technical schools, professional and business colleges, even secretarial schools—charged tuition. Despite the democratization instituted by Weimar Germany and the Nazis' professions of class equality in education, the German system of higher education remained the elitist male bastion it had become in the nineteenth century. In Germany, girls had generally been excluded from that educational system, restricted as they were to all-female high schools that offered little or no access to university study. This exclusion ceased—at least formally—in 1909 as a result of the long struggle for equal access waged by the first women's movement. The Nazis, however, reversed the trend, at least during the prewar years, discouraging higher education for women, particularly education preparatory to university study.

This well-regulated, exclusive, conservative school system had given the Weimar Republic and the German Reich alike their extraordinary class stability. Middle- and upper-class parents ensured their children's future at age ten by enrolling them in either the high school or the middle school entrance exam. After passing the respective examinations, ten-year-olds, depending on their ability and their parents' wishes, left grammar school for either a six-year middle school (which prepared them for further study in high school or for business careers) or an eight-year high school. Most high schools, including the one in Strehlen, had two branches: a *Realschule,* which provided education in the sciences, mathematics, and modern languages, and a *Gymnasium,* which taught Greek and Latin and offered a classical education. Only graduates of a *Gymnasium* or *Realschule* could attend a university. Children who stayed in grammar school graduated at age fourteen and entered the workforce, either as unskilled laborers or as apprentices to a trade.

There was little or no chance of receiving a university education if you were not enrolled in these exams, which were constructed so as to favor pupils of middle- and upper-class backgrounds. Access to career paths in the state and the civil service was available only through some form of higher education—from which the working class, because of tuition costs, class prejudice on the part of teachers, and sheer lack of information, was largely excluded (although with their taxes they paid the greatest share of its cost). But the entrance examinations, and a few stipends for tuition support for the poor, maintained at least the illusion that higher education was accessible to all gifted German children regardless of class.

When Jochen was ten and Mother asked him if he wished to go to high school, he refused. He wanted to become a farmer, he said, and administer a big farm, like Uncle Kurt. He did not need high school for that—an apprenticeship in farming, and agricultural school after eight years of grammar school, would suffice.

Jochen's refusal would leave me out in the cold. It was early 1940; I had turned ten the previous October. I definitely wanted to go at least to middle school, like my friends. Both my parents had gone to high school; Father had even gone to the Technische Hochschule (engineering college) in Hanover. I wanted to learn a foreign language, just as my friends would. Even then I was fascinated by history, geography, and books in general. In Mother's family it had not been the practice to send girls to high school, but she had attended the lycée on Promenade Street, a school for girls from "good families" who went on to cooking school and marriage. My friends' parents had signed them up for the same lycée, which was now a six-year middle school for girls. Boys were to be sent to the local *Gymnasium*. Only one very bright and ambitious girl from my fourth-grade class, Gretl Hartmann, had applied to take the entrance examination for the *Gymnasium*. And somehow I was already aware that not going to either high school or middle school would condemn me to a working-class existence for the rest of my life.

"It's not right that you should be better educated than your brother," said Mother, even though she prided herself on having been a feminist in the 1920s. "Besides, you'd have to get a scholarship. I don't have the money to pay twenty or forty marks a month in tuition and support you for another two or four years of education beyond age fourteen when you graduate from grammar school. And when I went to the lycée," she said, clinching her argument, "we all looked down on the scholarship students. I wouldn't want that for you."

All the kids in fourth grade whose parents were anybody in town were going to go to middle or high school. Bärbel and Elli, with whom I played frequently, had been signed up. I did not want to be left in grammar school with the quarry girls and have to go to work at fourteen in the local cigar factory, or do housework for other people, or, at best, as Mother planned for me, be apprenticed to a beautician. She did not want me to become a dressmaker and have to deal with customers who were never satisfied and who never paid her on time. "Beauticians are paid right away," she would tell me, "and you don't have to give credit, or work nights, as I do."

Becoming a beautician seemed grotesque to me. I hated artificial hairdos and found cosmetics revolting; I wanted my hair straight and natural. I did not want to be cooped up in a salon smelly with permanent-wave lotions and noisy with chattering, gossiping women. I took it as a matter of course that

I, like Mother, would have to have a job and earn my keep when I grew up. Mother, I knew, could not afford to give me a dowry, so marriage was out. At the very least, I wanted to go to middle school. For the time being I begged Mother to change her decision, to go talk to Fräulein Schäfer and tell her how badly I wanted to take the entrance exam. "You know I won't have another chance to go to middle school if I don't go now," I argued.

She finally did go. "Fräulein Schäfer says you are an average student," she told me when she came back. "You would have trouble making it in middle school, because your spelling and your handwriting are poor." This was true, but I certainly read and wrote better than, say, Bärbel, who had tutoring help. I clung to the faint hope that Fräulein Schäfer would act on her own and register me for the middle school entrance exam. When she began reading aloud the names of the children she had registered, I watched her like a hawk, my heart racing. I promised God I'd be in church every Sunday if she called my name. All the girls who I thought would be called were called; I was not among them. Anna, the best student in the class and the daughter of Bohemian day laborers, was registered for the exam as a scholarship girl. A week later, they all passed— all except Anna. Even Bärbel, who we all knew could hardly write. Higher education was a matter of class: Anna's parents didn't cut it; Bärbel's did.

"I knew it," commented Agatha, who was a year older and wiser than we were. She spoke with the cynicism that the quarry girls adopted to protect themselves from humiliation. I had no such defenses. I withdrew further into biking and reading, refusing to do my homework from then on and copying problems and essays from Anna during break, just in case I had to show something to the teacher.

As it happens, I was grateful later in life that I had not gone on to middle or high school; I gained immeasurably in social awareness and understanding and never acquired the snobbery that children learn when they are segregated at an early age from those who, because of poverty, race, ethnicity, or other prejudice, are excluded from opportunity. Most of the girls in my fifth-grade form, now forever barred from higher education, had talents none of their teachers suspected. All were street smart. They had wit and were quick with words. They talked freely about matters that were taboo in my family—like sex, their parents' fights, their work life, their quarrels with neighbors, brawls in pubs, "making out" in parks. This was a world different from my book world or my mother's work life at home—a world repulsive and frightening to me, yet fascinating. I was shy with my classmates most of the time; at any rate, they left me alone and did not tease me by calling me a bookworm. Many of them, possibly because their parents had been either socialists or communists, showed no enthusiasm for what our teachers thought should inspire us—neither for the glorious history of our country nor for our good fortune at living during a time of national victories under Hitler's leadership. They participated minimally and with obvious dislike in the activities of the Hitler Youth, doing just enough to keep from being reported to the authorities. At the time I neither cared about nor understood what interested them. (I would soon lose touch with Agatha, my only access to that world, because she was not promoted after fifth grade and transferred to remedial school.) Their preoccupations were different from mine; they liked boys, film stars, romances, the current hits of popular culture, having fun and being silly. I accepted their indifference to history, geography, and the great causes espoused in the kind of propaganda literature I was beginning to read. I saw them as apathetic about my enthusiasms, just as I was about theirs.

That same spring, together with my classmates, I was registered with the Hitler Jugend, or HJ (Hitler Youth). In 1939 membership in the Hitler Youth had become compulsory for all boys and girls aged ten to eighteen, and our teacher told us ten-year-olds to gather in the schoolyard for our first meeting as Jungmädel. Our school had undoubtedly provided our names to the local Hitler Youth leadership. From then on we would spend Wednesday afternoons in these meetings, and our parents had to buy us our Jungmädel uniforms, or at least a dark skirt and a white blouse, to wear to them. HJ *Dienst* (service), as we called it, was little more to me than a chore like any other the adults required of us.

After Easter break, when the "upper crust," as Agatha called them, had left, we got a new teacher: Fräulein Pelzer, a thin, nervous, middle-aged woman with a high-pitched voice, a black bobbed hairdo, and bangs. She told us that she was religious and professed great enthusiasm for the Führer, almost in the same breath. "God will protect our beloved Führer," she crooned. "You are blessed to have him as a leader. He has erased the shame of the Treaty of Versailles and regained for us the territories that Germany lost after the Great War." Our soldiers were never just soldiers: "Our courageous heroes fought most ferociously." Most of the girls made fun of her. Helga, as good a caricaturist at twelve as any I came to appreciate later, drew pictures of her seated in her chair on the dais, thin legs with rolled stockings visible beneath her hitched-up skirt, pot belly, thin, low-slung breasts, triangular face, compressed lips, bangs. Pinocchio nose, teardrops on cheeks and tip of nose.

Fräulein Pelzer had no control over us. We did whatever we wanted to; four-somes played cards on their desk, two of them with their backs to the teacher; others gossiped and giggled. I would read or daydream through most of the riotous bedlam, unaware both of my classmates and of poor Fräulein Pelzer.

Then, one day, *Bang!* Pelzer's desktop came crashing down—not just once but repeatedly. Pencils scattered, paper flew about, books hit the floor. *Bang, bang!* She smashed down the desktop again and again until everyone stopped talking and looked at her in growing consternation. Loud sobs followed; her head down, crying convulsively into a huge white polka-dotted handkerchief that covered her face, she sobbed on and on. For the rest of the day we kept quiet. My face burned with shame—for her, for me, for us?

But even after that I kept on reading. The school inspector came twice a year to examine us on what we had learned. When he did, I put my book away and answered his questions. Not that I had learned any of the geography or history, the poems or vocabulary, in class. My own reading and my curiosity about maps and encyclopedias provided all of that, and the inspector was satisfied. Fräulein Pelzer was happy with this arrangement and left me alone to read.

From fifth through eighth grade, whenever former classmates and friends now in middle or high school saw me, they whispered to each other, giggled, and turned away. I learned to ignore them. Once, when I went by Bärbel's house to ask her to come and play, she sent me away with, "Mother says I shouldn't play with you." Humiliated and betrayed, I withdrew. Hanne Knor-reck, a housepainter's daughter from the Boxhammers' apartment house and a dyslexic who had difficulty reading and misspelled every word in dictation, had stayed in my grammar school class. Fräulein Schäfer had dismissed her as stupid in the first grade, and only Hanne's facility with figures saved her from staying behind. Always ready to go for a walk, to imitate the latest popular singer or play a game, she could be counted on to lighten my bleak moods with her good humor and silly jokes, and so we drew closer together. Rita Box-hammer, whom I knew only as one fourth-grade classmate among many who had left for middle school, returned to our grammar school a year later. Both her parents had died of tuberculosis, and she too had contracted TB and had spent many months in a sanatorium before she was declared cured. She had missed almost a year of school and was too delicate to catch up. She lived with her Aunt Agnes, a dressmaker like my mother, in two upstairs rooms above the former Boxhammer smithy, on the corner of Promenade and Woiselwitz streets; the family's old apartment, downstairs off the smithy, could not be used or even leased because it was deemed too damp and unhealthy. I liked Rita, a quiet and thoughtful girl. Most of the time she was too tired—I now think too depressed—to come out and play with Hanne and me, though we often invited her.

I also became friends with Erika, a classmate whose father worked as a foreman in the quarries. They lived in the new settlement houses, duplexes that had replaced the barracks out on Breslauer Street. Like myself, Erika was a reader, and we spent endless afternoons reading penny novels in her parents' attic dormer, which served as her and her sister's bedroom. As we became teenagers, reading boys' books and playing with Jochen and his friends gradually came to an end. Erika's penny novels were mostly romances; we consumed them by the pound and talked about our daydreams. Erika, with long, silky, ash-blond hair, regular features, and a petite figure, wanted to become a famous film star, and I dreamed of being a world traveler—a spy or an explorer, slashing my way through primeval forests, climbing the Himalayas, swimming the Amazon, trekking across African savannahs.

My family's meager bookshelf provided the Auerbach's Children's Calendar—yearly editions of stories, riddles, and games from the turn of the century—of which we had a score. Father had also left us several popular historical novels, a few volumes of an encyclopedia, an atlas, and a medical encyclopedia, which held no interest for girls our age with the exception of its illustrations of human reproductive organs. Needless to say, I shared the medical encyclopedia illustrations with my friends, until Mother caught us giggling over them and locked the book up in her desk.

The winter of 1939–40 passed with the adults speculating as to which country, France or England, Hitler would move against next. What did happen next was another blitzkrieg (lightning war). On April 9, 1940, the German navy, assisted by army and parachute divisions, attacked Denmark and Norway, both neutral countries. Hitler and his generals had decided to risk a fast takeover of these two countries so as to protect Germany's northern border from potential surprises by the British, to secure access to Swedish iron ore through the harbor of Narvik, and to acquire stations for the German fleet in preparation for a planned invasion of the British Isles. Neither the Norwegians nor the Danes had more than a few hours of warning.

During the preceding weeks, the radio had repeatedly interrupted regular programming with a signature fanfare (taken from Liszt's preludes, I believe). An announcer would bark the *Achtung! Achtung!* and then would come: "A Special News Report! On the Führer's orders, our navy has launched landing parties along the coast of Norway, from Narvik to Christiansand. A beachhead has been established in Narvik Harbor." The national anthem followed. News report after special news report kept us glued to the radio in the living room, intoxicated by the victories of our troops. "British warship sunk off Narvik!" "Narvik taken by our paratroopers!" "German troops in Oslo!" "Trondheim in German hands!" "The King of Denmark has escaped!" "Denmark has surrendered!" Marching music would fill our living room in the interim between these bulletins.

Fräulein Pelzer started our class with a new project. She asked us each to bring to class a fresh lined copybook and the last week's newspapers, scissors, and glue. The *Strehlen Daily* displayed pictures of our troops at war, and these we cut out in class and pasted into our copybooks. We added maps of Norway and Denmark printed in the paper, and located the movement of German troops on them. Battles got a blue star drawn with colored pencil. We marked victories with red stars. Fräulein Pelzer replaced the map of Germany that hung next to Hitler's picture with a huge map of Europe. At about this time, a framed Nazi slogan in Gothic lettering—"Du bist Nichts, Dein Volk ist Alles" (You are nothing, Your people are everything)—replaced the earlier "Gott behüte dieses Haus" (God protect this house) above the door of our classroom. I wondered about these impositions from above and learned to provide my own interpretations of them, without, however, communicating my understanding to anyone. I did believe that I was nothing, unimportant, as the sign in our classroom said. All that mattered was the fatherland. When I overheard the other girls in my class grumbling about all these tasks and slogans, I envied their rowdy camaraderie but took no part in it, feeling that to do so would be disloyal to the causes that our teacher, the radio, and everyone I knew espoused.

France, in order to ensure that it would never again be attacked by Germany as it had been in the Franco-Prussian War and again in 1914, had built, we were told, the world's strongest fortifications—the Maginot Line—all along its border with Germany. But its northern border with Belgium, a neutral country, was open. At the outbreak of the war, Britain and its allies had stationed an Expeditionary Force of ten divisions of infantry, a tank brigade, and a detachment of the Royal Air Force at this border, in the event of a German attack. And through this "back door," Hitler attacked France on May 10, 1940. Our radio announcer ridiculed the French and British defense strategy, as Hitler's armies marched quickly through the Netherlands and Belgium and engaged the Expeditionary Force. Meanwhile, German tank divisions were entering France over the Ardennes Mountains, to the north of the Maginot Line, a route that the French had believed impassable to tanks. These tank divisions cut off communication between the French and British forces. The French attempted an attack on the approaching Germans but were defeated. The Expeditionary Force, poorly coordinated and not practiced in the field of battle, was driven back. After a futile counterattack near Arras, the Expeditionary Force pulled back toward Dunkirk. Between May 27 and June 4, close to 860 vessels—from destroyers to small yachts—rescued some 340,000 British soldiers and 140,000 French from falling into German hands. Paris fell on June 14. German troops marched in a victory parade along the Champs-Elysées on June 21. By the following day, two-thirds of France was occupied and the French, under Marshal Pétain, surrendered. With that, Italy and Japan joined Hitler's war against England, the three powers calling themselves the Axis.

After the fall of France and the defeat of the British Expeditionary Force at Dunkirk, Hitler believed that Britain would seek peace. When the British failed to surrender, the Luftwaffe attacked British airfields and finally bombed London and Coventry. The Battle of Britain lingered into the late fall of 1940 before the Royal Air Force defeated the Luftwaffe. Because of British superiority in the air, Hitler would abandon his plans for an amphibious assault on the British Isles.

I can recall none of the specifics of these major events of the summer and fall of 1940—except for a continuous sense of exhilaration. But I do remember vividly several newspaper reports about the French campaign. One photograph showed Marshal Pétain and Hitler in a railroad coach in the Compiègne Forest, with Pétain bent over, signing the capitulation. "That is the place where the dishonorable armistice was imposed on our army at the end of WWI," I noted in my copybook beneath the picture. Another picture showed a jumble of battered, burned, and shot-up tanks and trucks and armaments abandoned by the British at Dunkirk. I don't recall my inscription beneath this photo, nor do I remember the beginning of the Battle of Britain in July 1940. By July I was back at the Schultes' farm in Zülzendorf, where I had no access to news from either radio or newspaper.

Over the next two years we would trace the advance of German troops in blue and red. (We got all the way to a blue Stalingrad. After the German Sixth Army capitulated at Stalingrad in early 1943, Fräulein Pelzer would give up the exercise of following the movements of our troops.) I learned the geography of Europe, filling copybook after copybook with maps and pictures of soldiers and conquered countries and cities. We were told to accompany the pictures with a narration of the news and whatever we thought noteworthy about the picture. Before our troops had invaded Poland, newscasts had reported attacks by Poles against the German minorities in Poland; therefore, when Hitler ordered the German army to attack, I understood that we were defending our own people. The attack against Norway and Denmark came as a surprise—but I soon learned to write in my copybook that Hitler had acted only to foil British and French plans to invade those neutral countries. And of course France and Britain had been our archenemies since World War I, and long before that besides! It was our historic mission to fight them! It was always the fault of the other side, as I filled my copybooks with pictures of German soldiers in Holland, Belgium, and France. I absorbed the national rationalization game like a sponge.

Before I left home for the summer vacation at Zülzendorf, we had been told in school and in Jungmädel that Germany needed our help in bringing in the harvest. Having a purpose this time around, I enjoyed my stay. Much had changed since my last visit. Almost all of the male field hands had been called up, so my offer of help in the fields was accepted as a matter of course. I took a much more active interest in what was going on around me, now that I knew the routines of the household and was no longer constantly afraid. I loved everything about Friday, the baking day. Thursday night, after Herta, Selma, and I had cleaned up the huge farm kitchen, Aunt Helene poured a large sack of flour into a wooden trough that she placed next to the warm oven. She made a dell in the middle of the heap of flour and poured sourdough riser into it, mixing it with a little of the flour and covering the thickened paste with a little more flour. An hour or so later, she prepared the dough by adding water, salt, and butter and kneading it into one large roll. During the next few hours, the roll swelled so that it almost overflowed the sides of the trough. Just before bedtime, she would slap the risen mass so that the air escaped and then she would knead the dough once again and put it next to the stove for another rising. I never got to see her form the loaves or whatever else happened at daybreak, because by the time I got to the kitchen in the morning, three or four loaves still sat rising on wooden trays, while Herta and Selma had already carried half a dozen or so over to the huge brick oven in the bake house, next to the cow stable. The entire farmyard smelled of baking bread.

Before going out to the fields, I would go over to the bake house to watch the first load of shiny chestnut-brown loaves taken out of the oven with a big flat wooden paddle. While Herta took out the loaves, Aunt Helene painted the remaining loaves with a milky-looking mixture to ready them for the oven. Trays of *Streusselkuchen,* a cake topped with a crumble of butter and sugar, stood ready to follow the loaves into the oven, and some of the village farm women brought their trays of cakes to fill up any space left. When we returned from the fields at night and trudged through the kitchen on our way to wash up, Herta often handed me a slice of bread still warm and dripping with fresh butter. I have never again tasted bread half as delicious as these fresh slices, with their heavy crust.

Together with all the other women, I worked a full eight-hour day in the fields, every day except most Sundays. The men drove the mower and trucks, and older boys, the horse-drawn wagons. A farm boy my age was allowed to drive a wagon, and I thought it was a much easier task than mine, which was to bind the sheaves of wheat and pile them upright against each other to dry out. It took me a few days to learn how to twist the blades of straw into a thick rope and tie it around the sheaf without the knot slipping apart when I picked up the sheaf and stacked it against the others.

The foreman had me join a team of two other women the first week, and I could barely keep up with them. The second week, he paired me with Wanda, a Polish woman—huge, powerful, truly majestic. Even with my mind poisoned by the regional Silesian prejudice ("Poles are lazy," "Poles are stupid"), I did not think of being anything but respectful to her. By midmorning I was so exhausted that I began to sob involuntarily as the foreman kept yelling at us to catch up with the others. Wanda slowed down, daring the foreman to make her move faster by muttering what I thought were curses in Polish. Occasionally she tied a sheaf for me that would not stay tied. From the first day I trusted her, and at every new assignment I would stand next to her so I could work with her. She spoke very little German and I spoke no Polish at all, but over the summer our language skills improved.

The team working next to us was usually two Italian women, Anita and Maria. Anita and Wanda kidded each other good-humoredly by gesture and in broken German. That is how I found out that Wanda was working on the Schultes' farm as *Fremdarbeiterin* (forced labor) and hailed from defeated Poland. Anita and Maria, however, were *Gastarbeiterinnen* (guest workers), part of a seasonal labor force that came in early summer and left for Italy after the October potato harvest. Anita and Maria talked of going home after the harvest, of buying finery and of giving the money they had earned to their mothers. Wanda, I learned from her silence, would not be going home, nor would she be paid any money. Anita and Maria could go to the Saturday night dances at the local pub, while Wanda could not even leave her room after dark. I took all this in, feeling vaguely troubled even as I accepted her slave status. It would not even have occurred to me to think it was unjust.

I liked these workers much better than the German field hands. I felt comfortable with Wanda, Anita, and Maria, while I resented the coarse sexual jokes and rough bantering of the German women. I had little commerce with them, in part, I am sure, because I was the niece of the administrator. They dealt with me at a distance and exempted me from their often brutal teasing. Many of the German women brought along their teenage children and subjected them, particularly the daughters, to humiliations that terrified me. One day, an especially mean-looking woman grabbed one of the thirteen-year-olds and bellowed with laughter: "Let's see if you're a virgin!" Holding the girl under one huge elbow, she reached down with her other hand to fumble between the girl's legs. The girl screamed, while the other women (and the foreman, too) laughed uproariously. The foreign workers did not laugh. Wanda moved close to the woman, like a huge shadow, and looked down on her silently, her face rigid with anger. The woman let the girl go, grumbled a few curse words in Wanda's direction, and turned back to her work.

All of the field hands hated the foreman, and I came to share their hatred. He rang a bell in the morning, calling us to work. He had a lyric that accompanied the rhythmical ringing: "Kommt schinden und schuften, ihr Hunde, verfluchten" (Come toil and slave, you damned bitches). He drove us all relentlessly with curses and threats. Uncle Richard, who knew of this, never interfered (perhaps he knew that the coarser the foreman appeared, the more gentlemanly he himself would seem). I liked Uncle Richard, though, and was flattered when he occasionally allowed me to come along with him in the evenings in his buggy to inspect the fields. We drove through the quiet dusk and he answered all my questions. He told me what crops grew best where, and why; how to know when to harvest wheat, barley, and rye; how to judge soils by color and consistency; how to estimate losses from rainstorms. Even today when I ride by fields, I know at a glance what the crop is and the quality of the soil. I loved the rides in his buggy through the mild evening, with the sun casting its last rays over the fields of ripe, dark yellow wheat and a breeze rippling through that endless golden sea.

I soon came to understand, from my uncle's joking at the dinner table, that the Schultes had little reverence for anything related to the Nazi Party. Willy, Aunt Helene's younger brother and the family ne'er-do-well, had advanced to the position of an important-sounding party functionary and served as the butt of many jokes when he visited the family. His right arm had been damaged at birth and remained withered, making him unsuitable for a career in farming or the military, as was the family's wont. A tall, otherwise nimble, loquacious bachelor, he compensated for his handicap by playing the jokester, and when teased he gave as good as he got. His clowning embarrassed me, especially when he put a sofa cushion between his legs to demonstrate the size of his balls; such foolery seemed at odds with the seriousness that, to my mind, his brown-shirt uniform required.

Tired out as I was from the field work, I still read into the night. Among the books in the attic, I made a new discovery: a volume of poetry. We had learned poetry by heart since first grade, and I memorized verses easily. A few readings aloud would fix a poem in my mind, the rhythm and rhymes carrying me along. The year before, I had pushed the volume of poems to the back of the attic bookcase. This year, as I looked for a poem I knew from school, a poem by Joseph Freiherr von Eichendorff caught my eye:

> Kaiserkron' und Päonien roth,
> Die müssen verzaubert sein,
> Denn Vater und Mutter sind lange todt,
> Was blühn sie hier so allein?

> Sweet Williams and red peonies,
> Must be enchanted,
> Father and Mother died long ago,
> Why do they stand so alone?

What enchanted me in this and another favorite poem, by Eduard Mörike, was the fairy-tale atmosphere of languid melancholy, the forsaken and ghostly young women who mourned loved ones, the music of simple folk song rhythms and rhymes, and the vivid metaphors—red flowers and flames against the dark of night.

Früh, wann die Hähne krähn,
Eh' die Sternlein verschwinden,
Muß ich am Herde stehn,
Muß Feuer zünden.

Schön ist der Flammen Schein,
Es springen die Funken;
Ich schaue so drein,
In Leid versunken.

Early when the cocks crow
Before the stars grow pale,
I have to stand at the hearth,
And light the fire.

Beautiful is the glow of the flames,
Sparks fly about;
I look at them,
Sunk in grief.

I relished their gloomy atmosphere and sorrowful sentiment. In poetry I discovered another way out of reality. Whenever I found work in the fields too hard, when I felt threatened by the roughhousing of the field workers, when I had to sit through dinner conversations that bored me, I escaped into a poem, reciting it silently to myself, taking shelter in it.

The payment of another hefty sum for my summer's work brought me down to earth. I decided to buy some sky-blue woolen material for a winter dress and ask Mother to make it for me. On the train ride home, I designed the dress in my mind. After the summer in the country, this year's return was even harder than last year's. I couldn't help but see the shabbiness of our furniture, the grime of our kitchen, as compared with the elegance and cleanliness of the Schultes' household. My engagement with Hitler Youth would soon fill the void Oma's death had left and compensate me for my disappointment over my failed hopes for higher education.

Chapter Four

TODAY GERMANY BELONGS TO US —
TOMORROW, THE WHOLE WORLD, 1940–1941

WHEN I AND MY TEN-YEAR-OLD PEERS were inducted into the Hitler Youth, the HJ, in 1940, we joined a well-established, tightly structured national organization. During the Weimar Republic, the Hitler Youth, then a division of Hitler's SA, had been only one of many youth organizations and clubs that originated in the late nineteenth-century rebellion of male, middle- and lower-middle-class youth against their bourgeois parents and an industrial, mechanized, highly regimented society. Those early, largely apolitical organizations, the best known of which was Wandervogel (migratory bird), glorified youth as a vital, idealistic force of social renewal, inspired by the ideals of German romanticism. Like their romantic predecessors, Wandervogel groups tramped through the open countryside and explored the simple customs of the German peasantry, their tales, songs, and folk dances. They adopted a simple lifestyle—dressing in shorts, open-necked shirts, and solid hiking boots, living communally in their camps and on their hikes, and aspiring to individual self-realization and personal responsibility. Much of the Wandervogel spirit, its romanticism, its ethos of youth being led by youth, its romantic communalism, its stress on simplicity and naturalness of lifestyle, its songs, campfires, and hiking and camping practices survived into the Hitler Youth, as my generation came to know it. Even though none of us knew of its origins, this Wandervogel spirit was for many of us one of the attractive features of the Hitler Youth.

The German youth movement changed profoundly after World War I. Many groups became radicalized, moving to the political Left and Right. Those young people whose families believed in the betrayal of the troops by the home front joined the youth groups on the Right, of which the Hitler Youth was the most extreme. Those whose fathers believed in the exploitation of working people by the industrial-military establishment joined the Left. Both sides adopted soldierly values and attitudes—a reverence for heroism, discipline, group spirit—and hierarchical leadership principles. Uniforms and military ranks and organizational structure reflected this new postwar martial spirit. The apparent distinction between political Left and Right was often little more than a difference in shirt color.

From his early political beginnings, Hitler formulated the structure and aims of a mass youth organization within his party. Subordinated to his Storm Troopers, the SA, it was to have the same hierarchical military structure. Hence its shirts were brown and its insignia—swastika armband, leather belt—similar to those of the SA. Shorts rather than SA jodhpurs and boots, and a black kerchief held in place around the neck by a leather knot, recalled the dress of the Wandervogel. Hitler conceived of German youth united against the injustices of the Versailles Treaty, which he, like many conservative Germans, deplored. Instead of being divided by class or religion, German youth were to be one community of race and blood. The youth movement was to fight against the international conspiracy of Jewry, Bolshevism, and materialism and foster everything Germanic—of German blood and German *Volksgemeinschaft,* the community of the people. The Hitler Youth would be inculcated with these aims through weekly meetings, lectures, hiking, camping, singing, physical and military activities, and competitions. For us, the cohort born between about 1925 and 1930 and socialized from age ten on by the Hitler Youth, being German and being National Socialist became indistinguishable.

At the 1926 Nazi Party rally at Weimar, Hitler formally established the Hitler Youth for boys aged fourteen to eighteen. In 1931 he extended the organization by two subgroups, the Jungvolk for boys aged ten to fourteen, and the Bund Deutscher Mädchen, the BDM, or League of German Girls, for girls aged fourteen to eighteen. In 1933 the organization for girls aged ten to fourteen, the Jungmädel, completed the ranks of Hitler Youth. Thus almost from the beginning of this misogynist party's assuming a key role in the Germany of the 1930s, females in large numbers were to be socialized in Nazi ideology and included in public life. If the few Nazi women's auxiliaries of the 1920s that supported the SA had had their way, the Nazi organizations for girls would have stressed the learning of domestic roles for girls rather than the Wander-vogel ideals of the HJ. But Baldur von Schirach, appointed the party leader of Hitler Youth in 1926, wrested control over the BDM from the women's aux-iliaries and firmly incorporated BDM and Jungmädel into the Hitler Youth's administration and the party's pyramidal paramilitary structure. In sync with the Nazis' belief in separate spheres for men and women, the girls' organiza-tion, at least up to the HJ top leader, Baldur von Schirach, was led by girls and young women.

The consequences for girls and young women growing up under the Nazis were momentous. In their early years as Jungmädel, girls could enjoy a freer and less restricted modern life outside the boundaries of their families than had previous generations of German women. Jungmädel could travel with their groups to rallies, in their "separate sphere" compete in sports, and in fact enjoy most of the activities boys enjoyed. They could feel fully included when Hitler, or any party or HJ leader, addressed the HJ as the fatherland's glorious future. And the ambitious girl, particularly the girl rebelling against parents or social background, could rise within the female hierarchy and even build a professional career within it. These opportunities for fun, social advancement, and self-development made the girls' organizations of the HJ, especially the Jungmädel, attractive for lower-middle- and middle-class girls. For me, who from earliest awareness had chafed at my brother's preferred status, Jung-mädel would provide an illusory feeling of equality, of being just as valuable as he was.

From the beginning the HJ had a complex administration, consisting of var-ious departments dealing with education, welfare, the press, physical activities, even a department responsible for German youth abroad. In this administra-tion young women could reach the highest positions in their separate sphere at all ranks. The HJ was divided into five geographic sections, each subdivided into *Gaue* (often corresponding to provinces) and again into *Oberbanne* and *Banne* (regions and subregions) corresponding to counties, cities, and towns. Higher offices increasingly were headed by male and female professional leaders who had risen through HJ ranks. The hierarchy, as in the military, ranged from the lowest, a squad leader responsible for fifteen boys or girls, to troop leaders, who led three to four squads of up to fifty young people, to the *Gefolgschaftsführer*, the cadre leader, with responsibility for five hundred youngsters, to the highest of all, the party leader of the Hitler Youth, Baldur von Schirach, a young party stalwart who had earlier abandoned his studies in art history and German literature at the University of Munich to further the Nazi cause. With Schirach's ascension, the nationalist middle-class wing of the Hitler Youth won out over competing working-class HJ factions. The idea of the HJ's working-class origins, however—like those of the party, whose name, after all, was the National Socialist Workers' Party—informed its overall program, which was directed toward the disadvantaged and the common good, of Germans only, of course. During my first year in the organization, as a ten-year-old Jungmädel in late 1940, I would collect money from passersby on City Hall Square for the Winterhilfe, the assistance program for families in need. My enthusiasm for the HJ would have been dampened considerably had I not understood that the HJ's ideals of *Volksgemeinschaft*, of a classless community of all the folk, included me and my working-class friends.

In its early years the Hitler Youth was hobbled by a lack of finances, a shortage of meeting places for group activities, sports, and indoctrination, and the absence of a trained leadership cadre at all levels. Membership dues had to be kept low because of unemployment and the Depression. Basements, attics, and even public spaces served as the *Heim,* the home base that each HJ unit needed. Except for Schirach and a few of his colleagues in the HJ national administration, all leadership was unpaid and voluntary. Despite these handicaps the HJ grew rapidly after 1929, as did the Nazi Party as a whole. Attracted by its spirit and success, youth organizations of the political Right merged with the HJ, whose enthusiasm and aggressiveness played an important role in the elections, rallies, and street fighting of the party in the early 1930s.

A number of boys ranging in age from twelve to eighteen were killed in the street fighting and joined the ranks of party martyrs. One of these was Herbert Norkus, the fifteen-year-old boy who was celebrated in *Hitlerjunge Quex,* a sentimental novel and movie of 1933 for young people. Both novel and movie bear the hallmarks of Nazi martyr tales for the young: a generational conflict, a hero of impeccable character despite having grown up in a bad environment, his attraction to the clean-cut and upright Hitler Youth, HJ reenactment of Germanic fire-worship festivals at the summer and winter solstice, the comradeship of the HJ boys regardless of social class, the venality and cowardice of Nazi enemies, service to and sacrifice of one's life for the Nazi cause. The plot is simple. The son of a working-class family, Heini Völker ("Quex" is his later, Hitler Youth nickname), under pressure from his father, has joined a communist youth group, whose laziness and lax morals dismay him. He meets a group of Nazi boys and is attracted by their disciplined and comradely demeanor. He becomes friendly with them and reveals that his communist fellows intend to attack them in their meeting place. In revenge, his former friends drive his mother to commit suicide, and they finally stab Heini to death as he distributes Nazi election leaflets.

Shortly after assuming the chancellorship in 1933, Hitler made Schirach directly responsible to him and no longer under SA tutelage. Henceforth the administrative apparatus of the Hitler Youth would be shared between the Ministry of the Interior (the police) and the Ministry of Justice—that is to say, Hitler placed the entire Hitler Youth in the very heart of the police state. Youth organizations of the political Left, both communist and socialist, were proscribed, along with the parties of the Left. By 1935 most other youth organizations had been dissolved, prohibited, or integrated into the HJ. As a result of *Gleichschaltung* and the growing domination of the Nazi Party, HJ membership (which was still strictly voluntary) had increased from its original few hundred to some six million children. Financial difficulties had been resolved by confiscation or assumption of the funds and properties of all prohibited, disbanded, and integrated youth organizations. For example, the independent German Youth Hostel Association, which had served all the various youth organizations, was now controlled solely by the HJ. However, the inflow of other youth organizations did not resolve the leadership shortage, since Schirach did not trust their leaders. In 1933 he therefore established training centers all over the country to produce, in three-week workshops, a leadership cadre for the lower ranks to accommodate the increase in membership—seven thousand new members in 1933 alone. Even so, the lack of trained leaders at all ranks, and the consequent differences between the discipline and practice of local, regional, and national HJ units, remained a problem throughout the Nazi years. The problem became particularly grave when attendance increased again in 1939, when membership became compulsory for all "Aryan" Germans, male and female, ages ten to eighteen. In some localities and regions, attendance and discipline were strictly enforced and negligence and absenteeism reported and punished; in others, minimal standards were upheld, and in a few, particularly in the countryside, it was possible to ignore the Hitler Youth altogether.

The ideology of the Hitler Youth was a hodgepodge of old and new ideas. Foremost was the quasi-religious cult of the supreme leader, Adolf Hitler himself. The myth created by Nazi hagiography served as model to the young.

Rising from obscure beginnings and near poverty, Hitler had served his country as a common soldier in World War I. Through long and arduous struggle, he had attained national leadership and glory for his nation. The strength, courage, wisdom, and love of young people that the myth attributed to him made him a supreme loving father. At age ten, when I heard him and my HJ leaders call us "his Hitler Youth," I understood that phrase literally. I was his, as I was my mother's child.

Hitler, and the Nazi Party as a whole, held youth to be the vital force of the German *Volk*. Its enthusiasm was to bring about the nation's renewal. Never before or since has German youth enjoyed—in word if not in deed—such attention and glorification. This vital force of youth, so the ideology held, had to be channeled: boys and girls up to age fourteen were to be guided and strengthened by physical activity, education, and sports. Their actual programs became quite different for the mass of adolescents beyond age fourteen: military exercises and discipline in preparation for the military for boys, and, for girls in the BDM, training in health, child care, domestic skills, and self-improvement in preparation for motherhood, domesticity, and comradeship in marriage, hence a limited chance for self-development. Boys had a greater variety of HJ groups to choose from, provided that their families had the means to buy the necessary equipment: the motorized HJ; the navy HJ, with its own sailing yachts; the HJ air force, with its own sailplanes; the equestrian HJ. For girls, particularly in poorer towns or districts, nothing comparable existed. I remember well my envy as I stood, ten years old, near the runway of the sailplane port on Windmill Hill, watching as an older friend of Jochen's, in HJ uniform and flying helmet, climbed into his glider. But I also believed, having read of glider pilot Hanna Reitsch's world records, that exceptional girls and women had a chance to do anything boys and men did.

Physical struggle and exertion for both genders were thought to bring about moral strengthening. As Hitler put it time and again, "I want my Hitler Youth to be tough as leather, hard as Krupp steel, and fast as *Windhunde*," that is, greyhounds. The Hitler Youth instituted competitions in athletics, in useful activities like recycling, and in the mastery of weapon use between individuals, groups, and regions; achievement was rewarded by public recognition and medals. According to its ideology, neither rank, class, wealth, nor birth earned you leadership status but rather the achievement of aims larger than yourself—service performed for the Hitler Youth, *Führer, Volk, und Vaterland*. Dedication to service, unquestioning subordination to a leader, loyalty to Hitler, to the comrades of one's group, to the Hitler Youth itself, were the values that the HJ fostered. It also preached veneration of the German community, forged from a common history and a mystical union through race and blood. It glorified the German landscape, German soil, forests, and mountains, German rural and regional styles of folk art and architecture. It rejected rationalism, intellectualism, and the European Enlightenment.

At least in theory, one's private life, one's own personal, intimate sphere, did not exist for Hitler Youth. Each member was required to serve a cause larger than him- or herself, in ceaseless effort; thus activity triumphed over thought and reflection. From eligible males and females the Nazi Party demanded total involvement and lifelong service—for males from age ten to eighteen, in the Hitler Youth; for the next six months, in the Arbeitsdienst; for the next two years, in the military; and beyond that, lifelong party membership and service to party causes. For females from age ten to eighteen, total involvement and service in the Jungmädel and the BDM; for the next six months, in the Arbeitsdienst; and beyond that, lifelong membership in the party and its women's groups, the Frauenschaft and the Frauenwerk, the former the strictly political auxiliary, the latter the result of integrating middle-class women's groups of the Right through *Gleichschaltung*.

At the beginning of the Nazi regime, family and school still competed for the attention of the nation's young people, but in the course of Hitler's ascendancy and, later, the war, the hours spent in HJ activity increased, from one afternoon or evening a week to additional weekend days and finally to weeks and months at a time. Once enemy bombings of the cities started, entire school classes of children and their teachers were removed from their families and placed into HJ camps in the country. As the war went on, during school vacations long and short, entire HJ units and school classes and ever younger children were pressed into helping with the harvest and relieving other labor shortages on the home front. Some of their duties were military, including manning antiaircraft guns and digging trenches. Schirach expressed this absolutism of his organization's claims on the lives of its members with the words "You are either for us or against us." Neutrality, once the Hitler Youth got ahold of you, was impossible.

On the whole, early in the regime, the educational system and the teaching profession were not in conflict, as German schools claimed the morning hours of instruction and the Hitler Youth the afternoons. Moreover, our teachers—like the middle class as a whole—shared the nationalism of the Nazis. In 1933, when the HJ became an organization of the German state, local HJ units could freely use public school and sports facilities as meeting places and arenas. As time went on the party's influence over the schools and their instructional materials became dominant, so that the schools and the Hitler Youth followed the same goals. By 1936 most textbooks parroted Nazi ideology. Even the problems in our arithmetic exercise book had ideological content: "The inmate of a mental hospital costs the state 5.20 marks a day. How much does that come to in a month? A year?" The comment my teacher offered, of course, was, "All hereditary illnesses are a heavy burden for the community." I never heard her justify euthanasia or sterilization as a solution, but that was certainly the implication. Academic subjects became contaminated by ideology and diluted by indoctrination. Academic standards fell drastically, while HJ activity and service replaced instruction.

As instructional material and entertainment for the Hitler Youth, Nazi publishers (and soon most publishing houses) favored fairy tales and sagas, Germanic myth and heroic epics—particularly popular adaptations of its national epic, the *Nibelungenlied,* glorifying Siegfried's radiant strength and Hagen's loyalty to his king. (Later, in graduate school, I came to understand how grossly these popular nationalist versions trivialized and distorted the medieval epic.) Medieval heroes, like the Hohenstauffen and Saxon emperors, populated novels for young people, as did the kings, nobles, and officers of Prussian history. And of course the heroic feats of "our soldiers" in the two world wars and the treachery of "our enemies" formed the plots of much juvenile literature. Avid reader that I was, I consumed these HJ volumes whenever I could get ahold of them. By age fifteen I had read almost all of them. Like many intellectuals of my generation, after the Nazi defeat I would never again want to read a fairy tale or Germanic saga, nor could I tolerate a folk proverb or folk song except in a satirical context. It took me years to recover for myself, as a student and teacher of German literature, the literary romantic tradition of folk literature and to decontaminate it from Nazi perversion and abuse. To this day, German folk songs make me uncomfortable.

Jochen preceded me (as usual) into the Hitler Youth, and (as usual) he did not like attending the meetings, just as he did not like going to school. I was still smarting from not having been allowed to go to middle school and did not look forward to anything. As far as I was concerned, HJ was just another chore. Fräulein Schäfer, our fourth-grade teacher, had told us to assemble after school on Wednesday in Red School play yard. She gave us a pep talk about how lucky we were to become Jungmädel. "When I was growing up before the Great War, girls did not have your opportunities. We had to stay home and help our mothers. Like your brothers, you will be able to go on camping trips, have fun with your girls' group in singing and playing games, get to know your *Heimat* [home region] by exploring its forests and mountains, learning its myths and its fairy tales. You will have your own groups, led by older girls; you'll know a comradeship we never did." Her tone became wistful, and I stopped listening. I could not imagine her ever having been young.

When I try to recall the details of my actual induction into the Hitler Youth after Easter vacation in 1940, my mind resists remembering, refuses to focus. I cannot see the individual faces of the girls in my squad, as I can, for example, see Hanne's screwed-up nose when she giggled. I try to remember the names of the girls in my squad—nothing. Then suddenly I hear Marlis, our fourteen-year-old squad leader, call out the list of our names, which was how she would start every Wednesday afternoon meeting. My name, in the middle of the list, comes into focus: *Mahlendorf, Ursula*. And then the names that precede and follow it: *Kupka, Ursula; Lemke, Hannelore; Nitzsche, Helga*. I cannot see their faces, but other details emerge. I see myself standing in the schoolyard of Red School among a large group of girls my age, few of whom I know. It is two o'clock on Wednesday afternoon, after school has let out. I am alone in the crowd and miss Hanne, who is late. My former friends, who left for middle school and high school just a few days ago, stand together in a circle some distance away, and I know they will snub me if I approach. I feel angry and isolated, turn my back on them. Later, several older girls arrive with one of the middle school teachers, Lotte Turnow, all in HJ uniforms—navy blue skirt, white blouse, black kerchief held in place by a leather knot. Braided silk cords defining their leadership status, some red and white, some green and white, dangle atop the kerchief to the left blouse pocket. The older girls hold lists and begin calling out our names, asking us to form a circle around them. After a while, a pale, freckled girl in dark blond pigtails summons me to her group. By the time she has read aloud the last name, we are fifteen in her group.

"I am Marlis," she introduces herself, "and I'll be your *Schaftführerin* [squad leader]. We are four squads to a troop. Helga"—she points to a girl who stands next to Lotte Turnow—"will be our *Scharführerin* [troop leader]. Lotte leads all Jungmädel in town; she is our *Ringführerin* [cadre leader]. We'll always meet right here, in Red School yard, and begin our activities from here." Her tone now changes to command mode: "Line up by size!" The fifteen of us are practiced in lining up by size, as we have done it since first grade. I am the third tallest.

"Count!" is the next command.

The tallest girl begins: "One!" and snaps her head to the right for the next girl. My heart begins to pound. "Two!" yells the girl next to her, and swivels her head toward me. I hesitate; my mind has gone blank.

"Three!" Marlis barks for me. "Pay attention!"

I freeze, while my mind races, words, silent words, echoing within me. "Stupid, can't you even count?" I scream silently at myself. Because I have missed my turn, the entire squad has to repeat the count.

Next we practice marching in formation. We form five rows of three girls each, again graduated by size. That puts me in front row, right. "Forward, *march!*" comes Marlis's command. "*Right,* two, three, four, *right,* two three, four," and at each loud "*right,*" our right foot, knee slightly bent, is to move forward. We first practice marching in formation straight ahead. One of us falls out of step and Marlis bellows," Formation, *stop!*" After a brief pause and an admonition to pay attention, we start again. "Formation, *march! Right,* two, three, four, *one,* two, three, four."

Next come more complicated maneuvers: "Formation, *right!*" means that I have to perform my "*one,* two, three, four" by lifting my feet in place while turning forty-five degrees to the right. "Formation, *left!*" means that I have to take giant steps to the left at the "*one,* two, three, four" while making a quarter-turn without adding an extra step, which would put me out of step with the formation. Marlis's first "Formation, *right!*" prompts me to start my turn to the left, and when I see that my neighbor is turning toward me I reverse. "Formation, stop!" Marlis howls. "Don't you know right from left?"

At that moment, I learned that I (like most people) had some difficulty distinguishing right from left under pressure. Armed with this insight and paying close attention, I managed most of the ensuing "Formation, *right!*"s and "*left!*"s just fine.

After an hour and a half, Marlis stopped the drill and led us into one of the larger classrooms in the middle school next door, where we found the other squads of newly fledged Jungmädel waiting for us. I was so exhausted from trying to pay attention to the marching maneuvers that I slumped down onto one of the benches. Marlis shot me a glance, and I knew it meant that I ought to sit up straight. Lotte Turnow entered after a while and went up front to the teacher's platform. She looked down at us, her face stern. "Welcome to the HJ, girls," she addressed us. "You are beginning an important phase of your life today. From now on, you will serve our Führer and fatherland through Jung-mädel. For the next few months, you will be on probation and learn the first steps in becoming the kind of Jungmädel the Führer wants you to be. Once you have been tested, you will take your oath to the Führer after you return from your summer break."

Like all my future HJ leaders, once they got started, she went on and on, and I stopped listening. (The "probation" was a fiction: No one did or could fail, as we were required to attend.) I woke up from my daydream when she started to sing "Deutschland, Deutschland, über Alles," and I joined in, raising my right arm and feeling guilty, as always, about not having listened—and, as the song went on, proud that I was ten years old and a Jungmädel now.

Marlis led our squad to another, smaller classroom. "Let's learn a few songs for marching. It's easier to keep step when you sing." She began, in a clear soprano voice, "O beautiful western forest . . ." We had all heard this song when the HJ troops marched through town, so we knew the melody, and soon we learned all the words. After that, Marlis warbled the martial Hitler Youth theme song in her incongruously bright soprano, and when she had run through it she taught us the words line by line:

> Vorwärts! Vorwärts! Schmettern die hellen Fanfaren,
> Vorwärts! Vorwärts! Jugend kennt keine Gefahren,
> Deutschland, du wirst leuchtend stehn
> Mögen wir auch untergehn.
> Vorwärts! Vorwärts!
> Schmettern die hellen Fanfaren,
> Vorwärts! Vorwärts! Jugend kennt keine Gefahren.
> Ist das Ziel auch noch so hoch,
> Jugend zwingt es doch.
>
> Refrain:
>
> Uns're Fahne flattert uns voran.
> In die Zukunft ziehen wir Mann für Mann.
> Wir marschieren für Hitler
> Durch Nacht und durch Not
> Mit der Fahne der Jugend
> Für Freiheit und Brot.
> Uns're Fahne flattert uns voran,

Uns're Fahne ist die neue Zeit.
Und die Fahne führt uns in die Ewigkeit!
Ja die Fahne ist mehr als der Tod!

Forward! Forward! Let the fanfares ring.
Forward! Forward! Youth knows no dangers.
Germany, you will triumph
Even if we perish.
Forward! Forward! Let the fanfares ring.
Forward! Forward!
Youth knows no dangers.
Let our goals be ever so high,
We will conquer them!

Refrain:

Our banner leads us ahead!
We march into the future, man by man,
We march for Hitler through night and distress
With the banner of youth for freedom and bread.
Our banner leads us ahead.
Our banner is the new age!
And our banner leads us into eternity!
Our banner is greater than death!

None of us understood that we had just absorbed the key concepts that were to guide our lives as HJ members—that we were a special, valuable class, representing a new age for Germany; that we would serve Germany and Hitler, whatever the danger or hardship; that we were ready to sacrifice our lives so that Germany could live free of her enemies.

For the next four Wednesday afternoons we practiced marching and learned a repertoire of marching songs. I never lost my nervousness about marching ("*Right,* two, three, four!"), and since I stayed in the front row all year thanks to my height, I was highly visible. Why was I so awkward at marching? It was all the more striking to me because I was a whiz as a biker and a swimmer and good at games of physical skill. My best guess now is that I distrusted and resisted conforming to group activity and the orders of even a minor authority.

After marching we would repair to the classroom to learn more songs, marching songs at first, and later folk songs, most of which I already knew from having sung them with my mother and brothers. Sometimes, as a reward when we had completed our marching practice without too many of us falling out of step, we played parlor games like charades. Gradually I came to enjoy this routine, particularly the singing. Just before summer vacation, our Jungmädel troop was allowed to accompany the older girls' troops to a rally in Münsterberg, a few miles away. "You have really made progress in keeping in formation," Marlis told us. "I hope you won't embarrass us at the rally when we march into the stadium."

I worried about making mistakes even as I looked forward to the train ride—a rare event for me—to the neighboring town. We sang on the train, hundreds of boys and girls going to the rally. We marched into the stadium, and it was easy to keep in formation because we followed the more experienced Hitler Youth troops. We were part of what seemed an endless stream of boys and girls marching to the tunes of the large band on a platform at the far end of the stadium. Arriving at our designated spot on the stadium floor, we stood at attention while the flags and standards were carried in and the HJ leadership entered the stadium. Finally, after a long pause, the province leader of Silesia, a stocky, middle-aged man in brown SA uniform who was the rally speaker, marched in all alone, with measured step, to our repeated cheers of "Sieg Heil! Sieg Heil!" I was impressed by the dignity of this slow, deliberate advance, and thrilled to be part of such a ceremony. I understood only years later that, with his late arrival and solemn procession to the speaker's platform, he was imitating one of Hitler's techniques of mass manipulation.

Standing in the hot June sun soon became uncomfortable, as the province leader's speech droned on: "We are at war," he told us, rather unnecessarily. "Our brave soldiers have conquered France. England is next. We must all help the Führer in his difficult task of leading Germany. . . . We must all do our part in helping to win the victory. You, the future of Germany, can help: help with bringing in the harvest this summer, help with collecting herbs and recyclables—scrap iron, rags, bones, paper—with which to make guns, uniforms, medical supplies for our troops." I was greatly relieved when the time came for us to sing "Deutschland, Deutschland, über Alles" and the Horst Wessel song, our right arms raised in the Hitler salute. Since my group was standing in the middle of the stadium, with rows and rows of girls both in front and behind, I could rest my arm on the shoulder of the girl in front of me as the verses dragged on. Early in my HJ career I felt a certain amount of guilt over this undisciplined laxness in sustaining the salute. But during the many rallies that followed this one, even the keenest enthusiasm would dissipate by the time the final strophes had sounded. We sang again on the train back home, tired and sunburned but happy to be part of a great cause. I was aflame with zeal to do my part in the war effort. This summer at Zülzendorf, I swore to myself, I would work full days in the fields without protest, every weekend with no complaining, for the full six weeks of my vacation.

By the late fall of 1940, the war and the Hitler Youth had begun to take over my life. Because of war shortages it was difficult to keep the tires on our bikes in repair—even I got good at patching inner tubes—and this limited our riding around the countryside. When my inner tubes consisted almost entirely of patches and the tires were almost in shreds, I thought twice about going very far from home; walking home with a flat was no fun. And the daily news broadcasts and "special reports," preceded by march music and trumpets and "Achtung! Achtung! Here is radio Germany," kept us busy. Newspaper photographs of submarine heroes and reports on the beginning of the submarine war had to be cut out and labeled.

The party's new national youth leader, Arthur Axmann—in August 1940 Hitler had replaced Baldur von Schirach, whom he no longer trusted—called on all HJ troops to serve the fatherland as replacements for the men who had been called to the front. The older Hitler Youth began to serve as streetcar ticket collectors and as factory workers in munitions works. Toward the end of the war the boys would man antiaircraft guns and dig trenches at the German borders and in the streets of German cities; finally, even fourteen-year-old boys would be called up and sent to the front. The girls of the BDM acted as nurses' aides, took over as streetcar conductors when the men and boys were called up, worked in munitions factories, helped ethnic German farmers settle in annexed Polish territories—some even assisted in the forcible eviction of Polish farmers—and finally dug trenches as well.

It fell to the ten- to fourteen-year-olds of the Jungvolk and Jungmädel to go from house to house to collect recyclables and to help during the harvest. I participated in the recycling efforts once a week for the next four years. We collected paper, scrap iron, rags, and bones (to be used for soap making, we were told) from our families and neighbors. The barrels in the schoolyard into which we dumped the bones left over from family dinners crawled with maggots by the time a week had passed. Each time we lifted the barrels into our cart and then emptied them into a vat at the rag collector's on Adolf Hitler

Street six or seven interminable blocks away, I gagged. The place reeked of rotting meat; rats scampered among mountains of old papers, clothes, and rags; rusted bikes lay heaped atop mountains of scrap metal. Our task was much easier on Saturday afternoons, when we helped bring in the potato harvest at nearby farms in Segen, Striege, or Lauden. Horse-drawn wagons transported us back and forth from school to the farmers' fields. Going out to the fields we sang; coming home at dusk, in the flickering light of bonfires of dried potato stalks, we were tired and silent. Our wagons rumbled over Breslauer Street, turned onto Promenade Street with its canopy of yellowing linden leaves, and disgorged us in the schoolyard. I dragged myself across the street to the Baronie, past Werner and his friends playing in the front yard, and fell asleep even as I ate my supper at the kitchen table.

Gradually the town emptied of younger men, and older men and women took their jobs. The fathers of my classmates and the husbands of the Baronie's families went to war. Herr Gurn's truck driver, who delivered the beer and lemonade bottled in the Baronie's shed, disappeared to the front; his drunkenness had disturbed our peace every Saturday night for years, and while Jochen regretted the loss of rides with him, I was happy to see him go. Uncle Kurt, who was deemed indispensable as a farm administrator, and the one-legged Herr Gurn remained the only male presences for the rest of my childhood.

At our Wednesday afternoon HJ meetings all through 1940 and 1941, we practiced running, broad jumping, and throwing baseballs as far as we could in the middle school playground. Since I had tossed pebbles with Jochen and his friends for years, I had developed good wrist action and threw the ball proficiently, but I ranked as one of the poorest runners and broad jumpers of the entire troop. "Didn't you say that you were good at sports?" Marlis teased me. Hanne, who was in the same troop but another squad, took turns with me as the lowest scorer, and I talked her into additional practice on our own on the athletic field on Adolf Hitler Street (formerly Linden Street), which we occasionally used with our squads. But the older kids, who dominated the track, soon chased us off.

Then I had an idea. In the back of the Gurns' property there was a sand-pit. I spent a week spreading and leveling the sand until finally I had about ten meters of racetrack with a broad-jump pit at the end. Hanne had long since lost interest in the project, but I ran and jumped for hours on end for the rest of the year, until the first snow in early December, and began again after snowmelt in March. Gradually my broad-jump score improved, and in running I now scored close to the troop's average. I took pleasure in my athletic achievement and I began to enjoy the Wednesday afternoons; even the marching practice seemed less onerous.

During the winter months and the heavy Silesian snows, sports stopped altogether, and our Wednesday afternoons were spent in singing and political instruction. Marlis taught us about the beginnings of the National Socialist Party after World War I, about Hitler's struggles during the Weimar Republic. "The communists fought his movement in Munich," she said. "The Führer was betrayed by the army. He was imprisoned in Landsberg Fortress after he tried to win power. He wrote *Mein Kampf* there, and you'll read that when you're older." She told us about the Munich putsch of 1923, and how one of Hitler's comrades threw himself in front of Hitler and received a bullet in his stead. Her stories were all of martyrdom and sacrifice, betrayal and heroism. I remember the mood they conveyed more clearly than the facts of the putsch itself, which we learned to call "the march on the Feldherrn Halle," after the Munich war memorial where it occurred. I already knew (and thus resonated with) this glorification of comradeship, of sacrifice for the fatherland, of loyalty and heroism, from the World War I novels Jochen and I had been reading—books such as Richard Euringer's 1929 *Flight School: Book of the Crew* (the Nazi antidote to Erich Maria Remarque's antiwar novel *All Quiet on the Western Front,* published the same year) and Fritz Steuben's *Breakthrough 1918: A Frontline Experience* (1933). We also were encouraged to memorize short biographies of the Nazi leadership, starting with Hitler and going all the way down to such minor functionaries as Robert Ley, leader of the Nazi Labor Front. These hagiographies were not unlike the stories about the ever so pious and frightfully good children that Aunt Magda had told us about in kindergarten, except that as children these men were frightfully brave, loyal, and patriotic rather than frightfully pious and good.

Marlis followed up her tales by teaching us new songs about "the movement"—songs that raised our spirits and made me wish I had lived through the struggle with "Him." We learned the song of the "good comrade"—the man who, more loyal than anyone, dies for his comrade *als wär's ein Stück von mir* (as if he were part of me). My eyes filled with tears every time we sang it, and I found it difficult to sing along. And we learned a song that seemed to upset some of the adults—like Manfred Riedel's father, who a little while later was briefly imprisoned by the Gestapo for (as I heard Mother whisper to a customer) "defeatism":

Es zittern die morschen Knochen
Der Welt vor dem roten Krieg,
Wir haben die Knechtschaft gebrochen,
Für uns war's ein grosser Sieg.

Refrain:

Wir werden weiter marschieren
Wenn alles in Scherben fällt,
Denn heute gehört uns Deutschland
Und morgen die ganze Welt.

The ancient brittle bones of the world tremble
Before the Red war.
We have broken its slavery,
For us it was a mighty victory.

Refrain:

We will march on,
Even if everything sinks into dust,
Because today Germany belongs to us
And tomorrow the whole world.

We introduced a significant change into the song. The original read, "today Germany listens [*hört*] to us"; we sang, "today Germany belongs [*gehört*] to us."

Marlis was certainly an effective propaganda tool, the perfect realization of Hitler's HJ ideal that youth should lead youth. I admired her because she was cheerful and forceful, and because she went to high school but was not arrogant. Not particularly good-looking, Marlis was long-limbed, athletic, slender, and freckled, with dark blond hair and gray eyes. I could imagine that I might be like her in another few years, and I wanted to be like her. During summers in Zülzendorf I kept in touch with her by postcard. I don't think she was especially well schooled, but she was a skillful leader, appealing to our adolescent desire to embrace a "great cause"—to aggrandize ourselves by it, be loyal to it, sacrifice ourselves for it.

At one Wednesday meeting in late 1941, Marlis exhorted us to help clothe the embattled troops of the beginning Russian campaign: "Our soldiers in

Russia need warm clothes, particularly coats made of fur. Even small pieces can be sewn into coats. Get from your family whatever you can, and bring it here to the next meeting. Let's see that our squad collects more fur than the others." I knew that Mother kept an old coat with a fur collar in a trunk in the attic. And my own coat also had a collar of fur! I cut the fur off both coats and was about to run off to the meeting with my contributions when Mother surprised me. "What did you do with your coat? And where is that fur from?" she asked, pointing to the fur from the coat in the attic.

"I got it from your old coat," I replied, as coolly as possible. "I don't need a fur collar. They're for our soldiers."

"You didn't ask me if you could give them away!" she exclaimed, horrified by this act of independent butchery, and I ran off, knowing there would be hell to pay when I got back but feeling heroic. Mother refused to speak to me for a week, and though her silence terrified me, I was content, knowing that I had done the right thing for the Führer.

Was Marlis aware that this propaganda about the rebellion of the young against their elders, of devotion to a cause, of comradeship and sacrifice, fed right into our fantasies of omnipotence? That they provided roles for young teenagers who were struggling to acquire a sense of personal power? This much I know: she shared our enthusiasm and was as inspired as we were by the HJ's energizing, upbeat songs. The leadership principles that the Hitler Youth had borrowed from the turn-of-the-century German youth movement were an excellent fit. Twelve- to fourteen-year-olds led ten-year-olds, so that there was only a two- to four-year age gap between the leaders and the led in the lower echelons. Lotte Turnow, then a young teacher, served as our town leader, just as in other towns other young teachers served in the higher echelons. The slogan "youth led by youth" proved a powerful tool, welding us into what we thought of as comradeship but was in fact mass manipulation, down to the smallest unit. We thought of ourselves as different from our mothers. The HJ gave us different, new ideals and new tasks on behalf of our nation.

Many years later, Jochen and I talked about our Hitler Youth experience. We agreed that it would have been enormously helpful to us if even one of the adults around us had attempted to counteract this indoctrination, had told us that other values existed besides bravery, toughness, obedience, and loyalty unto death—that other nations, races, and peoples valued their way of life as much as we did ours and were worthy of respect. We both envied friends we made later in life whose parents tried to keep them out of Hitler Youth, sometimes succeeding. I don't remember talking much to my mother, let alone to my aunts, about what we were learning in school and in the Hitler Youth, or about what I thought and felt.

Not that we were silent at our noon meal, which was the only time we spent together as a family: "Fräulein Pelzer threw her key chain at Hanne today, and Hanne was almost knocked out," or some such other report, generally exhausted my contribution to the family conversation, and Jochen was no different in this respect. We bragged or complained or talked about the mundane misadventures of the schoolyard. Or we would ask Mother to tell us about her childhood, about Oma, about the farm she grew up on, about the dances she went to and the trips she took as a teenager. Home life during my teens provided neither intellectual stimuli nor ethical values and moral guidance. Explicit ideals and values, such as they were, existed only within the framework of the Hitler Youth.

I must have learned very early not to express my feelings, to keep my thoughts to myself. I remember one incident, at age nine or ten, that made me realize that my emotional or reflective life was separate from that of my family and indeed the everyday community. Mother, Jochen, Werner, and I were on a day's excursion with Mother's dressmakers' union. Trudi and Ida, Mother's apprentices, were sitting near me on the bus as we rode through the Eulengebirge in the Silesian mountains. I had a window seat, and all that day I had enjoyed looking at the passing landscape and daydreaming as the gentle swaying of the bus rocked me into a trance. (I still enjoy the comfort of a vehicle in motion passing through the early dusk, just as I did then.) The road went along the crest of a hill; a meadow slowly turning blue-gray in the fading daylight lay below us. Chains of hills, in ever paler shades of gray, stretched beyond the meadow. Mists rose from the depth of the valley, and I felt a sob rising in my chest. An ache engulfed me, ebbing through me in a gentle, euphoric swell. I quelled the sob but could not stop the tears. Ida noticed.

"What's wrong, Ulla?" she blurted out. I felt as though the entire bus could hear her. "I have a stomachache," I muttered—aware for the first time that I could not speak about what I felt. Was I afraid of ridicule? I don't know. What I did know, with a pervasive sense of sadness, was that I was alone with my emotions.

"Did you eat all the plums for dessert?" Ida worried. "Maybe that's why your stomach hurts!"

A little later we stopped for supper at a country inn and restaurant, and while everyone danced to the music of the village brass band I pretended that the stomachache was still with me. The feeling of being different, of being moved to tears by a landscape, from then on would keep me a pace away from everyone I knew.

By the late spring of 1941, I had scored the highest of my troop in the broad jump, and Marlis had stopped her teasing. "Some of you will be going to the Middle Silesian athletic competitions at Breslau stadium before the summer break," she announced one Wednesday. Pausing for effect, she called out three names. Mine was the last. I was dumbfounded, as my running score was still mediocre. "Your parents will have to pay for your rail ticket," said Marlis. "The HJ will house you with private families and provide meals at the stadium."

I had long since run out of last summer's money and had to ask Mother for the fare. She turned me down, saying that several customers had not yet paid her and she did not know when they would. I would just have to tell Marlis that I could not go. I begged and cajoled and promised that I would pay back a loan if she made me one, all to no avail. At her urging, I visited several of the delinquent customers, also with no success. They offered the usual excuses: they would pay at the end of the month; they had had a shortfall because the children needed shoes; a family member had died and they had to come up with money for the funeral; their husbands had not paid that month's child support. Uncle Kurt heard my griping for several weekends and finally gave in and handed me a twenty-mark bill for the fare and pocket money.

The Breslau meet was to take place at the end of June. We were to meet at the Strehlen railroad station at seven in the morning. I arrived at the station much too early and all alone. A few adults were waiting for the local train to Wansen. I felt shy and out of place in my uniform—my dark blue skirt cleaned and brushed with cold chicory coffee the night before, my white blouse, the obligatory black scarf cinched by a braided leather knot. I clutched my gym bag to my chest. Finally several girls my age arrived and called to me. My shyness evaporated as I greeted them enthusiastically, even though I knew them only by sight. We pushed one another around, joking and teasing as the adults looked on disapprovingly. Their disapproval didn't bother me at all. Like Heini Völker, I was part of a group now and I was happy about it. This sense of instant comradeship in Jungmädel contrasted sharply with my usual melancholy isolation and distance from others. I lost myself in the group, and that is probably why I remember none of my "comrades," apart from Marlis, as individuals—neither their first names nor what they might have meant to me at the time, nor even individual interactions with them. No faces, no voices emerge from these recollections.

I don't recall how I performed in the hundred-meter race or the ball throwing. But I was disappointed with my broad-jump scores. The gravel course slowed my run, as I could feel the stones through the thin soles of my gym shoes. The unfamiliarly shallow pit cut short my jump. Still, my comrades labored under the same handicap, so that I did not do too badly in comparison. To my surprise, at the award ceremony, I won a small brass medal. The regional troops whose members had won medals, ours among them, stood at the front of the stadium in the glaring afternoon sun—for ages, it seemed to me. Finally my *Ring*, Strehlen, was called. "Four medals: One silver, three brass," a voice rang out from the podium. All four of us marched up. At the top of the stairs, a hand stretched out to meet us. We shook it, one after the other. Back among the ranks of white and dark blue I felt enormous relief: I had not missed a step! I had not stumbled! I was half asleep from the sun when Marlis's voice summoned me. Looking up, I saw that our flag bearer on the platform had fainted. "Take her place, Ursel," she hissed. As the Red Cross helpers carried the girl to the Red Cross tent, I remounted the steps, took the flag that the girl's neighbor had picked up, and stepped into the line of the other flag bearers. I felt honored that Marlis had called on me. I had wanted to be the troop's flag bearer all along, but she had passed me over. I looked down into the sea of faces staring up at me, and after a short while they began to sway and grew hazy in the terrible heat. I was suddenly frightened, as the mass of faces faded and then grew sharp again. "I don't want to faint," I admonished myself. "I cannot let her down too!" As I struggled to stand upright, holding myself up by the flagpole, the ceremony stretched into eternity. At last the final medal winners descended the stairs and the boys' trumpets blared out a signal. We sang, I don't remember what. Finally a speaker in black uniform moved to the microphone. As he began to speak, I gripped the flag more firmly and held on.

"The Führer has ordered our troops to cross the border into Russia to avenge Stalin's treachery," he rasped. "We will win the huge spaces of Russia and earn *Lebensraum* for our people."

I stopped listening, as my mind went blank and then started racing: No. No. The grown-ups had said that Hitler would see to it that our soldiers did not have to fight on two fronts, as we did in the last war. He made a pact with

Stalin that the Russians would not attack us. The leader on the platform continued speaking of the glory our brave soldiers would win, and of the sacrifices we would have to make to be worthy of them. But amid the waves of *Sieg Heil!* that interrupted every sentence, I saw our globe on Father's desk at home—the tiny pink spot that was Germany and the large pale green blob stretching over almost half the globe that was Russia. I froze in fright and stared down at the mouths opening rhythmically with "Sieg Heil! Sieg Heil!" Mouths opening and closing, opening and closing. I don't know how I managed to stay upright for the rest of the ceremony, but I did. The spot that was Germany on the globe and the blob that was Russia hovered before my mind's eye; spot and blob, blob and spot.

On my return home I heard Mother and some of her customers repeating my worry—the huge expanse of Russia, the tremendous length of the Russian front, and tiny Germany. But my fear dissipated during the next few days, as our troops moved forward into Russia and one special radio report followed the other. Smolensk, Kiev. At school, I started a new copybook with pictures of the Russian campaign and learned the spelling of Russian towns and cities. We moved the little flags from the Polish Ukraine into the Russian Ukraine, toward Leningrad and Moscow, farther north. Over the radio we heard the jubilant shouts of the White Russians, rejoicing at being freed from Red domination, and we felt reassured and resumed our daily activities, as day by day the radio announced the victories of our side.

Just as the war had accelerated in 1940–41, my life sped up during my first year of HJ. I no longer sat on the steps of Frau Gurn's kitchen listening to her stories and getting comfort from her steady and loving presence. It seems to me now that I spent most of my days cleaning my uniform—I still had only one dark skirt and one blazer, both of which needed constant attention. We spent hours marching, listening to Marlis's propaganda tales, learning songs, and preparing for meets and rallies. I had little time to daydream, to spend summer evenings in the street playing with the neighborhood children, or to meander aimlessly through town. Years later I read that the Nazis put the end of childhood at age ten, and that was certainly true for me.

Chapter Five

YOU ARE THE FUTURE LEADERSHIP OF
THE HITLER YOUTH, 1941–1942

ON THE WEDNESDAY BEFORE SCHOOL LET OUT for the summer in July 1941, our troop of some fifty girls lined up in the middle school playground to be addressed by Lotte Turnow, the middle school teacher who headed the town's Jungmädel, the junior girls' HJ. She walked slowly along our formation, and as she did so I wondered, as I often did when I saw her: Does she remember me? Does she remember that she was friends with my father and shared meals with my grandparents? Usually she walked right past me, but this time she stopped and called my name, "Ursel Mahlendorf, to the front." I hated the diminutive Ursel, preferring the family's Ulla by far. I stepped out of the formation even as she called out other names. Finally, about six of us stood together.

"You'll be in a leadership training squad this coming year," Lotte told us. "You have proved to us that you have leadership ability. Marlis and I will train you this next year to be squad leaders. Another few girls from other troops around town will join you after the summer. We will ask more of you. You will have to attend HJ twice a week now, Wednesday afternoons and Saturday afternoons. If you do well, some of you will be promoted and lead your own squads. We'll go on a number of camping weekends. And we'll end our training with a weeklong camping trip. You will have to ask your parents if you can participate in the trip."

I do not know how the lower-echelon leadership of the various branches of the HJ in other localities or regions was chosen or trained. I do know, though, that almost all local nonpaid HJ leaders were middle or high school students. They had Wednesday afternoons free till age sixteen or eighteen, while primary school students went to work at age fourteen and were treated as adults. They had neither the time nor, many, the inclination to lead a group of youngsters. The very contingencies of schooling and working made it inevitable that local Nazi youth leadership, once HJ included all children from ten to fourteen, became middle class regardless of the ideology of social equality within the *Volksgemeinschaft*.

Books on Hitler Youth speak only about the training institutions set up for the higher echelon of leaders who aimed for careers working with youth. Soon after his appointment as the national youth leader in 1933, Baldur von Schirach created a number of leadership training institutions. The first, located in Potsdam, close to Berlin, was to serve as a model for all the others. Schirach claimed that twenty-one had been opened by 1934. By 1938 a full training program had been developed, modeling what the Nazis expected of their leaders in general and the HJ leadership in particular.

A member of the HJ could be asked to apply for leadership training if he or she could bring proof of being of pure German, Aryan descent and in excellent physical health without any trace of hereditary illness. The applicant had to display the proper National Socialist attitude, have served successfully as a local HJ leader, be physically and mentally fit, and have completed occupational/professional training or be matriculated at a university. The suitability of the applicant was to be tested in a preliminary training course; after successfully completing the course, the candidate had to finish the required labor service as well as military service. For young women, leadership in the Jungmädel, the BDM, and the Labor Service opened up a wide spectrum of entirely new careers with prospects of rising in the HJ hierarchy all the way to the highest level, the Reichsjugendführung, the national youth leadership.

The actual leadership training program was to consist of a four-month practicum in a regional HJ administrative office; a two-month training course at the Potsdam Leadership Institution; a yearlong period of study at the Academy of Youth Leadership in Braunschweig, in northern Germany; a three-week practicum in an industry in the candidate's home region; a six-month training program in a foreign country with a German minority; and a final examination. Needless to say, the war foiled these ambitious plans because personnel and resources became increasingly scarce. For that reason HJ leadership training at all levels was haphazard, and local groups very unevenly led.

For instance, in my hometown, where Lotte held the reins for the Jungmädel, and a young ss man and judge at the juvenile court for the Jungvolk, discipline was rigorous and organization tight. But at the villages in the counties where I spent my summer vacations, attendance was not enforced and organization was nonexistent.

Of my squad only Erika was called up, and we remained the only primary school girls of the new leadership squad. I was glad that I knew at least one person in the new group. Then I recognized another girl, Gretl Hartmann, who had left our class for high school. Gretl had never turned up her nose at me as Bärbel and Elli had, and so I looked forward to being in a group with her. I recognized a few other middle school and high school girls. Lotte motioned to Marlis: "She will be your leader."

Then Lotte called up another ten names or so. "You'll be in the *Spielgruppe* [the entertainment squad]. You will learn how to perform plays for our wounded soldiers." The *Berufschule* (trade school) next to Stone School had recently been converted into an army hospital. "You'll also practice folk dances and folk songs to entertain the soldiers. You'll have the opportunity to learn an instrument so that some of you can accompany your choir. You will also serve your country."

I envied the girls called up for the entertainment squad; they would have fun, learn songs and dances, play charades, participate in choir, act and put on plays for our soldiers and for special occasions like rallies or the song competition Marlis had taken us to a few weeks earlier. Heaven knew what we would learn.

Lotte must have read my disappointment. She turned to us and said, "You are the future leadership of the HJ. You will guarantee the success of HJ's mission to train the German youth of the future to be strong in body and spirit. Many new tasks on behalf of our nation await you. I know you'll do your duty competently and enthusiastically."

I was to hear speeches about our being the "future leadership" over and over again from Lotte and from numerous HJ leaders on any and all occasions; they became the theme song of my early teens. I never questioned them, and they fired my enthusiasm, but the responsibility they demanded also weighed on me. At that moment, though, I felt proud to be chosen and eager to participate. I dreaded Mother's reaction to my asking if I could join the leadership training group. I knew she would say, "We don't have the money for camping trips, you know that." And she did do exactly that.

"Why can't I use the money in my savings book?" I countered, knowing full well what she would say.

"That money is for your dowry. In time, you'll be grateful that I made you save it."

Nevertheless, Lotte's appeal to our vanity excited me, and I decided to start saving the tips I made from delivering dresses to Mother's customers. I don't remember if I told Mother how elated I was about being chosen for leadership group, but I must have, because since my bout with scarlet fever the previous year, I sometimes did talk to her about my enthusiasms for friends, leaders, and HJ. Usually she just listened without saying anything. If I pressed her to join the Women's League or become a party member—as I began to do, seeing that other girls' mothers participated in party activities—she waved me off. When Marlis told us that the Women's League needed women who could sew, to make coats from the furs we had collected, I hesitated, still smarting from Mother's anger after I cut up our coats. But I finally did ask her.

"I cannot afford the time for anything except making a living for us, and I certainly would not want to sew fur coats without being paid," she explained. I did not argue the point, for she often worked late into the night putting the last touches on a dress, particularly as weekends approached. Yet her refusal to become involved continued to irk me.

When I was sixteen and the regime ended, she told me that she had worried about my being so enthusiastic about the HJ. Her belated concern angered me. You are too late with that worry, I thought sarcastically. I took care of myself just fine. Now, at seventy-five, I still wish she had done more than merely listen. Would I have heard her? Did she know what we were indoctrinated in and how she might have countered it? I do not know. But since she did not, at that time, have a philosophical, religious, or political position from which to counteract that indoctrination, I doubt that she could have done more than dampen my fervor. Given my ever-ready distrust of her, she might even have increased my commitment to the HJ.

I received a different message about my enthusiasm for HJ when I got to the Schultes' for the summer break. Immediately upon arrival I asked Uncle Richard's secretary if there was an HJ group in the village I could join. "I don't think you need to do that," she replied. "You'll do your part for the war effort by working in the fields." When I boasted about being chosen for leadership training, Uncle Richard, who was excused from army service as an indispensable farming administrator, answered me by turning away as if he had not heard me. To my regret, I noticed that my relationship with him had changed. He no longer took me for evening rides to plan the next day's work. He stopped telling jokes about Hitler and the party bigwigs at the dinner table. The previous summer, not knowing that telling jokes about Hitler could have dire consequences, I had enjoyed the scatological pun in a Silesian-dialect joke he told, more because of the shocked look Aunt Helen shot him than because the joke was that funny. He exaggerated the Silesian difficulty in pronouncing umlauts. The dialect employs long *ee* sounds for the umlauted *ü*, and therefore the word for leader, *Führer*, sounds identical to the word for a four o'clock train: *Vierer*.

"An old man stands waiting on one of the platforms of the Breslau station," he began. "He yells loudly, 'Shit on the Feerer [*Führer*], shit on the Feerer.' A crowd gathers around him and looks at him in shock. 'Shit on the Feerer,' he yells again." Uncle Richard drew out the long *ees* and relished the *shits*. " 'Shit on the Veerer [the four o'clock train]. I'll take the five o'clock.' "

"Richard!" Aunt Helen admonished him as he chuckled.

This summer, when Uncle Richard had important guests from estates in the neighborhood, Aunt Helen asked her apprentice, Herta, and me to eat supper in the kitchen. She did not say that we were not welcome but told us that we'd be bored by the conversation, and that there wasn't enough seating space in the dining room besides. Sometimes when I entered the living room, the adults stopped talking. I felt but did not understand their disapproval and withdrew into reading when the field work did not claim my time.

Gradually, as I worked in the fields with Wanda and Anita, HJ life receded. It simply was not relevant. Remembering Fräulein Pelzer's sermonizing when we had harvested potatoes the previous fall together with guest workers and forced laborers, I knew that I, a proud German girl, should not fraternize with Poles (Italians, being allies, were still acceptable), and acted as most of the adults did: I denied to myself that Wanda was Polish and befriended her, joked around, and let her help me, as she had the previous year. I did not notice other forced laborers, though I now know that their number must have increased, because there were fewer Italian guest workers. Wanda became for me the good Pole with whom I shared my sandwich at afternoon break, while I kept my distance from the other laborers. My dishonesty did not strike me till years later, in my early twenties. At the time I thought of myself as loyal, honest, and loving and would have been horrified at anyone's thinking me otherwise. I enjoyed the summer less than the previous one, though, and was glad to get home. It was only when I wrote of this summer, much later, that I understood the full significance of a mental habit that I began to acquire then. Like many of my countrymen, I learned to dissociate the discrepant realities I lived. Increasingly I learned to overlook connections, separated what I thought from what I did, what I felt from what I acted on. I forgot who Oma had wanted me to be and did what was expedient. Except for feeling uneasy at times, I adjusted to the current HJ requirements without giving any thought to, or having any awareness of, what they meant. It took me years to understand the full dimensions of this mental habit and to wean myself from it as an adult.

I fell ill just after returning home from Zülzendorf, just as I did after every summer vacation for the rest of the war years. I do not know if I got sick because that was the only way to get Mother's attention, or because I was so exhausted from the physical and emotional demands put on me all year that I was prone to catch any bug that was around. Each time, my illness earned me an additional four- to five-week vacation from school and HJ.

After I went back to school, HJ meetings took more and more time, as leadership group had started. We met not only from 2:00 to 6:00 P.M. on Wednesday afternoons but also Saturday afternoons and Sunday mornings. Marlis and Lotte assumed different roles in our training. Marlis took charge of all practical training, such as teaching us how to lead a squad in singing, or how to enforce discipline in a squad by reward and punishment. She took us on most of the hikes and instructed us in how to take care of our squads on excursions.

Lotte saw to our ideological training and spoke to us about what the country and the Führer expected of us as leaders, future wives, and mothers. She lectured us on the party's ideological positions. And of course, like all Jungmädel, we still participated in recycling, in rounding up children's clothing and household utensils for bombing victims, and in working in the fields at harvest time. With winter approaching, we collected wool clothing for our soldiers in Russia from our families, neighbors, and friends. We usually went from house to house in groups of three and competed against each other to see who could collect the most. I emptied my family's closets of any wool object that we did not immediately need. In addition to the fur collar that I had appropriated earlier, Mother unwillingly contributed a fur boa she had worn before she was married. Protesting loudly, my seven-year-old brother Werner sacrificed a favorite pair of pants he had outgrown for bombed-out children. We delivered the collections we amassed at the middle school. I now wonder

if they ever reached the front or the bombing victims. But I felt we were helping the war effort.

Aside from these war-related activities, I remember long afternoons in
a middle school classroom in political instruction. Together with Marlis we
studied the biographies of Nazi leaders we had learned by heart previously.
She taught us the poems of Nazi and nationalist poets, such as the odes to the
Führer by Will Vesper and the historical ballads of Borries von Münchhausen,
so that we could recite them to our squads at solstice or other festivals. I still
remember fragments of a Vesper poem to Hitler that legitimized his leadership by putting him, the most capable son of his people, into the framework
of ancient Germanic hero worship.

> So gelte denn wieder
> Urväter Sitte:
> Es steige der Führer
> aus Volkes Mitte.
>
> Refrain:
>
> Herzog des Reiches,
> wie wir es meinen,
> bist du schon lange
> im Herzen der Deinen.
>
> Let our ancestors' customs
> be valid.
> Let our leader
> emerge from among our people.
>
> Refrain:
>
> Leader of the realm
> as we think of you.
> You have been in our hearts
> from days of old.

Marlis demonstrated to us how you lead a group in singing and how to
keep the beat. We practiced conducting in 3/4 and 4/4 time. My dread of
being called on to conduct the squad's singing replaced my dread of marching in formation; I was equally inept in both and totally lacked a sense of
rhythm. We memorized party history and party organization and hierarchy.
It is curious that I have forgotten most of the biographies and the hierarchy

of the party, probably because the former were such sentimental, monotonously propagandistic trash and the latter dry and uninteresting. Yet some of the poems, with their easy rhymes and rhythms, stuck. Years later, when I analyzed with my students how seductive appeals to nationalist sentiment can be, I could still recite samples of what I learned then.

Lotte's instructions centered on the basic principles of Nazi ideology, most significantly on issues of personal and what we called national hygiene, on the leader principle, and on Aryan supremacy. These lessons reinforced ideas I had run across in Norse sagas, in nationalist World War I literature about male heroism, and in Nazi "Blood and Soil" literature about German hunger for farmland and the need for conquest and settlement of the territories to Germany's east.

A sample of Blood and Soil peasant and nationalist Great War literature still sticks in my mind. It may be a generic plotline, since I have not been able to ascertain its exact title or author, but it contains Nazi ideology and its buzzwords in their purest form: a Westphalian farmer, having fought bravely and barely escaped death, returns home from the Great War, his face badly disfigured by shrapnel. He finds that his drunkard father has become heavily indebted to a Jewish land speculator. For many years the veteran works day and night to purchase enough seed and fertilizer to increase the land's productivity and free the farm from debt; but drought one year, floods another, and hail still another do not allow him to pay even the interest, which is, of course, usurious. His debt keeps mounting. Yet the stubborn peasant clings on, acquiring a wife and child after child to help him in the struggle for his ancestral land. The author heaps misfortune upon misfortune, threat upon threat to foreclose by the Jewish speculator, until the farmer has relinquished to him all but one barren field. A new law is enacted prohibiting Jews from owning land in Germany, and the usurer has to return the land to its rightful owner. The grateful farmer and his family celebrate their victory over adversity and the farmer joins the Nazi Party.

Novels like this abounded, filled with sturdy Nordic types and their Jewish or foreign antagonists. The taciturn hardiness of their protagonists hides the self-pity implied by the improbable chain of misfortunes. Moreover, extravagant descriptions of the vast and heroic expanses of the Westphalian heath appealed to my deluded eyes more than the gently rolling hills of our pastoral Silesia. The novel's ancient gabled farmhouse, with its giant open hearth, Wotan's horse heads shielding its roof, provided an atmosphere of primeval somberness appropriate to the Nazi ideals I came to espouse. And, of course, Hitler's assuming power in 1933 brought "justice" and resolved all undeserved misfortune!

I am still mortified that I felt edified rather than nauseated by such trash. Yet, truth to tell, these examples of Nazi and pre-Nazi literature, with their nature descriptions, engaged me more than the equally propagandistic, sentimental HJ examples of urban heroism like the story of *Hitlerjunge Quex,* the Berlin twelve-year-old murdered by the Reds. For long periods of time, reading such novels, I completely forgot I was a girl who, by virtue of her gender, was excluded from all these heroics. I identified with the stubborn farmer and never once saw myself as the selfless, morose wife who returned to toil in the fields the same day she gave birth.

Of course, I learned from the Germanic sagas that women participated in heroism as mothers and wives. Unafraid, they stood behind their men in battle and cheered them on to victory. But women who preferred that their fathers, husbands, brothers, and sons die in battle rather than be seen as cowards struck me as monstrous even then. The female roles that Lotte advocated for us bored me, and most of the time I thought that I would rather be a soldier and fight like a man. The story of a sixteen-year-old girl suited me—I no longer remember its author or title. This adventuresome teen, dressed as an ensign, joined her brothers in the war of 1813 against Napoleon; she led the advance and died holding the Prussian flag.

Yet one day, possibly noticing the lack of enthusiasm some of us felt for the roles she proposed, Lotte took a few of us aside, Gretl and me among them. "Leadership in the Jungmädel and BDM," she began, "for some of you with natural leadership ability can lead to a career. With the opening up of new territories to the east, you may be asked by the Führer to staff the organizations for German girls and women who choose to settle there. Some of you, I have seen, have been disappointed that you were too young to participate in the Führer's struggle for power. There are equally great, heroic tasks waiting for you and for all of us in the future." From that day on, I redoubled my efforts to please her and Marlis.

At twelve, we were still too young to be sent to leadership schools or inducted into the rank and the lore of the wives. As Lotte told us, we were women and wives in training, and that training for us was called personal hygiene and for the time being meant attending to cleanliness and purity. As a ten-year-old I had been very casual about cleanliness. I simply could not keep food spots and the dust and dirt of our unpaved front yard off my weekday dress, which had to last me all week before being washed on Saturday night. Afraid to draw Marlis's or Lotte's disapproval, I now began to wash my clothes myself and to take daily sponge baths, so much so that I annoyed Mother with the amount of scarce cleaning supplies I consumed. Purity to a twelve-year-old meant curbing my curiosity about sex and restricting my thinking to heroic deeds and the beauties of nature. Passages from Nietzsche—"The purest shall be lords of the earth," or "Man is a bridge between beast and overman"—quoted by Lotte and other HJ leaders when they spoke of our heroic future fueled my obsession with unworldly purity. Attempting to avoid mundane contamination, I did not participate with the other girls in class or in my squad in their bantering about cosmetics, dresses, boyfriends, and dances. I began to despise them as "the rabble" who did not strive to become leaders and "supermen." Of course, I was familiar with the dirty talk of the street. I had, after all, played with the street kids for years. I understood what the boys meant when they yelled after Agatha and me, sneering, laughing, "Girls, let's go fuck in the outhouse," while they accompanied their words with suggestive thrusts of the pelvis.

Fortunately for me, Nazi ideology as taught by Lotte allowed the cultivation of a love of nature. Whenever my HJ duties did not claim me, I took solitary hikes in the woods and twilight walks across the fields. As I walked through the meadows and fields, I indulged myself in turning the familiar landscape into a fantastic one of wild, jagged mountains, glaciers, and waterfalls. Even with all the activities that filled my daily life, I was desperately lonely and yearned for friendship with a like-minded soul. At the same time, made arrogant by my membership in the leadership group and by recently acquired theories of racial superiority, I believed that I belonged to an elite that had nothing in common with ordinary townsfolk, the "rabble."

One afternoon late in the fall of 1941, we neighborhood children played dodgeball in the playground of Red School. We got heated up, and I threw a particularly hard ball at Elli, the teacher's daughter and my former friend, who lived up on the third floor. She returned my shot with one equally fierce; it hit me so hard in the abdomen that I doubled over with pain. We played on and finished the game. When I went inside, I noticed that my panties were wet and I was bleeding. I was baffled and, as usual, feared that an injury might mean a doctor's visit and Mother's scolding about needless expense. That evening, when the bleeding still had not stopped, I told Mother. She looked at me in consternation and horror, and I had the feeling that I had done something terribly wrong.

I offered an explanation about the ball game, which she brushed aside with, "No, you will need to wear napkins once a month; you must not bathe or swim during this period; it will probably be painful; you must not be alone with men." My belly started hurting the moment she mentioned pain. For the rest, I was utterly bewildered, but judging by her look I did not dare ask any questions and felt guilty. She gave me some folded rags and several safety pins and told me to fasten them to my panties. I had no one to ask what was wrong with me, or anyone, either female or male, who could have explained my mother's reaction or the bleeding itself. The closest I could figure out was that this condition was something she was ashamed of, something despicable, sexual, and therefore lower class. It would not even have occurred to me to ask Marlis or any of the girls in leadership group.

Desperate and perplexed during the next few weeks, I found myself watching my classmates to see if any of them had blood-soiled panties. After two months of agonizing, I decided to ask Frau Gurn's kitchen help, a farm girl named Martha, if she knew what was the matter with me. We had always teased her about necking with her boyfriend on the park benches of the Marienberg. She seemed less intimidating to me than anyone else. She laughed at my naïveté. "Didn't anyone tell you that you are a woman now? Women have their period. When your boyfriend fucks you, you might get pregnant. So you'll have to be careful." It was another year or so before I acquired a basic understanding of female reproductive function from books in the local lending library and Mother's health encyclopedia, and the meaning of Mother's remark about "being alone with men." She had replaced the forbidden encyclopedia on the bookshelf after providing her awkward instructions.

As for Mother's other advice, I did what I had learned to do earlier: discover by trial and error whether she was right. I loved swimming, and in the spring I went to the pool, period or no period. Since it did me no harm, I figured that bathing was probably all right too. I went to bed with a hot water bottle for a few months on the first day of my period. Then one day I had to participate in a broad-jumping meet, and in the excitement of the competition forgot all about being unwell. From then on I sought vigorous physical exercise on the first day of my period. What I did lose at this time was the enjoyment of my body, its suppleness, the confidence with which I had moved in playing, running, swimming, and riding my bike. As my breasts started to develop and my figure changed, I shrank into myself and tried to make myself invisible. The uniform we wore for the Jungmädel served a new purpose, and I now wore it almost constantly; its very rectangularity drew attention away from breast and hips. The feeling of being dirty, of not being acceptable, poisoned my adolescence and young adulthood.

My enjoyment of sculpting the human form in my late thirties led me back to the comfort and ease I had felt about my body until my teenage years. Worst for me at age twelve, however, was that my isolation and alienation from others increased because the silence about physical and sexual intimacy extended to emotional intimacy. I could not express myself when I was confused, angry, or frightened. I could not find words for affection and love. Even Erika and I never talked about anything emotionally meaningful to either of us.

When I no longer needed it, two years later at age fourteen, I did receive a lecture about intercourse and impregnation, Nazi style. All fourteen-year-old HJ girls, about forty of us, met with Lotte in a middle school classroom. She had our immediate attention when she began with how difficult it was for mothers to talk to their daughters about sex. Most of us nodded our heads in assent. For that reason, she was going to tell us about sex and our future function as wives of German men and as mothers of a new generation. "Some of your families will doubtless not want me to talk about these matters." We understood this to mean, don't tell your parents.

"But rather than your hearing about sex in the gutter talk of the street, as you no doubt will in future years," Lotte continued, "I will provide you with factual information."

I am sure that by this time most of us had some information from parents or contemporaries; we were, after all, fourteen years old.

"You will enjoy having many children for the Führer, and that is why you must keep yourself pure." Of course I knew what that meant. Don't talk or think about sex, and keep clean.

"When your future husband makes you a mother, he will put his member into you like a sword thrusts itself into its sheath, and his seed will impregnate the ovum in your belly."

Silence—and that was it!

I still have difficulty understanding how a young teacher could be as alienated from her own body as to use such a violent, obscene metaphor. I still
cannot believe that a sane adult could delude herself into thinking that she
was doing us some good. Despite her prohibition, some of the girls did speak
to their parents, but they had a better relationship to their mothers than I
did. Several parents lodged complaints with the middle school principal about
this strange attempt at sex education, and that ended any future essays into
the subject.

Throughout the year in leadership group, we continued following war
events in our war diaries at grammar school, cutting pictures out of the *Strehlen
Daily* and supplying our paste-ins with explanations. I remember the invasions
of Greece and Yugoslavia, and the quick surrender of those countries in the
late spring of 1941, particularly vividly because Greece as well as our Axis
ally Italy had played an important role in my imagination ever since I read
Schwab's *Tales of Classical Antiquity*. They were the lands where actual gods
used to live—heathen gods to be sure, as my former Bible school teacher had
said, and not real gods like our Lord and Christ. When our troops raised the
German flag on Mount Olympus, the seat of the ancient gods, the radio and
the illustrated papers rejoiced, "Greek antiquity in our hands!" I pasted a picture of this scene into my war diary and wrote beneath it: "Greece Is Ours."

All through 1941–42 we celebrated one victory after another. An enthusiastic smile replaced Fräulein Pelzer's usually sour mien as she helped us choose
illustrations for our diaries and suggested wording for our descriptions of the
pictures. The victories also had concrete material consequences. Fruit we had
almost forgotten existed from the warmer regions of Europe appeared in the
greengrocer's store, oranges and lemons from Greece and Italy and watermelons from the Balkans and Crimea. Since Mother had more customers now—
coupons for new ready-made dresses were scarce and women kept their
wardrobe up to date by alterations—she had the money to buy at least the
cheaper watermelons. We were so intoxicated by our triumphs that we hardly
worried, or even noticed, that America, as we called the United States, entered
the war on the Allies' side in December 1941. For me, America, just like our
ally Japan, was so distant that it simply did not count. Caricatures of Churchill
and Roosevelt in the illustrated magazines showed them as bungling and
laughable cartoon characters like Laurel and Hardy, or rather their German,
prewar equivalents, Pat and Patachon. "Our U-boats will sink the cargo ships

America is sending to Britain," sneered Goebbels, the minister of propaganda. And, indeed, special report after special report in 1942 announced: "Attention! Attention! Here is Radio Germany! Führer Headquarters: Our proud navy has destroyed . . ." and then followed the names of the ships sunk and the tons of cargo that had gone to the bottom of the Atlantic.

Lotte's favorite subject in her occasional lectures was national and racial hygiene. We learned that our nation, just like us, had to keep itself physically and mentally healthy and pure of blood. "Only a nation that allows the fittest to reproduce will have a glorious future!" she sermonized. "Mental as well as physical illness, alcoholism, vagrancy, and criminality are hereditary illnesses passed on to offspring by Mendelian law." We understood this to mean that she was talking about unquestionable scientific fact.

"If even *one* of your ancestors has been mentally ill, you may have inherited a gene for mental illness and might pass on the illness to one of your children even though you yourself are healthy. That is why you should know your family's heredity and have your parents research your family's history," she added, personalizing her message. "Most of you, no doubt, are of pure German blood. But you must be able to prove by a genealogy going back to the early nineteenth century that you are of sound Aryan stock." Then she returned to a generality: "If mental illness or a physical deformity is frequent in a family, people should not have children and contaminate the *Volksblut*—the people's blood. They should be sterilized or not marry."

Was suicide a mental illness? I worried. After all, Father's sister Magdalene had killed herself. Did I have the gene? Could I go mad? Then I looked at Lotte speaking up front. Was she talking to me? She'd known my family when my aunt killed herself. For weeks after that lecture, I worried. I looked into the mirror obsessively as I tried to find out. Who am I? Am I mad? In my adolescent quest for identity, my eyes opened wide. I searched the image in the mirror with desperate intensity. Was that insane?

On another occasion Lotte spoke of the cost of mental illness and physical deformity to the nation. People confined in mental institutions suffer, I understood her to say. They are a burden to themselves, to their families, and to the state. The money used to care for them could be better used to raise healthy children, children who would contribute to the welfare of the nation. "Are the incurably ill, like schizophrenics or Mongoloids, not better off relieved of their suffering? That is what euthanasia, mercy killing, is about." I thought of the "Mongoloid" daughter of my mother's friend and knew what her death from pneumonia had been about. The sudden death of a healthy teen had been murder. But now, at age twelve, I was not horrified and indignant, as I had been earlier. I no longer felt empathy for her. Still, the disquieting question remained: Did *I* have bad genes? Did Lotte know I did?

Lotte's teaching was not just Nazi ideology but reflected Nazi policy. Beginning with a 1933 law, the party conducted an extensive mass sterilization program in which children and adults who were physically deformed or disabled, epileptic, or mentally ill underwent sterilization. In the early 1940s, about the time Lotte was talking to us, institutionalized patients in psychiatric hospitals such as Leubus, Sonnenstein, and Brandenburg were killed by injection, starvation, or overdose for being what the Nazis called "unfit life." Hitler ordered the cessation of the program by the end of 1941 because of protests by the churches and relatives. Yet the informal killings in institutions for the chronically ill and disabled continued until 1945 and later. I am certain that Lotte knew this and approved of the policy. She defended it to me as late as 1947, when we paid a visit to an institution for epileptics.

Lotte's discussions of "racial types" gave me another reason to obsess. She described each of the types in terms of their mental, psychological, and physical characteristics. "Germans derive their characteristics from a mixture of five distinct racial types," she told us. "The Nordic type is the best: They are creative and spiritual. They are tall and slender, athletic and courageous. They are fair-skinned, red-haired or gold blond, blue- and gray-eyed. Their skull is elongated." She pointed to illustrations of the types on the walls of the classroom. Her pointer traced the geographical regions in which the Nordic type constituted a majority on the map of contemporary Europe: northern Germany along the North Sea, all of Holland, Scandinavia, and southern England. "Nordics are contemporary descendants of the Germanic tribes about whom your history books tell us," she concluded.

Her piercing eyes scrutinized our expectant faces, but then she turned to the next type, when none of us seemed to measure up to the Nordic ideal. Pointing to the next illustration, she continued, "He is the Westphalian type. Soulful and slow of speech, he dominates in middle and northwest Germany. Westphalians are heavyset, with a large frame, have darker blond hair and blue eyes. They are stoic and loyal." Next came the Slavic type. Small of frame but heavy, round-headed, gray-, green-, or amber-eyed, with ash blond to dark blond hair and prominent cheekbones, the Slavic type was decidedly inferior to the first two types. "His mind is deceitful and his psyche slavish. Germany east of the Elbe River and, of course, your home province, Silesia, has the heaviest concentration of the Slavic type," she summed up.

She consoled us by adding that "a Silesian can be a mixture of many types, since Silesia is old German settlement territory. During the Middle Ages, the kings of Poland called on Swabians, Bavarians, Dutchmen, and Westphalians to settle on both sides of the Oder River. They came in great numbers and intermarried with the native Slavs. I have told you who the Dutchmen and Westphalians were. Who then were the Swabians and Bavarians? They lived in Austria and southern Germany all the way to the Main River; they were descendants of Nordic and Westphalian Germanic tribesmen who inter-married with the Romans, who occupied all of that territory during the second and third centuries A.D. We call them Dinarians. They are hawk-nosed—no, they are not Jewish," she added. "Of tall and slender frame, they may be blue- or brown-eyed; they have dark or auburn hair and have keen senses and intel-lect. Hitler is a Dinarian."

I cannot recall the name of the last type. It must have been the Latin type, the descendants of the Romans who had settled in the south German regions and who had remained pure-blooded. She described the Latin type as dark-haired and dark-skinned, of small frame and dark eyes, sensuous and lighthearted. It still amazes me that a person like Lotte, who had some edu-cation in biology and the sciences, could have taken such nonsense for scien-tific fact. Of course, Nazi biology textbooks promulgated this racial theory as legitimate science. When I got to know her better as my tutor after the war, I used to wonder: Did she, with her jet-black hair and sallow complexion, her huge, piercing, gray-yellowish eyes, hawk nose, and scrawny body, fancy her-self a Dinarian like Hitler? As a twelve- or thirteen-year-old, it would not have occurred to me to wonder. I took in this unholy brew of racialized biology, geography, and Nazi mythologizing as gospel truth.

It was a gospel that caused me some uneasiness at the time, and not only on account of my fears about a "madness gene." I don't know if other girls my age spent as much time as I did in front of a mirror trying to determine if they were Nordic or Westphalian—I did not even consider another possibility for myself. I was blond, tall for my age, sturdy and athletic, and had gray eyes. I think it was my mother who pointed out to me, observing my obsession with the mirror and finding out its cause, that our high cheekbones definitely put some Slavic or Mongolian ancestors into the picture. I was angry about her ironic skepticism.

The racial types occupied us in school as well as in Hitler Youth. In the upper two forms of primary school, during my thirteenth and fourteenth years, a new teacher for history, the new principal of Red School, replaced Fräulein Pelzer. By 1942–43, all male teachers under age fifty had disappeared into the army, and therefore Herr Schmidt stuck out as the only male left. Erika, whose father had served at the front since 1939, called him a draft dodger and party bigwig. He was the only teacher who wore a uniform to school that identified him as a member of the SA. He added some illustrations of Mendelian genetics to his discussion of German racial types for extra scientific weight. These illustrations showed two pea flowers of different color and the percentages of differently colored offspring if you cross-fertilized a red with a white flower. He threw around words like *genotype* and *phenotype,* but I don't think any one of us understood what he meant. Having never had a male teacher, and growing up without a father or any other meaningful male figure in my life, I was fascinated by Herr Schmidt. His subject, history, interested me even more than he did, though I joined my classmates in snickering behind his back about his ridiculous bearing. His mustard-colored jodhpur breeches and the black riding boots displayed his bowlegs prominently. He had the voice, the oily black hair, the sallow complexion, and the small stature of Dr. Goebbels, the minister of propaganda, and he identified with him down to the leather gloves. Needless to say, I would have been blind to these features if Erika and the other working-class kids had not brought them home to me and had I not overheard Mother's customers call him, like Goebbels, "the unbleached, shrunken Teuton."

Despite his ridiculousness, I listened to Herr Schmidt's instruction attentively. I had read a lot of historical fiction of the *völkisch* variety by this time and was all too willing to take in what he had to say. He in his turn appreciated my interest. He used our physiognomy to exemplify the historical racial types. For him I represented the Nordic/Westphalian type; Hanne, whose parents hailed from the Bohemian village close to town, good-naturedly accepted the Slavic type designation.

His history instruction parroted the Nazi Party line down to the minutest detail. It began with the migration of peoples and the movements of the different Germanic tribes through Europe and Africa, and continued down to the struggles between the Ghibellines and the Guelfs and a succession of popes during the Middle Ages. Herr Schmidt favored the Guelfs because they were Saxons and were "less corrupted by Italy" than were the Ghibellines. But based on the historical novels I read at the time, like Otto Gmelin's, I was intrigued with the Ghibelline emperors, particularly Frederic II, the courtliest of the Ghibellines, who held court in sunny Sicily, and his grandson, the tragic sixteen-year-old prince Konradin, who fought and died for his vision of the Holy Roman Empire. Despite Herr Schmidt's efforts, I found Gmelin's "Germanic passion for Italy" much more appealing than Herr Schmidt's brave and hardy Saxons. For me the oranges, grapes, and melons of our prewar years, the decorative, splendid costumes, and the marble luxury of Sicilian palaces held much greater fascination than the wooden throne of the Saxon kings.

Successors to the medieval emperors, I learned, were the Prussian kings, mostly military men, particularly Frederick the Great, who took Silesia away from Austria and made it part of Prussia and us Silesians, Prussians. Here Herr Schmidt's instruction touched upon my earliest interest in the history of the Silesian wars and my hometown's role in Frederick the Great's campaign. From there his history instruction went straight to Hitler, who was "the final fulfillment of the ancient Germanic longing for freedom." Freedom for him meant freedom from foreign domination. "Our" oppressors had been the Romans, the popes (we were Protestants, to be sure), the French, and the English. Herr Schmidt thought Slavic populations inferior peoples and Poles despicable cowards. He characterized the Russians as Bolshevik hordes driven at gunpoint into battle by Jewish commissars. Fräulein Pelzer, who listened in during our instruction, praised Herr Schmidt's teaching methods enthusiastically.

"He speaks straight from the heart. He does not confuse you with too many different points of view," she gushed, then added, "When I was attending teachers' seminary during the 1920s, our teachers held so many different, confusing opinions. How fortunate you are!" Fortunate indeed!

As our troops moved farther into Russia in the spring of 1942, Herr Schmidt began to outline to us the party's settlement plans for the east in Poland and Russia. Exultantly he told us that as of this date—it was September 1942— Hitler had achieved the Hohenstaufen emperors' goal of uniting all of Europe under German hegemony.

"Our armies dominate Europe from Narvik, Norway, in the north to North Africa in the south, as Field Marshal Rommel helps the Italians win back their colonies," he proclaimed proudly.

"They hold the east-west axis from Stalingrad and the Caucasus all the way to the French Atlantic coast. You, the younger generation, will never have to worry about *Lebensraum* [enough space to live]. Large farms in the Ukraine and southern Russia with fertile soil will be yours for the asking. Prepare yourselves to become settlers in the east!"

Three summers of helping bring in the harvest had taught me one thing: I was not ever going to be a field hand or a farmer in the east or anywhere else. Not that I did not enjoy being paid by Uncle Richard. But the talk of the field hands and my own observations of how they lived and worked told me that farm life was not for me. Settlement in the east? Not for me. Maybe a farm of his own for my brother Jochen; it would provide him with a splendid opportunity. Africa and Rommel's African campaign held greater appeal for me. Ever since Rommel had gone to assist the Italian army in Tunisia in March 1941, I had followed the progress of his tanks through the desert. For my war diaries I cut out illustrations of German tanks and trucks moving over sandy hills. Would Rommel's army reach Germany's former colonies, Kenya and Togo? I thought of Father's brother, Willi, who had gone down there to build roads. Maybe after the war I could join him there and live in Africa, marry a farmer, and have orange trees in my garden. Having read a fair amount about colonial life in Africa, I knew that whites did not work the fields. Blacks did that. Hence my willingness to contemplate becoming the wife of a white farmer.

As I think about my childhood ideas of colonization, I wonder, did I really accept Herr Schmidt's colonial fantasies? Did I not object to our stealing land from Russians, Poles, and Africans? Of course, I did not see this then in terms of theft. I knew that it was wrong of Helga, my bench mate in first grade, to steal my pencil. After all, I had learned the Ten Commandments in our Protestant nursery school and in Bible lessons and had taken them to heart. Besides, I was much too frightened of the police ever to think of stealing. Was it the scale of the theft that made conquest different? In part I think that it was. In part, however, I accepted Herr Schmidt's colonialist argument that we were a superior race, an elite who would bring German culture to an inferior race of Slavs and Africans. By 1942–43 I had forgotten my friendship with Wanda as well as the 1939 newsreels showing Polish refugees—and my compassion for them. It was only in the 1990s, when reading about the role BDM leaders like Melitta Maschmann had played in ethnic cleansing, and in driving Polish and Jewish farmers from their lands, that I realized where Lotte's appeal to my vanity to think of myself as a leader of women might have led me, namely, to a leadership role in Germanizing the conquered east.

The best part of the year's leadership training was the many hikes and overnight camping trips we took as a squad. Since I knew the villages and towns as well as the countryside and the forests from my days as a biker, I often served as a guide or scout. We played games designed to teach us map reading and to orient ourselves in the country without the help of a compass. I loved the long hikes and did not mind being sweaty or exhausted. And I enjoyed learning about the mushrooms, wild plants, and roots that Lotte pointed out when she accompanied us. She designated some as safe to eat and others as poisonous. "You can survive in the forest in case you lose your way if you can identify what is safe to eat," she said. Sometimes I fantasized about our squad getting lost and my rescuing them. We stayed overnight in barns when their owners allowed us to sleep in the hay.

On such overnight trips I loved singing folk songs in the gathering dusk, huddled around a few burning logs in the safety of a farmyard, resting after our long hikes through meadows and woods. As we gazed lazily up at the stars, Marlis sang the song with which we ended each such evening and we hummed along:

> Kein schöner Land in dieser Zeit
> als hier das unsre weit und breit.

> No land more beautiful
> than ours around us.

In the darkness of the barn, one of the girls would start telling ghost stories, and others joined in. Since I had heard my share of them in the Gurn kitchen, I found it easy to contribute my headless horseman story. Such evenings— and there quite a few of them—came to mean *Heimat,* my Silesian home, to me. When I looked back after the war, my disillusionment with the HJ, and our expulsion from Silesia, these evenings and the feeling of *Heimat* they had inspired seemed to me a seduction into a sentimentality that harbored dangerous illusions: the illusion that Germany was a special country, more beautiful than any other, a land ours since time immemorial and for all eternity.

The culmination of our training was to be a weeklong stay at one of the youth hostels in the Silesian mountains. Scheduled for the week before the summer vacation of 1942, our participation in the activities was to test our leadership abilities. I earned part of the money to participate by delivering dresses to Mother's customers. Uncle Kurt, on my pleading, paid for the rest. I had looked forward to going with the group. I do not remember much about this trip except a few moments of intense discomfort, the reasons for which escape me. Was it that we shared the hostel with squads from all over Silesia and were crowded? Was it that we all felt we had to compete against each other? Was I running short on the still unaccustomed and uninterrupted feeling of good fellowship? I do not remember what we were tested in or how I acquitted myself. But I must have passed, because at the end of the week I was promoted to squad leader.

The hostel was located on the side of a hill overlooking the mountain ranges in the distance. We shared the large dormitory with several other groups. At morning rallies before breakfast, we raised the flag on the sports field next to the dark wooden building. Staring into the distance, I scarcely noticed the mountains I had so yearned to see, barely paid attention to the ceremony of singing and choral recitation of poems that usually moved me deeply. I just wanted to be away from the others, away from being cooped up in meetings and herded to sports competitions, away from the girls and their leaders, many of whom I did not know. I did not feel the comfort I had recently come to enjoy as I lost myself in the group of my comrades. Nor did I, at the end of the trip, take any pleasure in having been promoted or look forward to leading a squad, as some of the other girls did.

When I started leadership training I looked forward to what I would learn and felt proud to be chosen. There is no doubt in my mind that the training and the good times on hikes increased my enthusiasm for Nazi causes. I believed that with the Führer as our leader, our country had achieved its mission to lead the world, that the cause demanded personal sacrifice and devotion to the HJ's goal of training German youth, which would keep its blood pure and its body and spirit strong. My voice became shrill when I defended these goals to the occasional adult who expressed disapproval of HJ activities, like some of Mother's customers who objected to Sunday sports meets as substitutes for church. I cringe with embarrassment now at the memory of my strident adolescent voice.

I had hoped that I would make new friends in the leadership group. The truth is that I lost what little intimacy I had had with Erika and never got to know Gretl or any of the other girls. HJ comradeship did not allow for individual friendship of any depth. I became even lonelier than before. I have no doubt that the depression that settled on me at the end of the training resulted from this isolation and from the continuous demand to be passionately involved in the Hitler Youth.

When I first read feminist studies on the role of gender and social class in the HJ, in preparation for a class on Christa Wolf's autobiographical novel of her Jungmädel experience, *Patterns of Childhood* (1976), I was struck forcibly by how thoroughly I had absorbed Marlis's and Lotte's lessons. Like most German girls at the time, I had learned early that I was "only a girl," less valuable and beloved than my brother. Early on I had dealt with the blow to my self-esteem by denial. Becoming a tomboy and sharing my brother's and his friends' activities, I proved to myself that I was not really a girl. In my reading as well I identified with males, their adventures, their work life, and their heroic exploits. My middle-class elders had taught me to look down on the working class. The communal Wandervogel spirit I encountered in my first years as a Jungmädel allowed me to forget the realities of being female and my family's having sunk into the working class. When I entered Jungmädel I was still smarting from the rejection of my middle school friends. Much of my intense involvement in Jungmädel, I came to see, was an attempt to compensate for the hurt. By hiking and competing in sports, by marching in rallies and being recognized as a full member of the HJ, I could again identify with the boys, even as I could dismiss my former friends' snobbery as merely an "uncomradely" character flaw. I took comfort in the Nazi slogan that the HJ knew no social classes but only comrades. I could daydream: I'll show you! I am just as good a Jungmädel as you and better—hence the extraordinary lengths I went to in practicing the broad jump. Being chosen for leadership group undid the blows to my ego inflicted by my former friends' rejection and the humiliation of being left behind in grade school. I had leadership potential! I would be someone they would have to pay attention to! And, of course, my early adolescent rebellion against my mother found ample reinforcement in the Hitler Youth ideology of the superiority of the young. As my body became womanly like Mother's, I could differentiate myself, the Jungmädel idealist leader in the service of the Führer, from her realist concern with "just" making a living. My deluded, thoughtless arrogance and ingratitude certainly did not strike me then.

Chapter Six

BETWEEN CONFORMITY AND REBELLION,
1942–1944

DURING THE YEAR IN LEADERSHIP GROUP I lost my friendship with Hanne and Rita. Hanne stayed back in my first HJ troop, and since she had no interest in either books or HJ, we had nothing in common. Besides, as we became teenagers the silliness that had cheered and put me at ease now annoyed me. Corrupted by the HJ's sneering at what the Nazis called "Americanized" mass culture, I began to feel contempt for Hanne's fascination with popular music and movie stars. Because of a recurrence of her tuberculosis, Rita did not attend HJ at all. I continued visiting Rita and her aunt, but Rita withdrew more and more into herself. I saw more of Erika, as both of us participated in the leadership squad. She had more sense than I did, however, because she never volunteered for anything, and she offered to help with as few extra tasks as she could get away with, coming up with plenty of excuses as to why she could not take part. Without saying so, I disapproved of her lackadaisical attitude, and my silence increased our distance from each other. She particularly hated sporting events, and I could never get her to come with me to practice running and broad jump.

After Easter 1942 and the beginning of the new school year, Lotte called together the leadership squad for something like a graduation ceremony. We swore an oath that we would serve the Führer until our death. My former classmate Gretl stood next to me at the ceremony. I did not feel ready to take on the leadership of a squad, yet when Lotte promoted Gretl and me to squad leaders I was elated. Then my apprehension returned, and I envied the girls who were going to continue for another year in the newly constituted leadership group and remain with Marlis as their squad leader. Erika and several others of the leadership squad were transferred to the entertainment squad as unsuitable for leadership.

"You are needed as leaders," Lotte told us, probably seeing Gretl's and my lack of enthusiasm. "You have shown that you have natural leadership ability. You are ready to teach your squads to march and sing and to supervise them in sports. We'll put several squads together for political schooling so that you won't need to worry about that task. Your new troop leader will take it on." I have no recollection at all of this troop leader.

On the Wednesday following the graduation, I went with Lotte, the new troop leader, and four other squad leaders to meet the ten-year-olds who had been inducted into Jungmädel that afternoon. We had each been given orders to take attendance from a list of fifteen names. I felt awkward and worried but called out the fifteen names as the girls gathered around me. I remember neither their names nor their faces. I knew none of them. I felt better after Lotte left, having told us to use the afternoon for marching practice. It took me a while to take charge of my squad. When I asked "my" girls to line up by size, they lined up helter-skelter. While it was easy to put the tallest in front, it took valuable time to sort out the rest. Meanwhile, they giggled with embarrassment, pushed each other around, and squealed. "Silence! Attention!" I yelled. I looked over at the other squads and saw that they had already begun their marching practice. It took more time to have them form rows of three. Then I moved to the front of the formation, shouting, "One, two, three, four," and marched ahead. They did not follow me. I went back to the first row of my girls and yelled, "Straight ahead, march!" and made them march next to me. Finally the other rows followed and we were on our way, marching straight ahead. We never got to formation right or to formation left. I was exhausted when we broke up.

During the next few weeks we practiced marching, and my squad gradually learned to line up, to form into rows, to follow my commands. I gained confidence when I realized that it's a lot easier to give commands than to obey them when you have trouble knowing right from left. Teaching the squad to sing was a problem, and marching to a song even more of a disaster. Someone must have noticed my difficulties because after a few attempts I was relieved of the task and Gretl took over singing practice for both of our squads. After that we improved quickly, so that we could take our squads out of the school-yard and into town.

It must have been after I had gained some confidence that I decided to show off my leadership skills on my own. It was, I think, the only time I consciously misused the squad for my own purposes. The troop leader had told each of us squad leaders to march our girls through a few streets of town so as to prepare them for marching in a rally the following week. I see myself leading my squad down Münsterberger Street and right into Frankensteiner Steet, running up and down along the four rows of three, yelling, "One, two, three, four!" We started a new song, with me in the lead. Up comes Aunt Lene's, the home of my childhood nemesis. I hear myself coach them, "Louder!" and sing along with them in full voice: "The ancient brittle bones of the world tremble," all the way through to "today Germany belongs to us / And tomorrow, the whole world!" We march right past her living room windows. I look up and hope desperately that she will come to the window and see me. I don't think she did. I am still embarrassed to recall this pathetic attempt to gain her recognition.

Though no longer thrown together, Erika and I sometimes still met in her room to read, and occasionally I could entice her to come for a walk around town, through the Ohle River meadows, or up to Marienberg. Erika preferred going to City Hall Square instead of taking boring "nature walks," as she called my meanderings. During most of the year, particularly on spring and summer evenings, teens met on the square till the nine or ten o'clock curfew enforced by the HJ Patrol Service—the Streifendienst. Girls circled the wide sidewalks of the square clockwise, boys counterclockwise, and when a group of girls passed a group of boys, the shyer ones exchanged meaningful glances or bashful greetings and the bolder ones called out to each other. A particularly forward group of girls that Erika liked to join would ask several boys to circle the square with them. This group received catcalls from the other boys and girls as they passed by, and it took boldness like Erika's to go around as a mixed group. I, feeling awkward, put on a brave front and only a few times accompanied Erika in exchange for a walk with me during the afternoon.

One secret united us in an almost silent comradeship for a few months. Our way from Erika's house to town led past our favorite candy store, which now, in the third year of the war, displayed only dusty dummies of old chocolate boxes and a plate of cookies with artificially pink and green icing. By

The author at age twelve,
passport photo

this time everything from potatoes and flour to shoes could be gotten only
with coupons. Chocolates and candies had disappeared altogether, as sugar
was scarce. Because Uncle Kurt provided us with basic foods such as potatoes,
flour, some butter, and poultry, we were better off than many townsfolk, including Erika's family. They lived exclusively on ever-shorter rations, while
Mother could use the little sugar we were rationed for baking cakes for Sunday afternoon coffee hour. One Friday afternoon, Erika and I stopped at the
store window. We knew that we could not buy sweets without coupons, but
hungry as we were for treats of any kind, we pressed our faces against the
store window to check for any possible strokes of good fortune. To our surprise, the owner motioned us in. We went in and stood at the counter wordlessly. No one else was in the store. We stared at the grim-faced middle-aged
woman behind the counter, who stared back at us and then suddenly smiled.
She took a bag from the counter and filled it from a cookie jar.

"Share it," she said, as she handed Erika the bag of pink and green cookies.

"But we don't have sugar and bread coupons," I stammered, and my face fell. "That's fine, take the bag," the woman insisted. "I don't need coupons."

We ran out of the store before she could change her mind. Wordlessly we continued our walk and headed up to Gallows Hill behind the railroad station. Gallows Hill overlooked the town, and I loved the scramble up the rocks of the steep hillside. Up on top you could either sit on the rocks and gaze down on the town or move along the rim of the adjacent quarry and watch tiny men working, running tiny lorries along rails that looked like pencil marks, so deep was the quarry. We sat down on a large, flat rock with our treasure, looking down at the town. Erika took the cookies out of the bag one by one and, counting them, divided them into two heaps. We sat there silently and munched them slowly, one after the other. They were small animal forms covered with an icing of powdered sugar and pink and green food coloring. The green cookies tasted of mint and the pink ones of rose water. We did not say a word as we consumed the entire bagful.

The following Friday we went by the store and the woman motioned us in again. But this time, when she handed me the bag, she said, "That will be thirty pennies."

I was about to hand back the bag, as I had no money, when Erika dug into her skirt pocket and produced three ten-penny coins. This time we remembered to say thank you as we left the store. Up we went to the quarry again, where we sat on a rock and silently ate the cookies.

"I'll get the money for next time," I promised.

Fortunately, Mother had me deliver several dresses that weekend to customers who tipped, so that I had enough money by the following Friday. We continued the cookie jaunts without speaking about it to anyone or even acknowledging it to each other. We never exchanged any words with the woman apart from "good day," "thank you," and "goodbye." We never greeted her with *Heil Hitler,* as we used to greet everyone else. We alternated paying for our loot. Sometime during the year, we found the store closed, the shutters down, and the cookie lady gone forever. I always remembered her gratefully. She was the only adult during the war years who offered us a gratuitous kindness, and I sometimes still wonder, why did she invite us in, and how did she manage without our coupons? Was she just touched by our noses pressed against the window and our obvious hunger for sweets? Did she remember herself as a sweet-starved child of the Great War and satisfy her own past hunger by gratifying us?

Getting ahold of reading matter became an increasingly difficult task. By age twelve I had begun to despise the plentiful cheap romances in Frau Gurn's spare room. Since rationing cards had been introduced, I no longer had lunch with the two women who ran the dress shop and therefore lost access to their books. Erika, Rita, and I had exhausted our families' meager supplies of books. The local lending library, where each book cost at least fifty pennies a week, carried mostly popular novels and romances. I had read the few novels from that library that I liked, Mereschkowski's *Leonardo da Vinci*, Felix Dahn's *The Strugggle for Rome*, and several translations of Dickens and Mark Twain novels, three times or more.

Mother's customers, therefore, took on a new importance for me as owners of books. To be sure, in most homes in this Silesian backwater, the pickings were slim. Only one customer, Frau Dunisch, the wife of a physician and herself a young home economics teacher at the local trade school, offered better prospects. At least that is what I surmised when I delivered a dress and was asked to wait to be paid in her living room. Two walls of the large, airy room held immense bookshelves. But it was not only the books that drew me. For the first time in my life I saw a room in which every object pleased me. Large windows, white linen curtains opened wide, looked out on Marienberg Park and the houses below by the Ohle River. A comfortable low couch covered in beige, brown, and blue-patterned wool stood below one window; several armchairs of the same material made a set. Low coffee and side tables in gleaming blond woods were placed around casually. Two sculptures that suggested human figures dancing, imitations of Kolbe's bronzes, I learned, without understanding who Kolbe was, sat on blond wooden stands. Several large colorful prints whose brilliant blobs of paint looked like giant flowers or butterflies drew my attention. Shimmering hardwood floors and a hand-woven wool rug with bold semicircles completed the furnishings. And forsythias in unglazed clay vases everywhere lit up the room.

How can I ask Frau Dunisch to lend me a book? I thought as I inched closer to the bookcase nearest the door. I recognized a lot of thin Insel Publishing House volumes from their patterned bindings. I did not think much of them because they usually contained prose sketches or short narratives, for which I had not yet developed a taste. I still preferred a voluminous novel into whose world I could disappear, the more pages, the better. I noticed a few gold and brown bound editions of classical plays, Schiller and Goethe, which I had tried to read but which failed to hold my interest. From the bookshelves of my Schulte relatives I recognized the bindings of a few nineteenth-century novels and novellas by Theodore Storm, Wilhelm Raabe, and Gottfried Keller. But most of the books I did not know. They were linen-bound hardcovers in paper jackets with sparse designs in Gothic script, contemporary novels of the historical variety, as I found out later. How could I ask her to lend me any one of them?

It took me a month to watch for Frau Dunisch to bring another dress to be altered. During the war years, most of Mother's business was alterations, as coupons for textiles grew ever scarcer. I stayed in the background by a living room window, reading, and sure enough, Frau Dunisch, seeing me engaged with a book, asked, "What are you reading?" I had one of the lending library's better novels, Jo von Ammers-Kueller's *The Wives of the Coornvelts,* at the ready and gave her the name of the novel.

"Do you read a lot?" she asked. "That is a long novel."

I nodded, adding, "I have read the novel twice because I like it. But I can't find much in the lending library I haven't read."

Fortunately Mother intervened. "She spends all her free time reading and complains that she cannot find enough to read."

To my delight Frau Dunisch invited me right then and there to come that evening and pick out something from her library. After that, I spent many an evening in her living room selecting another book, after a few days return-ing each volume carefully wrapped in newspaper because I was always afraid that I might spill something on an obviously well-cared-for possession. I loved going to her house out by Old Town Road, just below the park of Marienberg. Since she taught till four in the afternoon, I went in the early evening hours, and I treasured my anticipatory mood. I used the time it took to get there to muse on the book I was returning and to plan what I would ask for next. Many of the nineteenth-century novels by Mörike, Raabe, and Keller, which I read then for the first time, still remind me of that route. In my mind it is still associated with my first love of the German bildungsroman, the novel that traces the childhood, youth, and the educational and emotional experience of an adolescent. I identified with the heroes of these novels, who are in conflict with their environments, who pursue an inchoate quest for a life of the spirit, a life devoted to art, literature, and music beyond the mundane shop-keeping lives their parents led. At the time I had no idea that the world I came to love through these books represented a gentler, more melancholic Germany than the militant and aggressive one I was still entranced by. I read with equal enthusiasm—though less personally, emotionally engaged—Frau Dunisch's Gothic-lettered books of the nationalist-militarist variety, like the World War I war novels of E. E. Dwinger or the historical novels of Gustav Frenssen.

At the beginning of the summer of 1942, Mother told me that I would not be going to the Schultes' for the summer vacation. "You'll stay with the Frenzel relatives at Senitz. It is closer to home, just four railroad stops away on the local to Nimpsch. Cousin Oskar and his new wife, Marianne, have promised to take you in, and Oma's sister Ida will keep an eye on you." I was not too sorry not to be going back to Zülzendorf, but I minded being shunted about from one relative to the next and envied Jochen, who always went to Uncle Kurt's. Though I had visited the Senitz farm once with the family, just before Father died, and had met Aunt Ida at Oma's funeral, I dreaded the change. But there was nothing to be done.

A week later I arrived at Senitz station and walked the mile over to the village, lugging my suitcase. It was an inauspicious beginning, at any rate, and I felt apprehensive. Once arrived, however, I was pleasantly surprised. Unlike most of my other relatives, Aunt Marianne welcomed me with a friendly smile. She was pregnant with her first child and impressed even me as very young. "I am almost as new here as you are," she greeted me. "I don't know my way about the house or the farmyard yet, and my mother-in-law is a mystery to me." I warmed to her immediately. On evenings I would harvest pears and apples with her in their orchard across the road from the comfortable residence, talking with her about the baby to be born in a few months, or about the family. Uncle Oskar, a tall, straight-backed man with piercing blue eyes, seemed much older than his wife. The first in his family to be a university-trained farmer, he ran the farm himself without an overseer. Unlike Oma, Aunt Ida, a stooped, white-haired, heavyset widow, was a formidable presence who still ruled the house and everyone in it. She wore black and was in deep mourning because her youngest son, a twenty-year-old gunner in a tank division, had died the previous year on the eastern front. I could literally feel the weight of her and the family's grief and shock at his terrible end in the burning tank when I met them all at the evening meal. But except for the usually silent breakfast and supper, I did not see much of either Aunt Ida or Uncle Oskar, as I worked a full day with the other field hands bringing in the harvest.

I missed the companionable work with my Polish and Italian friends, Wanda, Maria, and Anita, and found no substitutes for them, probably because by this time I was too heavily indoctrinated to seek friends among foreigners. I remember one telling incident about my attitudes toward them at the time, however. Once, as I walked through the village on Sunday, some youngsters who did not know me called after me, "Dirty Pole." I felt ashamed, shrank into myself, walked on, did not look back, and berated myself for looking like a Pole. Uncle Oskar's farm was not as large as Uncle Richard's, and he employed mostly German field hands. The few Polish women and a few Russian POWs in rags kept to themselves. Unlike at Zülzendorf, none of the German field hands lived on the farm but rather somewhere in the village. The Poles and Russians had their separate quarters in a dilapidated house my uncle rented on a neighboring farm. By this time I had learned to keep my distance from them and hardly noticed their presence. I remember only one time when I could not ignore the apprehension I felt about them. It was late, and I overheard Uncle Oskar tell his wife as he got a rifle from a locked case in the hall, "I am on night watch with the *Ortsgruppenleiter* [the Nazi village leader]. Don't worry. He thinks the foreign workers might cause trouble. They won't. They have just been restless."

In the mornings Uncle Oskar directed the work crews to whatever field needed tending. Coming in from the fields at five, I helped Aunt Marianne feed the pigs and a few times even tried, unsuccessfully, to assist with the milking. By this time I could hold my own in field work with any adult and still had energy left for evening chores. Aunt Marianne was training an apprentice, and unlike Herta at the Schultes', Wally was only two years older than I and already very good at milking. On weekends the two of us went for hikes together and sometimes swam in the local swimming hole out past Uncle Oskar's fields by the railroad tracks. Once again I checked out the attic for books but only found a few schoolbooks. Since we all worked long hours, I did not miss the reading much and fell asleep even as I was undressing.

Only two incidents during the two summers I spent at Senitz stand out in my memory. Aunt Ida's second son, an officer in Guderian's tank division, visited her after he had received the Knight's Cross for bravery in battle. Though short and almost bald, he impressed me immensely when I saw him in uniform, but he lost his heroic aura once he put on civilian dress. At dinner during his overnight visit, he broke the usual silence and talked about being received by Hitler at the decoration ceremony.

"Many people," he said, "even the bravest soldiers, freeze when Hitler talks to them. His eyes bore through you so that you are almost transfixed."

Even though he was awed, he reported with a laugh, "I answered Hitler's question easily about how many enemy tanks we destroyed. I should know, shouldn't I?"

I was fascinated by the idea that Hitler's eyes could have such a powerful effect. I had been reading about men of demonic power, like the healer Rasputin, who could stop the flow of blood merely by the force of his eyes. A few days later in the local grocery store, while I was looking at a Hitler portrait with its piercing eyes, the thought suddenly struck me: What if he is mad? I brushed the idea guiltily away. Don't even think that, I told myself.

Another visitor at Senitz, another of the family's four sons, my uncle Willy, whom I had met at the Schultes' the previous summers, appeared a few times to pick up food supplies. After dinner, when his mother had retired, Uncle Oskar teased his younger brother, "Aren't you sick yet of your canary outfit?" He was referring to the color of his mustard-yellow SA uniform. "When is your business going to collapse? Isn't it about time?" In the kitchen, Aunt Marianne explained to me, "Willy failed at a number of businesses the family set him up in, and Oskar had to bail him out. That's why he teases him. A few years ago Willy had better luck and found a job with the party. It's not much of a job, but he is doing well." At other times Uncle Oskar teased Willy for boasting and exaggerating. "Has Hitler crossed the channel yet? I suppose he has a lot of time for that. After all, he has a thousand years"—a reference to the thousand-year Reich that the Nazis anticipated.

To ingratiate himself, Uncle Willy responded with jokes about Göring or Goebbels, or made fun of his involvement with the party. "The other day, I had to go to Berlin to ask if Dr. Goebbels would speak at the party rally I am organizing in Breslau. He could not see me; he had an all-day appointment with Lale Anderson." Lale Anderson was the most famous, sexiest actress under the Nazis, the equivalent in voice and sex appeal of Marlene Dietrich. I understood, of course, having listened to the gossip of Mother's customers, that Goebbels's well-known infatuation with actresses and Willy's lowly standing in the party were the point of this anecdote. I picked up my relatives' disrespect for Uncle Willy and the party. Yet the disrespect did not conflict with my idealization of Hitler and his cause. That year in leadership group I had learned that we, the HJ, were different from the adults around us and from the Nazi Party and some of its corrupt bosses. We were youth being led by and leading youth. We were idealists loyal to the cause; we served the country and did not take advantage of it the way some party bosses did—Göring, for instance, who confiscated pictures in the museums of occupied countries for his own estate. And Hitler, I was convinced, did not know what the bad apples in the party were doing. As the war went on, these discrepancies between my idealization of the cause and rumors of corruption became ever more glaring. Adults, I was more and more certain, could not be trusted. They betrayed the Führer. We, the young, would remain loyal. My definition of "young" included, of course, a few special adults such as Frau Dunisch.

After the summer and throughout the winter, I grew increasingly unhappy about my leadership role. As squad leaders we were responsible for the girls' attendance. When too many girls were absent, the squad and I looked bad and I got a reproof from the troop leader. My squad had the worst attendance record of the troop—we had been issued small black record books in which to take attendance. Looking across the middle school's yard, I saw that few of Gretl's fifteen girls ever missed. Most of my girls were working-class grade school students who lived in the new apartment houses close to the quarries and the sugar beet factory out on Frankensteiner Street. Even though we only met Wednesdays, I spent at least two or three more afternoons a week visiting the mothers of the girls who had failed to show up. As squad leaders we were supposed to report any girl who missed two or more times in a row. By going and begging their mothers please to send them, I would not have to report them to Lotte at monthly meetings. I managed to have at least eight girls present every Wednesday. For the rest, I learned innumerable excuses for nonattendance and thus I remember the mothers better than the girls. If I could get a mother to write an excuse for a series of absences, I could let it slide. Of course, the husbands of most of these women were at the front, and their daughters, I could see, were needed at home for babysitting and helping with their many siblings and their mothers' usually chaotic households. I don't remember if I ever did report a girl to Lotte; I must have, because I was conscientious. I do know that I tried hard not to, and I visited the mothers I could not reach on my first attempt over and over again. In part I tried so desperately to have the girls attend because I felt I had to compensate for not being a good enough leader. Had I been able to make our activities more interesting and fun, I figured, the girls might have shown up.

I wonder now what the mothers thought of me and of what I was doing. Most actually were friendly. By this time, too, I had forgotten that many of their husbands had been socialists and communists, a fact I had been aware of a few years earlier, when I had seen quarry workers being deported at the railroad station. With some of the women I had long conversations about their husbands at the front, about insufficient food coupons for growing children, about shortages of shoes and clothing for them, about gangs of fatherless fourteen-year-olds who tyrannized the younger children, and about fights among neighbors of the overcrowded apartment houses. I gained from these conversations at least some understanding of what it meant to be a working-class mother. I liked them better than their children, with none of whom could I establish a relationship.

The routine of leading a squad was mind numbing. Marching was a bore and supervising sports without participating myself, frustrating. Fortunately, Lotte had decided to have the troop leader take over political schooling so that I did not need to worry about teaching my squad the biographies of party leaders or party hierarchy; but sitting through endless repetitions of the material I had learned twice before was exasperating. Since I had failed at leading my squad in singing, Gretl was in charge of that for both our squads. She was unable to inspire the fun that Marlis had provided by alternating solo with group singing, nor could she direct us in canon singing. And none of us could do a credible second voice like Erika could. We sounded monotonous and usually lost an octave in the course of a longer song. We both missed the leadership squad and its comradeship. The only other task left for us squad leaders was to take girls to the fields surrounding town to collect herbs and plants for teas to be used in military hospitals.

I was good at this task because Oma and Lotte had taught me about the medicinal plants and herbs of the region during our hikes together. I knew the fields, the meadows, the roads, and the creek sides where they grew. It was the only activity during the two years as squad leader that I enjoyed, even if the girls found it boring. Week after week, except in the depths of winter and during summer vacation, we filled basket after basket with linden blooms, horsetail, colt's foot, and yarrow. At afternoon's end we brought our baskets to the middle school and spread the plants on drying racks in the attic. On winter days, when snow covered the ground, we sometimes went to sing for wounded soldiers at the local hospital and at the trade school, which had been converted into a hospital. I felt embarrassed by our attempts at singing, but the soldiers seemed pleased by our presence.

At the beginning of my second year as squad leader, Lotte Turnow lined up the four squads of our troop in the middle school yard. Without much ceremony she called Gretl to the front. "Gretl will be your troop leader from now on," she announced. "She has already led you well in singing. We need [here she named another girl] to lead another troop." As Gretl walked up front, I was overcome with disappointment and humiliation and wanted to disappear. Of course, I thought resentfully, thinking of what Agatha would have said about the advantages of the "upper crust," they only promote high school girls to troop leader.

Though my HJ leadership took up much time and effort for the rest of these two years, I do not remember a single girl in my squad, nor did Gretl and I sustain our earlier bond of comradeship from our days in leadership group. I felt alone, angry, and frustrated in managing a totally unrewarding job. The two years as squad leader felt like a sentence in purgatory for sins I could not fathom. In my last year I could not wait to finish being a squad leader, graduate from grade school, and take up something else, anything— I did not know what.

When I began sculpting in my late thirties I was surprised that my hands knew how to form clay, carve wood, and use tools. And then I suddenly remembered the toys I made in my teens. As the war went on, fewer and fewer nonnecessities were available. Even when Mother had money at Christmastime, she could not buy toys for us. This was hard on my younger brother, Werner. Ever since I had begun to acknowledge him as a person a few years back, I had made presents for him, paper dolls, boys and girls, which I drew and for which I made paper dresses, pants, and shirts. At Christmas 1941 I found a wooden box and decided to get more wood and make a castle and soldiers for him. A friend of Mother's who owned a soap shop gave me a few more wooden boxes. Some of the wood I used for making soldiers, the rest for the castle. In the attic I located an old fret saw and a few blades that had belonged to my father but had not been used for years. A few drops of oil made the saw serviceable. I even found some old rasps and some sandpaper, leftovers from the time Father had made a dollhouse for me. It was lucky that I had several blades, because I broke a few in the course of making the soldiers, the outlines of which I had drawn on paper and copied onto the wood. But soon I was skilled enough to cut out a few horses as well. Sure, they looked a little like dogs, but then, using a bit of material and glue to make saddles, they could pass. It was easier to glue together a few biplanes made from tongue depressors. The castle even had battlements, and a drawbridge on leather hinges that actually worked. I found some old paint, gray and black, in the attic, and some brushes, so that two weeks before Christmas I had a creditable present.

The problem was that I could work only on the kitchen table, and so my brother, of course, knew that I was constructing a castle and soldiers. In fact, I even got his help—such as it was; he was only six—with sanding the cutouts. I told him I was making a present for a neighbor boy whose father had just died at the front. I loved working with him at the kitchen table, showing him what to do, telling him stories and humming folk songs with him as we worked.

Since there was time left until Christmas, I made myself a present, a peasant cradle painted with a flower garland for the only doll I sometimes still played with surreptitiously. As I was putting the parts of the cradle together, one of the headboards broke. A customer of my mother's who was just walking through to the living room saw my frustration. The wife of the owner of a furniture factory, she said, "That wood is difficult to work—you need plywood."

"I don't think I can get any," I replied.

"Why don't you come and get some of the bits and pieces left over at the factory?" she offered. I did, and the plywood worked even when nailed.

On Christmas Eve, before leaving for church, I covered the castle with a sheet and had Mother put it under the tree. As we sang "Silent Night" I lifted off the sheet and looked at Werner. "For me?" he stammered, his face lighting up. "So it was for me after all!"

In November 1942 I started my Christmas shop in the kitchen again. This time around I had wood aplenty, plywood for cut-out figures of dolls, soldiers, horses with actual legs and hooves, dollhouse furniture, but also wood blocks suitable for making toy houses and church steeples, and curled wood shavings for trees. At first I only wanted to make a toy village for my brother and some dollhouse furniture for myself, but customers of Mother's saw me work, liked what they saw, and asked if I would make some toys for their children. Soon I was at work making doll furniture, toy soldiers, cradles, cannons on wheels, even airplanes. I had seen Mother make out bills, so I did too, and the adults actually paid me. I earned enough money that Christmas season to buy myself a new uniform skirt and blue blazer.

I had great plans for the following Christmas, 1943, and I got ready early. The furniture factory again provided as much wood as I could use. Another customer of Mother's got me new fret saw blades and plenty of sandpaper. And I even found some more paint in the attic. I had gotten plenty of orders. It must have been on the second or third day into the work that a policeman came into our kitchen.

"Can I see your trading license?" he demanded.

"Trading license?" I replied, suddenly afraid that I had done something bad. "I don't know what that is."

"If you want to sell something, like these toys"—he pointed to a completed set of a woodblock village—"you have to have a license from city hall." I was stunned. I don't know who reported me, but the police had been informed that I was selling toys without a license.

"We won't prosecute you," he added. "But you must report to your troop leader. The HJ will take appropriate action." For the rest of the day, I worried about what action the HJ would take, and I stopped working on my toys.

The next day Lotte Turnow gave me a talking to. "You are undermining our HJ effort of toy making for the HJ toy shop," she said. Since I had been leading my squad and working hard keeping up its attendance record, I knew neither of a toy-making effort nor of an official HJ toy shop.

"You are taking wood, saw blades, sandpaper for your private use that rightly should have been donated to our toy-making efforts," she berated me. "You will not be disciplined, but you will put in five hours a week every Saturday till Christmas, fret sawing for our toy shop. You will also bring along and hand over your supplies."

I felt thunderstruck, mortified at having done something wrong, and then numb. I had not meant any harm, I told myself, but that did not make me feel better about the reproof. I showed up for the HJ toy-making workshop in a middle school classroom several days later with my saw blades, sandpaper, and the wood I had intended to use. I was given a piece of plywood stenciled with a clown form—a body and two separate arms and legs. Not just one form but five. Some of the other girls were already sawing away, also making clowns. Others were sanding, while a few painted the sanded clown forms, copying the colors from a sample. I set to work. My blade broke after a few strokes. I put in a new blade. Puzzled and embarrassed, I had difficulty following the clown's body outline on the wood and broke the next blade as well.

The girl in charge looked at me sternly. "I was told you are an expert sawyer."

"I was—am." But try as I might, I just was not able to do it. I was demoted to sanding that afternoon. After I finished that assignment at Christmas, I did not touch another tool for more than twenty years.

I felt humiliation and fury only years later, when I told an artist friend the entire story. So that was why tools, working with my hands, felt so familiar. So that was why I had rejected producing anything concrete, visual, with my hands for years. What had happened to me? My memory went further back. When I was three, four, five, Father used to make us toys, and I sat at the kitchen table, barely looking over its top at first, and had helped, watched, and learned how to use tools. After he died, and my younger brother needed toys, I had taken his place and made them. The fun in toy making was in designing the castle, the drawbridge, the planes, in drawing the soldiers myself and transforming my fear of soldiers, planes, and war into a creative activity in which I controlled what they looked like and could do. Toy making was about creating and controlling my own world, a world I could design however I wanted. The resistance of the materials—doing a clean cut-out, not breaking blades while sawing a difficult pattern, not splintering the wood when nailing pieces together—was a challenge that, once met, gave me a feeling of mastery. My hands refused serial production!

And the doll furniture, too, had meanings I understood only later. My chore at the Schultes' during the summers had been to put the fake-garlanded peasant chairs in the hall on top of the bulky peasant table, roll up the long rug, and put it on the fake peasant chest. I had hated the job, which seemed totally pointless to me, a sort of routine punishment, because the chairs were heavy and the rug full of dirt and dust. And I never got it right, either; my aunt always complained. I had not understood—and my aunt never explained— that I was to sweep the floor, and that putting the furniture up was only preparation for cleaning. Designing and painting my own peasant furniture, I was no longer dependent on adults; I could follow plans that made sense to me and do whatever I wanted to. And Mother's customers all encouraged me. They found my toys beautiful and wanted to buy them. The furniture factory owner's wife and the owner of the hardware shop supported me. And I could even earn enough money to buy myself a new uniform. Designing meant that I could have my own life, could be independent. At the HJ toy shop, I understood, my hands, my body, refused HJ regimentation and imposed conformity. Without knowing it, I was beginning to resist HJ activities.

Jochen graduated from grammar school in the spring of 1943. He was sent to a farm for his *Landdienst,* a year of obligatory service in farming, as many grade school graduates were. I knew it was going to be my turn to leave home in a year. I was impatient to be an adult and looked forward to graduation from grade school and confirmation by the church, at which point I would be addressed by the formal appellation *Sie* and no longer by *Du,* reserved for children and social inferiors. Once a week now I joined a confirmation class of the local Protestant church held in a classroom at the Red School. Almost all the girls in my class attended. The teacher, Pastor Thomas, an elderly man with a lugubrious voice, entered the classroom with his right arm raised, greeting us with "Heil Hitler, Grüss Gott, liebe Kinderchen." I resented the address "dear little children." We were not four years old! The other girls scoffed at his saluting Hitler and God in the same breath, and even I did not need Agatha's cynicism to recognize the ignominious pairing. The indoctrination of the HJ had had its effect on me. As a proud Jungmädel and a future leader, I had come to see religious belief as a faith for weaklings who could not stand on their own two feet. I do not know from which books I picked up the Nazi misinterpretation of Nietzsche's "God is dead" —probably from a pocket Nietzsche in Frau Dunisch's library, a volume for youths aspiring to become "supermen." I had stopped praying at age ten or so, but not for ideological reasons. I first stopped praying during my first stay at the Schultes', out of spite. I had asked God to make my mother write to me, and she did not. In anger, I stopped praying, fully expecting that God would make me feel his displeasure. When nothing happened, I prayed only occasionally, usually when I was in some kind of a scrape and in need of help. Since sometimes I did get out of the scrape, I did not entirely lose my faith. But it was, as I realized during confirmation class, a purely mercenary belief in God, a kind of quid pro quo that had nothing to do with trust or faith in a supreme being.

Pastor Thomas fit the picture of the spineless Protestant clergy who had joined the German Christians, the Protestants subservient to the Nazis. Sometime in late 1935, shortly after Father's death, when the Gestapo had jailed some members of the Confessional Church, among them Pastor Niemöller, the police had taken Pastor Thomas as well as several clergymen of our town from their pastoral residence next to St. Gotthardt's, which we called Little Church, and arrested them for the day. I remember standing with Oma at the entrance to Little Church that day, a Sunday morning. On coming home, the adults spoke excitedly about the event. I was upset and did not understand why they had taken our pastor to jail. I gathered that Oma and Grand-father Mahlendorf, though anticlerical in orientation, objected to the Gestapo action and thought that the charges against the clergymen were trumped up. The next day, all of the local Protestant pastors were released. After the Nazi period, when I read of Pastor Niemöller's role in the Confessional Church, the Protestant resistance to Hitler, I understood that our local clergy probably be-longed to the faction that had come to a compromise with the regime. But in 1935 I sensed that Oma, though she continued to go to Little Church services, for some reason no longer respected Pastor Thomas.

At any rate, Pastor Thomas's greeting at confirmation class, "Heil Hitler and God's Greetings," represented the compromise of the nationalist German Christians, the so-called SA Christians who had parted ways with Niemöller's Confessional Church. Pastor Thomas prayed that the Führer might be granted strength, and the German troops, victory. For the rest, I remember little about Pastor Thomas's weekly instruction. We had to memorize the Ten Command-ments—which I knew from the Bible lessons in early grammar school and kindergarten—the explanations of the commandments in the catechism, and the Lutheran confession of faith. These were the subjects in which we were to be examined before the congregation during the public confirmation cer-emony. Most of us jeered at Pastor Thomas, paid no attention to what he said, and subjected him to the same disrespectful treatment that we had meted out to Fräulein Pelzer, our grade school teacher for the last three years. While I had felt sorry after a while for Fräulein Pelzer, I felt no sympathy for Pastor Thomas. I took a book along to the instruction and read. Since it was easy for me, I did memorize the explanations of the catechism and the confession of faith. I liked Luther's sonorous oratorical repetitions, and I did not want Mother to be ashamed of me at the ceremony.

A special news bulletin in the late summer of 1942 had celebrated the vic-torious battle of Stalingrad. We rejoiced at the simultaneous taking of the Crimea by gorging ourselves on watermelons shipped in from the Crimea. It was a brief pleasure. At Christmas 1942, both at school and at HJ, we all sent let-ters to the soldiers at Stalingrad, urging them to hold fast because they would soon be relieved by Hitler's miraculous breakthrough maneuver. Needless to say, I never got an answer to my letters. The radio announced the fall of Stalin-grad in January '43 with somber march music and blamed it on the betrayal of Paulus, the commanding general who had surrendered against Hitler's express orders. From then on, most of the retreats of the German army figured as betrayals of our heroic soldiers by whomever could be blamed, or whoever committed suicide and could thus be called a coward, like my former hero, Field Marshal Rommel. The only prominent general I remember distinctly is Rommel, if for no other reason than that I had once copied his portrait from a postcard.

At school during that last school year, we stopped keeping our war diaries on the fate of our troops. The *Strehlen Daily* and the illustrated papers no longer published pictures of the army's retreats. That is why I don't remember later events of the war, even decisive ones, neither the capitulation of Rommel's Africa corps in early 1943 nor the Allied invasion of Sicily in May 1943, nor Italy's surrender in July 1943, nor even D-Day. In newscasts the former "courageous Italian ally" became "the cowardly, undependable Italians." For a while, Herr Schmidt had still marked some of the retreats on the Russian front on the large map of Europe, telling us, "In any war, strategic retreats to straighten an extended frontline assure eventual advantage." But after a while the map of Europe disappeared from our classroom and Herr Schmidt concentrated his efforts on earlier historical heroics. The radio once again became my source of information, but the enthusiasm for news disappeared. Partisans suddenly dominated the news. They were everywhere, in the Ukraine, Poland, Greece, the Balkans, in France and in Italy, and they treacherously attacked our soldiers. They could not be distinguished from civilians. That's why entire villages had to be shot if one of our soldiers was shot, the radio reported. Traitors surfaced everywhere. I had memorized the progress of our troops on the European map well enough that I could locate in my mind where our troops had retreated to—or rather where "the front line was straightened," as the newscasters had it. But I soon lost interest altogether and my world grew ever narrower, just as the territories that Germany had occupied shrank.

The denial of our true situation is almost incomprehensible to me now. Like my peers and most of the adults around me, I gave no thought to where the country was heading, just as I refused to take in the true horror of the bombings of the large industrial cities of the western parts of Germany and of Berlin. The town and the shops filled with bombing victims. I could not go shopping for Mother without running into them.

"Our house was in flames and we ran from the cellar through the burning street; even the asphalt was on fire. The firestorm roared around us, my dress caught fire, and I would have burned to death if . . ." I did not want to hear what Aunt Klara's cousin from Hamburg was telling a crowd of us at

Hartmann's dry goods store. I did not listen, and I felt no sympathy for her or for others like her. Instead, and this is painful to remember, I felt angry at them for what we in Jungmädel called their defeatist attitude.

Instead of keeping notebooks on the war, we learned in school about first aid and nutrition, about the calories, minerals, and vitamins the human body needed. The hard dark bread called *Kommisbrot*, which contained bits of straw, was good for us, Fräulein Pelzer told us. Unpeeled potatoes and vegetables contained healthy vitamins. "Only degenerates eat the quantities of butter, cheese, meat, and sausages that we used to consume before rationing," she argued, even as rations for these foods got smaller and smaller. For children over age twelve, milk rations went down to a liter per week, I believe. "You are almost grown up now. Your bones don't need the calcium of milk they used to need for growth," she explained. Whatever the scarcity, she came up with a rationalization that it was good for us. I have resented calorie counting and diet minding ever since.

I came to appreciate Mother's relatives in the country now. Many a late summer and fall evening we—Mother, Werner, and I—went to Striege or Segen, villages close to home, to visit a cousin here or an aunt there. We always went home with a liter of milk or pitcher full of molasses, some cottage cheese or fruit in season. "You city dwellers," the cousin or aunt would say, "surely can use some extras." On walks back home in the gathering darkness, on a footpath through the harvested fields, still fragrant from ears of ripe wheat littered on the ground, Mother, Werner, and I drew closer together as a family—brother Jochen had left for his *Landdienst*, his war service helping farmers. We sang to the accompaniment of chirping cicadas, Mother told stories about the relatives we had left, and best of all, we made plans for what we would do after the war, when we would no longer have shortages of food and living space. My favorite *Zukunftsmusik*—music of the future—was building a house with a separate room for every one of us, a huge dressmaker's studio for Mother, a living room like Frau Dunisch's. The plans got more extravagant and the house larger and more elaborate as the war approached its end. On some evenings I was keenly aware that this kind of future was an illusion, a game we indulged in until—but I never dared think further.

In HJ we practiced what to do in an air raid and how to assist the air-raid warden. Many families, like Aunt Klara's, had relatives living with them who had been evacuated after bombing raids. I was terrified of air raids, and my terror was all the greater because I could not show or admit it. Instead, I insisted stridently that we keep strictly to the blackouts. This was not an easy task, for we had shutters only for the kitchen and living room windows, none for Father's office and our bedroom. Several old blankets draped over the window frames served instead of blackout curtains. Afraid of light shining through gaps, we dared use only low-wattage bulbs. Even so, Herr Gurn, the air-raid warden, asked us again and again to turn off the lights altogether. Nighttime reading became impossible. A few times we had to go into the deepest of the Baronie's cellars, our air-raid shelter, from which the secret passage was said to lead to Rummelsberg Castle. I did not find the heavy, arched walls reassuring, having heard of buildings collapsing and burying people under them. We were lucky, however. Few enemy planes flew over our town on their way to the Upper Silesian mines. Only once, from far away, we heard a few bombs falling on Breslau, some thirty kilometers away. Several times in the later war years I discovered that Mother listened to foreign radio stations late at night. We had been told in the HJ that this was a criminal act and I begged Mother to stop, being thoroughly frightened about what might happen to us if she went to prison. The nightmares I had after Father died returned in 1943.

As the fronts receded back to Germany's borders during the course of 1943–44, party leaders and the radio began referring to a secret miracle weapon that German scientists were working on. "Hitler and our scientists will prevail, if our nation will but hold out bravely! . . . We must be steadfast! . . . Report defeatists," Dr. Goebbels shrieked into the loudspeaker, turning our inadmissible fears into public paranoia. Being a defeatist meant not just doubting "final victory" but also complaining about shortages. A PR persona similar to Smokey the Bear, posted in schools, municipal offices, banks, and other public places, warned of Kohlenklau (coal thief) and admonished us to conserve energy for the war effort. Hoarding food supplies or obtaining rationing cards by some pretext or other counted as felonies. The worst offense was to defame Hitler. Another sign in railroad cars, streetcars, and buses proclaimed, "Caution: Enemy Listening In," and warned about speaking of the whereabouts of relatives at the front or of the damage done by the bombings of the cities. The sign displayed two train passengers talking, with the sinister shadow of a big-eared man towering over them. Increasingly I felt that no remark was harmless. Apprehension poisoned everything, and on the rare occasions when we visited Grandfather Mahlendorf by train, I noticed that people sat in their seats silently and morosely. When a contrary soul dared speak up about "Goebbels's idiotic speech about final victory," a neighbor berated him,

"Don't you know that the enemy is listening?" Retaining respectful manners from Oma's training, I was too shy and inhibited to reprimand adults about what I considered defeatist behavior. I remember a few times, however, when I wanted to, and felt outraged by the adults' lack of loyalty to the Führer.

I spent the summer vacation of 1943 in Senitz again and worked in the fields as I had before. With the birth of an heir, Aunt Marianne and Wally, her apprentice, were busier than they'd been the year before. In the farmhouse attic, among my uncle's old schoolbooks, I found a little treasure trove of books and spent all my spare time reading. I discovered the lyrical and melancholy novellas of Storm and Keller, *Immensee* and *A Village Romeo and Juliet*. They spoke to me of unfulfilled love, tragic family hatreds, and yearning for death. They encouraged in me a morbid sensitivity. I reread both novellas at least half a dozen times that summer, relishing sentences as if they were poems, identifying for the first time with the female characters of a narrative. Looking back, I see this as an unfortunate identification, that I was seduced by the concept of female passivity in affection, passion, and love.

My Senitz relatives lived in a far different world from that of sentiment and melancholy. Since nobody out in the country bothered much about blackouts, I could keep the light on and read undisturbed. But one night Aunt Ida saw the light from my window and chided me the next morning at breakfast.

"It's unfortunate if a girl has her nose in a book as much as you do."

Fortunately, Mother, an avid reader herself, had never objected to Jochen's and my reading. When relatives told her that I read too much and would come to a bad end unless I learned to help around the house, she answered, "She is out of harm's way when she is reading. Besides, she'll have to work soon enough."

I was fascinated by all love stories, both literary classics like those of Keller and Storm and popular sentimental novels like Ludwig Ganghofer's *Silence in the Forest*, based on a neoromantic Böcklin painting of the same title, a copy of which graced Aunt Lene's living room. I consumed the literary classics and Ganghofer's melodramatic novel indiscriminately, but the latter excited me more because of its dramatic plot and its grossly passionate, treacherous characters who almost succeed in destroying the novel's melancholy protagonist, a world-weary prince, and his love, a young woman artist. Set in a villa in the Alps, with long descriptions of glaciers, mountain peaks, and forests—favorite Nazi subject matter!—the action was simple enough. On his solitary wanderings in the forest, the prince sees a young woman painter who reminds him of

Böcklin's painting. He comes to love her; his love is returned. Another man, a violently jealous poacher who also seeks to gain the painter's affections, observes the lovers and vows to destroy the painter if he cannot win her. The prince's divorced wife, a rapacious plotter, attempts to regain her estranged husband by inciting the poacher to set fire to the forest and destroy the painter with it. As the flames engulf the mountains, both men attempt to save the painter. In a grand finale, the conflagration consumes the evil characters while the intrepid prince and the artist emerge from the flames unscathed and purified.

Yet, after every reading of the sentimental and suggestively erotic love scenes and rescues, I felt vaguely ashamed, as if I had indulged in something forbidden. I never regretted reading as much romantic trash as I did growing up. If nothing else, it helped me develop a fine ear for what was and was not turgid prose.

Mother came to visit me in Senitz one weekend that summer. When I went to church with her and Aunt Ida, a couple of village teenagers whistled after us and called out to me. I was embarrassed when Aunt Ida commented, "You are filling out. The boys are noticing you." When I walked Mother to the station that afternoon, she admonished me, "Don't do anything with these boys. Be careful." I was furious with her for distrusting me and for evading the sexual issues I was struggling with.

Back at home, with Jochen gone, I began to be troubled by what I would do after graduation, just eight months away. I knew that I did not want to be a dressmaker or a beautician; nor did I want to be apprenticed to a shopkeeper and become a salesperson. After this last boring farm summer, I did not ever again want to work on a farm, however much Herr Schmidt and the HJ promised that German youth would be given lands in the east. His talk of lands for the asking did not stop even as the Russians closed in on our borders. After all, the miracle weapons were going to secure all of Russia to the Ural Mountains and the Caucasus for Germany. I did not want to learn shorthand and typing and work in an office. I dreamed of being allowed to go to the high school of the Ursuline convent in Breslau—a school that accepted girls who had missed years of schooling—even as I recognized this as a vain fantasy.

It was Frau Dunisch who, knowing my love of reading, came up with a solution to the career problem.

"The government is setting up a new institution for teacher training modeled on Austrian teacher-training seminaries. Graduates of middle schools and specially gifted grade school graduates qualify," she told Mother and me.

"Seminary attendance is free if Ulla signs up to teach for five years wherever they need teachers after she graduates. Graduation from one of these seminaries grants the graduate the equivalent of a high school diploma." I was ecstatic. I could go on to high school after all.

This time around, my teachers, Fräulein Pelzer and Herr Schmidt, supported my application. Late in the fall, Mother received notification that I should report to a selection camp where applicants would be tested for their suitability to become teachers. I remember only a few details about the week-long examinations that took place in a mountain youth hostel. We were to write an essay on a theme of our choosing about our family. As I looked out a large window of the mountain cabin at the tall firs that surrounded us, I wondered what I should say about my family. Then it came to me. I wrote about Oma's jewelry box, about the time Oma's mother went to the village spinning room, where women in the early nineteenth century gathered to gossip as they spun cloth together. She told the women assembled there, "I've lost the key to the jewelry box. I have looked everywhere and cannot find it." This was during the Franco-Prussian War of 1870, when women gave their gold jewelry for the war effort.

"If I cannot find it," Oma's mother continued, "I can't contribute any of my jewelry to the village effort." She felt embarrassed and offered to donate a large sum of money instead. The story went on to describe further attempts to find the key, and how finally her little daughter, Oma, at age four, solved the mystery. "I took it to Wuff's [the yard dog's] house," she confessed to her nanny. The dog, a nasty, snarling, outdoor creature, strangely enough was her friend—but that is another of the many stories my mother was full of.

As usual when I got to writing a story, I lost my sense of time as well as my sense of what the actual family tale had been. Embroidering and making a point took precedence over the truth. I had finished the story, except for a concluding summary sentence, when the examining teacher called the time. I felt good about the essay and even thought that the somewhat abrupt ending might be especially effective. Next came a dictation, my weak point, and I tried hard not to be sloppy.

That night, as I was trying to fall asleep in the attic dormitory to the sound of a gentle rain pattering on the wooden roof, I became more and more agitated. I worried about how many mistakes I had made in the dictation. Then my thoughts went to the essay. What if the examiners noticed my embroidering and exaggerations? After all, though, I consoled myself, good storytelling needs exaggeration. What I did not acknowledge to myself was how carefully I had chosen the theme, to give my judges just what they would want to hear. I half knew that a nationalistic theme, like the sacrifice of family heirlooms for the fatherland, would reveal a properly patriotic attitude and leave a positive impression. I chose a village spinning room for the setting, although the action took place at the village pub. I knew that spinning rooms no longer existed by the 1870s, but a spinning room provided the folk atmosphere obligatory in Nazi writing. Was I aware of why I had made these choices? Did I know how well I was able to fit into the system if I really wanted to? I do not know. All I knew then was that I wanted to be admitted to the seminary and that I could not afford to be rejected. Despite my poor spelling in essay and dictation, I received the letter of admission just before Christmas.

In the German Protestant Reformed Church, children were confirmed at age fourteen in a public ceremony on the Sunday before Easter. Presents by relatives were mandatory, as was a new dress for the occasion. This played a larger role for all of us than the religious meaning of the ceremony—namely, our acceptance into the church as confessors of faith. After confirmation, we grade school graduates were defined as adults, able to go to work, old enough to help support the family.

As this was the fourth year of the war, a new dress was out of the question. But Mother insisted that I oblige her by getting my hair coifed. I had never had my hair done. I felt as hypocritical about such a beauty treatment as I did about the show of religiosity—the distinctions still escaped me. Looking at my curled head in the mirror after coming home from the hairdresser's, I felt disgusted and washed out the curls, leaving a halo of frizz.

Since I did not believe in any kind of confession of faith, I refused to say the words during the ceremony. But I did begin to answer correctly one of the questions I was asked during the public examination, even though all of us knew that no one had ever failed. As luck would have it, Pastor Thomas asked me to recite the commandment concerning adultery.

"Thou shalt not commit adultery," I began, as my fellow communicants tittered. I never finished, and Pastor Thomas motioned to me to stop so as to forestall further merriment. Embarrassed by the tittering and the sexual subject, as I was by the entire communion ceremony, I almost did not hear that Jochen, up in the organ loft, had begun, softly and tentatively, to play Handel's *Largo*, the one piece of music we both loved at the time. Unlike me, he had developed his early love of music and had taken organ lessons. Now he had come from the country, from quite a distance, and had talked the organist into letting him play. I noticed the melody's solemn sweep only as he concluded. I appreciated his thoughtfulness but felt too conflicted at the time to thank him. After my thoroughly two-faced performance in church, I decided that I would never again get involved in pretending to a faith I did not have.

Graduation from grammar school also came with a celebration. Our class decided that those of us who wanted to would contribute a song, a poem, or a skit of some sort to entertain our teachers and fellow students. Our democratic process of arriving at a decision tells me how resistant we, as a group, remained to our teachers' and the HJ leaders' efforts to instill Nazi principles in us. When we finished discussing what to do, we decided to vote on several options. Herr Schmidt was horrified by our voting and told us in no uncertain terms that voting was the wrong approach for members of National Socialist society. Since I was his favorite, he chose me to be the class leader and decide for the class. As much as I sometimes now looked down on my classmates, I felt a basic loyalty to them when it came to our teachers. After he left the classroom, I asked the others what they wanted to do, and after some back and forth, we opted for a free-for-all, everyone contributing what they felt like contributing. I did not think us rebellious in doing what we did. We simply did not want to leave anyone out.

I settled on doing a one-person skit of Till Eulenspiegel's pranks. By assuming the role of the prankster and boaster, I intended to poke fun at my reputation as a teller of tall tales, a reputation I had maintained since the second or third grade, when I made up homework essays even as I "read" them in class. I designed and sewed my own costume and was particularly proud of my tri-colored foolscap. The words were my own, freely adapted from one of Till's pranks in the collection of Till Eulenspiegel stories I owned. It was the story of Till's tricking the citizens of the proud and wealthy city of Magdeburg by the boast that he could fly and would prove it by flying from the steeple of City Hall. All I needed as props were a chair and the top of a desk. The assembled class, as well as our teachers, Fräulein Pelzer, Fräulein Schäfer, and Herr Schmidt, the principal, automatically constituted the citizenry of Magdeburg.

When my turn came, I marched in, reciting Till's arrival in the city, his ill treatment at the hands of some magistrates, and his boast in the marketplace that he could fly. I then slowly ascended the teacher's desk, acting out the motions of climbing a steeple and arriving at its peak. Once there, I stopped, looked around, and then waved my arms in the air. My classmates began to laugh, as I had expected they would.

"Fools!" I addressed the assembly. "Of course I cannot fly. You think me a dunce, but it is you who are the dunces for coming here and expecting me to fly."

As I strutted around on the desktop, I was suffused by a wonderful sense of self-assurance and pride. But as I jumped off my perch and noticed the disapproving expressions of my teachers, misgivings and embarrassment overcame me, and I rushed out to take off my costume. At the time, I was not aware of the rebellious meanings attached to the folk figure of Till Eulenspiegel, that of the trickster who defies authority, the rich and powerful, by ridiculing them in a way that makes it impossible for them to fault him without losing face. As Herr Schmidt handed me my diploma an hour later and my teachers shook my hand, I half understood my offense when I saw their stern expressions and felt waves of hostility coming at me. But at that point, I no longer cared. I only wanted to leave grammar school and never come back.

Looking back from the perspective of 2008, I realize that frustration with leading my uncooperative squad, my disappointment about not being promoted, my hands' refusal to cooperate in official toy making, and my mind's unconscious choice of a story of rebellion were leading me away from conformity to Nazi causes. But my admission to the teacher seminary, the only chance I believed I had for the higher education I craved, placed me right at the heart of the Nazi educational establishment, right in the belly of the beast.

Chapter Seven

IN THE BELLY OF THE BEAST
The Teacher Seminary, 1944–1945

RIGHT FROM THE BEGINNING, IN 1933, Hitler's goal was the Nazification of German schools. Since very few private schools existed and the teaching staffs largely preferred the political Right, this goal was not hard to achieve. The private Waldorf schools were an exception, but since their graduates were excluded from higher education beyond high school, they scarcely competed with the public schools. All professional organizations of teachers in the process of *Gleichschaltung* automatically became Nazi organizations. Additionally, all teachers were encouraged to join the Nazi Party. Those who objected— as some communist, socialist, and Catholic educators did—either retired or were fired. By the mid-1930s new textbooks had been issued for all levels, all of them—including those in the sciences and even mathematics—infused by Nazi ideology.

In their lingering distrust of the higher education establishment, which they suspected of still harboring the democratic ideals of the Weimar Republic, the Nazis created their own system of academies to educate their future leadership elite: the Adolf Hitler Schools, founded by Baldur von Schirach, the national leader of the HJ, and the NAPOLAS, the National Political Educational Institutions, run by the SS. The former, eleven boarding schools in all, followed party guidelines and trained the party elite in Nazi ideology; the latter, thirty-nine elite boarding schools by the early 1940s, resembled the older Prussian military academies and were to educate the future leadership of the SS and the government. Nazi misogyny for the most part excluded girls from Nazi higher education. Only three NAPOLAS educated girls. Adolf Hitler Schools and NAPOLAS accepted only pupils of pure Aryan stock, from ten to twelve years of age, who could demonstrate intellectual and athletic superiority and pass an entrance examination. Adolf Hitler Schools recruited their students primarily from the lower and lower middle classes; NAPOLAS from the middle and upper classes. The academic standards of the Adolf Hitler Schools were said to be lower than those of the traditional German public high schools, the gymnasia, while those of the NAPOLAS were equivalent to them and also included the engineering, science, and ballistics training given by the former military academies. In both systems, Nazi ideology dominated all subject matter.

The teacher seminaries for future grammar school teachers of the Weimar Republic and early Nazi period had trained gymnasia graduates in a two- to three-year course in educational theory and practice. Because graduates of the high schools from 1935 on had to enter the Labor Service and males also had to perform military service, a shortage of applicants to the seminaries as well as of graduate teachers developed that was soon exacerbated by younger and prospective teachers being called up to fight in the war. The early victories over Poland and Russia encouraged the Nazi leadership to look for an additional source of future teachers to teach the German colonists they planned to send east. Relatively late in the regime, in 1942, the government therefore instituted a new kind of teacher-training seminary based on an older Austrian model. The teacher seminary into which I had been accepted was one of these new institutions that took its applicants from grammar school graduates and middle schools. Its academic program—minus Latin or Greek—included thorough National Socialist ideological training in addition to a traditional high school curriculum for the first four years. During the final year students were to study pedagogy and begin supervised practice teaching. Students were expected to continue their HJ membership and wear the BDM (League of German Girls) uniform at all times while in their institutions. They were to pursue rigorous athletic training and participate in the usual wartime activities under HJ auspices. Criteria for admission were proof of being of German, Aryan stock—an uncle of mine had prepared a genealogy back to the great-grandparental generation—certification of excellent health, superior academic standing and athletic ability, graduation from grammar or middle school, an entrance examination, and recommendations by teachers and party members.

I was exactly fourteen and a half when, shortly after Easter 1944, I started teacher training at Obernigk Seminary. Obernigk, in Lower Silesia, a small town and a health spa of some eight thousand inhabitants, was situated about twelve miles to the north of Breslau, on the east side of the Oder River, and about twenty miles away from the Polish border to the east. With one train change in Breslau, I arrived at Obernigk station in about two hours. The train trip had taken me through open fields and a meadow landscape with groves of firs here and there. An avenue lined with rubinia trees in bloom led past suburban villas from the station to the former spa hotel, now the seminary. Apart from a few visits to a local physician, I never got to know the town, as a rigid schedule restricted us to the campus except when we marched in troop formation to the off-campus school building. Each class of about thirty students made up one BDM troop. The campus consisted of two large buildings of an older, somewhat run-down hotel and spa, built, to judge by its utilitarian architecture, immediately after World War I. Until the month before our arrival, the buildings had housed a rehabilitation center for wounded soldiers. We were the first residents of this new and spartan establishment. For the time being, we were only some sixty girls in their first year of teacher training.

I was lucky in arriving early, because I could claim the bed and locker next to the window of a long, narrow, bare-walled twelve-bed dormitory. After settling into my space and putting away my clothes and underwear in a metal locker next to my bed, I asked the girl who had come in with me, Adelheid, to go with me to explore the park that surrounded the spa hotel. After Adelheid had unpacked a few items, we left together as other girls began moving in.

The park was much older than the hotel buildings; huge horse chestnut trees towered over our building, their spiked blooms piercing the tree's fanned-out leaves. A walk hemmed in by winter lindens just leafing out and by rubinias scattering their blooms at our feet led us through a gate into a neglected, overgrown garden with a pavilion in which, during the heyday of the spa, musicians must have performed for the guests.

Walking next to me, Adelheid was almost a head taller than I and, as she told me, two years older. She had graduated from a middle school in Breslau and would be in the class above mine. Her almost ink-black hair hung in long curls down both sides of her face and, like my older brother's, her eyes were a deep dark blue. I envied her looks. She seemed very grown up to me and spoke somewhat condescendingly in a big city accent. She immediately made me aware of my own Silesian accent, my difficulties in pronouncing the *ü* and *ö* sounds of umlauted words like *über* (above) and *schön* (beautiful), which turned into plebian *īber* and *schēn* when I said them. In replying to her, I tried to answer her questions in as clear a High German as I could muster. But I reverted to my natural speech once I noticed that I sounded as affected as Aunt Helene at Zülzendorf.

Adelheid awed me, particularly her name, which suggested nobility, even though I thought her manner conceited and affected. Like me, she was a reader, and soon, standing in the pavilion, she declaimed a poem to me in a style I had never heard before: rhythmically, solemnly, like saying a prayer in church. I liked reciting ballads to myself or in class, if called on, but I would have been embarrassed to declaim it in such an elevated style to another person. Adelheid brought a kind of hothouse atmosphere to the threadbare existence I knew from home, and I was soon entranced by it. Even during this first walk we took, she talked of several boyfriends and of crushes she had had on teachers in her school, a notion more extravagant to me than the alpine romances of Ganghofer's that I had read the year before. A crush on a teacher! I imagined Herr Schmidt and Fräulein Pelzer and flinched.

That evening after supper (we always had soup and bread, with pudding for dessert), the principal, Frau Braun, introduced our housemothers and our teachers, outlined our schedule, and gave us some directions on how we were to behave in school as well as on leaving the premises. They were, I realized, simple rules of polite and inoffensive behavior such as pointers concerning table manners, silence during study hours, neither shouting nor horsing around nor even singing when out in public. They impressed me because the rules of our hometown HJ imposed no such restrictions. There, when we marched with the HJ, we always bellowed out our songs as loudly as we could.

Next she introduced the two housemothers, each of whom would supervise the some thirty girls housed in each of the buildings. Ours was an elderly, gray-haired, gaunt matron dressed in a striped shift that resembled a Red Cross uniform. As she nodded to us, Frau Braun explained, "Your housemother is in charge of house discipline; she will wake you at 6:30 and turn off the dormitory lights at 10:30. For the rest, she will supervise you in doing your chores."

Except for a cook and her helper, there was no staff, and our fare was sparse: bread, a saccharine marmalade, and barley coffee for breakfast, and *Eintopf,* a stew, for the noon meal. Students, in pairs, cleaned the floors of the dormitories and classrooms, set the tables, washed up after meals, and hosed down the washrooms and showers. Every morning, after a single-file run through the grounds and a hasty scrub down in the washroom, our housemother inspected our beds and our closets, having taught us to make a bed and keep a closet military style. She tore apart any bed whose sheets showed a single crease and whose blankets were not properly folded. She emptied onto the floor the entire contents of any closet in which even a single handkerchief was out of its proper place. Most humiliating were her inspections of personal cleanliness, such as properly clean, short-cut fingernails and a lint-free belly button. At night she watched us take our cold showers before herding us to bed. I submitted to her discipline without question. It was the price I paid for being at the seminary. Besides, Jochen, who had been on home leave after finishing his *Landdienst* year with his HJ troop, had given me some valuable advice on how to get along in an HJ camp setting. "Fit in. Don't stand out either negatively or positively. Don't call attention to yourself!" I understood the obsession with discipline and military precision that ruled Frau Braun and her housemothers only later. By submitting to them we were to be habituated to a Nazi way of thinking and being.

Of the teachers I remember only three: Frau Braun herself, Fräulein Müller, our history and geography teacher, and Frau Scherzer, our German and English teacher. We must have had a mathematics instructor and a science teacher, and a gym teacher, as athletics played a supremely important role in any Nazi educational institution. But I don't recall either a person or any instruction in these subjects. Frau Braun, Austrian by birth, still spoke with a tinge of Viennese accent. Far from melodious, however, on her lips the Austrian soft cadences were sharp, penetrating, harsh, a female version of Hitler's rasping speech. She introduced herself as an early party member, a proud compatriot of Hitler's. I wondered, "What does it feel like to be Austrian, like the Führer?" Of course, Silesians had been Austrian under Maria Theresa, empress of Austria, but that was two hundred years ago. Besides, Father's family came from north of Berlin, so I was part Prussian.

I don't remember Frau Braun having many functions other than presiding at meals, where she watched our table manners and made announcements about schedules and news. She also led the morning flag-raising ceremony, which she conducted almost in the manner of a religious service. She used these services as a kind of Nazi moral and ideological training and gave us homilies on our future role as Nazi teachers in the eastern settlements of the annexed territories in Poland. We were to inspire the ethnic German settlers by our courage, comradeship, and such Germanic virtues as silent strength, toughness, and loyalty. Years later, when I read of BDM girls just a little older ·than we were then serving in these eastern settlements, participating in driving out the native Polish population and introducing the ethnic German settlers to Germanic values, I shuddered to think what my future might have held. But then, because I was familiar from my leadership training with most of her admonitions on how to be a model leader, her speeches bored me. Since we had no access to radios or newspapers, we knew nothing about the world outside except what she belched out to us—hymns to the Führer, his secret weapons, and final victory. In the course of the summer and fall of 1944, we knew nothing about the landing of the Allies in Normandy and their progress through France. Nor did we hear about the uprising and the final annihilation of the Warsaw ghetto, or about the Russian army closing in on the German border of Poland in the east. Truth to tell, by the time I arrived at Obernigk, politics and the war had lost all interest for me, and I barely listened to whatever she did tell us. But, like my classmates, I firmly believed in German secret weapons and our ultimate victory.

I remember fondly Fräulein Müller, our history teacher. She started us out on classical Greek and Roman history and taught us the geography and natural resources of our home province, Silesia, so well that I impressed my later high school geography teacher with the thoroughness of my knowledge. She had been given the task of reorganizing the school library, which consisted of the books left by the spa hotel, the rehabilitation center, and a discontinued local high school, whose building we used for classrooms. Skimping on the afternoon homework, I volunteered to help her and read out titles and authors to her, which she entered on a card. Even as I read out a title, she interrupted me with a dark voice, "Slower, please." I liked the warmth emanating from her voice and the calm of her "Please repeat," when I read too fast. I spent all my free time helping her, hoping, of course, that in addition to getting acquainted with the collection, my assistance would secure me a permanent claim to the library. It did, and I soon received the key to it, together with the job of assistant lending librarian.

Unfortunately, so I thought, Fräulein Müller declined the supervision of the library after finishing the cataloguing. Frau Scherzer, our German and English teacher, took over the task. Frau Scherzer wore her bleached blond hair short in a smartly cut pageboy style. Unlike the natural, healthy, plain-looking German woman the HJ proclaimed as its ideal, Frau Scherzer wore lipstick, and heavy eye makeup accentuated the soft blue irises under her heavily lidded slit eyes. Long-limbed, perfumed, and elegantly dressed, she was also, Adelheid and I discovered, the only university-trained member of the teaching staff. We put her into the role of an Englishwoman, an exotic upper-class lady, about whom we read in one of George Warwick Deeping's novels, a book from the former spa library. The only contradictions in her sophisticated appearance were broad cheekbones and a slightly upturned nose that suggested the urchin hidden in the woman. Frau Scherzer soon noticed that I knew the location of most of the books I lent out to the students, and that I had read many of them.

When we catalogued the books, Fräulein Müller had set aside a number of volumes as unsuitable reading for us. I asked her why.

"They are by authors you should read only when you are more mature and have better judgment," she replied. Of course her words only piqued my curiosity. As assistant to the librarian, however, I knew the location of the "special collection" and of its key. Alone in the library during homework hours, I started reading these books. That was how I first read Heinrich Heine's *Travels in the Harz Mountains,* which I found boring at the time except for the jokes about the city of Göttingen. I knew from a reproof I once got from Fräulein Pelzer that Heine was Jewish, but I could not understand why I needed maturity to read him. At home, when we sang folk songs to Mother's piano accompaniment, we loved his Lorelei ballad just as much as the folk songs we all sang in Jungmädel.

One day Frau Scherzer surprised me as I was reading another novel from the "special collection," Wiechert's *The Baroness.*

"Do you like it?" she asked, rather than scolding me as I had expected.

"Very much," I answered. "I like the way Wiechert sounds and what he says, his ideas. I am copying some of his sentences into my diary. They sound like poetry. I don't understand, though, why I should not read his novel. The hero is disillusioned with modern life. What is wrong with that?"

After a pause I added, "Actually, he raves about how corrupt modern city life is. I don't know anything about cities. But I would like to live in Berlin, for instance, and go to concerts, and the opera, and maybe the theater. Why not?" I had done none of these things, of course, but I had imagined doing them and knew that this was exactly what I wanted to do when I was an adult.

She looked at me and then said, almost to herself, "That must be confusing. But don't worry. I like Wiechert. He was in a concentration camp for a while, in Buchenwald. He got into difficulties with the party, and that is why you should not read him until you are older."

"In a concentration camp?" and then I stopped and remembered Manfred's father. The previous year the police had taken him away, and he returned from a camp after a month. Mother had explained that Manfred's father went around saying that, after Stalingrad, defeat was inevitable. Someone had reported him to the Gestapo. That is why he had been sent away, and the adults said that he came back beaten up, but would not talk about it.

I felt that Frau Scherzer liked my questions and me. I mistrusted her for her elegance and her difference from the teachers I was used to. I disliked her for her patronizing tone — "until you are older" — and found her turned-up nose ridiculous. But she never disturbed me again when I read books from the special collection. And a few days later she assigned me the coveted job of class speaker and leader of my BDM troop.

In literature class Frau Scherzer started us out on Voss's translation of Homer's *Iliad*. I loved reading the sonorous hexameters aloud to myself and soon had memorized the beginning of the first book. It was not so much the story of the Trojan War that fascinated me as the relationship of its characters, including the poet himself, to their gods — a personal relationship, as if the gods were fellow humans, some friends, others adversaries. Frau Scherzer explained that a Greek poet thought of the muse of music and poetry as his companion, as a friend who accompanied him and helped him out with words and ideas. Such an unseen companion made a lot of sense to me. I did not like Agamemnon, who sacrificed his daughter, or the boisterous and bullying Achilles. I feared for Hector as he prepared for battle. But one day, as Frau Scherzer spoke of Achilles' and Patroclus's friendship, and Achilles' rage and fury about Hector's killing Patroclus, and his grief afterward, tears welled up in my eyes. With Frau Scherzer teaching us, the stories we read came alive. I later realized that she had opened up a new way of reading for me, reading beyond the storyline into the emotional meaning of actions, into the emotional world of characters that the poet meant us to identify with.

This way of reading literature readied me to explore the world of German literature and poetry. When Frau Scherzer found out that I had memorized the lines of Achilles' wrath and grief, she pointed to a large anthology of poetry in the library.

"Why don't you read some Hölderlin and, of course, Rilke!"

From grade school I already knew and loved ballads like Fontane's "Archibald Douglas." Simple, brief romantic lyric poems like Eichendorff's and Storm's had for several years charmed and comforted me with their melodious melancholy. Satisfied by sound, I paid little attention to their meaning. But as my teacher read Hölderlin's poem "Youth" to us, I understood the poem's emotion with a strength of feeling new to me.

> Da ich ein Knabe war,
> > Rettet' ein Gott mich oft
> > > Vom Geschrei und der Ruthe der Menschen,
> > > > Da spielt' ich sicher und gut
> > > > > Mit den Blumen des Hains,
> > > > > > Und die Lüftchen des Himmels
> > > > > > > Spielten mit mir.

> When I was a boy
> > A god saved me
> > > From the shouting and caning of men.
> > > > I played, safe and well,
> > > > > With the flowers of the grove,
> > > > > > And the breezes of the sky
> > > > > > > Played with me.

The sonorous words called forth in my mind meanings and feelings I had not understood or felt before. In my enthusiasm for this newly revealed confluence of meaning, emotion, and melody, I began to understand Adelheid and her love for declaiming poetry, even though her recitations still embarrassed me.

Adelheid and I had a crush on Frau Scherzer. We observed her every move and speculated about what kind of person she was. I noticed that Adelheid imitated her in speech and gesture but failed to see that I did the same. I competed with the other girls in class for Frau Scherzer's attention and worried that they would call me teacher's pet. Inge, a pale, thin, oily-haired girl whom no one wanted on their dodge ball team and who tattled to teachers, finally did. "Hey, Ursel, you are playing up to her."

I felt like lashing out at her as I had at Jochen when he teased me. But I turned away, ashamed to acknowledge that I did want Frau Scherzer's attention, and wanted it badly. A few years later I understood why Frau Scherzer had been so meaningful to me. She was the first adult I met who offered herself as a model to emulate. She did not dismiss my enthusiasms as my other teachers had. She listened to me, and she talked to me as if I were her equal. She radiated warmth and she spoke with an emotional intensity that turned every encounter I had with her into an emotional adventure. Until that time I had not known that such relationships could exist between people. I knew she was the kind of woman I wanted to become, though I did not know how. Adelheid and I found out that, unlike the other teachers, Frau Scherzer was married. She had an apartment in Breslau in the "exclusive" West End. Her husband served as a journalist with a press unit at the front. Unlike the other teachers at the school, she was not a party member. She had volunteered to teach at the school because she thought that at a party-approved boarding school in the country she would be safe from air raids and food shortages. She kept her apartment in Breslau and often stayed away overnight from her room in our dormitory. In our eyes, that fact alone lent her an air of mystery.

She used her German literature class to teach us Homer and Greek mythology as preconditions for understanding German literature. By the teaching of Greco-Roman ideals of friendship, loyalty to family, and compassion for fellow humans, she introduced us to the ideals of classical humanism and a love of beauty and poetry that differed markedly from the ideology of nationalism, racial superiority, individual toughness, duty, and loyalty to the leader that we were supposed to absorb. Only years later did I come to appreciate that she was deliberately undermining the Nazi ideology she was supposed to be teaching us. At the time, I wondered why she gave short shrift to the excerpts from the Norse sagas in our textbook, with their heroes outlawed by Fehme courts, blood bans, and strife, and enlarged on the Homer section instead, supplementing it with readings from Gustav Schwab's *The Most Beautiful Tales of Classical Antiquity*, with which I was already familiar. She drew our attention to the moving scene in which grief-stricken King Priam pleads with the enraged Achilles for his slain son's body, and to the graciousness and compassion with which Achilles accedes to the old man's plea. I remember this particular lesson so well because it stood in such stark contrast to everything I had been taught before. It strikes me now as ironic that at a school where her task was our indoctrination in Nazi ideology, Frau Scherzer's instruction opened up for me a world beyond the national and introduced me to the common European and Western heritage of humanism. I owe to her my love of literature, and to her teaching the illumination of the mind that the study of literature and poetry can bring about.

In about early July, my headaches began, violent headaches that never stopped. They kept me awake at night; they almost blinded me during the day. After four to five days of this, I reported to the infirmary. It was not migraine, the doctor decided, and it was not meningitis. After a week, I went back to class. I participated in the hikes we took, though almost incapacitated by pain. I could not concentrate on anything except the twinges radiating out from the back of my head to my forehead, a ring of flickering stabs of pain, a pressure in my head that never stopped.

After another week, Fräulein Müller took me to the neurological polyclinic of the University of Breslau, a forbidding red brick building, the mere sight of which terrified me. But I followed Fräulein Müller into a waiting room filled with strange-looking people—a teenager with a dirty, turban-like bandage around his head, a baldheaded woman with a permanent grimace on her face, a distraught old man who muttered to himself. A string of interns, medical students, and professors looked me over, poked me, and tested my reflexes while my head throbbed away. A technician took X-rays of my head, my neck, and again my head from side and front. A day later, I was told that I was to return to the clinic to be operated on. The doctors had located a tumor in my cerebellum. I did not want to leave school. I was afraid I was never going to be able to return, never study with Frau Scherzer again. That thought terrified me much more than the surgery itself.

After packing my suitcase late in the afternoon, I stood in the hallway of the dormitory staring out at the park, desolate and afraid, my head throbbing, thinking I might go down for a walk while the other girls were in study hall. A hand touched my shoulder, and I turned to see Frau Scherzer standing behind me. I turned away again because I did not want her to see my tears or how devastated I felt and how alone.

"I'll go to the hospital with you tomorrow," she said. "You remember the story of Achilles' and Patroclus's friendship, don't you?" I nodded.

"Friends support and give each other comfort," she continued. "I will help you get through this! Let's go for a walk now, and you tell me what worries you."

A load fell from my shoulders, and as we walked, first through the tree-lined streets of the town and then the open fields, I don't know for how long, I poured out my fears: how afraid I was that I would not be allowed back into school, that I might lose my capacity to think, to learn, that I would become like the morose, baldheaded people I had seen in the clinic waiting room. I told her that I wanted to become a teacher like her, a person who could—I did not know really what, but someone who was not like my aunts, my mother, my other teachers, or any of the other women I knew.

The next morning, accompanied by Frau Scherzer, I met with my mother and Professor Hardenberg, who was to operate on me the following day. After a few minutes they sent me out of the consulting room to the reception area to be assigned a bed in the ward. I was furious to be excluded from their conversation with the professor, not to be told what the operation entailed. Mother told me a few months later that the professor had informed her that I might not survive the operation, or that I might lose my sight, or be paralyzed.

As I talked with my neighbor in the ward, a young woman who had developed a disturbing tic on the right side of her face, Mother and Frau Scherzer came in to say goodbye. Frau Scherzer, looking concerned, took my hand in both of hers and said, "I'll do everything I can to get you back to school." As I walked Mother off the ward and down through penetrating cabbage and Lysol smells to the iron front gate of the institution, she remarked, "Child, you always worry me. Every summer for the last few years you have been very ill, with scarlet fever, with boils and furunculosis, and now with a brain tumor." True enough, there was not much I could say to that.

That evening, I left the ward to take a walk in the clinic garden. Large chestnut trees seemed to stand guard silently. I remembered Frau Scherzer's talking about tree nymphs like Daphne, about the Greeks imagining that divine personages were alive in trees. I had thought that not just mythical female creatures should be represented as trees but ancient, mighty creatures like the ones I sensed in these trees. Years later, when I read of Celtic tree myths and their giant ancient tree men, I recalled that evening in the hospital garden. During the night, unable to sleep, I talked to my neighbor on the other side of me, who also was awake and who had had a tumor removed from her head. She whispered to me, "You'll be shaved in the morning. They keep you awake during the operation; but they give you injections into the skin of the skull so that cutting won't hurt. Drilling through the bone is painless because bone and brain are insensitive to pain. The sound of the drill is bad, though." I would have to talk to the surgeon all through the operation, she went on, so that he could monitor me and not harm vital functions.

"You'll be all right," she assured me, as my head throbbed. "At least the pain in your head will be gone," she added. "Mine is."

I was not going to show how afraid I was as I walked into the operating room. You walked in; they wheeled you out. My head was shaved; I was dressed in a white hospital gown. Before lying down on the table, I asked the nurse to show me the instruments the doctor was going to use; she wisely refused. As my neighbor had said, the injection into my scalp did not hurt much, but as the drill started hammering on the back of my skull, I felt as if a huge knocking noise was shaking me, shaking and shaking.

A man's voice ordered me to count, "One, two, three. Start and continue counting."

"One, two, three," I began, and had counted to I don't know to what number when another voice said, "She is bleeding a lot. Stop. Get me a sponge."

After that I felt as if my head were gradually being blown up like a balloon, and I lost consciousness. I came to under the X-ray machine and then went out again. I woke up in intensive care, my head bandaged, the ring of pain still in place. As I opened my eyes, I saw only gray, no forms, no room, no light, only a gray dense fog. I fell asleep again, I don't know for how long. When I woke up, a radio was playing marching music that was intolerably loud. I rubbed my eyes and then it came back to me — everything had been gray before, and it was gray still.

"Nurse, I can't see!" I shouted. "I am blind!"

My heart raced and I breathed rapidly, trying to control my rising panic. "I am blind!"

The panic receded as I felt the needle prick of an injection and a wave of warmth and comfort swept me away. In the distance I heard voices, my mother's and Frau Scherzer's. I did not really care. The radio came on again with martial music, a clear date, July 20, 1944, an excited announcer. "There has been an assassination attempt against our beloved Führer. He was not hurt. A miracle of fate. The traitors will be found. Executed." The national anthem played as I swam in a sea of indifference.

When I woke up next, I could see shadowy forms through the gray veil over my eyes. I could discern the light of the window.

"I can see, nurse!" I cried. A figure in a white nurse's cap leaned over me and I could make out kind eyes.

"I am glad," she said as she looked down on me. I fell back to sleep. The radio was still playing when I woke up again. The announcer's stern voice told of a conspiracy of officers who had tried to kill the Führer. They had been caught, the main leaders had been executed, and others would be tried. They were only a small group; their families would be placed under arrest. Which family members? I asked myself. I suddenly felt frightened for their children. What would arrest mean? Would the children be taken away to prison, too? Or taken somewhere else? Where?

"The war effort of all loyal Germans will continue to final victory," the voice in the radio concluded. Repetitive announcements about the assassination plot came to me through a veil that kept everything at a distance, just as it did the light from the window. My headache remained the only reality.

My head still throbbing, I was dismissed from the hospital after a week and sent to a private clinic in Breslau's West End. One of Mother's relatives arranged for my stay there. I was told that the surgeon had not found a tumor. Professor Hardenberg explained that the lack of toe reflexes, protruding visual nerves, and shadows on the cerebellum in my X-rays were probably caused by an inflammation of my visual nerves. A few weeks of treatment with mercury ointments, he believed, would heal the inflammation and cure my headaches.

The clinic, with its garden setting, made for a stark contrast to the sinister, Lysol-smelling polyclinic. Instead of a bed in a ward, I had a comfortable room and bath to myself. My room was bathed in soothing, rich green light from linden trees outside my windows. Every morning and evening a nurse gently rubbed a silvery-black ointment all over my body, both massages preceded by long soaks in the bathtub. Gradually my headaches ceased, and the ring of pain around my head dissolved.

I still believe it was the luxury and kindness of the private clinic environment rather than the mercury ointment that brought about the cure. I was not supposed to read in order to spare my eyes. Frau Scherzer brought me the book of poems I had used at school, and I started learning by heart the poems I liked best. Memorization required little use of my eyes and helped me feel comforted. Hölderlin's womanly ideal Diotima and Rilke's images of Roman fountains and exotic wild animals engaged my imagination, and their rhythms and melodious, sensuous language soothed me, so that after several weeks I was ready to be released. I wanted to return to school, but a grim-faced doctor at the polyclinic, to whom I had to report again, insisted that I should recover further at home. Besides, my fellow students had been sent off to work in a munitions plant and the doctor did not think I was ready for physical labor. I was told that I would need his permission to get back into school.

Back at home by mid-August, I was at a loss as to what to do. The following six weeks were probably the most anxious and uncomfortable of my entire adolescence. I feared that by my headaches—had they been psychosomatic?—I had cast myself out of school. Excellent health, after all, had been a prerequisite for admission. Superficially, life continued on its normal course. Yet I dreaded something, had the vague apprehension that something, I did not know what, was profoundly wrong. At home, without the distractions of the rigid discipline and constant activity of our program at the seminary, I no longer had the comforting protection of mindless obedience or the occupation with classes and lessons. My enforced leisure, I believe, allowed me to feel what the adults around me feared without admitting it: the approaching collapse of the regime, which would confront them with the consequences of their complicity.

My usual escape through poetry and reading failed me. I could not concentrate on reading, and the language of the poems I loved seemed empty and dead. I seemed to see everything and everyone as if through a wall of glass. My former friends were unavailable. Hanne and Erika were serving their *Haushaltsjahr*, that is, working all day as mothers' helpers. They all seemed light years away from me, busy as they were with their own working lives. Only Elli, the teacher's daughter from upstairs, still in middle school, offered some company in exchange for my key to the apartment house. At night, before curfew, we strolled around City Hall Square together, but that bored me even more than it had before, because now I knew only a few of the passersby.

Mother, too, had changed, as had her seamstresses. Trudi, whose gay laughter and vivaciousness I had enjoyed, had left to serve as a Red Cross nurse at the Stone School, which had been converted into a military hospital. Mother went out a lot, sometimes dating an uncle of mine stationed in town and sometimes the owner of the mill on Mill Street. When I did see them, Trudi acted subdued and Mother distracted. They talked hectically, in loud voices, about news of the war and other matters I could hardly fathom. The adults drank more alcohol; even Mother once came home tipsy from lunch, as Ida told me with a malicious grin. Only Ida, the hunchback, took care of the sewing business as usual, while supervising two new apprentices.

Frau Dunisch lent me books from her library, but I had difficulty reading them. Once I visited Adelheid at the munitions plant in Breslau where my schoolmates were working. Frau Scherzer sent me books that I hardly touched and gave me an insincere-sounding pep talk when I met her while visiting Adelheid. News blackouts at home were not as thorough as they had been at the seminary. Both the eastern and, especially, the western front crept slowly toward Germany's borders, as I heard on the radio as I sat with Ida and the apprentices in the living room. But, Goebbels assured us in one speech after another, v-1s were demolishing London and southern England, and more powerful secret weapons would soon be ready for deployment. I can still hear the staccato cadence of his voice: "Then, five minutes to twelve, final victory will be ours." In all of his speeches until May 1945, when he committed suicide, the clock stayed at five minutes to twelve. Sometime that fall, the Allies on the western front arrived on German soil. But either we did not hear about it or I did not take it in, being totally preoccupied with anxious ruminations about how to get back to school.

On a few weekends Mother had parties, inviting my uncle's fellow officers and Trudi and her friends. Werner and I helped Mother free up space for dancing in the living room. They played cards, sometimes danced; they always drank heavily. They laughed wildly. I was invited, now that I had been confirmed and was an "adult," but I liked neither the card games nor the home-brewed liquor that Herr Breiler, Mother's friend, supplied in great quantities. I was perplexed and sometimes frightened by the abandon with which everybody emptied jiggers of schnapps, and by the crude jokes the officers told. I particularly remember one grossly sentimental story from the front with which a cousin of Mother's, an elderly reservist lieutenant recalled to duty, entertained us—a story starkly at odds with the jokes preceding it.

"We had just ended a hard day at the front and were sitting around in the market square of town [a Polish town whose name escapes me]," he began. "There were several hundred of us. Suddenly one of the men started singing 'Am Brunnen vor dem Tore' [At the well before the town gate, by Schubert], and all of us joined in. We sang all of its stanzas, every one of us. As one voice, our song rang through the town. We Germans and our culture against the Bolshevik hordes!" I did not wonder about the mixture of sentimentality and jingoism then, but I find it revolting now and shudder to think what reality he was hiding behind the sentimentality. A mass shooting of Jews? A massacre of women and children?

In the smoke-filled living room they belched out popular songs like Lale Andersen's "Vor der Laterne" (Under the lantern I'll wait for you). I did not know what to make of their saying, when they were intoxicated, "Kinder, genießt den Krieg, der Frieden wird schrecklich" (Children, enjoy this war, peace will be terrible). I guessed it was nothing good. They seemed disgusting and crazy to me, all of them. To calm myself, I often stayed out late, walking through the cemetery along Promenade Street. I did not need to fear the HJ Streifendienst, the patrol service, there, whose combing through the pubs and town square ruled out the adolescent nighttime amblings through town of years past.

The cemetery's dense panoply of huge old chestnut trees, their dead leaves rustling beneath my feet as I sloshed through them, provided peace and comfort. The trees felt like powerful protectors from my obsessive worry about being allowed back into the seminary. As children we had run about in the cemetery during daylight and played hide-and-seek among the gravestones, and were often chased away by the cemetery attendant. Fear of ghosts sent us home at nightfall. Now ghosts struck me as irrelevant. I loved the safety of darkness and its sadness. Every evening I visited the grave of a student who, Mother told us, had committed suicide some years before. I wondered about his history. What kind of person had he been? His parents had had an inscription chiseled on his gravestone, a simple block of rough granite. It was a quotation from Goethe's *Faust:* "All that is transitory is only a parable." I had no idea what this meant, only that it was from the masterwork of our greatest poet. But I savored the words. *Alles Vergängliche ist nur ein Gleichnis.* I knew the individual words but could not imagine how they hung together. Did they say something about the meaning—of what? Life? The student's life? His death? The kind of person he had been? I identified with him. I liked to imagine him as a poet who could not tolerate this town and its people, who just wanted to get out, as I did, and did not know how to do it any other way. Although I did not understand them, the sound of Goethe's words pacified me as I spoke them to myself as I walked.

During daylight hours I took a great many solitary hikes into the woods beyond Windmill Hill, where the leaves of the oak trees were turning a dull yellow, while those of the birches flickered bright yellow against the black trunks of the fir trees. A few times, to exhaust myself and to quell my anxiety about school, I jogged all the way up to the top of the Rummelsberg. On one of my shorter walks along Mill Creek one Saturday afternoon, my unease found something to settle on when I witnessed several ss men taking some teenage boys, boys I knew by sight, into the town's ss headquarters. One of several women standing around commented, "The boys have been caught committing acts of sabotage. They will be incarcerated for the weekend."

Another of the bystanders whispered, "Many boys in the cities like Hamburg belong to a gang of hoodlums. They call themselves *Edelweisspiraten"* — Edelweiss pirates. Another woman, addressing no one in particular, asked, "Do you think these Strehlen boys are *Edelweisspiraten?"* "No," a soldier on leave chimed in. "They probably stole something or violated the curfew." I agreed with him, because I could not imagine that boys I knew might have done more than violate the curfew. Yet an atmosphere of uncanny threat from traitors in our midst clings to my memory of the ss villa across from Mill Creek.

I recalled that episode when I remembered that all through my early teens I had been ashamed of Jochen's intermittent refusal to attend HJ, from the time he was eleven until he left home at fourteen. I was afraid that the police would pick him up; he would have to attend the HJ squad for delinquents or, worse, go to jail and dishonor the family. This fear was not entirely groundless, as I found out much later, for Strehlen youths were tyrannized by a fanatical juvenile judge. I recalled the same episode again, in the 1970s, when I taught my students about the German resistance and thought that this was the first time I had heard about a working-class resistance group like the *Edelweisspiraten.* It was only when I researched the history of the HJ in the 1990s that I understood that, by 1944, the Gestapo and police were paranoid about losing control of German youth. They placed a small contingent of young people in camps for their spontaneous resistance, Hamburg apprentices of the *Edelweisspiraten* and several urban jazz groups that they designated as delinquents. And they took in for weekend arrests a larger number of HJ boys who came into conflict with the ever more numerous and stringent HJ regulations that the Gestapo imposed. In late 1944 I heard rumors of resistance groups in the large cities, and I thought of them as traitors who should be punished. It is difficult now, if not impossible, to decide exactly what I knew, and when. But by the fall of 1944 I sensed that our world was coming apart, and I was frightened. I was still an ardent young member of the HJ, but I was afraid that I had somehow put myself outside its bounds. I wanted nothing else but to go back into my BDM troop and the seminary.

At the beginning of October I had an appointment with the grim-faced doctor at the neuropsychiatric polyclinic whose permission I needed to get back to school or to join my fellow students at the munitions factory. I was determined to wrest the permit from him. There was nothing wrong with me; my headaches had ceased and my eyesight had been restored to normal with the glasses I had received before leaving the private clinic. Left to myself, I was going crazy with nothing to do.

"Even if I have no toe reflexes, I can work. There is nothing wrong with my mind," I insisted, as the neurologist looked at me doubtfully.

I persisted, "My classmates are working here at Breslau munitions works— just let me join them. I'll work hard. I won't be any trouble to anyone."

"Well, good," he finally relented. "Go to work." And he handed me a piece of paper with his signature.

I telephoned Frau Scherzer as soon as I got home.

"I have permission to join the class at the factory!" I shouted into the receiver, not being used to long-distance calls.

"Calm down. Great. The class has just been released from the factory. We are returning to school. Meet us in Obernigk on Monday. Tell me then how you got the doctor to sign the permit."

I left home with a sense of elation. Mother was relieved to see me go. My classmates had arrived at school a few hours earlier and we all went to supper together. Frau Braun, the director, welcomed us back. "The second V-rockets are flying to London as we speak. Our scientists are designing larger and more devastating secret weapons that will bring the war to an end. *Der Endsieg ist unser!*" (Final victory will be ours). Although I had overheard some skeptical comments at Mother's parties about the new secret weapons that would turn the tide, Frau Braun's earnestness reassured me. The front was not collapsing, as Mother's reserve officers had blurted out in their drunken stupor. Everything was going to be fine. We were back at school, after all. Obernigk was close to the Polish border. The authorities would not have us come back here if it was not safe. I glanced over at Frau Scherzer, standing in the doorway. Her face was without expression, as it always was when Frau Braun spoke.

I understood my psychosomatic illness some twenty years later. Away from home, affirmed by a teacher I loved, by the first person who showed me who I wanted to be, I could not tolerate the strong emotions that she, and the subject matter she taught, inspired in me. These emotions conflicted with the repressive school discipline and my Nazi training. My headaches were the result of this conflict, and they were real enough to me. But since I was a good student, an athlete, and well liked by my fellow students, my teachers and the physicians thought my headaches had a neurological and not a neurotic origin. Many later physicians found my toe reflexes irregular, as had the neurologists at the clinic, and I assured them that this had always been the case. My ophthalmologist recently made me a photo of my protruding visual nerves and told me that some patients "just have them like that." Heaven knows what the primitive X-rays of 1944 showed. I am certain that, when they failed to find the tumor they suspected, the neurologists took me for a hysteric and, by the ideology of the time, a degenerate. When I made my case to the physician about being fit to return to school, he must have felt that with the war being as good as lost, nothing much mattered anymore, so he let me go.

Lessons resumed the morning after we returned. I remember little about them except that after a few weeks classroom hours were reduced and we all, together with our teachers, went to a refugee camp in town for practice teaching. The refugees were ethnic Germans from the Baltic provinces who had been resettled in the annexed territories in Poland and then fled westward from the approaching Russian army. I did not put it together at the time that these ethnic Germans were the kind of students for whose benefit we were in training, since I had paid little attention to Frau Braun's earlier sermons about our mission on behalf of the settlers in the east. The irony struck me much later: the ethnic Germans we were to teach in the conquered east had come *heim ins Reich*—home to the Reich—as Hitler had promised. I also had no comprehension of what being a refugee must have meant to them, nor did I feel anything about them except that they were material on which to practice.

My class of ten girls ranged in age from nine to twenty-seven, and I was surprised that girls much older than I obeyed my directions. They barely spoke German. Since I did not know Russian or Lithuanian, I used what I would much later come to know as the direct method of teaching. As I got up from my chair I said, "Get up," and they followed my direction, repeating, "Get up!" We practiced similar everyday phrases for hours on end. Nobody had told me what to teach and nobody supervised what I was doing. After I got over my initial awkwardness, I actually enjoyed teaching, and the girls seemed to have fun and even learned some German. In the few hours we had for our own lessons, Frau Scherzer concentrated on our English textbook.

We went home for Christmas. My brothers and I went to the Christmas Eve service together and exchanged gifts; I had bought them each a book with the pocket money I received at school. We celebrated with Mother by cooking the usual Christmas Eve dinner, and Aunt Lene and Martha spent the evening with us as they had every year. We did not know that the local authorities had already received the order not to plan an evacuation of the civilian population should the enemy break through the front line. On January 2, I returned to school, and Jochen went back to the farm where he was apprenticed.

In mid-January a Russian breakthrough occurred in East Prussia, and when the German village the Russians had occupied was retaken by our troops, our soldiers found the raped and mutilated bodies of women, children, and old men. Goebbels's propaganda machine made the most of it. "This," he shouted into the microphone, "this, my fellow countrymen, is what awaits you if you surrender! We will never surrender! You must fight to the last drop of blood!" Frau Braun played his speech for us at supper as she began to prepare us for being moved to another seminary in the "heart of Germany," at Weissenburg/Saale, though she also told us we might be called to dig trenches at the nearby border. "Our soldiers will stop the Russians. Our scientists' new weapons are almost ready to end the war," she said, trying to calm our fears.

Late one evening at the end of January, as we were preparing for bed, the alarm bell that called us for meals rang insistently, as if for an air raid. It was pitch dark and snowing outside. We ran across the yard to the main building, the cellar of which served as an air-raid shelter. We found Frau Braun on the outside steps, dressed in her robe and ready to address us. She looked agitated and pale and began speaking immediately, without letting us into the building. Her hoarse voice trembled.

"I just had a call from Breslau, the ministry. The Russians have broken through the front. Their tanks will arrive in a few hours, maybe any time. Pack a few things into your knapsacks and get to the station as fast as you can. They expect that a few trains will still go to Breslau. If you miss the next one, don't wait. Start walking on the Breslau road till you reach the Oder River. Our soldiers will stop the advance at the river. I will be in touch with you about Weissenburg seminary." I realized with a profound sense of shock that all the talk about group loyalty had been just that: talk. Every one of us was on her own.

Adelheid and I raced back to the dormitory, threw a few items into our knapsacks, and stumbled through the deep January snow to the railroad station. The platform was crowded. We had not exchanged a single word, but as we waited she told me that Frau Scherzer had not been in her room when the bell rang and therefore must be at her apartment in Breslau. We were both still in sweats and sneakers; in our panic, we had forgotten to put on coats and boots. The cold cut into us, the icy wind whipping up the falling snow. We huddled close together and pressed ourselves into the crowd for warmth. A train rolled in after what seemed only a few minutes, but it was so jammed with people and soldiers spilling out onto the steps, couplings, and roof that it did not even stop. "I am going to start walking toward the Oder River," Adelheid said. "Come along, the road is just over there, and it's only a few stations away. We'll be faster than the tanks." A few of the other girls who had joined us ran after her. I don't know why, but I decided to wait for the next train. I pressed myself into the crowd of people waiting, shaking with fear and cold. Another train arrived an endless time later, during which I thought I heard tanks crushing the cobblestones of the icy road by the station. This time it stopped.

I hurled myself through the crowd toward an open compartment door, crying to the people inside, "I have to get home. My mother is ill. She cannot do without me. Let me in." Miraculously a man's arm hauled me up, as my knapsack fell off my shoulders, and deposited me in the luggage rack on top of a pile of bedding and baggage. As the train lurched out of the station I supported myself against the ceiling, so as not to fall on the heads of the people jammed into the compartment. My face burned with shame for my lie and for my cowardice. As I held on to the ceiling and the train hurtled through the night, I was still shaking uncontrollably. I could barely breathe. Was it because the air was so thick with steaming, sweating bodies, or was it from shame? Right then and there, my face burning, I decided that I would never beg like that again, never humiliate myself by begging for my life like a coward. The shame blunted my fear and my sense of loss. My comrades were gone. I had done nothing to help anyone. I had just hidden in the crowd to save my life. I do not know what happened to Adelheid or to any of my classmates or teachers. Events moved too quickly; there simply was no time to find out—the Russians were upon us before we quite knew what had happened to us. Except for Frau Scherzer, I never heard from any of my fellow students or teachers again, though I looked for them after the war.

The train took only half an hour to Breslau, and it did not make the first two Breslau stops, which it normally would have done. An air-raid siren howled as the train pulled into Breslau's main station, and everyone ran for shelter. I waited for a connecting train home in the underpass instead of the shelter and stayed close to the stairs so that I could dash up should the train come in during the raid. A locomotive with just a few passenger cars soon pulled in and I boarded it, before the crowd surged up the stairs when the sirens announced the end of the alarm. Then we waited in the unheated train. Finally it moved out, only to stop again at a suburban station for what seemed an eternity. The usual thirty-minute trip lasted into the early morning hours, the train repeatedly stopping and then lurching ahead again. Fortunately, the compartment was so packed that we warmed each other. Somewhere before we arrived at Strehlen, a newly arrived passenger reported that the Russian tanks had been stopped at the Oder River. I knew enough local geography to understand that, for the time being, we were safe on the west side of the river, unless the Russians made another massive attempt to cross the Oder. As I walked home through the dawn and in the still falling snow, my hometown seemed strangely changed. Military vehicles, some motorized, some horse drawn, were parked everywhere. Straw, abandoned suitcases, papers, and horse manure littered the streets.

The few months I had spent at the teacher seminary proved crucial to my later life. The discipline and intellectual content, such as it was, of Frau Braun's teaching, which repeated much of what I had learned in the HJ leadership group, began to evaporate in the heat of my disillusionment with the Nazi leadership during the last days of the war. In the seminary, despite my earlier disenchantment with being a leader in the Jungmädel, my commitment to the HJ revived, at first because the regime offered me what I craved, an education, and later because it offered a way of hiding from the reality that we were losing the war. On returning home I clung for a while to the illusion that I might be called to the Weissenburg seminary, but Mother finally disabused me of the notion: "With the Russians at our doors, the government has better things to do than open a new seminary!" It is ironic that it was in the seminary, where I was to be trained as a Nazi teacher, that I made my first acquaintance with the Western humanistic tradition that weaned my mind away from Nazi nationalism and chauvinism. Even more important, Frau Scherzer modeled for me a new way of being a woman, one totally different from and opposed to the stereotypes propagated by the HJ—the fertile earth mother or the loyal follower of Hitler, preferably dressed in Bavarian dirndl and sturdy shoes and wearing no makeup. Even as a thirteen-year-old Jungmädel I had found these Nazi versions of womanhood equally unattractive. Frau Scherzer gave me an idea of who I could be as a woman that sustained me when the world I knew fell apart around me. She showed me who I wanted to become:

educated, above all else. A lover of literature. A friend when a friend is needed. A person who tries to understand others and to be helpful and compassionate. An elegant and sophisticated woman who rejects the Nazi patriarchal cult of the heroic mother and loyal helpmate just as much as the passive nineteenth-century woman of my adolescent novels. In the following months, during my training as a Red Cross nurse and my service at the military hospital during the Russian invasion, other women and men became my role models. But none influenced me as profoundly as my first real teacher, Frau Scherzer.

Chapter Eight

THE BIG WHEELS ARE LEAVING FOR THE WEST, JANUARY–MARCH 1945

THE DAY I ARRIVED IN STREHLEN from Obernigk, when the Russians had been stopped at the Oder, a division, formed from several army units, had taken position to defend Breslau. Gradually, over the next weeks, the Russians crossed the river in several places and surrounded what became known as "Fortress Breslau." The encircled German troops in the city held out a few days beyond Germany's unconditional surrender on May 7, 1945. During February and March, Strehlen, like several towns in the neighborhood of Breslau, changed hands several times as the Russian army crossed the Oder and in the north prepared for the assault on Berlin in April. By late April or early May only the Silesian mountains had not yet been occupied by the Russians.

At the Baronie, I found our apartment taken over by soldiers of the German army units in charge of defending Breslau. Some slept on sleeping bags all over the living room and bedroom floors. A few sat smoking in the kitchen. Others had set up a telecommunications center in Father's former office, where several field radios crackled, hissed, and occasionally spit forth clipped commands. All the doors stood wide open, and a constant stream of uniformed strangers washed in and out of our apartment house. The men told me that Mother and Werner had gone to stay at a friend's apartment, but they did not know where. I knocked at the Gurns' apartment, which was also jammed with soldiers. Finally, in a back room, I managed to rouse Frau Gurn, who told me that Mother had gone to sleep at the house of her friend Aunt

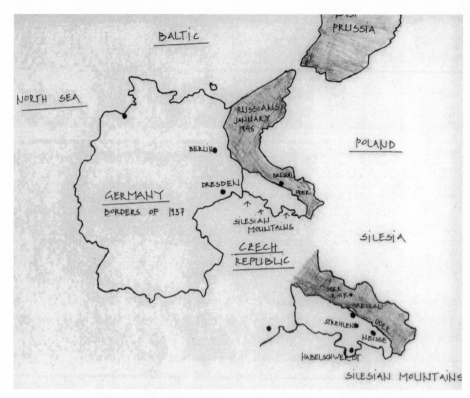

Map of Germany and Silesia, January 1945, showing Russian advance. Copied from *Der Spiegel*. Copyright, *Der Spiegel*, drawing by Annette Mahlendorf

Lenchen, who owned a soap and perfume store on City Hall Square. Frau Gurn let me sleep a few hours on a stuffed chair in their small guestroom. I returned to our apartment sometime late in the morning. The soldiers were still underfoot, but Mother had come home to pack our belongings and was in the bedroom, which was strewn with empty sleeping bags.

"We are staying at Aunt Lenchen's," she said. "I don't know for how long. I guess till it's no longer safe here." Then she gave up packing and went to the living room.

"I suppose we should return dresses and materials to customers," she muttered, as she dug into a closet in which she kept dressmaking materials. She handed me a dress and some material I recognized as Frau Dunisch's.

"I'll take that," I offered, glad to have an excuse to get out.

Walking down Promenade Street, I checked on the Boxhammers' apartment house. Hanne and her parents were gone, as were Rita and her aunt.

At the mill on Mill Street, Herr Breiler's windows were still lit. I found it reassuring that he had not left yet. Mill Creek was completely frozen over, a sign that it had been very cold the past few days. Along Old Town Street some of the apartment houses looked deserted, but a whole crowd of people, dragging suitcases and bundled up in layers of clothing, moved along the street to Ring Road and beyond. Ring Road had been built at the beginning of the war as a detour around the town center; it came from points east, intersected Old Town Street by the Ohle River, went all the way to Frankensteiner Street, and from there led to points south and west of Strehlen. As I passed Ring Road itself, I saw that it was thick with traffic: horse-drawn wagons piled high with suitcases, bedding, bales of hay, old people, children. People fleeing, people bedraggled, stone faced, silent, wheels crunching on snow. Old men and women drivers whipped exhausted horses to force them forward. When would it be our turn to flee?

I went quickly to Frau Dunisch's house, but she had left. Returning to Ring Road, I walked alongside the wagons to the turnoff for Mill Creek Promenade, when I noticed that the innkeeper at Winter Garden Inn was handing out hot tea and barley coffee to the refugees on the wagons. I went over and offered to help, as had another few girls in HJ uniforms. We carried hot drinks to the passing refugees all afternoon. I was cold, my toes frozen, and I could barely walk when I arrived home after dark. Mother was furious.

"Why didn't you come back when Frau Dunisch wasn't home? Where is her stuff?"

"I don't remember. I probably left it at Winter Garden Inn. I'll pick it up tomorrow." My gym shoes were soaked through.

"Where are your boots?" she asked.

"At Obernigk. I forgot to change into boots. My coat is gone too," I added. "There wasn't time to pack." Instead of continuing with her angry outburst, Mother said, "Jochen called. He was drafted last week. He is in boot camp in Glatz for the next few weeks. He won't need the ski boots he left here last Christmas. Put them on. We'll leave for Aunt Lenchen's now."

As we walked along Grosse Kirchstrasse, the town seemed even quieter and darker than it had the previous night, its houses dark and eerily silent. City Hall Square was deserted; its dimmed gaslights had gone out altogether. The far distant roar of trucks and the rumbling of horse-drawn wagons could be heard from far-off Ring Road. Aunt Lenchen opened the front door after we had been knocking for a while.

"The whole house is empty; all the families left during the day. They are all taking the railroad south, up to the Glatz Mountains," she explained. "There is no other way out of town. The Russians have cut off the line to Breslau." She quartered my brother and me in her living room, just behind her store. Mother and she shared her bedroom. We had brought along a few featherbeds from home, rolled up in sheeting, and spread them on the couch. Mother and Aunt Lenchen listened to the radio, which was still playing marching music. Occasionally an announcer interrupted the program to read official bulletins or notifications to the population about which towns or villages were being called to evacuate to make room for the German troops defending Breslau. I slept fitfully, hot and apprehensive. Would the Russians break through again?

The next morning Mother went back to our apartment to pack a few more things to bring to Aunt Lenchen's house. Lenchen gave us her door key. "I think I may leave in the course of the day. Depends on what the radio says. But I might see you tonight." I told Mother that I was going back to Ring Road to help with the refugees. She let me go but asked me to come back home before dark. Ring Road was still thick with people. But yesterday's wagons and trucks bearing the wealthier farmers had been replaced by poorly dressed people pulling handcarts, teenagers pushing bicycles and baby carriages loaded with blankets, pans, and bedding, with now and then a bundled-up toddler sitting on top. I started helping with bringing out hot drinks but gave up after a few hours. I felt exhausted; despite the cold I was hot.

Mother took one look at me when I got back and said, "You have a fever, child." She asked the soldiers to let me rest in the bedroom. She packed me into bed and took my temperature; it was 104°F. One of the soldiers offered her a flask of vodka to make me a hot drink. My head hurt and my eyes were burning. Mother used Oma's remedy for breaking a high fever, a sweat cure. She filled me up with a strong punch made from the vodka, wrapped me tightly into a cold wet sheet from head to toe, and piled a featherbed and blankets on top of me. I shivered from the wet sheet. My head spun, and then I broke out in a sweat. An hour later, I was drenched. She unwrapped me, washed me off with lukewarm water, and toweled me off. In the midst of being dried off, I fell asleep. When she woke me later, I felt cooler and better. We returned to Aunt Lenchen's house, dragging another pile of our stuff through the now deserted town. I begged Mother to let us leave tomorrow. Aunt Lenchen was gone when we arrived at her house. As I was falling asleep with the help of another hot punch, I heard the radio playing marching music from a long way off. At daybreak Mother woke us, saying, "Ulla, Werner, the radio went off the air. Get ready fast. We have to leave."

We dressed quickly and then shouldered our knapsacks and took our bed-rolls. Each of us dragging a suitcase, we made our way to the station along City Hall Square into Cloister Street. Werner had difficulty keeping up with us and sniffled, "I cannot carry this suitcase. It's too heavy. Wait." We met a few people going our way, loaded down as we were. I still felt groggy from the punch of the night before and stumbled along half asleep. As we rounded the corner from Münsterberger Street into Railroad Station Street I looked back toward City Hall Square. About halfway up Münsterberger Street I saw a gallows, a huge beam that extended almost all the way across Münsterberger Street, with three dark figures dangling from ropes.

"Deserters," a woman behind us said. "They have been stringing up all the men and boys who try to run."

"Who?" Mother asked.

"The ss or the party bosses," the woman said quietly as she moved past us.

I stood transfixed, unable to move. They were three boys, slender, small shouldered. Fifteen or sixteen, in dark blue HJ uniforms, their armbands torn off.

"Move on," Mother said very quietly. "Jochen is away at boot camp."

We both thought it couldn't be him, and felt relieved. We did not know that he had just made a crucial decision, alone in his boot camp up in the mountains. He, who had fought going to HJ meetings and submitting to their disci-pline through all these years, in a fit of patriotism and loyalty to our father had volunteered for the ss, hoping to stem the Russian invasion.

By early February 1945 trains in Silesia ran irregularly, if at all. They ran only in one direction, to Glatz and the Silesian mountains. By the time we got to the station, Strehlen was at the end of the line; the stationmaster had to wait for empty trains to be sent back from the mountains to pick up refugees. Everybody went to the platform, though, so as to be in front when a train was ready for boarding. It was bright but still icy cold. The day before, Mother had allowed me to put on the pants and windbreaker Jochen had left behind in addition to the boots. The crowd was not too thick when we arrived on the platform. As the hours passed and we waited, Mother wanted to go back to our house repeatedly, to fetch this or that. Impatiently, I tried to talk her out of it.

"What if the train comes and we get separated?"

"It won't leave that fast. It has to be turned around. I'll be back in half an hour."

I was frightened she would do it and was angry with her for making me feel like a coward. I suddenly lost my temper and started raging against her, "Damn it, stop! Stupid cow, stupid, stupid, don't leave us here. Stop, stop!" I screamed and railed as startled onlookers turned toward us and then away.

"We should have left days ago. We won't get out! The train won't come. Damn it, damn!" I finally collapsed on the station platform, still sobbing, and Mother left.

It did not occur to me till years later, still ashamed of my outburst then, how hard it must have been for Mother to leave her apartment, everything she had owned and known in her life, and to go, without any of her friends or neighbors, none of us knew where. Even now I am astounded that she had not made plans with her brothers, her friends, or our many relatives about where to go, how to meet when separated, how to help each other in an emergency. Was it inconceivable to them that they might have to flee from the approaching enemy armies? Had they been deluded by Goebbels's promise of last-minute miracle weapons, seduced, even those who had been skeptics, into an almost torpid passivity? Or was everybody on their own as far as they were concerned?

Of course, they had gotten no official warning that enemy troops had broken through the German lines to the east. The national and regional leadership, whether civil or military, had made no evacuation plans for the civilian population. In fact, as late as early January 1945, any person who publicly advised or ordered civilians to flee from the enemy could be, and in some cases was, dealt with as a traitor and shot. At least in Strehlen, individuals and families fled when they deemed the front too close. In the course of the morning hours, as we waited for a train, many of the people who joined us on the platform grumbled under their breath about the gallows on Münsterberger Street. Finally, one woman started shouting. "The dirty swine, the Nazi bastards, they are hanging children who are only doing what we all are doing, running away!"

People tried to hush her up, but she continued screaming for quite a while. Finally, just after Mother, out of breath, returned from her visit to our apartment, an empty train arrived and was turned around and ready for boarding. Jammed into a small compartment, we waited and waited. The sky darkened and it began to snow again. The train did not move. Then, without the usual public announcement, it started up with a jerk.

The journey, which normally takes two hours or so, took from about five in the afternoon till nine the next morning. I slept fitfully standing up, leaning uncomfortably halfway across a couple; Mother had obtained a seat, and someone had lifted my brother into the baggage rack. Sometime during the night the man offered me his seat. I took it gratefully and fell asleep at once.

I woke up to hear the couple whispering to each other. Obviously upset, the woman grumbled, "Why doesn't she give you back your seat?" I felt embarrassed about being impolite but stubbornly kept my seat until the train pulled into Glatz station. We followed signs to a rescue mission and from there were sent to another train that went farther up into the mountains to Habelschwerdt. Hungry and cold, we waited on the platform where the train to Habelschwerdt was to arrive. Mother remembered that she had prepared sandwiches. Our train came in just as we started looking for the sandwiches in our baggage. In the hurry to pack up again and board, we left one of the suitcases on the platform.

This time we arrived early in the afternoon, only to be loaded into trucks to be taken to the surrounding villages. Somehow we managed to stay together. Our truck and two others went farther up into the backwoods, to a village called Lomnitz, almost all the way to the Czech border. We were unloaded at a village pub and led, with our baggage, into what must have served as a dance hall on Saturday nights. We were asked to group ourselves as family units, and then farmers and their wives and an official, the mayor, slowly examined us. "They are auctioning us off," I whispered to Mother when I observed that the mayor was asking adult refugees what skills they had and how they were prepared to compensate their hosts for shelter. "Be quiet," Mother hissed back. "Don't be fresh or nobody will want to take us."

Most of the family groupings had left with their hosts when we were finally approached. After Mother identified herself as a dressmaker willing to work for two women who owned a farm, she and Werner went with them. Shortly thereafter, their next-door neighbors, a heavyset farmer and his wife, beckoned me to come with them. I was much too tired and disoriented to undress or look at the small attic room into which the farmer's wife led me. In the middle of the night I woke up from a rattle at my door; heavy footsteps approached my bed. In the dark I could make out the massive shape of the farmer who had brought me to his house. I jumped out of bed, flew to the window, and swung myself down, the narrow window frame scraping my face. I fell into the deep snow. When I arrived at the house next door where my mother was staying, everyone was asleep and the door locked. I fled into the hayloft, burrowed into the hay, and waited out the night. From that day on I stayed at Mother's hosts' and shared Mother's bed. Explaining what had happened, I had the sense that neither Mother nor the two women, despite my scratches, believed that the farmer had invaded my room. "She just got frightened by herself," Mother explained to the two women. They never mentioned the incident again, or the broken window. After a few days I forgot about it too, and remembered it only as I was writing this account.

Snow fell every day. The farm women's radio reported as it had for weeks that powerful V-2 rockets were flying into London—a guarantee, the radio announcer proclaimed, that even with the Russians standing at the Oder River, the British would soon surrender and Final Victory Would Be Ours. I forgot that I had fled home from the tanks, that our town was probably in Russian hands. I was certain that we would return home victorious in a few weeks. Still fired by Goebbels's voice calling on us to sacrifice ourselves, I could not imagine a Germany without Hitler and the Nazi Party. If the unthinkable happened and Hitler died in the upcoming Battle of Berlin, we would all die, I was sure. I would be loyal—loyal unto death.

Several days or so after settling into the two women's farmhouse, the three of us walked down into Habelschwerdt to inquire at the refugee office about whether they had lists of refugees in the region. They did, and we found out that Aunt Lene and Aunt Martha had found shelter closer to Habelschwerdt and that Mother's friend, the miller, was in a neighboring village. "Our soldiers are still holding on to Strehlen," a neighbor from Woiselwitz Street explained. "The furniture factory on Fisherman's Alley was bombed but the Russians have not gotten further than Gross Lauden village. I just got here yesterday and I'll go back home tomorrow to pick up dry goods and blankets I left behind, if it is still safe."

At this point there was no holding Mother back. "I'll go with you," she told her. "We lost a suitcase with most of my clothes. If it's safe to go, as you seem to think, I could get what I left back home." Early the following morning, with Werner and me protesting, we walked back to Habelschwerdt. Mother had wanted to go alone, but we both were far too worried to let her do so. "It's still safe," the women we met at the station explained as we boarded the train back to Glatz. From there, the train home, almost empty, went only to Münsterberg, three stations from Strehlen. "We'll have to walk back but should manage that in three hours. That's how long it took me last time." It took us longer, and the trek through the almost deserted, eerily quiet villages—neither dogs barking nor the usual sounds of farm machinery—seemed endless. The day had turned warm, and the snow was melting on the asphalt of the road. Now one, now the other, of us slipped and fell into the sludge as we hurried along. Nonetheless it took us until the late afternoon to get home. The town seemed strange without civilians, overrun as it was with soldiers and men of the Volkssturm (the home defense, men over the age of fifty who had been called up). None of them had uniforms; you recognized them by their white armbands. At our apartment, with rifles and field gear strewn about, we found the same soldiers we had left a few days earlier, but this time they cleared the bedroom so that we could stay overnight. I felt reassured by their presence. "You must leave in the morning," their sergeant admonished Mother. "The Russians may attack at any moment; we have been waiting for them for days."

Our return to the mountains remains a blur in my mind. We were awakened at daybreak and told to move on fast. "Russian planes have been strafing the roads every day. Watch out for them and take cover in the roadside ditch when you hear them. They sound like sewing machines but they aren't harmless." We took the back way to Frankensteiner Street by the municipal swimming pool and across the Ohle meadows. The refrozen snow crunched hard underfoot and the road, once we reached it, was no longer slippery. Mother had put the clothes she had picked up in old knapsacks so that we were not handicapped by lugging a suitcase. She swore that this was the last time she would want to go back. The next day, at the Habelschwerdt refugee office, she found out that the Russians had taken Strehlen on the very day we left home a second time. Up until then the town had held out.

A few weeks into our stay at Lomnitz, when I picked up our rationing cards at the mayor's office, I saw an announcement asking fourteen- to sixteen-year-old girls to volunteer for Red Cross training in a three-week course and to work at a military hospital after completing it. Here, I realized, was my chance to get away, and I jumped at it. Enthusiastically I put in my application. In my daydreams I saw myself bandaging wounded soldiers in a field hospital under fire from enemy machine guns.

A week later, toward the end of February, I was en route to a Red Cross training center at a textile mill village outside Habelschwerdt, higher up in the mountains. It had turned bitter cold again. The training center, an art-nouveau villa, was surrounded by towering snow-laden blue firs in a large garden, a breathtaking view. This villa, I realize now, with its dark wood paneling, its stained-glass windows, its magnificent but now dulled oak staircase leading from the downstairs hall to a wide upper landing and adjoining bedrooms, must have belonged to the owner of the mill some time before. Or was it one of the opulent places the Nazis requisitioned for their own use when they forced Jewish citizens from their homes and the country in the early and mid-1930s? I do not know. At the time I did not know its history, but the villa's gloomy splendor, still discernible despite boot marks and years of neglect, impressed me powerfully. Exhausted and distressed as I was most of the time, I appreciated its beauty as I did the stately blue firs. The house and its environs made me forget the double-decker metal beds, thin, gray, dirty blankets, and sparse meals we were served on crude tables in the former staff dining room in the basement. Looking at the grand fieldstone fireplaces, I forgave them that they did not dispel the penetrating cold that decorated the leaded windows with ice frost flowers. Because I suffered from the cold more than the other girls did, I put myself in charge of the fireplaces and stoked them constantly with logs from the woodshed, but with little success. During the first few days we practiced putting bandages on every conceivable body part. I took great pride in the skill with which I wound the crepe paper bands into elaborate crisscross patterns around elbows and knees. We learned how to take a temperature, how to set a simple break. A Red Cross nurse taught us how to give hypodermic shots subcutaneously, intravenously, and into muscle.

After the first week, most of the girls were signed up to practice at neighborhood military hospitals. Monika, one of my roommates, and I were sent by bus to work at an infant ward in a pleasant, modern mountain lodge in the next village. I had made friends with Monika, a few months my senior, in the kind of easy friendship you make with a dormitory roommate at age fifteen. She was as tall as I was but lank and willowy, a black-eyed brunette with a shock of short hair that she tossed when she was annoyed as if she were tossing off a fly. She had a ready tongue and I, nervous, sputtering, and awkward of speech, envied her gift for the quick, snide comment. She had her own, mostly negative opinions about the BDM leaders of the training camp. Early in the morning the bus delivered us to the maternity ward. If we had not been buddies able to share duties and thoughts, our work there would have been even harder than it was. The hours were long and we had no food until we came home after dark. The maternity facility was as cold as our villa. It had central heating, but they had run out of coal. Only in the infant ward did a few small electric heaters dispel the worst of the cold.

The nurses at the ward were a tough lot, but I don't remember any of them individually. They taught us to give the infants their baths, to lift them by their feet onto the changing table, to put crumpled, rough paper diapers on bottoms red and sore with rash. We changed the infants only twice a day, the paper soaked through with urine and runny diarrhea. We had neither baby powder nor cream to ease their discomfort. Yet the infants were strangely quiet; they hardly cried. Their arms and legs were pitifully thin, their skin gray and clammy, their bellies distended, and when we arrived at the ward in the biting morning cold, several of them were always gone.

"Froze to death during the night," the gruff head nurse explained without further comment, and her glance told us not to ask more.

The most disturbing thing about the ward was that many of the mothers shrank from holding their infants when we delivered them to their rooms, refused to cuddle them even though we had just cleaned and diapered them, and could be brought to feed them only with repeated cajoling. With dark army blankets thrown over their shoulders, these women with their bloated faces shuffled aimlessly around their dayroom or hid in their rooms. Only the nurses could make them sit down in preparation for feeding.

"Your beauty will die if you don't give him your breast." The head nurse shook a particularly heavyset woman with ample breasts. "Hold him and be done with it!" she snapped, ripping open the woman's sweater and placing the infant against her. "Just see how hungry he is!"

The woman held the baby awkwardly and removed him from her nipple once the head nurse moved on to the next mother. Some women refused altogether to nurse their infants, claiming they had no milk or their breasts were too sore. Since the ward had no milk to feed either mothers or infants, we made do for the babies with a thin, gray gruel made of water, flour, or oatmeal. Once we had prepared the bottles with the infant feed, we could get only two or three of the fifteen or so mothers to come to the nursery to help us. Even then they failed to hold the babies when feeding them, and we, too busy washing and drying the infants' bedding and cleaning up, had no time for snuggling with them either. Monika cried every evening when the bus came to take us back to the training camp, sobbing with exhaustion and despair, "Why don't they care, why doesn't anyone care?"

As we stood waiting for the bus, I glanced up at the snowflakes dancing around the lamplight from a single dim streetlight. It seemed to me as if the dense cloud of tiny shining crystals was performing a deadly dance that would turn us both into columns of ice as they silently spiraled lower and lower.

That night, chopping wood, as I did every evening instead of helping clean the supper dishes, I saw again the spiraling snowflakes against the lamp outside the woodshed. Hot from the chopping, I stopped to watch them as they sank slowly into the sudden silence around me. The tall firs pointed against the night's blue as if demanding something from me. A storm of curse words flooded my mind, "Verdammte Sau, Schwein, lerge, lerge, Sau verdammte" (damned sow, pig, damned), I raged as I lifted the axe against the next bole of pinewood and crashed it apart. "Verdammt, verdammt!" I cried over and over as I tackled the next block and the next. When I came back in, Monika sat huddled in a blanket in one of the carved seats by the fireplace. Her dark, spiky hair was caught by the intense glow of the flames that roared in the grate. I stood transfixed in the doorway, staring at the fiery halo over her forehead. She looked like an angry, overgrown sprite. As I came closer I saw that she had been crying. I sat down next to her and said, my voice still choked with anger, "I know, none of them care if the babies die. You are right. I don't ever want to have children."

One afternoon late in our training, a soldier came to teach us how to shoot a rifle.

"When the Russians break through," he explained, "you will have to know how to defend yourself and the wounded you are going to take care of."

I could hardly lift the rifle he handed me. I was terrified of it and found it hard to listen to the soldier's instructions. When it was my turn to shoot, I failed to place the rifle correctly against my shoulder and its backfire almost broke my collarbone. The next day we were to be trained in using antitank guns. The soldier in charge explained the model he had brought along, a simple metal pipe with a projectile in front, a charge inside, and a trigger. He assured us that it was safe and easy to use. We were to take the pipe under our right arms, being careful to leave room for clearance for the backfire so that we wouldn't get burned. "Its range is short, so you'll have to be close to the tank," he said, concluding his lesson. My friend Monika was the only one in our group of some fifty who objected to the paces he put us through.

"There is no way I'll fire that thing," she told him in a flat voice. "I am not strong and stupid enough."

Fortunately, someone among the trainers who had some common sense left must have shared her opinion, because we never practiced with anti-tank guns.

The alarm bell shrilled, yanking me out of a deep sleep. Voices barked, "Get up." It was still dark; it couldn't be morning yet. Alarm.

"What the hell is it now?" Monika said next to me as we pulled on our tracksuits over the underwear that we never shed because of the cold.

"Dress uniform," the squad leader yelled. "The *Gebietsführerin* [province leader] is going to address you."

"Damn it! Why in the middle of the night?"

I stumbled out of my warm suit into the thin blouse that had once been white and pulled the blue skirt over my head. My fingers were so numb that I could hardly push the black kerchief through the leather knot. Shivering, I followed the others into the downstairs hall as I slipped into my blue blazer and took my place in the formation we had been drilled in for the last few weeks. Then we waited, shivering in the leaden cold, the room lit only by a low-wattage bulb. It seemed hours before we heard the crunch of tires on the harsh frozen snow outside.

A woman in her thirties, clad in a fur-lined air force leather jacket, heavy wool riding pants, and black boots, swept through the front door in a flurry of snow. We stood at attention.

Our troop leader stepped forward, shouting, "BDM troop Habelschwerdt fifty-three, at your command."

"At ease," the heavyset figure rasped.

"I have come . . ." I heard through the thick fog of half sleep. "When the Russians come, use your rifles: fight. You may die, die bravely . . . you might be taken prisoner . . . they'll take you to Siberia, but remember, you are proud German girls. Keep your purity, even if you're starving and cold, be neat and clean, always scrub yourself all over, comb your hair, stand straight and tall, remain chaste German girls true to the Führer." She droned on and on as I stared at the faint, intricate blue and ruby meander that the hall's stained-glass window, backlit by the waiting car's headlights, painted above the now dead fireplace.

"Sieg Heil, Sieg Heil . . ." I must have chimed in.

The next thing I heard through my trance was the command, "At attention."

"Dis—missed." The front door slammed shut and the car shot away. We stumbled up the stairs, back to bed.

"Purity, sponge baths, I'll be damned. The bastards," Monika gasped under her breath to me. "The big wheels are leaving for the west and letting us kids take the shit." I tried to contradict her, but I was too numb with cold and despair and finally fell asleep.

From that night alarm in late February on, once I understood that our "leaders" were forsaking us, I walked through the events of the Russian invasion into Silesia on automatic pilot, in a daze. I turned into an automaton that registered and reacted to what was happening around me without feeling, a daytime sleepwalker. Only my senses stayed alive, keenly and even painfully acute, particularly my vision—as when my eyes hallucinated the fiery halo around Monika's head. Occasionally, I would become suddenly intensely aware of myself when, on a break, in the garden of the training camp villa, I saw an incredibly blue sky explode through the white snow on the branches of the fir trees. Or my chest would constrict with intense pain when I opened a diaper to a grayish-white infant bottom with purplish-red oozing sores. Then I sank back into my trance, no longer listening to news, no longer focused on anything but sleep and my work at the ward.

My emotional numbness did not lift till years later, long after the war, when I began to feel my rage at the adults of that time in my life and began to understand where I had been. The maternity ward had been, I now believe, a part of Hitler's pure race *Lebensborn* program, a eugenic experiment the Nazis designed in the late 1930s in which women of supposedly pure Germanic stock were encouraged to have children with blond Aryan ss men. Those women who became pregnant gave birth to their infants in state-run clinics and infant wards like the one in which Monika and I were trained. Compensated and assisted by the state to raise these children through infancy, these mothers were to relinquish their offspring at school age to Nazi training institutions. As the Nazi state disintegrated in 1945, the infants we cared for were the issue of ss men and their "racially pure" consorts that nobody wanted anymore. That explained the callousness of the mothers, the absence of physicians, and the indifference of the nurses. We teenagers, ignorant of the purpose of the ward and the origin of the babies, had been their stooges. No one had explained to us what it all meant, and we, obedient as we had been taught to be, had asked no questions.

The higher-echelon Hitler Youth leaders of that alarm night went west-ward as the Russian troops advanced. The leather-clad province leader who had talked to us that winter night about death and cleanliness in Siberia, I found out later, had fled to South America, leaving us to the fury of an enemy that Goebbels's propaganda all through these last days portrayed as ruthless rapists and killers. It amazes me, thinking back, that I was not frightened out of my wits of the approaching enemy, but I was not. I was numb. I do not know at what point exactly I turned into a kind of robot that did not feel and just went through the motions of living. At the same time, I was convinced I was going to die soon. I no longer thought of or planned for a tomorrow. Long training in marching from Jungmädel on had accustomed me to bear pain and fatigue without complaint. Gradually now I became even more insensitive to pain, whether physical pain such as hunger pangs or open sores on heels and toes from shoes that did not fit. Nor did I feel psychic pain from such things as my mother's rejection, or sadness at having lost my teachers, my school friends, the only home I knew. Most of the time I was indifferent to the pain of others around me and felt no empathy for anyone. As far as other humans were concerned, I saw them, observed them, reacted to their commands and requests, but rarely allowed myself to have feelings about them. And yet, at the same time, I experienced some of the most intense moments of my life during this period. I could suddenly break into a wave of fury, directed par-ticularly at adults, and rage at them, abusing them verbally in my mind or with my mouth, something I had never experienced before and have not since. But I also experienced, for brief moments, the natural world around me so poignantly, with a physical pleasure in sight, sound, touch, taste, and smell so strong that it engulfed me with an ecstasy that I have rarely felt since and that I have never forgotten.

I realize, in looking back, that another crucial and permanent change had begun to occur within me from the time when we fled from the seminary in late January to the time at the Red Cross training camp in March when I understood that our leaders were abandoning us. Flight from the enemy and betrayal by leaders proved to be a great social equalizer. For the child growing up at the edge of the middle class, social position, rank, status, leadership titles seemed supremely important and desirable. Getting an education and becom-ing a teacher meant for me then gaining rank and respect. When, as a fifteen-year-old at the teacher seminary, I read Rilke's *Cornet*, his tale of an eroticized death in battle, I glorified the young soldier not least because he was an officer and a nobleman. Six months later I saw pretensions to nobility, desire for rank and title and privilege, as irrelevant if not downright despicable. I had other concerns.

When we had completed our training a week later, Monika and I were assigned to serve as nurses' aides at the Habelschwerdt field hospital. We worked there until a few days before Germany's surrender in early May.

Chapter Nine

WE DON'T KILL, WE HEAL
The Russian Invasion, 1945

WHEN I REPORTED TO THE MILITARY HOSPITAL in mid-March 1945, the melting snow made the streets of Habelschwerdt slippery. The local HJ office assigned me a space at the town youth hostel, which housed refugees. I shared the dormitory with ever-changing families in transit but kept my bed and a locker in a corner next to a window. I took my meals at the hostel, and because I made friends with one of the cooks, I had enough to eat even when I missed mealtimes because of the arrival of too many casualties from the front. She was a short, bony, older woman from East Prussia who spoke with the droll singsong accent typical of East Prussians. She reminded me of Oma as she moved calmly about, helping now this, now that refugee. Monika, who reported to the hospital the same day I did and who was a Habelschwerdt native, lived at home.

A two-minute walk took me from the hostel to the hospital, a former school that was housed on the grounds of a convent and staffed mainly by Franciscan nuns. A number of Red Cross nurses, a group of orderlies, several surgeons, and a tenth-semester medical student completed the personnel. The head nurse, Sister Prudentia, a tall, even majestic middle-aged nun in black habit, the white band of her headdress framing her large, pale, severe face, assigned me as an assistant to two wards on the second floor. Monika was assigned to another two wards downstairs. Our duties were to serve meals, take temperatures, fetch and empty bedpans and urinals, and help wash patients who could not wash themselves. Some days, when too many cases came in from the Breslau front for the nuns to handle by themselves, both Monika and I helped with washing the worst dirt and blood off the new cases before they went to the operating room. I found those the most exhausting days because I tensed up when any of the young soldiers cried out in pain at the mere sight of our approach. Bespattered with dried blood, their HJ uniforms encrusted with dirt, they smelled of shit, urine, and acrid sweat.

Most evenings, even when we had worked overtime, Monika and I accompanied each other home, talking as we meandered back and forth between our two houses. Her father had a carpenter's shop and her family lived above the shop. Her father was a World War I veteran who had lost a leg and had fashioned his own prosthesis, as Monika proudly told me.

"He hates war," she said, shocking me with what struck me as heresy. War, I had learned in my HJ training and from my reading, is the master of all things. It hardens you and makes you courageous. Sometimes our meanderings would take several hours. Just as she had at the infant ward, Monika expressed her distress more openly than I did about the torn limbs, the oozing wounds, the penetrating sweet smell of iodine and pus, the groaning of the wounded men.

"They are just like the boys I go to school with," she cried as the tears ran down her face. I was embarrassed by what I thought of as her weakness, and I could think of nothing to say to console her. Indeed, about half of the soldiers were our age or a little older. When you went through some wards, you thought you were going through a youth hostel dormitory. The other half of the wounded were older men in their forties or fifties, members of the Volkssturm (home defense), much like my uncle Kurt, called up, just like the boys, in a last-ditch effort to hold off the Russians. Both of us feared that we might see badly disfigured boys we knew.

One of the wards I worked in was occupied by boys, the other by the older men. I liked working at the hospital; I felt that I was finally useful, and some days I tried talking Monika into seeing the carnage and misery we witnessed this way.

"We are doing something useful; we are helping them," I told her. But she only cried harder and got angry with me.

"Don't you see how horrible, how senseless it is?"

I did see that it was horrible, but I automatically started in again about being useful in the defense of our country.

The hospital was short on everything: pain medication, ether, hypodermics, dressings, bandages—even those made from paper—and sulfa drugs to fight infections. The operating room was downstairs from the two wards where I worked regularly. The muffled shouts coming from behind its double doors disturbed even me if I was sweeping the hallway and made me work faster. The soldiers called me "girl" when they wanted me for something, and soon the hospital staff followed suit. I wanted to learn about the different kinds of wounds. At first, the nuns kept me away from daily rounds on one pretext or another, when the staff removed the dressings and examined the wounds. One day, as I tried to see what the seam of a leg amputated at the knee looked like, Paul, the medical student, noticed my curiosity. "Come on and look, girl. Find out what this is all about." I did not know how to respond to his angry challenge but moved closer. He sounded furious, and his critical tone stung. After rounds, he confronted me in the hall, his high forehead creased with an angry scowl.

"How old are you, girl?"

"Fifteen," I replied, surprised by the attention, and then did not know what else to say.

"You want to be a nurse when you grow up?"

I felt insulted; I was grown up, after all.

"No," I improvised, "I'd like to study medicine and become a doctor."

Actually, I had never thought about becoming a doctor, but at this point I felt sure that I wanted to do just that.

From then on, the staff tolerated my joining them on rounds. I got used to seeing flesh wounds to arms and legs laced with pus. Harder to tolerate were bullet wounds where the bone had been shattered, and worst of all were belly shots. Invariably, there was not much the surgeon could do but remove the bullet and flush the wound with sulfa solutions. Men with bowel wounds screamed when they were moved for washing or rebandaging. They always ran high temperatures. Most died within a few days.

The first man I saw die was a pale, freckled, red-haired eighteen-year-old. He had a high fever from the time he arrived on the ward. Sometimes he shouted and raved in delirium; at other times he lay quietly, unconscious, and then began crying. Quickly, it seemed to me, his voice got weaker and the periods of unconsciousness longer. Sister Prudentia called a priest to administer last rites to him. Just as the priest entered, the redhead woke up. Wide-eyed, he stared as the priest approached his bed.

"I don't want the sacrament, I don't want to die, I don't want to die." His face convulsed with sobs as he cried out again and again, "I don't want to die." Not deterred by the protest, the priest began to chant his prayers as his acolyte swung the incense vessel back and forth. The smell of incense filled the room as the boy mercifully lost consciousness. I was furious with Sister Prudentia and the priest. Why couldn't they just let the boy die without his knowing what was happening to him? I turned away from the ritual and stared out the window, resting my forehead against the soothing cool glass. The other men in the ward behind me seemed to hold their breath. There was no sound except for the priest's murmuring his prayers. Death behind me—and outside a glorious warm spring day, the trees leafing out in tiny yellow-green fingers. And I, cut off from their fresh, tickling fragrance by a wall of glass. The next morning, when I came back to the ward, the red-haired soldier's bed had been stripped and remade afresh. "He died last night," Sister Prudentia told me. "The good Lord took him into his merciful arms."

A few days after we began working in the hospital, both Monika and I were called to the town's HJ office and presented with twisted silk cords in green and white, an emblem of troop leadership. "You are getting these in recognition of having passed the Red Cross training," the local HJ leader said as she fastened the cords over our black kerchiefs and pressed a small white cotton oval embroidered with a red caduceus into our hands. "Sew these on the pocket of your blouses." A few weeks earlier I would have given almost anything for these insignia. Now, like Monika, I glared at the older HJ girl, feeling a sneer pass over my face. Just like Monika, I attached the embroidered caduceus to my uniform blouse but never wore the cord again.

I gradually lost my initial distrust and anger at the nuns as I saw how devoted they were to easing the men's pain and making them comfortable. They started every day with early Mass and at six o'clock they relieved the nuns on nightshift. Except for half an hour for the noon meal and a prayer at the convent, they stayed on duty till nine at night. At any hour of the day you saw the swift swirl of their black-and-white habits as they scurried through the hallways. Highly skilled in nursing, most of them were gentle when they removed bandages or moved a patient. They knew every patient's name. They cheered the men by asking about their families, how they had been wounded, where they were from; they even helped them write letters when they had a free moment. They donated blood if their blood type was needed. They made toddies of wine, eggs, and sugar, which they brought from the convent for those soldiers who needed more energy to fight for their lives than the gruel from the hospital kitchen provided. They stayed on duty when the front moved closer during the next two months, and they remained when physicians, orderlies, and one Red Cross nurse after another left for the west. The nuns took up the slack without complaint. Their images in my memory blend into each other, except for Sister Prudentia, who stands out.

The nuns had been mistrustful of me when I first started to work, probably because I still wore my HJ uniform. Actually, aside from my ski pants and my brother's heavy jacket, it was the only outfit I owned after I lost my knapsack getting into the train at Obernigk—a few white blouses, two dark blue skirts, and a dark blue blazer. After I'd been on the ward for a few weeks, the nuns began to trust me and assigned me special tasks like handing out medications. They spoke to me in just as friendly a way as they used with the soldiers and with Paul, the medical student. During my frequent nosebleeds, Sister Prudentia put an icepack on the back of my neck to stop the bleeding and let me rest on quieter afternoons. By the time I left, I admired all of them for their kindness and calm devotion to service. This admiration began to take the place of my former awe of rank and title. I wanted to be as devoted to the soldiers as they were.

Nobody liked the ss man in the ward of older men. He teased me mercilessly. "Come on, girl, you fucked your boyfriend just last night, I can see it in your eyes!" He leered at me and I, to my embarrassment, turned scarlet.

"Leave her be, you swine," one of the other men scolded, trying to shut him up. But the ss man gave up teasing me only when he saw me hurry out in humiliation. Whenever I left the room of the older men, the ss man called for me, called even louder when I came running, and sent me to get this or that. I would do as he asked, and then he did not want what I brought, no matter what it was. The entire ward of fourteen men—seven beds on each side of the door—seethed with anger at him. Most of the men in his ward were home defense men in their fifties and sixties who had been wounded at their very first enemy encounter. He occupied the third bed to the left from the door. One of his legs had been amputated. Around age forty, he spoke with a sharp nasal rasp that grated against your eardrums. You could hear his loud voice out in the hallway when he talked to his bed neighbor, another older man who had been in the military police on the eastern front.

It was late one evening when a new contingent arrived from the front. I had helped wash the incoming cases down in the front hall. Ready to leave, I had gone upstairs to my two wards just to make sure that everyone was all right for the night. Even from the stairway I could hear the ss man and his neighbor talking. I stopped, reluctant to enter.

"We must have shot the entire village when one of ours got a bullet from a partisan—old men, women, and even the kids. They screamed like crazy, I can still hear them. But we didn't have any choice in the matter. They all were involved in the resistance. We burned down the village after that." This was the military policeman, I realized.

"We killed a lot of civilians. Particularly the Jews. Don't tell me you couldn't take it, you didn't have the balls," the ss man sneered. "You guys were harmless idiots. Now, we had some fun with . . ." I did not want to hear more. I was afraid to hear confirmation of the atrocities that Mother's customers and her officer cousin had whispered about when I was home after my operation.

"What are you going to do," I heard the military policeman ask his neighbor another time when I worked late, "when the Russians come? You can play the ordinary soldier, but they'll know from your tattoo that you were in the ss." That was the first time I heard that ss soldiers had their blood type tattooed on their upper arms. "They won't know I am ss. I'll ask the surgeon to cut it out and it'll look just like the other shrapnel scars I have," the ss man laughed. "And they aren't going to get me. I'll disappear. I have connections."

At night the ss man had nightmares and walked in his sleep, the other soldiers said. He hopped out of the room on his crutches cursing and screaming, "I got to get out of here." Sometimes he was delirious, and the others said they heard him rave about what the ss unit he belonged to had done in the Russian hinterland of the front. Even unflappable Sister Prudentia snapped at him when she lost patience with his obnoxious remarks and constant demands. I was afraid of him and had difficulty not showing it.

One day, standing in a corner of the hallway, I overheard Sister Prudentia talking to Paul in the room that served as the nurses' station. I had seen Paul enter dressed in his army corporal's tunic, as if he were going out.

"You aren't leaving?" Sister Prudentia said with a worried intonation that made my heart beat faster.

"No, of course not! I just need to take a break," Paul replied. "I've been on duty too long and I need to clear my head."

"How far did you get in your studies?" she inquired.

"I'm in my tenth semester. I started at Breslau University the winter semester of 1938 and finished my preclinical exams then. They drafted me right after the Polish campaign and sent me to Norway as a medic. I served during the first winter of the Russian campaign at the front. I was lucky that I got frostbite and was sent home. They reassigned me to continue medical training and recalled me for hospital duties as an orderly just a few months ago."

Listening to them, I realized that I had almost overlooked the fact that Paul limped. It must have been because of the frostbite. Feeling ashamed of eavesdropping, I slunk away.

Usually I avoided going into the operating room, but one day Sister Prudentia needed some dressings and sent me to get them. The surgeons had just finished with an operation; the soldier still lay on the operating table under bright lights, covered by a sheet. Suddenly I froze, staring at the refuse can next to the table. From among bloody paper bandages and swabs a leg stuck out, a brilliantly white leg with short, dark stubble, a leg with a foot, toes with yellowed toenails, still dirty with mud. I steadied myself at the door and swallowed hard, trying to control my vagus reflex and the spinning of my head. Sister Prudentia, noticing my paleness when I handed her the dressings, offered me some of the toddy she had just finished making for one of the soldiers. I took it gratefully.

I was on duty with Sister Gisela, a young, energetic Red Cross nurse, in late April or early May, when the radio announced Hitler's death. "Our beloved Führer died a hero's death in the defense of Berlin," the announcer intoned. A heroic mourning march followed. I must have flinched as if from a blow, because Sister Gisela said, "Why don't you take off for a few hours. I'll stay around till you come back. We haven't got any new cases today." I was glad to be allowed to get out, go for a hike, be by myself, and yet I felt at loose ends, unmoored. As I walked up St. Florian's Hill, I considered going back and asking Monika to come with me, but I remembered that Monika had the day off, so I continued on alone. I learned the next day that Monika and her family had left for the west. I never saw her again.

It was a clear spring day. The lindens on St. Florian's Hill were just showing little reddish-green buds against the sky, and snowdrops and crocuses peeped out from grass still dead from winter frost in the few gardens I passed. It had rained in the night and the air was still fresh; a slight breeze cooled my hot face. I followed a dirt road out into the meadows lined with blooming cherry trees. As I walked on, I looked up into a sea of pink and white blossoms against a deep, brilliant blue sky. I could not think. I felt nothing. The pink and white against the dark, radiant blue filled my senses. In a trance, I repeated the words to myself, "White, pink, deep blue, the Führer died," as I walked, trying to drive the news into my head. The physical movement and speaking the words gave me relief, I did not know from what. I just wanted to keep moving and speaking aloud to the blooming trees above me. At the same time, I felt unpleasantly numb, as if I had been anaesthetized. I hoped that the fast movement and the speaking might help me come to myself. Suddenly, and for just the briefest second, I felt a keen, sharp stab of joy that flashed by as quickly as a bolt of lightning, then dullness again. Then: "I am alive." Then dullness and nothing.

I don't know how long I hiked that day, but I returned to the hospital by nightfall, exhausted. Sister Gisela was waiting for me; she had taken care of my duties by herself. I wanted to get right to work, but she stopped me.

"You are upset because Hitler killed himself."

"Killed himself?" The radio announcer had said that he died a soldier's death for the fatherland. I did not want to believe that he had died a coward's death. Despite myself, I listened to her.

"I only know that he shot himself and that he appointed Field Marshal Dönitz as successor," she continued. I wondered what had happened to loyal party followers like Göring, or Goebbels, then shrugged off further talk. I did not really want to know more. We found out about Eva Braun and his marriage only when we moved to West Germany in 1946.

"Life will go on," Sister Gisela insisted. "In fact, I know many people who are glad that he is dead and gone for good." That seemed strange to me. I had always thought that if Hitler died, we'd all die.

"Many people who are glad?" I asked.

"Maybe you should come and visit with my family and our friends. You'll see that they are loyal Germans but relieved he is dead. Germany won't cease to exist just because Hitler committed suicide. We will be defeated, and that's good, because defeat will destroy the party. Dönitz is a navy man, not a party boss. We have a chance with him to rebuild a better Germany."

I was utterly bewildered and confused. The Führer had died and I was alive; we were alive. Hitler had committed suicide, deserted us, and here Sister Gisela was telling me that people were happy about it. The paradoxical words still ran through my mind, ran on when, automatically, I resumed work on the ward for a few more hours. I did not want to stop. Most of the men on the wards slept soundly, a few groaned; no one else seemed upset that Hitler had died. When I walked back to the hostel after midnight, I thought, I like Sister Gisela; is she right that some Germans are glad he died? These people she talked of, could they be traitors like the men of July 20 last year? Why is nobody as troubled as I am? Everyone used to revere the Führer. Where are they? Maybe I should go visit Sister Gisela to find out more.

Back at the hostel, some of the refugees were still awake, talking. That day the army had opened its local supply depot to the town population, and everyone had gone and brought back food, cartons of cigarettes, blankets, shoes, even whole bars of chocolate. They were happy, excited. No one even mentioned Hitler's suicide.

The following day, when I returned to the hospital, Sister Prudentia told me that the last surgeon and even Sister Gisela, the operating room nurse, had left. She and Paul would have to take over the surgery and operate on emergency cases. The other nuns and I would have to assume Gisela's duties, and the older men would help me take care of the more severely wounded men on my wards (since Monika had left, I had taken on hers). With his perennial scowl of intense concentration, Paul seemed very capable to me. I was fascinated and awed by him. I could not tell if he liked me, but whenever I met him in the hallway, I was conscious that he noticed me, for he always acknowledged my presence with a curt "Hallo, girl." Once, when I had one of my heavy nosebleeds, he showed me how to compress my nose for minutes on end and breathe through my mouth. Later that day, when a new contingent of wounded arrived from the front, I heard Paul and Sister Prudentia talking in the downstairs hallway.

"Have you done an amputation?" Sister Prudentia asked. I could hear the tension in her voice.

"No, but I've assisted at plenty."

"I did a stint as operating nurse," Sister Prudentia said, "but that was a few years ago."

"We haven't any choice," Paul replied. "We have the Russian with the shattered knee in the operating room, and that leg over there"—he pointed to a man whom I had washed as I choked back a gag because of the nauseating smell—"that has to come off mid-thigh, or he'll die."

When I finished washing the new arrivals, Sister Prudentia sent me to fetch some dressings for her from the operating room. As I walked by its open door, I saw two orderlies preparing a man for surgery. They had swiped his bluish-red leg and bloodied knee up to his thigh with iodine, and its strong smell permeated the room. They motioned for me to come in and have a closer look. I took a few steps forward and they addressed me.

"He's Russian, a prisoner of war, the dog," one of the orderlies said.

"Wonder how many German women he has raped, the swine," the other added. "You know, don't you, girl, that the Russians are rapists?"

"What do you think, girl," the first turned to me, "should he be allowed to live?"

"Should we kill him? Just say the word. We'll give him enough ether to send him to the great beyond," cajoled the other as he took up the ether mask from a metal tray and placed it over the Russian's face.

I stood motionless. A wave of hatred swept over me. I wanted that man to die; he had raped, killed. I felt hot with fury. Blood went to my head, and I was about to cry out, "Do it, do it!" when Paul came in from the scrub room in back of the operating room. He had heard us, and he spit his words at us.

"What the hell do you think you're doing? Kill him? This is a hospital! We don't kill, we heal them, friend and foe alike, ours and theirs." Turning to me, he said, "Remember that, girl. Doctors take an oath: Never do harm!"

The angry bloodlust I had felt just a second before gave way to a rush of shame and remorse. How could I feel that way, wanting to kill? I was hateful—Aunt Lene was right. Later in my life, whenever I got into discussions about what crimes and acts of inhumanity people are capable of, I remembered Paul. I knew that I could have killed that Russian. I was lucky that Paul came in at just that minute and stopped us. I could have killed. I was just lucky that Nazi time was running out.

As hard as we worked the first few days after the new contingent of wounded arrived, a few days later there was a lull. No new cases from the front. One afternoon Sister Prudentia sent me home.

"Go get some sleep. You look like you need a rest. You'll need your strength soon enough."

You don't look too chipper yourself, I thought, though I would not have dared to be so familiar with her. I went back to the hostel and asked the East Prussian cook if she knew whose bike I could borrow. I felt like riding fast out into the spring weather. One of the hostelers lent me his bike. By this time in full spring all the trees had leafed out, cherry blossom time had passed, and the air stayed warm even after sundown. Out on the meadows, wild primroses bloomed in great profusion, covering the fields with a bright yellow carpet. "Death is so close," I said aloud to myself, "that's why the colors are so intense, why the sky radiates so brilliant a blue, why the wind in my hair feels so energizing." I pedaled more quickly and the meadow sped by. "I am alive, alive, alive." But my exhilaration vanished when I returned to the hospital.

Every day I became more afraid to go into the older men's ward. "Girl, you'd better leave soon, like the Red Cross nurses," said the ss man, his constant refrain during my last days at the hospital. "They know enough not to wait for the Russians to get here to rape them. They are leaving to be safe on the American side."

One of the men shouted him down. "If it hadn't been for guys like you, our women wouldn't need to be afraid. If you hadn't killed civilians like there was no day of reckoning and behaved like swine, they would be all right, invasion or no."

Though the ss man's talk frightened me because he was much more believable than the propaganda we had heard for weeks, I was determined not to run as the other staff had, and to stick it out with Paul and the nuns. At this point, a few retired nuns in their seventies came over from the convent to help us out. Yet we were still short of staff, and any one of us leaving was unimaginable. As it was, Sister Prudentia recruited every last man on the wards who could even hobble about to fetch bedpans, clean floors, and distribute food, while I was instructed to change dressings and even give shots. Most evenings I went back to the hostel alone after midnight, too tired to know what hour it was.

I don't remember who told me that the hospital would be moved by train to the west a few days later and that I should get ready to go. By this time everyone had heard rumors that the Russian invasion would be catastrophic. Just as in Strehlen, none of the town administrators had made plans to evacuate the population or given any kind of direction on what to do, where to go, or how to stay alive. To the end of the war, all officials were in complete denial. After what I had heard the ss man say, I didn't think we would live to the end of the week. The Russians would take their revenge. Their cities and towns had been devastated, their people forced into slave labor or killed. Almost everyone sought to get to the American side, because we had heard that the Western powers did not allow their soldiers to kill civilians or rape the women.

I asked Paul if I could bring along my mother and kid brother with me on the train. I received permission and set out that night to Lomnitz on a borrowed bike. The eight kilometers from Habelschwerdt to Lomnitz led uphill almost all the way, and I had to push the bike most of the way. As I struggled against the wind that blew through my threadbare jacket, it began to rain in torrents. I worried that the creek, roaring with snowmelt alongside the road, might flood my path and keep me from crossing. Drenched to the skin, I arrived at the farm where Mother and Werner lived. Everyone had gone to bed, and it took me a while to wake them.

I argued with Mother. "Come along. It is our only chance to escape the Russians. We'll have a place on the train."

She started packing a few things, and soon both she and Werner were ready to go. As I opened the door to the rain outside and she heard the fierceness of the raging storm, she stopped.

"This is madness. Not tonight, not in this weather. Let's wait till the storm stops."

"We can't wait," I countered. "The train is leaving in the morning." But she would not budge.

"Go ahead," she urged me. "We will leave with Herr Breiler tomorrow. He said that we will get a place on his truck." I found out later that she had received no such promise.

I finally left. In a few places the creek had flooded the road but I biked right through, hardly noticing the water sloshing against my pedals. I felt defeated and angry that Mother had not come with me, that my mission to save the family had failed; but it did not even occur to me to stay with her and not to go back to the hospital. It was Frau Dunisch, I think, who later asked Mother the obvious question: "Why did you let her go? A girl alone on the road had almost no chance to escape rape or worse. And you knew it was madness to try to flee at this point."

"I could not have stopped her," Mother replied.

She gave the same reply when asked why she had not kept my sixteen-year-old brother with her on his last furlough a week earlier. "I could not have stopped him." Her refusal to take responsibility as a parent cost him four years as a Czech prisoner of war. It almost cost me my life.

Returning to the hostel after midnight, I dozed for a few hours till daybreak and then went over to the hospital. Everyone was gone. The wards were empty, in disarray, littered with refuse, old blankets, sheeting, socks, and discarded slippers. The high iron gate that gave access to the convent next door remained closed, as much as I rang the bell and called. I hurried back to the hostel, but no one could tell me what had happened or had even heard that the hospital had been moved. My friend the cook said, "Come along with us. We are all leaving to try to get to the American side. We will have to walk; we will have a cart and a horse to load on baggage and the smaller children. We will cross over into Czechoslovakia, and then head west."

I joined them in the hope that I might find the hospital train. I dressed in my brother's pants and boots. Since my hair was still short from last year's operation, I thought I could pass for a boy if need be.

We left in the afternoon. The hostel manager assigned me the role of nurse to the hostel group and handed me a satchel filled with first aid supplies. Quitting town, we joined a steady stream of refugees that covered the entire width of the road. We adapted our speed to its slow and halting forward movement. An hour or so after we started, the children in the mass of refugees began to complain of blisters on their feet. As we could not stop, I lifted each child onto the back of the baggage cart and dealt with the blisters as we walked. I kept busy, applying iodine and bandages through most of the night. Nobody stopped to sleep. I lost track of the hours, and I believe that we walked all through the next day. In the middle of the next night, dragging myself along behind the baggage cart now loaded down with children, I had a temper tantrum.

"Damn it, shit, why can't we stop? Why can't we just drive the people in the next village out, take over their beds, and go to sleep?" I lashed out. I don't know whose voice it was who yelled back at me in the darkness, "Get used to it! You can't just take over a village! The days of the master race are gone forever. The Czechs will beat you up if you don't shut up." That sobered me. I went back on automatic pilot and put one foot in front of the other. We never stopped anywhere. We heard shouts and curses, cries, screams, moans. Occasionally a shot rang out in the darkness, an explosion; a sudden glare of headlights illuminated white faces, huge eyes, gaping mouths. In the darkness again motors roared, heavy trucks rumbled in the distance, horses neighed. Screaming, cursing, shouting, praying, weeping, wave after wave. A robot, I no longer knew whether I was moaning and screaming, too.

Later that night or the next, people ahead of us began shouting in panic through the pitch-black darkness, "The Russians are coming!" We tried to run but could not because the dense crowd just went on moving at its slow pace. But the panic spread. Some people praying, others cursing, others groaning or crying, louder and louder. In the gray dawn we realized that German soldiers had joined us. Most had already torn off the insignia on their uniforms. Some of the refugees screamed at them, "Why aren't you back at the front? You cowards!"

"What front?" came the grim reply. "Everybody is running for their lives."

I have no idea where exactly the Russians overtook us. Sometime in the chaos of the night, I had heard several voices behind me talk about committing suicide. At daybreak, as the owners of these voices tried to pass us, I recognized them by their impeccable uniforms, even though they had already removed their leadership insignia. They were several high-ranking HJ leaders, several men and a few women, all in their mid- to late twenties. One of them looked vaguely like Marlis, my first Jungmädel leader, but this woman was older and mousy-haired. Then the crowd's screaming—"They are coming!"—reached us again. The HJ leaders and one or two of the soldiers jumped across the road-side ditch and headed uphill, away from the roadbed jammed with refugees, over a meadow. I dashed madly after them up the meadow, down a small ravine and up again. I caught up to the group that was still running, and I knew that, like them, I did not want to live. Here was a way out, away from the Russians.

I came to myself, out of breath and gasping for air, as we arrived at the forest's edge and threw ourselves down. The mousy-haired HJ leader, whom I had trusted instinctively, sat down next to me. She trembled, her face gray with fear. I heard the men talk about suicide again. "Let's make it fast. We'll be killed anyway. . . . The Russians will take it out on us after what we did to them. . . . They'll torture and kill us when they find out who we are." The rest of the words trailed off. With my blood pounding in my ears, I heard only fragments. The words of the SS man at the hospital came back to me. "What we did . . . rape . . . shoot the swine . . . kill. Fast, come on, do it!"

As I regained my breath I felt far away, and their voices grew faint. I realized that I did not know any of the six people I was with at the forest's edge. The mousy-haired woman with her pointed nose no longer looked familiar and trustworthy. I disliked her. She disgusted me. It was light now, the sun shone into the meadow that sloped down toward the highway we had left. We could not see the road because it lay behind a rise in the meadow. I looked over at a black-haired, sallow-faced soldier who held a pistol in his hand. He had taken off his belt and was fumbling in his holster for something. Bullets, I realized. "I have enough for all of us," he said aloud. "Seven." I looked, and they were six. So he was including me. I watched as his slim fingers flipped the cylinder and loaded his pistol. My panic faded away and every detail of the scene around me came into vivid focus.

My feet planted firmly on the earth of the path that ran along the forest's edge, sitting on the rise formed by needles, brown leaves, and small brush, I looked away into the valley. I leaned back against a tree and felt the rough bark through my jacket, hearing the group as if from far away. My palms on a soft bed of moss and leaves, I felt the full sun on my hands now, and I looked down at a few early dandelions in the grass by the path. Fully awake now, every one of my senses keenly awake, I gazed into the spring world, into the valley with its distant mountains shrouded in a pale morning haze, fading into ever fainter bluish grays. I marveled at the yellow sea of flowers in the meadow. *Himmelsschlüssel,* I said to myself, wild primroses, keys to heaven in German. I savored the *mms* and the rounded, labial *lü* sound. A lark soared into the blue sky with a jubilant trill. A bird chirped and wrenched my gut. Suddenly the world was still except for the insistent murmuring of my companions. I felt alive. My heart started to race, and a surge of love for this morning valley rose up in me.

"I want to live!" Had I shouted these words? Fear. My heart pounded. "I don't want to die!" I don't think I screamed it aloud. "I don't belong with them. I haven't done anything. Why should I be shot!" And then I was running, ducking down for fear they would shoot me in the back. Was that a shot I heard? No. Falling, scrambling up again, running for my life. Nothing could be as bad as the death I was fleeing.

After I had gotten away and the shock had subsided, the entire suicide episode seemed as if I had imagined it. I am sure it happened, though, because I met the gray-faced HJ woman with her pointed nose again, three years later in West Germany, at the Bremen railroad station, in the winter of 1948. The group had not gone through with their suicide plan after all, she said.

"The group broke up once you broke the spell by running off."

My escape from this destructive group fantasy became a source of my later refusal to participate in anything resembling a group. For many years I prided myself on not belonging to anything—not to a family, a group of friends, a professional organization, not to anything that would bind me to anyone. Since that day in May and for years afterward, I felt invulnerable. Nothing would harm me. I would come through any experience unscathed, untouched, unhurt. Other people might commit suicide, not me. Other people could be shot, not me. Other women could be raped, not me. Other people might fail, not me. I trusted my mental and physical endurance, of getting through whatever danger confronted me, of knowing instinctively what to do, how to survive. It never occurred to me to hesitate or doubt my luck. I felt protected by an almost magical invulnerability. I was always going to be a survivor. This conviction sustained me for the next twenty years.

I returned to the road and melted into the crowd. The invading army had ordered the refugees off the road. Unit after unit of the invaders went past us, and none even gave us a look. Most of the fleeing German soldiers had changed into civilian clothes grabbed from possessions that the refugees had thrown into the ditches overnight. Others hid in the forest up the hill from where I had just come. Now and then, once the first units had passed, a Russian soldier broke rank, either to ask for a watch or some jewelry from a refugee or to pick up an object he fancied. Once, we even laughed at a Russian soldier as he pushed the tenth or eleventh watch up his arm. He grinned back at us.

From the time I escaped the suicide group till I reached home sometime in late May or early June, my memory holds only a whirl of scenes and images. For every other part of this year, I have a clear idea of the sequence of events and some memory of what I saw and experienced, but I lack a point of orientation for these days. This reflects, I believe, the chaos I experienced both within and outside myself. Part of the time, no doubt, I was in shock and numb with terror. Except for the suicide group, I do not believe that I was ever actually in danger for my life, nor was I raped or otherwise harmed. But for the first time since beginning this account, I feel reluctant to continue writing. I don't want to return to the chaos I lived through then.

Once the first units of Russian invaders had passed, we milled around. I looked at the ditches that lined the road and rummaged among the suitcases, blankets, pots and pans, bedding and toys that had been discarded by the fleeing refugees. I picked up a knapsack, some men's shoes, an old sweater, and an army blanket for the coming night.

One vivid image stayed with me of a dead white horse among the heaps of suitcases, torn bedding, discarded uniforms, thrown-away foodstuffs, and other debris in the roadside ditch. Its head, teeth bared, lay on its side on a bole of grass; a leaden, silvery-white open eye stared at the sky, as if in accusation. The image of that accusing eye stayed with me for years. I also remember a slim, twelve-year-old baby-faced boy picking up a pistol German soldiers had thrown away. A heavy older woman in a black peasant skirt and shawl tried to wrest it away from him, hitting him. "Put that down, Karlchen. Do you want to get shot?" A Russian soldier walks up to them. My heart skips a beat. Will he shoot? No. The boy throws away the pistol and the soldier picks it up.

Still another scene: I am looking for my hostel companions, keeping to the side of the road as I search the faces of the refugees. My eyes scan for them among wrecked horse-drawn wagons and overturned handcarts, castoff featherbeds and boxes, but I cannot find them. I look up at the road just as another wave of the Russians has passed. A small group of men in striped prison outfits drag themselves after the Russians, followed by women in loose, dirty dresses, and girls my age in rags. They drag dirty blankets. Emaciated, weary, hair shorn, they stagger along, sometimes stopping to stare at us by the roadside. But they don't see us; their huge, dead eyes are glazed over. I sit down until they pass. I don't want to be seen. "Concentration camp inmates," the woman next to me says under her breath. "We must be close to a camp here. Those women haven't eaten anything for weeks." I had heard Mother's customers and her officer friends talk of camps in the east, in occupied Poland, but this horror? My mind stopped and I refused to take in the full extent of what I saw as I continued to look for my companions.

Finally I flung myself down next to a group of girls and boys and stayed with them at the roadside. As we waited for the next wave of Russian soldiers to pass, we began to talk. The boys, all sturdy and still boisterous at fourteen years of age, had been drafted by the HJ in January to dig trenches. In the confusion of flight they had lost contact with their families and were trying to find them. Of the girls, only one stands out to me: Ellen. Like the boys, she was younger than I, fourteen; unlike them, she was frail and terrified. With long, straight hair the color of dark honey gathered in a ponytail, and huge, anxious, amber-colored eyes, she looked like a waif lost in the wilderness. She could not remember how she had been separated from her mother during the turmoil of the flight from her hometown, Ohlau, not far from my own. She did not know what had happened to her father. He had been drafted just before they left her hometown. As she talked in soft, perfect German, we all began to feel protective of her.

I don't remember if it was the first day of the invasion, or the second, or the third, when the Russian army had finally passed us and we could use the road again. Two of the boys in our group went ahead to scout out our location. They came back and reported that a railroad station with several trains waiting was just two kilometers ahead. Although some of the refugees turned around and went back the way we had come, our small group of five or six kids decided we would try to get to the railroad station and see if we could stay overnight in a freight car.

We reached the train tracks just before nightfall and followed them until we arrived at a train yard. There a number of trains were parked, some freight trains, some passenger trains, all of them without locomotives. We pounded at the doors of the freight train, asking if there was room for a few of us. We went along two of the passenger trains without anyone rolling down their windows or opening their doors. In the middle of a passenger train, at a mail and baggage wagon, a man in an undershirt, missing an arm, obviously a German soldier who had thrown away his tunic, stood looking out the open door.

"Well, in back of the baggage and parcel section," he said, "there are shelves and pigeonholes for letters and cabinets where the mail crew kept their provisions and personal stuff. We could probably fit you in there. You are small enough."

They were four of them, all wounded, all dressed in various pieces of uniforms, who had come this far in a hospital train. Those among them who could walk had left the train before the Russians overtook it. Three of the men, one whose leg had been amputated and two with belly shots, were bedded down on straw and blankets on the floor of the baggage section. The fourth, the one-armed man at the door, had stayed with his buddies because they had no one else to look after them. It was not the hospital train I had been hoping to find, but at this point any shelter would do. Ellen and I promised the soldier, "We'll help you to take care of the three wounded men." The boys added, "We'll scout for food and water tomorrow."

Ellen, the boys, the other girl, and I climbed into the back of the baggage section and soon were fast asleep in spite of our hunger. I don't remember who gave us blankets. I woke up several times with my stomach growling to hear cries and shouts coming from the other wagons. I was too exhausted to care what it was all about. I don't remember how long we were parked together with the other trains in this train yard or even the name of the station; it was somewhere in the neighborhood of Gablonz, on the Czech side of the Silesian mountains.

In the mornings, as long as the supply lasted, the soldiers shared their breakfast with us, leftovers from their hospital provisions, some hard bread and a canister full of artificial marmalade. Then Ellen and I went to look for bathrooms and for water to bring back to sponge-bathe "our patients." A long queue stood waiting at the filthy station bathrooms, and it took ages to get in. "The Russians searched the trains last night and took all the men away," an elderly woman said. So that's what last night's commotion had been about.

"They are taking them to prisoner-of-war camps, even the old men." Finally, after an hour or so of waiting, we made it to the toilets and sinks. Having neither soap nor towels, we rinsed our faces and hands in cold water. We filled several empty marmalade canisters the soldiers had given us with water and lugged them back with us. We repeated the toilet, washing, and water-fetching ritual every morning. Then Ellen—who learned fast—and I washed the three wounded men, emptied their one bedpan and the urinal, and I changed their dressings. Fortunately they still had a supply of sterile dressings and bandages in a metal case.

On our first day in the mail car, the one-armed man asked me how old I was. "Eighteen," I lied, hoping that he would trust me with the care of his buddies. "I served as a Red Cross nurse in Habelschwerdt hospital. I left there when they shipped the wounded to the west." He accepted my story without question. From then on, I kept to the age I had told the soldier, thinking that being taken for an adult would give me greater authority and freedom to move about.

After washing up, several of the boys went foraging for food. Most of the time they returned empty handed and we went hungry. Once they went into town and returned beaten up; they had been recognized as HJ members because they still wore parts of their uniforms, although without insignia. After that we restricted all sorties to the industrial sheds around the station. In one of them the boys discovered some discarded German army supplies. They returned surreptitiously from the shed with tins of dried milk, egg powder, and bags of dried vegetables. A later haul brought us several sides of bacon. Since we had no means of cooking anything, we chewed dried vegetables together with bites of bacon and mixed the egg and milk powders in water. Food dominated our thoughts and conversations. The first few days, we went along the trains to see if we recognized anyone we knew. One of the boys found his grandmother among the refugees in our train and happily left us for her. The other girl departed for a boyfriend. I don't know how long we lived in the mail wagon. Was it two weeks or three? Most days I spent lying on my blanket dozing and being hungry. After we told the soldiers our stories, there was not much to talk about except food.

On one of the first nights, the Russian soldiers stationed in barracks not far from the station were celebrating. Several came knocking at the wagons filled with refugees looking for German soldiers but also calling out, "Come, Frau," and dragging screaming women with them into the woods. We had anticipated such visits, and every night the soldier with the amputated leg moved himself next to the door, blocking it with his body. Ellen and I crawled into a space below the cabinets, and the boys bedded down wrapped in their blankets in front of us. When several of the Russians rolled back our door that night and shone in a flashlight, they saw only the wounded soldiers and the boys. Motioning the one-legged man by the door to move so that they could investigate further, he stretched his stump toward them, signaling that he could not move by himself. The Russians left it at that. All through the night, we heard women crying out, men cursing, children screaming, and wagon doors rolling open and shut. I held on to Ellen and covered her mouth so that her sobs would not give us away.

My understanding of the risk of being raped has changed over the years since 1945. Then I was terrified of the Russian soldiers, as a precaution dressed as a boy, and was firmly convinced that our fear was not based merely on Nazi propaganda, rumor, or our overwrought imaginations. During the postwar years, as I came to understand how the racist Nazi propaganda had portrayed the Russian population, namely, as lewd, rapacious Mongolian hordes, worse than beasts, *Untermenschen*—men lower than animals—I began to doubt that the danger of rape had actually been that great. To be sure, I had heard the women scream, but I had escaped it. Some of my and Mother's friends, some of the women in my hometown, had not. In the 1990s, when studies began to appear about the women and girls raped during the fall of Berlin from April to June 1945, I began to realize that my fear had been real enough and that my precautions had protected me. In Berlin, 7.1 percent of women of childbearing age had been seen in clinics after one or several rapes by Russian soldiers. How many did not report or did not seek medical help is not known. The number of rapes that contemporaries in 1945 cited—60 to 70 percent of women—was exaggerated. But the number of rapes, pregnancies, and health consequences documented by researchers in the 1990s was still considerable. No one knows how likely rape was for the refugee populations wandering like us in the countryside or living in temporary shelters where it was difficult to hide. At any rate, all through our stay at the railroad station we heard marauding Russians search the trains and take away the women. The fear of rape did not leave me until we got to western Germany in August 1946.

Rumors spread like wildfire among the refugees waiting in the trains: that a woman from this or that train had been killed during a rape; that the Americans would advance into Czechoslovakia; that the water in the washrooms was contaminated; that the international Red Cross would distribute food; that the trains would go to the border and everybody would be told to return to their homes; that the wounded soldiers would be taken to a hospital. The last two rumors turned out to be true, because one day a locomotive appeared. Our car was connected to it and without warning it began to pull out of the yard. It gained speed rapidly, thick forests speeding past us on both sides. Looking out the open door, I felt reassured by the changing greens of the woods, the dark green of crowded firs alternating with reddish-green spruce, yellowish-green birches, and with deep green oaks and maples. The woods filled me with a sense of tranquility. A few years later, when I read Mörike's tale of Mozart's journey to Prague, I recalled these dense forests and the peace seeing them had given me. As suddenly as it had begun to move, the train stopped at a small, yellow-brick stationhouse. Czech militia appeared from the stationmaster's office and a voice bellowed in German, "Everybody who can move, get off the train!" The militiamen herded the crowd of refugees to a road and pointed toward the east: "Go home!"

We hesitated, not wanting to leave the wounded soldiers to an unknown fate. Several militiamen came over and motioned to us, "Off, off. Wounded stay. Be okay. We take them to hospital." We climbed down reluctantly and joined the other refugees. The militia shouted, "Go! Go!" We began to move toward a guardhouse, passed a red and white barrier, and realized that we were back in Germany. After another four hours of walking, first uphill, then down, we arrived at the town of Waldenburg, center of the Lower Silesian mining industry. Someone directed us to a school building that served as a refugee center.

The school was packed, but we found space in a classroom upstairs with some thirty straw sacks on the floor for bedding. We took the last five by the door, as an older woman began shouting at us, since most of us still wore pieces of HJ uniforms. Her theme was "today's youth"—a kind of railing against young people that I would hear frequently over the next few years. It was an intergenerational anger and blame game by means of which each generation tried to make the other responsible for Nazism and the defeat of Germany.

"You just push yourselves in here without a greeting, without even asking permission if you can stay here. The HJ has completely corrupted you. Where are your parents? Show some respect for your elders!" She raged on and would not stop. To my own surprise, I lost my temper and started yelling back.

"So now it is our fault that we don't know where our families are? You bet we don't have any respect for you. Why should we? Sure, we were HJ. Sure, we loved Hitler. Until a few weeks ago, you all said you did, too."

I don't remember what else I said, but five minutes later I felt ashamed about my ranting. I left the room and considered what to do now. Ellen and I hung around the schoolyard late into the night until everyone was asleep. I remembered that Mother had had a friend in Waldenburg, Frau Kovak, the wife of a miner, but I did not know the address. The next day I went to the town hall and found that, fortunately, they still had an address book. I located the woman an hour later and asked if I could stay a few days until I found out what had happened to Mother and my brothers. She welcomed me, although she and her invalid husband had little room to spare in their one-bedroom apartment. They even let me bring Ellen, her amber eyes still wide with fear that I had deserted her when I went off in the morning from the refugee encampment. They shared their food with us until we left.

One episode of my stay with the Kovaks stands out, a grotesque return to the normalcy of a Sunday dinner. Herr Kovak and their neighbors had found a dead horse in their street a few weeks earlier. They had slaughtered the animal and divided the meat among them. For Sunday dinner, Frau Kovak made the typical Silesian fare of a roast with dumplings and red cabbage. Sharing the common aversion to horsemeat, I gagged at the thought of eating it. But the delicate texture of the meat, its delicious flavor, and my hunger made me dig into the hearty portion Frau Kovak put on my plate. I gorged myself on two helpings, but my stomach rebelled, no longer used to fat and bulk. I made it to the kitchen sink just in time.

Sometime during the dinner I had a conversation with Herr Kovak. I remember it clearly because he was the first adult whose criticism of the Nazis cut through my defenses. Still mouthing what I had learned in the HJ and still trying to be loyal to the Nazis, I argued that Hitler's labor policies had ended the unemployment of the Great Depression, that workers' lives had improved and that they had supported Hitler.

"That's the propaganda line you were fed," Herr Kovak replied calmly. "Our lives as miners"—he had worked in the Waldenburg coal mines—"certainly did not improve. We did not support Hitler. We kept quiet because we did not want to be beaten up or sent to a camp."

Ellen and I stayed with the Kovaks three or four more days, during which we learned that it would take months to reestablish telephone contact as well as mail delivery and train service. We had heard no news of what had happened since the Russians overtook us, only rumors. We had no idea if the war was over or what our future held. But on one of those days, as I walked by a street display case that used to display newspapers or public announcements by the authorities, I stopped to join a crowd of people to read a proclamation by the Russian occupation authority. It said something like, "Now that the war is over, German citizens should return to their place of origin." I did not take in what else it said. So this is the end, I thought. Not death or Siberia. Just go home.

Since Ellen was from Ohlau, a small town some twelve miles from my hometown toward the Oder River, we decided to hike back home together. I promised her that I would go halfway to Ohlau with her so that she would find her way. We thanked the Kovaks and said goodbye to the boys at the camp whose way home led in a direction different from ours.

We set out early in the morning. I figured that it would be a three-day hike to Strehlen and would take Ellen another day to reach Ohlau. Herr Kovac took us to the Reichenberg Road out of Waldenburg, and after that I found my way like a homing pigeon. As we left the town, its mineshafts and its hills behind us, Russian military vehicles overtook us several times. We decided to look for a back road and detour around villages so as not to meet any Russian soldiers. The sounds of the women screaming in the trains still rang in our ears.

The first village we passed lay silent and empty, no people, no domestic animals even. Scattered over the road through the village we saw only straw, horse manure, clothes, uniforms, blankets, empty shells, and army mess gear, remnants of the flight from the approaching enemy. Cast-off rain-soaked boxes and old suitcases told us that the civilians had not yet returned. The seams of Ellen's shoes were torn even before we left Waldenburg. Soon she began to limp. For a while we sat by a brook on the roadside so that she could bathe her sore feet. Luckily, she found an old rucksack with a pair of tennis shoes in it on the road. Though a size too large, the shoes were better than her own pair, and she put them on.

As we hiked along, I remembered that the Zopten, a mountain range in front of the Waldenburg Mountains, should be to our left—first ahead of us and then, as we approached Strehlen, behind us. By late afternoon the Zopten had come into view against the northeastern sky. What from home looked like two pale blue triangles, one smaller, a larger one joined to it, I recognized here

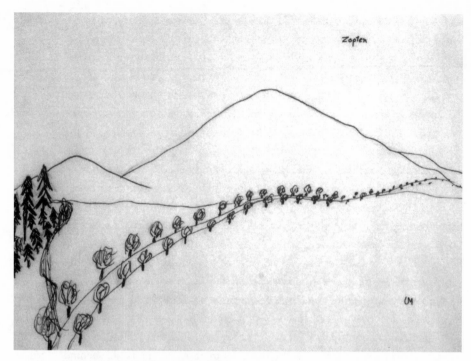

Zopten Mountain, drawing by author

as the silhouette of one bulky mountain with a smaller peak leaning against a larger one. Its mass felt as familiar to me as a childhood friend, and, the two triangles becoming ever more distinct, its outline accompanied us all the way home.

Only once, when we heard a truck in the distance, did we hide in the ditch by the road until it passed us and drove out of sight. At nightfall, exhausted, we came to a farm on the outskirts of a larger village, where we spotted a woman and several children. We entered a large farmyard and asked the owner, who had returned just the previous day, if we could stay in the barn. Except for the woman and her children, the farmhouse, barns, and stables were uninhabited. There was not even a dog. Dirty straw, manure all over the yard. Straggling grass grew between the cobblestones.

"We found only the buildings, unspeakably filthy with spoiled food, broken crockery, ripped apart featherbeds, heaped with refuse," the woman told us. "The soldiers of both armies killed all our farm animals. We don't have much to eat, but you are welcome to stay." She gave us some bread and herb tea before we bedded down in the hay. She warned us not to drink from the well. She did not know whether the passing armies might have polluted it.

The second day we stuck to the main road and by now had left the last hills behind us. Only now and then, when we heard a vehicle some distance off, did we hide, either lying flat in the roadside ditch or, if a stand of trees seemed dense enough, among the trees. The second night we reached Senitz and the farm of my relatives. I hardly recognized the yard, so covered was it with broken-down wagons and heaps of refuse. As we entered the farmyard a militiaman met us, and we were about to run from him when Aunt Marianne called me to stop. The militia had no interest in us. They were Poles and had come to tell my relatives that the family would be relocated to another farm in the morning. I don't recall what my relatives said to us or what we found out about them. I was still in a daze; the only thing I took in was that they did not know anything about my mother and brothers.

We started up again early the next morning, and I figured that we could reach Strehlen more easily if we did not take the road but went along the railroad tracks that I knew from my visits to Senitz. That was shorter and safer, as far as danger from passing Russians was concerned. We reckoned that we could get off the tracks and hide if we heard a train approaching. Most probably there would not be any, since railroad service had not been reestablished. We had a clear view of the countryside as the tracks were slightly elevated above the surrounding fields. On some of the fields we passed, winter wheat had come up, and its foot-high, deep green rows sparkled in the sun. Other fields lay fallow, and weeds had begun to grow. We soon found walking on the tracks difficult and tiring. We either had to jump and skip a tie, or we had to walk balancing ourselves on one of the rails. The bridge over a creek had been blown up, but the creek was low and we crossed it easily. From then on we knew that no train could pass us, and we felt safe.

The first station building we passed stared at us with burned-out windows, its bricks riddled with bullet and grenade holes. We realized that we were now passing though territory where fighting had taken place recently. The church steeples and houses of the villages we saw in the distance had lost their roofs, and their blackened rafters pierced the sky. Burned barns and fragments of brick buildings stood like empty shells. As we entered Strehlen at the crossing near Railroad Hill, a man signaled to us from a distance, waving both of his arms in a frenzy. As we began running to him, he frantically motioned us to the side. When we stopped and looked over to the side he was pointing to, we heard him shout excitedly, "Get off the rails, off the track, the line is mined!"

We jumped and fell to the side of the tracks in fright. Shaken, we sat in the grass by the tracks for a while. I reckoned that we had been too light to set off one of the mines, but that did not lessen my feeling of shock that we had just escaped being blown up. When we finally walked on, we met a woman whom I recognized as Frau Fischer, one of Mother's former customers.

"Your mother got here yesterday," she called out, "and the Baronie is still standing!"

I started crying from the double shock and did not stop crying till I reached our house. Ellen trudged behind me, weeping to keep me company.

I could see the damage to the town from up Railroad Hill. The towers of Great Church and of City Hall had disappeared. All the houses along Nimpscher Street and Münsterberger Street were heaps of rubble. Lenau's corner pub and the houses on the corner had been dynamited, leveled by tanks, and cleared away. The house where Aunt Lene's apartment had stood was a burned-out shell. Walking along Münsterberger Street toward City Hall Square, steel girders and beams obstructed our course. We climbed over cascades of bricks. All the houses of City Hall Square had burned down, their blackened, bullet-riddled, grenade-shattered façades still standing. The dynamited City Hall covered most of the south of the square, a huge mountain of rubble that had buried St. Florian's statue as well as the town's fountain. Entering Grosse Kirchstrasse we found stores and houses turned into heaps of brick, concrete, and half-burned beams. The tall bell tower of Great Church had crushed the Gothic nave of the church; the sky shone through the blackened arches of the crypt's windows. The lindens at the church porch had been transformed into leafless scorched stumps. At the end of Grosse Kirchstrasse stood one lone house, unharmed except for broken windows and bullet holes in the plaster. It was our house, the Baronie.

It was early June when I arrived at home. Mother and Werner had hiked in from Lomnitz the day before. They had not left Lomnitz the morning after I tried to get them to come with me, as Mother had promised. Except for their hosts' losing their last cow to the invaders, and the women having to hide from Russian soldiers during the first onslaught of the invasion, the arrival of the Russian army had been uneventful for them. A feeling of being safe at last came over me when I discovered that the Gurns, our landlords, were back as well. Home, finally, home.

We found our apartment in shocking shape. First German and then Russian troops had camped out in it, leaving behind on the floor food leftovers, now covered with mold, mixed in with straw, hay, even horse manure. A two-foot-deep layer of this refuse covered the floor. Intermingled in this mess were rags, military camping equipment, and plaster that had fallen from the ceiling from the impact of grenades. All the closets and cabinets had been torn open, their contents emptied onto the floor. Feathers were strewn over everything from a few featherbeds we had left behind, adding an almost whimsical touch to the scene. In the kitchen, dishes and dry goods from the kitchen cupboard had been scattered; glass containers of preserves and molasses had been smashed, their contents poured on the wooden floorboards. The sticky mass of syrup, glass shards, and bits of crockery made it difficult to sift through the mess for anything that might still prove usable.

For the first few nights we slept rolled up in soiled army blankets on top of the mountains of refuse. Gradually, with the help of shovels and buckets, we removed the debris out into the sandpit in the Gurns' garden. We soon realized that smaller inhabitants had taken up residence—rats, mice, and fleas. One night I woke with a start, a mouse in my hand that had scampered over my face. Once we moved the refuse out and set a few traps, we got rid of at least the rodent population. Neither electricity nor gas nor water service had been reestablished. Fortunately, the daylight hours were long, and the Gurn garden contained a well with a hand pump. After drinking its water for a few days, Frau Gurn, looking down into the well, discovered a dead Russian soldier in its depths. I don't know what happened to the body. I only know that for the next two months everyone got their water from the town well at the corner of City Hall Square and Horst Wessel Street. Its water ran constantly, pouring onto the pavement. As I hauled my two water buckets over four long city blocks, I had time to wonder at the speed with which Nazi names disappeared as if they had never existed. Horst Wessel Street again became Paul Ehrlich Street; Adolf Hitler Street returned to Linden Street. I thought it despicable that no one seemed to want to acknowledge that the Nazis had ever existed. Going for water always meant waiting in a long queue, because this well was the only clean water source for the town. Were any of the people standing in line aware of the irony that their only famous son, the Nobel Prize winner Paul Ehrlich, now provided a necessity of life for those who had forsaken him during the Nazi years? I certainly was not.

In the first days after our return, a few of the other families who had lived in the Baronie came back. On my second or third day home, Aunt Lene and her mother, Aunt Martha, arrived at our doorstep. Their house having burned down, it was a matter of course that Mother invited them to stay with us. I felt apprehensive about their moving in, as my relationship to both women had been poor all through my childhood. Gradually the apartment house filled up. Families who had lived there before the invasion took in friends and relations whose residences had been destroyed. About half of the former residents never returned; strangers who had lost their homes took over their apartments and possessions. Some days, Ellen and I scouted the town to find out who had come back and which buildings were still standing, keeping well away from Railroad Station Street, where the Russians had taken over a house as headquarters for the town commander.

The three-story façade of the burned-out Red School across the street from us threatened to collapse, so I hesitated to mount the one staircase still standing, which led up to my old classroom. Looking at it, I had a vague sense of guilt that the school had been consumed by fire, because I had wished for just such an event throughout my childhood. All the other schools in town, except the high school out on Breslauer Street, had likewise burned down. But the outlying districts past the center of town stood intact, their houses pockmarked by shells. All the houses on Promenade Street to Woiselwitz Street, Water Street, Old Town Street to the Ohle River, and Mill Street were in ruins, some burned down, a few, like the Eisenberg residence next door, flattened by bombs. On Mill Street, Herr Breiler's watermill still stood as one of the exceptions, and the miller, as Mother informed me, had returned. The chestnut trees in the schoolyards and cemeteries had survived and were in bloom. The lindens on Promenade Street had not been damaged. Occasionally, on rainy June evenings, their honeyed fragrance proved stronger than the stench from burned brick, mortar, and blackened beams that drifted over from Grosse Kirchstrasse. I often went by the Boxhammer property looking for Hanne and Rita, but their apartments were burned out. Sometimes people chalked notices on the burned walls, saying where they had gone, but not the Boxhammers. My short excursions left me depleted of energy and depressed. Despite later searches through the International Red Cross, I never found out what happened to Hanne or Rita. Neither they nor their families ever surfaced.

Ellen had not left for home after a short rest, as we had planned. The open sores that covered her feet after our three-day walk home needed to heal first. She helped with the cleaning, but as the days went by she became more and more lethargic and distraught. At night she screamed in her nightmares, and when I woke her she could not stop crying. Sometimes during the day she talked incoherent nonsense, as if she were delirious. My aunts agitated for her to strike out for home and find out what had happened to her family.

"We don't have enough food for us as it is," Aunt Lene said to me.

I felt like saying that the food we lived on was not hers to give or withhold. We all lived off Mother's potatoes, carrots, beets, and the preserves that had been stored as winter supplies in the cellar.

Finally, when her feet had healed, I gave in to the pressure and told Ellen, feeling like a coward, that she should make the effort to find out what had happened to her parents. She agreed listlessly. I had promised her, when we set out from Waldenburg, that I would accompany her halfway to Ohlau, her hometown. We set out early the next morning, after a night during which she awoke crying several times. This must have been about two weeks after we had arrived in Strehlen. Both of us were silent and morose. We walked past the abandoned brickyard at the edge of town. I steered us past the village of Kuschlau, where one could miss the turnoff to the Ohlau road. A few miles after we reached the Ohlau road, I felt nauseated and had a headache, and sat down on the grass of the roadside ditch thinking that I could not walk another mile. We had gone only a quarter of the way to Ohlau.

"Ellen, I don't think I have the strength to take you halfway and get myself back home again," I said, then gagged and threw up. She did not answer me, and I rationalized away my worry about her. She acted alert, and surely she could not fail to reach her destination if she just followed the main road with its signs. To my relief she finally said, "I'll be fine. Don't worry, I'll get there. I'll let you know somehow that I got there once I am home."

All the way back to Strehlen I reproached myself that I had not kept my promise to her. I arrived at home exhausted, my head hurting worse than it ever had before.

When I still could hardly move two days later, Mother consulted with Frau Dunisch, who had returned at about the same time as we had. They took me to the old Catholic hospital on Cloister Street, where Frau Dunisch knew the head nurse, Sister Anna. None of the local physicians had returned to town. In fact, almost the entire middle and upper middle class had departed for western

German destinations in January and February. Everyone who had relatives beyond the Elbe River, and had either means to leave or the imagination to conceive of what might happen if the Russians invaded, had fled. The Catholic priests and nuns at the local convent had stayed with their congregations. Sister Anna knew that a physician was expected from Breslau within the next few days. Meanwhile, the staff would keep me under observation. Aside from an incapacitating headache, I had the diarrhea all of us suffered from and a below-normal temperature.

Sister Bertha, the floor nurse, thought I was taking up space that could be better used by someone in greater need. After three or four days, my temperature suddenly shot up to 104. Sister Bertha, thinking I had cheated, measured again. For ten days my temperature stayed at 104–5. At some point the physician arrived and diagnosed typhoid fever after one look at my blackened oral mucous membranes and swollen neck glands. The other patients who had shared my room were moved as soon as the staff knew what ailed me. Since the hospital lacked sufficient staff, Mother came in daily and took over most of my care. I lost consciousness after the third day of the high fever and regained it only a few times. I remember once, when I woke up struggling for breath, my heart racing, that I was afraid I was going to die. I breathed more easily when Mother held me up in a sitting position.

"You have pneumonia and a kidney inflammation in addition to the typhoid fever," she told me.

Another time, a sharp pain on my neck roused me. My doctor stood over me, having just lanced a huge boil below my ear. I sank back into unconsciousness as the pulsing ache of the boil and its pressure subsided.

My temperature eventually came down to below normal in the mornings but shot up again to 104 late in the afternoon. During that phase of four to five days, I was delirious most of the time, haunted by the most colorful and vivid hallucinations. I strolled through an exotic garden with brilliantly green fruit trees laden with tropical fruit, costly, rare delicacies for a child raised in a northern clime: oranges, mandarins, bananas, apricots, mangos; again and again oranges, huge oranges of glorious color. I just needed to stretch out my hand, and I could almost reach them. But every time I was just about to touch an orange, the scene changed. Frustrated, crying with thirst, I found myself in my hospital bed again, my throat sore, burning, wanting something to drink.

At first Mother brought me juices and fruit from Herr Breiler's garden. But as my diarrhea got worse, the doctor did not allow me to have fruit or anything to drink. Mother swabbed my mouth with a wet washcloth, but that did not assuage the thirst. Driven by my thirst, when no one held me down, hallucinations of orange trees in Africa made me get out of bed to reach the fruit.

One day Sister Bertha found me collapsed on the floor after I had tried to climb onto a high closet shelf to take down my suitcase. Furious, she calmed down only when the doctor explained to her that I was not conscious of what I was doing. I had dreamed that Uncle Willi had invited me to come to Africa, and that the ship was going to take me there. I had the ship hallucination a number of times, and just when I was about to board and looked up the gang-way, the ceiling of my hospital room, coved with scalloped moldings, came into view again. Several times I tried to bribe the doctor and Sister Bertha, telling them that I would send them coffee, real African coffee from Kenya, if they would just let me board the ship. Then the world steadied; my fever leveled off. I was so exhausted that I could hardly lift a hand and simply dozed the days away, waiting for Mother to come.

Toward the end of my hospital stay, I was half asleep when Mother came in with a letter from Ohlau. It was from a woman whose name we did not recognize. Mother read it aloud to me. The woman introduced herself as a neighbor of Ellen's family. Ellen had stayed with her because neither her mother nor her father had returned to Ohlau. Shortly after her arrival, going out one morning to see if she could find her family, Ellen had run into a group of Russian soldiers.

They gang-raped her. A few days later, she fell ill. High fever, typhoid. The neighbor took her to the typhoid ward. She died a week later. I did not cry then; I only felt terribly guilty for not having accompanied and protected her. As I am writing her story now, I am crying. A girl alone and on her own had no chance of surviving. Without Mother nursing me through typhoid fever, I felt for years, I would not have survived either.

Mother took me home on a stretcher in a hand-drawn cart a few days later. Shortly after I came home from the hospital, both my aunts fell ill with typhoid fever. Fortunately for Mother, both of their cases were milder than mine, and they were up and about two weeks later. In the course of the summer many of the residents of our apartment house fell ill with typhoid fever. Several died, and the occupation authorities put up a large yellow warning sign: "Caution, Typhoid!" We were grateful for the sign because it protected us, at least for a while, from the marauding and revenge-seeking bands of

Ellen about to run from soldiers, bronze sculpture, 1995, by author

former slave laborers the Nazis had brought to Silesia. Mother thought she had brought me home to die, as the doctor held out little hope that I would get well. At the very least I would be left with damaged heart valves unless I grew a lot. I had to learn to walk again, but gradually, as late summer turned into fall, I regained strength.

To obtain food supplies Mother and Aunt Lene started sewing for the Russian soldiers. They made alterations to their uniforms, fixed buttons, or made dresses for a few of the women soldiers in exchange for butter, meat rations, bread, and cigarettes. In September the invading Russian army, except for a small command post, marched back to Russia. Some of the men for whom they had just finished alterations returned and, threatening us with rifle butts, confiscated both sewing machines. Fortunately, some of Mother's and Aunt Lene's German customers had kept their machines and lent them theirs so that they could resume work a few days later.

For days the departing Russian army divisions paraded down Grosse Kirchstrasse, turned right into Promenade Street, and marched out of town on Woiselwitz Street. From my bed I could hear them singing and was fascinated and frightened. It was dangerous, we felt, to draw their attention by looking at the marching columns out the window. Werner finally found a way to satisfy my curiosity. A high, wide wall separated the Gurn property from the Eisenbergs', the stonemason's property. In back, close to our bedroom window, it was easy to climb the wall. The wall terminated in a kind of triangular riser that overlooked the intersection of Grosse Kirchstrasse and Promenade that we could hide behind. Lying on my belly, peeking over the riser, I watched as unit after unit of troops passed beneath my perch. Musical bands with triangles, flutes, and hornpipes preceded some units. I knew them as Cossacks from encyclopedia illustrations. Some groups wore colorful native costumes instead of uniforms. Some were led by a small group of singers with sonorous bass voices. Indoors, I had been afraid of their singing and of the rhythmic stomp of their boots on the pavement; now in the open air, seeing them march by, I was entranced by the festive spectacle of a victorious army.

Until I wrote this account, I never really mourned the destruction of my childhood world and the loss of my childhood friends. I never understood until I wrote of Ellen that she represented my teenage self without the shell of numbness and toughness I had assumed. Instead of mourning, the dread of approaching catastrophe, the horror of bleeding, mangled, dying bodies, the sense of being abandoned, the fear of being raped, and the helplessness of being caught in social chaos haunted my nightmares for years. The safer my environment and the better my personal situation became, the worse the nightmares got. I dreaded two repetitive nightmares more than others. In one, I walk through a desolate village of burned-out houses. It is winter; the straggling trees at the roadside are dead. I am cold, and something sinister and catastrophic looms ahead in icy fog. I don't know what it is but I feel an unspeakable dread. I want to scream, I struggle to call out, but I cannot. In another dream I jump from railroad tie to railroad tie. I sense danger and know that the line is mined, but I don't know where the mines are. A man, a soldier in a black uniform, suddenly comes up behind me from out of nowhere. I try to run but my legs will not obey. I wake up as he grabs me. The nightmares receded only when, with time and support from friends, I could accept how terrified and how helpless I had actually been.

Chapter Ten

MY HOMETOWN BECOMES POLISH, 1945–1946

A FEW WEEKS AFTER THE RUSSIAN ARMY MOVED OUT during the late summer of 1945, we heard that trucks were bringing in Polish families and Polish militia. The Russian town commander had stayed at his local headquarters on Railroad Station Street together with a small contingent of Russian occupation soldiers. At the time, we, the German population who had returned to Strehlen from the Silesian mountains, did not know what the Allies had decided at Yalta in February 1945—namely, that all territories on the east side of the Neisse/Oder rivers, that is, all of Silesia, parts of Brandenburg, all of Pomerania, and most of East Prussia, were promised to Poland, while the Russians laid claim to some East Prussian harbors on the Baltic. We also had no idea that the Potsdam Treaty, in the summer of 1945, gave these German territories to Poland, while Poland lost the Polish Ukraine that Stalin had won from Hitler after the German victory over Poland in 1939. We did not know that Sudeten Silesia, which Hitler had occupied in 1938, had been returned to Czechoslovakia. We also did not know that according to Article XIII of the treaty the Allies had decided that in the following months the German population of some six and a half million people was to be removed from these territories and resettled evenly over the western and eastern Allied occupation zones of Germany. The transfer of the German population was to ensure that the border conflicts that had led to World War II would never again recur. The eviction was to be "effected in an orderly and humane manner."

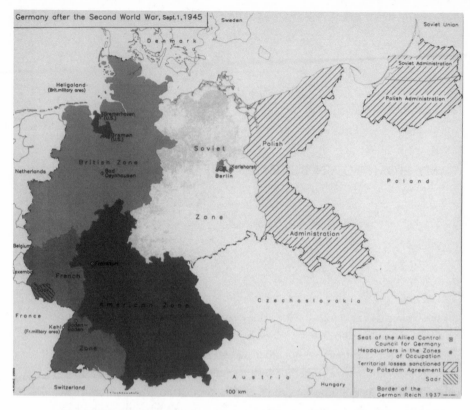

Map of Germany, September 1945, showing territories under Polish administration and the Occupation Zones. IEG Maps, Institute of European History, Mainz. Copyright A. Kunz, 2005

In the late summer of 1945, we gradually found out that the Poles who had come into our hometown were not former forced laborers who had stayed after the German defeat and taken over, with the consent of the Russian occupation forces, whatever businesses were left in town. The Polish families that now arrived hailed from Poland itself. Many of them, we found out gradually, had lost their homes in the Polish Ukraine. It was rumored that we were to live under Polish occupation in a Polish-administered zone and that the Polish newcomers were to settle in Silesia. But we were far too busy with mere survival to pay much attention to what the future might hold. Since the town center, with its shops and other businesses, administrative offices and savings banks, had burned down, the few remaining businesses—among them a grocery store and a bakery on Linden Street (formerly Adolf Hitler Street) and the internal revenue office near the railroad station—were taken over by Poles. A Polish militia commander had moved into a house down by the railroad station, and militia began to police the streets. The German population tried to keep out of their way because the militia picked up any Germans they found out in the street and herded them off to work cleaning the streets, unloading trucks, or clearing rubble.

But all of these changes, for the time being, remained rumors for us, because all the public announcements that began to be displayed in the town's kiosks were in Russian or Polish. And, at least in our house, the Baronie, the only house still standing on Promenade Street, no one read Polish or Russian. In the late summer and fall of 1945, the Baronie was still quarantined. Most of the families in the house had lost one or more family members to the typhoid epidemic. One entire family, the wife, the husband who had returned from the front, and their three-year-old daughter, died within a week, just after I got back from the hospital. In all, thirty of the ninety occupants who had crowded into the Baronie after our return died during the epidemic. Most were older residents and young children. Werner and I were the only young people left in the Baronie. Since we knew few of the new families well, their deaths did not affect us as they might have had they been our former neighbors. All we could really think about was that the yellow typhoid sign in Polish and Russian protected us from the militia and from plundering former forced laborers.

One late October afternoon, after the yellow typhoid sign had been removed from our apartment house, several militiamen herded Mother, Werner, my two aunts, and me at gunpoint from our kitchen and living room into our bedroom and Father's former office. We had just been preparing dinner. The militia men nailed the doors shut and sealed them with tape. They did not allow us to remove any of our possessions. It happened so quickly that we withdrew from the threatening rifles into the bedroom without even crying out. At the same time, other militia evicted the Gurns from their kitchen, living room, and bedrooms and restricted them to their former office, a windowless storeroom, and a former guestroom. I don't know how we acquired a stove, kitchen utensils, and sewing machines, which allowed us to turn Father's old office into a kitchen and sewing room. Nor do I know how the Gurns managed to obtain kitchen appliances and bedroom furniture. With the loss of our kitchens, both of our families had lost access to water. We were lucky that by this time the town had running water and that we could get it from an outlet in Herr Gurn's now unused stable in the backyard—his horses as well as the beer trucks had disappeared during the invasion. The eviction from part of our apartments brought about one advantageous change: the entire apartment house was now connected to the electric grid, which had been repaired. We had lived without electricity since our arrival, and with winter approaching, having electric light was almost compensation for our loss.

A few days after our eviction, a Polish couple moved into our kitchen and living room. The husband was the Polish militia commander's driver, and soon the backyard filled with various militia vehicles. Another Polish family, a woman pianist with a boy Werner's age and two daughters about my age, moved into the Gurns' kitchen, living room, and bedrooms. Polish families gradually took over several rooms in every apartment in the Baronie, while the Germans moved closer together. Polish customers began replacing the few Russians that still came occasionally. At first, neither Aunt Lene nor Mother dared demand payment for their dressmaking services. The first few customers paid whatever they felt like in produce, cigarettes, or a few zlotys. The two dressmakers established a going rate only gradually.

But whatever the two of them made from sewing did not suffice to feed us. During the time we lived among the Polish population, from the fall of 1945 to August 1946, we Germans lived a shadow existence. We did not receive rationing cards, nor could we earn zlotys or buy food. German reichsmarks could not be exchanged for zlotys, and we had no access to savings or accounts, since the town bank had been buried under City Hall tower. At any daylight hour the militia was liable to round us up from our houses, women, adolescents, and children alike, to clear away rubble or scrub militia headquarters. Most of us felt humiliated by the militia raids, but we submitted without protest.

Only a few of the older soldiers drafted in January for the home defense had returned, and they soon found out that they could survive only if they stayed hidden. The owner of the bicycle and radio shop, Herr Ernst, who had sold us our bikes and had moved in with a family upstairs, was one of these men who concealed themselves during raids. He was a bald, taciturn man, handy with any tool. He managed to make a living by repairing anything and everything for everyone in the house in exchange for a meal. Mother and Aunt Lene employed him to keep the barely functional replacement sewing machines running. All families had him make them carts and hand wagons from spare parts they found in the ruins, like the undercarriage and wheels of half-burned baby buggies. Everyone needed such wagons for fetching food from the countryside and for bringing home the firewood that we picked up from the ruins of dynamited houses or from gardens and parks all around town. In the course of the winter of 1945–46, we cut down every tree small enough to be hauled away quickly, before we could be caught by the militia.

Rumor had it that it was dangerous to speak German aloud in public because we could be robbed, beaten, or taken away to the militia prison. Since we had no access to a radio or newspaper, we lived off hearsay. There was no way to tell whether the rumors we heard were true or false. Did the Poles beat civilians they picked up or heard speaking German? I know only what I actually saw or experienced. I did not see it. I became very cautious, however, just in case the hearsay happened to be true, and sought to stay beneath the occupiers' radar screen. I still dressed as a boy, which was easy because I had lost my hair once again during the typhoid fever. I avoided the neighborhood of the railroad station, where the Russian and Polish authorities lived, and if I had to go anywhere through town, I cut through the ruins and bypassed the main thoroughfares.

Food became our constant preoccupation. I was never as ravenously hungry as I was after the typhoid fever. The few valuables we had left after our flight from home and the invasion, Aunt Lene, who was good at such dealings, bartered for butter, cheese, and raw bacon from the Russians and the few Poles we got to know through the dressmaking shop. The potatoes stored in our cellar had run out by July. Till the end of August 1945 Mother fed all of us with fruit and produce she received from her friend, the miller on Mill Street. This source of food dried up when he was evicted from his property by a Polish miller. Early that fall we harvested some apples from Oma's community gardens, but by the time we got to the trees, the owners of neighboring gardens had helped themselves to most of our fruit. By that time, notions of stealing and property had become very flexible. You did not take anything away from the people who lived in your apartment house. But picking up food, clothing, shoes, and other essentials from gardens, fields, and deserted or demolished houses we called "organizing." Everybody did it, and in fact, how skillful you were at "organizing" became a matter of prideful boasting.

By mid-September I had recovered enough strength to go with Mother and Werner to ask relatives who had returned and who lived close to town to help us put in supplies for the coming winter. Since many of the farmers had not been able to plant crops either the previous November or in the spring, the harvest was sparse. And no one knew if the planted fields were mined. Therefore nothing could be done except to bring in the harvest, even from mined fields. Fortunately none of us ever stepped on a mine. Mother and Werner, who had not contracted typhoid fever, had walked on mined fields close to town in late summer to harvest wheat, barley, and rapeseed for all of us, and they were lucky. Harvesting potatoes was no problem, because they had been planted in late spring after the invasion. If no one had been blown up during the late planting in June, then it was safe to harvest in early October. We got permission from various relatives to dig for potatoes and spent several weeks hauling hand wagons full of potatoes home. By late November, when we went to dig up sugar beets, everyone knew which fields were mined and avoided them.

Our trips to the country also revealed what had happened to Mother's extended family. Most of the women had returned to their farms. All of the men were dead or missing. Uncle Kurt, Mother's brother, we found out, had last been seen when he was given an antitank gun. "When exactly was that?" Mother asked the widow, Frau Jenatsch, Uncle Kurt had worked for. "In early February," she replied. "The home defense officer ordered him to stay to defend the village when we left. I hope the Russians took him prisoner and that he did not die here. We found several soldiers and a home defense man in shallow graves out in back of the barn. He was not among them. We reburied the bodies after searching for identification tags so that we could notify the relatives." For years Mother was haunted by the thought that Uncle Kurt had died as he had often imagined he would in his nightmares, run over—not by a tractor, as he had feared, but by a tank. Neither Mother nor Frau Jenatsch ever learned what happened to him, how he died or where.

After the hard work of harvesting and hauling potatoes and sugar beets, we had to get our yield past the militia sentries, who set up several, always changing control points around town. If they caught us, they confiscated our produce. On my first outing after my illness, a militiaman stopped us at one such control point. Every time I was held up on the road, I would start to tremble, freeze, and be unable to move even a foot. This first time, Werner, ten years old, panicked and started to run away from us. Both Mother and I, terrified that the militiaman might shoot him, yelled after him, "Werner! Stop! Don't move!" I can still see him standing there, his stick-thin legs shaking with fright, his white face stained with snot and tears. The militiaman approached us, pulled the cover from our load, saw the potatoes, and motioned us to unload them. Having no choice in the matter, we did so with shaking hands and were glad that he had not shot Werner. Still frightened, and aggrieved by our loss,

Werner cried all the way home. I wished I could have cried as well, but I felt that as the older one I had to keep face. Werner was pitifully thin then, and in the torn, soiled shorts and shirt that he had almost outgrown, he looked like a small scarecrow. Yet he faithfully came along with us and helped push the cart filled with whatever we had harvested.

Usually we met a few other families on our expeditions, townspeople like us on their way home with handcarts like ours. Sometimes, as we approached the first houses of town, someone from an upstairs window would call down to us, "There's a checkpoint up ahead at the corner of Breslauer and Kuschlau roads." Then we would backtrack and follow a footpath, first through fields high with weeds, then past the garbage dumps, and from there into Promenade Street by way of the cemeteries.

On our next excursion to get potatoes from the same relative's field, we started for home on an unpaved back road, hoping to avoid the militia. We did not know whether it was mined, since none of the tracks in the dirt were new. We were lucky and made it home safely. Happy about our success, Mother announced triumphantly, "Lene, we got more than a hundred kilos." Aunt Lene was not impressed.

"Fine and good. But what will we eat when these are gone?" she said, dampening our enthusiasm.

Every time we brought back potatoes for winter storage and sugar beets for making syrup, Mother and I, looking at each other and laughing, echoed her refrain, "And what will we eat when these are gone?" While the cooperation in our family left much to be desired, everyone in the house community of the Baronie cooperated in the tasks that none of us could have accomplished on our own. Everyone pitched in.

All of the families in the apartment house had gone to the country to harvest grain, rapeseed, potatoes, and sugar beets. Frau Gurn taught everyone how to make syrup from sugar beets and oil from rapeseed. Herr Gurn and the bike shop owner, Herr Ernst, the only adult males in an apartment house full of women and one little boy, constructed a press from bits and pieces of metal and wood in Herr Gurn's auto workshop for squeezing the juice from boiled beets. They devised another press for extracting oil from boiled rapeseed. All of the women living in the house worked together, sewing sacking and sheets into bags for the presses. The women took turns boiling the beets and rapeseed in the boilers of the cellar washroom—the Baronie had an old-fashioned basement washroom for common use with several boilers for boiling sheets, towels, and linens on washing day. We all collected firewood for the boilers. The women filled the steaming boiled beets or the heated rapeseed into the bags they had made. Everyone took turns working the presses. Finally, each family took its share of beet juice and raw oil. And within each family, everyone participated in boiling the beet juice into syrup and heated the rapeseed oil to purify it. Both the syrup and the oil had a raw, bitter taste. None of us cared much for it, but together with potatoes, our products stilled our hunger. After having proudly finished making a liter of syrup or oil for the winter, I would turn to Mother as we both laughed and said *uno voce,* "And what will we eat when this is gone?" The saying became our motto whenever Aunt Lene complained.

The entire process of syrup and oil making took us about two weeks and yielded enough oil and molasses for each family for the winter. Working together welded us into a community, undoing the isolation that the typhoid and the many deaths had wrought. The adults became companionable and, now that we had light, gathered in the evening in the upstairs apartments, where the crowding was not yet too great. They played skat or whiled away the evenings with gossiping and jokes. Werner and I, the only youngsters, drew closer, since neither the adults' talk nor their games held much interest for us. We played card games like rommè and I made up stories for him about what Jochen's and my life had been like when we were little.

Looking back, I realize that despite my grudges against my aunts, I was content. We all thought only of food and of keeping out of the Russians' and Poles' way. Every step I took as I learned to walk again was a triumph; every cartful of food we brought home from the fields and every liter of oil or syrup we produced gave us a rewarding sense of accomplishment. Most of the time we felt little need to look back at what we had participated in and what had happened to us. Attention to mere survival kept reflection and recollection, thought and emotion, at bay.

On and off all through the rest of 1945, the militia went from house to house to round up people for work crews. At one of the roundups in late October, I was detailed to help clean up the high school on Breslauer Street. I managed to get myself assigned to cleaning up the library, the natural science and map collections, and the teachers' lounge. Since grenades had hit the building and the plaster had fallen off the ceilings, every room was covered with plaster dust, and all the books had fallen off the shelves. The Polish school that had started in some of the classrooms could use the natural history objects and the maps, the German-speaking militiaman told me. "Dump the books into the garbage," he added contemptuously.

Needless to say, I did not get rid of all of the books. I "organized" quite a few for myself. Every day when I left work, I hid a few books under my coat. I chose carefully, and within a few days I had acquired some of the basic high school textbooks for English, Latin, physics, chemistry, and mathematics. In addition, I helped myself to the book of poetry I had used at the teacher seminary and, of course, any of the novels I could carry off.

On a rubble-clearing roundup in early autumn, I met my friend Erika again and also Lotte, the middle school teacher who had led the Strehlen Jungmädel. Talking with both of them as we worked in the ruins stacking bricks, I mentioned in passing that somehow I still wanted to get back to school. At the time, of course, the very idea was preposterous. We had no idea what the future had in store for us. We knew that the Polish authorities would never allow a German into their schools. I understood that during the German occupation their children had been deprived of an education. Now it was our turn. Revenge was the order of the day. Rumor had it that even taking private lessons was forbidden.

All through the days when I was working with various cleanup crews, I kept thinking of Wanda, the Polish woman who had befriended me in Zülzendorf. I had never asked her what she felt about doing forced labor; in fact, at the time I did not think about who she really was, where she was from, or what had happened to her family. Now I was in her shoes. She had never complained, as most of my family and current companions did. I did not really mind the physical work, as it left me time to daydream and plan what I might do. Besides, it got me out of the house and away from Aunt Lene and her mother, Aunt Martha, who nagged me continually. But I resented not having a choice about the work and felt humiliated by being picked up by the militia at any time and herded about.

Erika and her sister, who had lost track of their parents, lived in a room in an apartment house on Linden Street, close to the county hospital where both my father and Oma had died. Lotte and her mother, who had been a prompter in a provincial theater, occupied a room in the attic of the same house. Erika's sister had worked for the Russian commander and now held a job in the Polish militia commander's kitchen. Erika's ambition was to be taken on where her sister worked, and she soon managed to achieve her goal. I understood from fellow workers that the sister was the administrator's mistress. I asked Erika, when I visited her after she left our work crew, if this was true.

"Sure," she said to my bewilderment. "That is the way we'll get through this time. I am going to find myself a militiaman and then I won't have to scrub floors or peel potatoes. And we do have plenty to eat." Everyone I talked to in our apartment house despised Germans who had collaborated with the Russians and now were collaborating with the Poles. Here was my friend from a year before and she had no compunction about such collaboration. Yet I did not want to drop her. I understood that she had little choice in the matter and continued to be friends with her.

"Look, if you want to," she went on, "my sister can get you a job at the commander's too. Don't be stupid," she continued, noticing my disapproval. "Stop dreaming. The sooner you give up your hopes of becoming a teacher, the better off you'll be." I, for my part, felt sure of one thing by now: you could lose your home, your possessions. Your property could be confiscated, like that of my farming relatives. Your house could be bombed and burned down. Your loved ones could die or be killed. The only thing you could keep was what you had learned, what you knew. Your knowledge and your brain were the only things that remained. Learning and education protected against loss.

For fear she would give us away, I did not tell Erika that I had talked to Lotte about giving me private lessons in math, science, and English. Lotte had agreed, although I had nothing to pay her with. We started the lessons immediately, and since I had appropriated several math textbooks from the high school, Lotte could proceed to test me on what I knew and where to start. Our first lesson told her that I needed to start from the beginning of the basic high school math book. After several lessons at her place, Lotte decided it was not safe for her to see pupils there. She was afraid, no doubt, that someone might report her to the Polish authorities. Having been a prominent Nazi in town, she did not want to give anyone an opening for denunciation, particularly as the Polish authorities had begun to put Nazis who had returned into prison.

Mother readily agreed that it was safer to have the lessons in the bedroom we shared with the two aunts. Lotte's regular visits as a "customer" of the dressmaking business would be less noticeable than mine at her place. Mother also asked Lotte to teach Werner, whose schooling had stopped the previous December. At age ten, Werner was less than enthusiastic about lessons. Both my aunts heartily disapproved of our undertaking and constantly harped on our endangering everyone with the forbidden lessons. I wonder now if there was ever any real danger of being reported. All I know for certain is that everyone thought so. We paid Lotte by including her in the oil and syrup production as well as in our ongoing expeditions for food supplies from our relatives and from fields and gardens around town. In this way she became almost a member of the family.

I felt ambivalent about Lotte from the start. I was grateful to be taught and worked hard to learn what she offered. But I resented her comparing my work to that of other students she had taught. She called me undisciplined, a daydreamer, and that was true enough. I escaped her frequent reproofs through daydreaming. I felt I was never quite good enough. I could never relax and enjoy what I learned. She still supported Hitler's ideas avidly and denied that concentration camps had existed; and if they had, she asserted, then Hitler had known nothing about them. I listened to her and wished she would talk about something else. I was embarrassed and worried that the other adults might think her crazy. I felt too dependent on her as a teacher to contradict her with what I knew: that I had seen concentration camp inmates on the road, and that their condition confirmed the horrifying stories I heard adults on the work crews and at home occasionally tell with averted eyes, stories of mass shootings, of deliberate starvation, of beatings of inmates. Lotte assumed that I thought as she did and invited me when she held memorial services for Hitler or celebrated former Nazi holidays like November 9. She usually conducted these when the two of us went scrounging for food supplies, for mushrooms in the town woods or sugar beet greens that Mother made into a spinachlike puree. I would sit next to her at the edge of a ditch by a deserted roadside, silent and morose, as she sermonized and swore undying loyalty to Hitler. I felt mortified by my hypocrisy.

Early in the fall, water service in town had been reestablished, and electricity shortly thereafter. At least for the oncoming winter we did not have to carry water over icy streets or spend long hours standing in line in the darkness. But since the gasworks still supplied no gas, and coal for heating cost zlotys we did not have, we needed to collect fuel for cooking and heating. The house next door, the Eisenbergs' property, had been partly demolished by a bomb and contained masses of lumber, beams, wainscoting, doors, broken furniture, and books. For months we had gotten the fuel we needed from other sources as we waited for the Eisenbergs' return. We chased off people who wanted to loot what was left of the house. I picked through the rubble and rescued a number of books Frau Eisenberg had lent me years earlier, thinking that I would return them when they came back. Someone in the Baronie, however, started dismantling the heap of bricks and wood by removing half-buried clothing and suitcases, as well as small pieces of furniture. Wooden scaffolding from Herr Eisenberg's showroom and shop disappeared next. Once the demolition started, there was no stopping it, and family after family in our apartment house sawed away on beams, freed buried, broken furniture from brick and plaster, braved a standing façade in the back of the house, and pried loose window frames and doors. The Eisenbergs' house kept us warm all winter.

On another work crew that fall at the town commander's house, I met Frau Dunisch again. She told me that she and a friend of hers, Sister Gisela, were employed as Red Cross community nurses. I told her about my Red Cross training during the last months of the war and my work at the military hospital. After listening to me attentively, she asked, "Do you want to work for me? I supervise the community nurses in the villages close to town. We need more nurses. Too many left in January before the invasion." There was nothing I wanted more than to work for her, but I doubted that I had enough experience.

"You have enough for what is needed," she said. "You have learned to dress cuts and minor injuries. You know how to give injections. And you can always get help from me if you run into something you cannot handle." I couldn't say yes fast enough.

"You won't be paid, but the villagers will give you foodstuffs for helping them. I'll also get you an identification card in Polish so that you can move around safely and won't be picked up by the militia for cleaning crews." And sure enough, my identification card saved me from further work crews.

Much about Frau Dunisch's role in the town at this time is unclear to me now, and I am amazed by how little I knew about it or even wondered. As I report it now, I can give only the perspective of the mouse in the maze I was then. I do not know from whom she had the authority to assign me, at age sixteen, as community nurse to the village of Krippitz, or what relationship she had to the Polish authorities that enabled her to get me an identification card. Nevertheless, a few days after our conversation, I was on the way to Krippitz, five kilometers from Strehlen, to introduce myself to the Polish mayor. Frau Dunisch had equipped me with a black doctor's satchel that belonged to her missing husband, filled with first aid supplies as well as with the promised identification card, decorated with a large official seal.

"Ursula Mahlendorf is community nurse in Krzepice, Strzelin. Please give her what assistance you can," it read in Polish.

After presenting my newly acquired identification to the mayor, a large, friendly man who greeted me with many exclamations that I failed to understand, I was ushered next door to a house that served as his office. Realizing that I had no Polish, he led me by inviting gestures to a small room off the hallway that had been the last nurse's dispensary. I managed to mutter the few words of thanks in Polish that I remembered from Wanda. They sufficed, at any rate, to put me on a cordial footing with him from then on.

Frau Dunisch had told me to go to the next village after my introduction to the mayor for instructions from the nurse who had taken care of Krippitz up until then. I have no idea whether Nurse Klara had been informed of my coming, since there still were no telephone communications. She lived a twenty-minute walk from Krippitz through the Ohle meadows, close to where Agatha and I had picked snowdrops years earlier. A tight-lipped, gray-haired woman with gray eyes in a sallow face, she questioned me with some skepticism and then welcomed me as a helper. "I suppose you'll have to do." I never knew if she was reassured by what I told her or if she needed my help so badly that my meager qualifications did not bother her. At any rate, she gave me a list of the village people she had seen recently and told me what ailed them.

"Visit these patients first," she instructed me. "Send someone to get me if you cannot handle the situation. I went over twice a week," she concluded. "That should be enough." I promised to visit Krippitz twice a week as she had done and assured her I would send someone if I needed help.

For the next eight months I went to Krippitz twice a week. I am not sure whether I helped anyone, but the five-kilometer walk twice weekly, reciting poems or English vocabulary to myself, helped me overcome the last vestiges of weakness from typhoid fever. Moreover, while trudging along, I memorized the entire volume of lyrics that I had taken from the high school. Luckily it was an excellent collection, for it gave me a sample of every meter and rhythm of German poetry from the Middle Ages to the 1930s. I could still recite poem after poem by heart from this treasury when I taught lyric poetry many years later.

Fortunately I had few difficulties with my nursing duties. For the most part I visited households headed by women, talked to them, bandaged a few cuts, and provided ointments to fight the scabies that plagued almost all children and many adults as a result of poor hygiene—the village still depended on wells. Most of the German villagers were day laborers from the one large estate, whose owner had been relocated. Horses and cattle, even chickens and geese, had been appropriated by the troops some months before. The Polish authorities were planning to convert the farming operation into a state-owned enterprise. For the time being, the women individually harvested for their own use the few plots that they had been able to plant in late spring, and sometimes offered me produce for my help. An unknown number of fields were still mined.

We had one major accident when three teenagers stepped on a tank mine. I arrived at the scene after the families had already loaded the boys onto the mayor's horse-drawn wagon to transport them to the hospital. I only needed to deal with one boy's leg, which had been nearly severed at the knee. I steadied the leg with a splint and applied pressure to an artery that was spurting blood. Fortunately, the boy was unconscious. Together with the distraught mothers, and frightened out of my wits about the responsibility I had taken on, I delivered the children to the hospital.

Except for the two days I spent at Krippitz, I could now plan my days and had time to study and read. Lotte came for lessons several times a week unless she was stopped for a work crew. With five people living in two rooms, one of which we had refashioned into a kitchen and used as living and sewing room, and the other of which served as bedroom, study, and dressing room for customers, our various interests often conflicted. Worst were our conflicts over food. Aunt Lene and Mother worked together as dressmakers, but Aunt Lene, having been Mother's teacher, thought that she contributed more to the business. Therefore she claimed that the most valuable produce they received as payment, like meat, butter, eggs, sausage, and cheese, belonged to her. She claimed that the potatoes, oil, and syrup Mother, Werner, and I provided had less value. Therefore she and her mother could have their share of our products, but she could ration out her "valuable" foods in minute amounts. Needless to say, I protested; but since Mother did not support me, I could do little but sulk. Aunt Lene in turn objected ever more loudly to Lotte's coming to give us lessons. It did not help that Mother supported me when we were on our food collection missions, and agreed with Aunt Lene when I was not there to hear it.

I don't know exactly, but it must have been shortly after I started my duties at Krippitz that Frau Dunisch asked me if I would help her with a lifesaving and possibly dangerous task.

"I am not sure," she began, "if I should involve you in this. My husband left a basement full of medical supplies that he kept as county medical officer. I don't want these to fall into the hands of the militia. I want them used by the doctors and the village nurses in the county for those for whom they were originally intended. I hope that you can help me deliver them."

She stopped to look at me and, seeing my interest, continued, "A few times a week, I'll give you a knapsack filled with medical supplies. You'll have to deliver them without telling anyone where you got them. You'll be a great help to the people in the villages. The doctors and nurses there cannot get syringes, insulin, sulfa drugs, dressings, or any other medical supplies. They ran out of most some time ago. Some of the nurses are taking care of diabetics, and I know that they need insulin urgently." She paused, looking at me questioningly. I felt proud that she trusted me.

"Of course I'll do it. When do I start?"

"I'll provide you with the addresses, but under no circumstances tell anyone who you are or who is sending you." I was enthusiastic about this mission and about the secrecy. And, suddenly, I was also apprehensive.

"What if the militia stops me?"

"You'll need to see that they don't. If they do, they might put you in custody overnight, but I doubt that they'd do much else," she replied, adding, "of course, I understand if you think it is too risky and don't want to do it."

"To whom do I go first?" I wanted to know so as to have no time to think it over.

"We'll start with Nurse Klara. You know the way; the village militia in Krippitz knows you, so they won't stop you. And Sister Klara knows better than to ask any questions. Come by my house early tomorrow morning. And come in by the door in back so that the doctor does not hear you. I'll be waiting for you at the door." The doctor was a Polish physician who had taken over her apartment and her husband's practice. She, her parents, and her friend Sister Gisela lived in the attic.

I met her at the back door shortly after daybreak, when the curfew was lifted. We went down into the cellar. Behind some shelves at the back, she opened an almost invisible door into still another cellar filled with boxes. I recognized some of the boxes as similar to those from which she had filled my doctor's satchel for my duties at Krippitz. The knapsack was ready. I left quietly and without speaking by the back door, crossed a footpath up to the bushes and birches bordering on Marienberg, and was soon out of sight.

This first mission was uneventful because part of it was my usual walk to Krippitz. Nurse Klara accepted the supplies without comment, but I could see that she was happy. Her sallow face flushed with relief as she smiled.

"I was running very low—you saved my life."

The reactions of the doctors and nurses made the long hikes—often with a heavy rucksack and one or two buckets of sulfur salve for scabies—worth my effort. My next trip, a few days later, took me to Striege, my mother's birthplace. I knew a back way, a footpath along the Ohle River to the village on which there was no danger of meeting anyone. I hoped that it had not been mined. Again the nurse received me with open arms once she saw what I had brought.

Over the next eight months, sometimes twice weekly, I delivered knapsacks full of supplies and buckets of sulfa ointment. Neither Mother nor Aunt Lene knew what I was doing. I had told them at the start that Frau Dunisch had offered me space at her house and I would be studying there. My knowledge of the country and its byways and alleys from my biking days made my missions easier. I usually took a detour around the villages I had to pass. From my "customers" I learned the locations of the village militia posts so that I could avoid them on future trips. Only once was I stopped by a militiaman. I felt elated, like a real heroine on a secret mission. It was the perfect realization of the fantasized games Jochen and I had played as preteens, riding our bikes as spies and explorers. I don't think I ever again experienced a similar thrill. The game was exhilarating and seemed dangerous; and it probably was. I loved the surprised, relieved, and then happy look I received from doctors and nurses as I asked them to empty the knapsack. I never said where I came from or who had sent me, never gave them my name. I proudly turned them down if they wanted to reward me with anything but a sandwich or some water. As I think about it now, most of them probably knew who had sent me and who had given me their address. None of them questioned me much or wanted to know anything specific. I believe they felt it was safer for them and for me not to know. I never stayed long, partly because I often had to cover some ten to fifteen miles to get home before curfew at nightfall and partly for safety reasons. Occasionally my visit to a nurse's aroused the curiosity of the villagers who directed me to her dispensary. Then I felt it imperative to leave before the news of a stranger visiting spread through the village and reached the local militia.

Over the months we extended our reach to the outlying villages of the county. I loved the hikes over the fields, along the Ohle River beyond Krippitz, or up the hills south of town and through the town woods. I got to know the villages west of town where we had never gone before on our bikes, a region of the country with large estates. On some of the back roads there, I came through the moors that Frau Gurn had talked about years before in her kitchen. Walking along past the reeds and brackish meadows, I remembered how afraid I had been then of the will-o'-the-wisps that lived in the moor and tempted travelers off their course, so that they were sucked into the moor and drowned. I ventured off the road now on returning home and collected a few of the meadow saffron or other late moor flowers for Lotte to identify for me. Everywhere I went, I could orient myself by the silhouette of Zopten Mountain in the west. On most of my deliveries I took a book along, and on lonely stretches of the roads and byways I memorized English vocabulary or learned more poetry by heart. Reciting poems helped allay anxiety about being picked up by the militia.

There was only one problem: I was wearing down my brother's boots. The soles were worn through, and the seams had come apart in several places. I had no other shoes. I stitched some of the seams and Herr Gurn resoled the boots for me. But, not being a shoemaker, and lacking glue, he used nails, and the nails soon stuck into my feet. When she learned of my problem Frau Dunisch gave me a pair of boots that had belonged to her husband. Though they were too big and I got blisters, they were better than going barefoot. I used up several pairs of men's shoes donated by her. Sore feet and blisters were a constant annoyance and the price of my adventures.

After each delivery I went by Frau Dunisch's house to return the knapsack, to report on the mission, and to visit with her and her parents. I felt welcomed by them and we often talked. They encouraged my taking lessons and being intellectually curious. They lent me books and discussed them with me. While we at home lived from one day to the next, worrying only about the next meal, Frau Dunisch and her family conversed and bantered with each other on every conceivable subject. They made plans. They could conceive of a future for themselves and for me. They were committed to service to the community, whether as a nurse, a doctor, an organizer of the Olympics (as Frau Dunisch's father had been), or a teacher. They modeled for me the kind of life I wanted to lead.

After the New Year, I received a letter from Frau Scherzer in Breslau, who had been my mentor at the teacher seminary. She wrote that she had survived the siege of Breslau and asked me how I had fared and if I knew the whereabouts of any of the other students. It was the first time we received any mail, though we still had no public transportation. Train service to Breslau had not yet been restored because many of the rail bridges that had been blown up toward the end of the war still had not been rebuilt. The letter, at any rate, seemed like a message from another world. I did what no adult would even have considered—namely, hike all the way to Breslau, some thirty kilometers away, to visit her. I left at daybreak the day after I received the letter and arrived at the address she had given me shortly after dark.

I was used to hiking long distances, but the villages around Breslau frightened me; they were a fearful sight of destruction, still empty of people and animals. A few emaciated stray cats meowed at me; the façades of blackened farmhouses, barns, and outbuildings stood along desolate village streets, their roofs blown off by grenades. It was winter, but no snow had yet fallen to hide the devastation. Standing on the outskirts of Breslau among these ruins, I understood the starkness of defeat for the first time. I met no one, not even militia, all the way to the suburbs of Breslau, so the world I encountered felt eerie, unearthly. I was afraid, but I kept thinking about a poem I wanted to write about this dead world and about my brother Jochen, who we assumed had died during the last days of the war.

Frau Scherzer was surprised, of course, by my spontaneous visit. Fortunately I had had the sense to bring along two days' worth of food supplies for myself. She put me up in her one-room flat in Breslau's north end. Electricity in her neighborhood had not yet been restored and so we spent the evening talking in the darkness. She told me that she had stayed through the siege of Breslau, helping out as an aide in a hospital for shelter because she thought she would be safer there.

"It was curious," she explained. "You would think that when a city surrenders to the enemy, the invaders come in en masse and start burning, looting, and raping. That's not the way it happened. As the city's commander negotiated the surrender, small Russian convoys infiltrated every night, and gradually the city was taken over. When the surrender was finally declared, the Russian troops were everywhere. A few days later we were thrown out of the hospital, everyone who could walk. Out on the street, I looked for a place to stay. Some women took me in. A few days later, trying to see what had happened to my neighborhood, I found out that our apartment house had been flattened by artillery fire. Afterward I ran into a Russian convoy. I scrambled through some of the ruins but one of the soldiers caught me, threw me down, and raped me. If you cannot run, don't fight back once he throws you down. Remember that," she concluded.

"What did you do after that?" I asked, grateful that she told me frankly what had happened. Mother had clammed up about rape or what to do. Since my typhoid fever, whenever I talked to Mother or my aunts about rape, or about what had happened to Ellen, or even about the women at the infant ward where I had worked, they had made me feel that there was something wrong with me for being preoccupied with sex and rape.

"I went to the next hospital to be examined and treated," she replied. "The doctor flushed out my uterus with a saline solution so that I wouldn't get pregnant." Her answer was detailed and specific about the procedure she had undergone to make sure that she did not contract gonorrhea.

"The Russian commanding officers," she continued, "gave their troops leeway to rape the German women they found for twenty-four hours after the Germans surrendered. After that, soldiers who were reported for rape could be court-martialed. That's why I went to the Russian *Kommandatur* after the hospital and filed a report. I don't know what happened. I do know from the doctor at the hospital that other women were raped as I was."

The next day I went to look at what the siege had done to the city. To my surprise, Breslau was actually less devastated than my hometown of Strehlen. I went by the redbrick polyclinic near Frau Scherzer's house and found it still standing in all its ugliness. I searched for the houses of our relatives and of Adelheid's parents. All had burned to the ground without any indication of where their inhabitants had gone. I arrived back at Frau Scherzer's room depressed and discouraged. Once again we talked into the night. Generalizing from my own situation at the teacher seminary, I maintained that as bad as the Nazis had been, they had furthered women's opportunities and education.

"No, that is what the HJ told you," she corrected me. "You know better than that. It was education for motherhood only. They decreased the number of admissions for women to the universities significantly. I was fortunate that I could finish my degree. They founded the teacher seminaries only when they ran out of male teachers. You would never have had a chance to study.

"Stay with your lessons, even if you don't like everything that Lotte says. You can learn from her. And somehow our lives will return to some kind of normalcy and you will be able to go on with your schooling," she encouraged me. I left her strengthened in my resolve to persist with the lessons despite my relatives' nagging and my own resistance to Lotte's discipline. I left early the next day and was home by nightfall.

My sudden departure for Breslau had made me miss one of my weekly visits to Krippitz. I had justified this to myself by thinking that I would go three times the following week. My only important case in the village was a mother who had rejected her infant. The baby had been born a few weeks earlier with Sister Klara's assistance. When I first saw the mother and child, I felt like I was revisiting the infant ward where I had trained the year before. The baby boy, listless and pitifully thin, with a stone-hard swollen belly, lay in soggy rag diapers that had not been changed for at least a day. The mother had no milk and paid no attention to the child. Her sister, who lived with the mother and infant, had asked me to come and help her with the baby. Neither cow's nor goat's milk was to be had in the village, and therefore the sister fed the infant a flour-and-water mixture. At this first visit, the sister and I bathed the baby and found some old cotton sheeting for diapers. I left some cotton swabs and baby oil to wipe the baby's bottom, and told the sister that I would try to get more cotton sheeting for diapers.

I asked Frau Dunisch if she could get canned milk or milk powder for us. Two days later I set out for Krippitz with several tins of canned milk and a few old sheets. Frau Dunisch had promised to get me dried milk for the following week. I left for Breslau on Tuesday of the week I had promised to deliver the dried milk. I returned Thursday night and delivered the milk powder late Friday morning. When I arrived at the sisters' apartment, the mother had left, and her sister told me that the baby had died the day before. Looking at the tiny shriveled body covered by a piece of sheeting in its dirty hamper, I felt heartsick. I had been so sure that I could make a difference in the baby's survival. In my missionary zeal, I had fantasized that this time, unlike at the infant ward, I had control over the situation; I could help this infant. And I had failed! I was struck forcibly by the fragility of human life. You miss a few days and it is all over! I felt guilty whenever I remembered that I had been neglectful, followed my inclination, and broken my promise. Unfortunately I did not trust any adult sufficiently to speak about my failure and express my oppressive feelings of guilt. Because I could not, I did not gain a gentler, more forgiving perspective on my role in the infant's death, and guilt feelings continued to haunt me for years. My remorse had the effect, however, of my taking commitments in the village very seriously and being more thoughtful about any future promises I made.

On my next visit to Breslau that spring, I stopped to ask for a glass of water at a house in a suburb. With some hesitation, I recognized the woman who answered the door. She was Frau Friedrich, a woman of thirty-five or forty, whom Mother had met at one of her holidays and who had visited us a few times during my early teens. I had always looked forward to her visits because, unlike my aunts, she inquired about my interests and listened to my answers. She was married and had been a lively brunette, radiant, well dressed, with a ready smile and a sense of fun. The face of the woman I now saw was swollen, its formerly clear features blurred and pasty; her dress hung on her and her figure looked ungainly. But she greeted me with the same cordiality she had a few years earlier.

"My God, child, what are you doing out on the road!" she asked as she drew me into a darkened room. As in most houses at the time, the windows had been bashed out during the fighting and the panes replaced by cardboard and planks of wood. "You shouldn't be here. We just had Russians come through. It's not safe here. Where is your mother?" She calmed down after I told her my story. From then on, when I went to Breslau, I stayed overnight with her and gradually found out what had happened to her. She too had survived the Breslau siege. She had not left for the west because she was waiting for her husband to return.

"Our apartment burned down. I moved out into the suburb after the siege because I thought I'd be able to feed myself better being close to the country. I came from here and I have relatives here. But they don't talk to me now."

"Why not?" I wanted to know. It took her a while to answer me. But when she decided to talk, the story rushed out of her. "They think that it's my fault, that I wasn't careful enough. That I didn't hide well enough, that I didn't make myself ugly enough to drive the Russians away. I am pregnant, in the seventh month. I was raped. I tried to abort the baby but I couldn't. I know that my husband, like my relatives, won't believe me. He'll think it was my fault. That I had intercourse with the Russian because I wanted to."

I was too young and too inexperienced to understand the extent of her desperation, or her passivity—she had never tried to see a doctor or report the rape—of her fatalism and her fear of rejection. I did understand that she would be stuck with having to bring up a child she did not want and that her husband, if he returned, would reject her just as her relatives had. All I felt was sympathy and outrage that no one could or would help her. I went to see her every time I visited Breslau, talked to her as the baby's birth came closer. But once I stopped going to Breslau, I forgot her. Mother and I found out later in West Germany that she did have the child and that she brought it up by herself.

I visited Frau Scherzer a number of times in an effort, I realized later, to regain the idealized relationship that had helped me and supported me during the collapse of my HJ identity and beliefs. But that effort turned flat over the course of several visits. The everyday realities of Frau Scherzer's life could not sustain my fantasy of her. It was during a casual exchange that my disillusionment got the better of me. We had been discussing what the future held for Germany when she remarked about the young people she observed in her neighborhood, "I worry what will happen to German youth after their seduction by the HJ, and the turmoil and defeat they have experienced during these last few months." Looking back, of course, I can see that this was the reasonable concern of a caring teacher. But at the time I lacked that maturity. Personalizing her remark, I asked if she also worried about me.

"No, I don't worry about you. You will be fine," she replied. I could have seen her answer as an expression of confidence in me. But her remark hurt and continued to rankle over several weeks, because I felt far from fine or confident about myself. How could she assume that I would be fine without asking me how I felt? As usual, on every occasion when an adult expressed "concern" for my generation, I thought resentfully, "You should have thought about that when you let the Nazis teach us." I felt too awed by her to express my anger, though, and therefore gave her no chance to continue our discussion and clarify her position.

I answered a card from her a few weeks later by returning an empty envelope, an angry gesture I was ashamed of even as I dropped the envelope into the postbox. I knew it was evasively provocative—provocative because we believed that we lived under censorship, and receiving an empty envelope could mean any number of worrisome things. I decided that I would never return to Breslau for a visit, and I never found out what happened to her. I deeply regret that I lost touch with her, for she was, after all, the teacher who inspired me and helped me when I needed it most.

I feel sad now that I was unable to tell her how I had interpreted her remark, how desperately I wanted her or any adult to care about me. I realize that the adults who knew me at the time did not understand that I was still very much a child and lacked the perspective of an adult. I needed reassurance constantly and I got little of it, because almost everyone, including Frau Scherzer, expected me to be an adult.

Several times in the course of the winter and spring of 1946, militiamen for whom Mother and Aunt Lene had made alterations returned and confiscated their sewing machines. Twice, relatives and friends lent them their old sewing machines as replacements, and Herr Ernst, our former bicycle repairman, put them in working order. The third time this happened, my ten-year-old brother—much to our surprise—began addressing the men in Polish. With his Polish, he made enough of an impression on them that they left without the machines. Unlike all of us, and not handicapped by resentment and prejudice against Poles, he had learned the language while playing with the son of the Polish pianist who lived in the Gurns' apartment. From then on, I also made an effort to learn at least enough Polish to carry on a conversation and understand the Poles in Krippitz with whom I dealt as a nurse.

What helped me overcome my prejudice against Poles, which I had acquired through Nazi indoctrination, through our resentment against the militia, and through my ignorance of Polish culture, were not only my memory of Wanda but also my daily experiences with Polish civilians, with the ever-friendly mayor of Krippitz, and with the pianist who lived in the Gurns' apartment. For the most part the Polish families who lived in our apartment house ignored us and we them. I liked the looks of the Polish pianist, though. Her poise, her beautifully cut chestnut hair, her finely chiseled pale, sensitive face intrigued me. I first heard her play the piano from the hallway of the apartment house. Deprived of any source of music—our piano had been confiscated shortly after we returned—I was thrilled by her playing, particularly by her duets with a young violinist. Wanting to hear better, I asked Frau Gurn's permission to listen from the Gurns' former storeroom, separated from the music in the living room by only a thin wall.

From then on, if I had any free time on the afternoons when the violinist and the pianist practiced, I went to the Gurns' storeroom and listened. Sitting on a discarded beer keg in the windowless room, I heard sonatas I did not know by whom but later recognized as Beethoven and Chopin. It was the first live classical music I was exposed to. The intimate, subtle sound of the duo's chamber playing stirred and moved me. Their duets created in my mind a passionate and heartrending antithesis to the aggressive blare of symphonic and martial music transmitted by the radio during the Nazi period. It took me almost a lifetime to dissociate symphonic music from the violence and horror of Nazism. The pianist and her violin accompanist sensitized me to the intimacy and expressive power of chamber music, and I remained devoted to it forever after.

In May Mother received a letter from Grandfather Mahlendorf's second wife in Neisse. Grandfather, the letter told us, was mortally ill with pneumonia, and if she wanted to see him alive, she should come soon. Grandmother sent the letter on the chance that it might reach us at our old address. Their apartment in Neisse had burned down during the fighting and she gave us their new address. I volunteered immediately to go as the family's emissary. This time I notified Nurse Klara that I could not go to Krippitz for a week and asked Frau Dunisch if she could provide me with medications that might save Grandfather's life. By this time train service going south, at least part of the way, had been reestablished. Rumors about Germans being beaten or ejected from public transport were rife, and therefore I was apprehensive about traveling by train or being searched. But since I had to get to Neisse fast, and since we did not know how risky it might be to carry medication, Frau Dunisch put a heavy plaster cast on my left arm in which she embedded the medication for Grandfather. She also gave me the money for the ticket. Thanks to the cast and my arm being in a sling, everybody on the train was helpful and friendly. Instead of the hostility I expected of my Polish traveling companions, I was asked solicitously how I had broken my arm. I stuttered a few sentences in the little Polish I knew, and nobody minded my being German or questioned my using the train.

I had visited Grandfather in Neisse just before setting out for Obernigk, and he had been pleased that I was entering the teacher seminary. The city I arrived at two years later was as devastated as my hometown, because the battle for Neisse had raged back and forth several times. Nobody was at home when I knocked at the attic door of the address Grandmother's letter had given. The railroad bridges over the Neisse River had been blown up, so I had walked the last five miles into the city, and I fell asleep on the stairs while waiting for my relatives to return. I woke up with a start of apprehension as I heard steps approaching on the dark staircase. It was Grandmother Mahlendorf, her daughter Elfie, and Elfie's eight-year-old daughter. As we entered the twilight of their kitchen I gathered from the expressions on their faces that I had come too late. Grandmother confirmed that Grandfather had died the day before. They were returning from the cemetery, where they had arranged for a plot for his grave.

Over the following two days they told me their story. In early 1945 they had waited too long to flee and had stayed in their cellar as the city was overrun by the Russian army. A week later German troops retook the city and made them leave the town. On the road, Russians again overtook them. They got caught in the back-and-forth of the battle for the city several times. Each time, however, they were out on the road, and they did not know what to do but return to the city, even after their apartment had burned down. They moved from one apartment to another during the next months, as the Polish population moved in, because the militia requisitioned every new place they found in the ruins of the town. They received permission to stay in their current, rather spacious attic apartment only because Grandfather had found work at the municipal waterworks and was helping restore water service to the city.

A few weeks earlier, water service had been disrupted, and Grandfather was sent to repair the pipes. He caught a bad cold while at this work and refused to go back. The waterworks' overseer sent the militia to fetch him in an open truck; Grandfather had no choice but to go along. He had worked on the pipes all day and had returned home with a high fever, delirious. The next day the militiamen returned to fetch him for work. Being delirious, he resisted them. They beat him until he collapsed. That is when Grandmother decided to write to us. She managed to find a doctor, who examined him and told her that there was little hope for Grandfather's life; one of his lungs had detached from his chest wall. He was unable to move and went in and out of consciousness until he died. The militiamen had returned every day to see if he was awake and able to go back to work.

Even as they were telling me the story, we heard the militiamen coming up the stairs. They were four or five young men, hardly different from the young German soldiers of the Habelschwerdt hospital ward. They pushed us aside and went into the next room, where Grandfather's body still lay on his bed. I followed them into the room. I was awed by the stillness of his large, familiar frame lying on the bed, his face haggard and gray, cheeks fallen in, nose pointed, a dark red scabbed-over cut running diagonally across his high forehead. The militiamen stopped by the bed and one pushed his head off the pillow and examined the pillow, as if hoping to find something. I stood frozen at the headboard, livid with fury at their disrespect. They stayed for what seemed an eternity. Their callousness made no sense to me. What were they looking for? What did they believe was hidden under the dead man? I seethed with anger.

That night I slept in the room next to where Grandfather lay dead. Electricity had been cut off, and Grandmother gave me a candle to light my room. In the middle of the night, unable to sleep, I took the candle and went to stand by his bed. Gazing down on him, a faint high humming in my head, I felt only a kind of solemn awe. Suddenly Rilke's poem "Autumn Day" came to my mind, and slowly, under my breath, I recited the first two stanzas, repeating them over and over.

> Herr: es ist Zeit. Der Sommer war sehr groß.
> Leg deinen Schatten auf die Sonnenuhren,
> und auf den Fluren laß die Winde los.
>
> Befiehl den letzten Früchten voll zu sein;
> gieb ihnen noch zwei südlichere Tage,
> dränge sie zur Vollendung hin und jage
> die letzte Süße in den schweren Wein.
>
> Lord: it is time. Summer was huge.
> Place your shadow on the sun dials
> And unleash the winds on the fields.
>
> Command the late fruit to fill out;
> Give them two days of southerly warmth,
> Ripen them to perfection and press
> Final sweetness into heavy wine.

The poem's melancholy celebration of life's ending wrenched my chest with a few dry sobs but brought no tears to my burning eyes. With Rilke's demanding and desperate imperatives I called out to a God I did not believe in and attempted to squeeze some meaning from Grandfather's death. I realize now that the very form of the verse comforted me and carried me through the night.

In the morning I accompanied Grandmother on her errands related to the burial. She had to get a death certificate from a municipal office, check on a coffin she had ordered built from a wardrobe they had found in the apartment, solicit a Protestant clergyman to perform the funeral service. Though a Catholic herself, she wanted the right kind of preacher for the funeral. I took an immediate dislike to the man and protested that Grandfather had been an atheist and would not want a sermon, particularly the lugubrious sermon I was sure he would (and in fact did) give. I was too young to know that the purpose of the sermon was to console Grandmother and her daughter, both of whom were genuinely grieving. I felt self-righteously that my service for him of the night before would have been more to his liking.

While we were gone, a woman had come to dress the body and the carpenter had come and placed it in the coffin. They had left the casket open so that Grandmother could put into it some of the objects Grandfather prized, like his toothbrush and a ring. On a bookshelf in his room, among books on plants and birds, I found a small volume of nineteenth-century poems, many of which I knew by heart. I spent the following night at Grandfather's side again, reading poems to him and to myself. They helped me through the night. In the morning I put the book into his coffin. We buried him that day. On the train on the way home, I realized that I had forgotten to take off the cast containing the medications.

I did not cry when I told Mother how Grandfather had died. (Indeed, I never cried during these years.) Outrage at the callousness of the militiamen dominated my thoughts. Resentment of the clergyman and his total lack of comprehension of my grandfather's life and death choked me as I talked to Mother about the funeral (the clergyman had asked God for mercy for the dead man's atheism and berated me for sharing Grandfather's beliefs). I felt my fury over Grandfather's violent death and my grief at his loss only years later. Until then I remained unaware of what I owed to him: my love of nature and my capacity, developed on childhood walks with him, to experience the soothing of emotional pain in nature's presence. At the time, in the spring of 1946, I rushed back into the activities that dominated my life, delivering medications, attending to my duties at Krippitz, and studying for Lotte's lessons.

None of us ever profited personally from the medical supplies that I delivered all through that winter and spring. I admired Frau Dunisch's ingenuity and courage in taking the risk of hiding the supplies from the militia, all the more so as we had to be careful that the physician who lived and practiced in her house did not find out what we were doing. I always managed to evade the militia on my trips and prided myself on my endurance and skill. As I got used to walking the countryside, my anxiety about the militia diminished. Particularly when I passed through the woods on the way to villages south of town like Krummendorf or Riegersdorf, I stopped in the woods for a rest, moving some distance off the side of the road. One day early in the spring, when the trees had not yet leafed out and patches of snow still covered the ground by the underbrush of small conifers and bushes, I noticed a strong, sweet odor that overpowered the smell of wet dead leaves. I looked around and spied a low, still leafless bush with several dense clusters of tiny, deep pink blossoms. Daphne, I remembered. I'd been here with Oma an eternity ago. "They are very rare; they grow here wild," Oma had said. "Don't disturb them. Don't pick them." I went closer to the bush that was almost hidden by brush and leaves. The small, radiant, almost lilac-colored blossom clusters with their strong sweetness transported me out of myself into the comfort I had felt with Oma.

Only once, carrying a heavy knapsack and two buckets of sulfa ointment, was I stopped by a boyish-looking militiaman who biked by me on a back road. Surprised by his silent approach, I impulsively produced my Polish identification card. He took the paper from me, studied it, looked for a long time at the seal, and handed it back. Murmuring something in Polish, he motioned for me to proceed without checking my knapsack. Relieved and reflecting on the matter once he had passed me, I realized that he could not read and had judged the situation on the basis of the impressive seal. As I passed by the next village, I made a large detour through the woods, just in case he decided to double back looking for me, once he had had time to think. At the time I felt contemptuous of the militiaman because he could not read. Later I recalled that during the German occupation of Poland, Polish children had had no schooling. But for Lotte's instruction, my brother, in a few years, might not have been able to read either.

By June 1946 we were hearing rumors that Germans in Silesia would be resettled. We still knew nothing of the decisions at Potsdam or of any other political developments. Some rumors had it that we were going to be shipped to central Germany, some to Siberia, some to the west. We did not know that in 1945 occupied Germany had been divided into four zones: the Russian, British, American, and French zones. In fact, one of the most frustrating and anxiety-provoking aspects of living without news was that rumor ruled our mental lives. Sometimes these rumors were florid exaggerations of some measure that the Polish administration was planning; sometimes, wild fantasies about events taking place in other towns of Silesia; still other times, fabrications of fearful people about what had happened or might happen. Even Frau Dunisch, who had some connections to the woman who had been appointed "mayor" of the Germans living in Strehlen and therefore had some access to official news, knew only that we would be resettled. She did not know when or where.

Knowing that we would have to leave, we began to prepare. At the time, we believed that we would be resettled only until a final peace treaty was signed and would then come back. We learned that each person was allowed to take only what he or she could carry. Therefore we made bedrolls with sheeting to transport our feather beds under one arm. We packed our knapsacks with personal items to carry on our shoulders. Herr Ernst helped us fasten wheels to two aluminum washtubs for household and cooking essentials. My aunts did the same. Each tub had a rope tied to it for us to pull with our free hand. While we waited, packed and ready to go at a moment's notice for the next several months, Frau Dunisch and I stepped up the distribution of medical supplies to the county's nurses and physicians.

Early that summer, with the permission of the militia and the cooperation of the "German" mayor, Frau Dunisch and Sister Gisela inoculated the German population against typhus and typhoid. Nobody wanted a repeat of the previous year's epidemic. I helped them, and met the mayor for the first and only time as a result. Frau Dunisch had told me earlier that the mayor was the daughter of a prominent local communist who had served on the town council during the Weimar Republic and that both she and her father had been imprisoned in Buchenwald. He had died, but she survived. Though a young woman in her late twenties, she had a presence that impressed me. She was flippant and, unlike most of us, unafraid of the militiamen. Frau Dunisch introduced me as her "helper with the supplies." I now understood where my identification card had come from and who was likely to have provided the addresses of the community nurses. On a hunch, I asked the young mayor if she was making up the lists of names for resettlement and had any control over who would be sent with which of the several train transports from Strehlen.

"I make the lists," she replied with a laugh. "Do you want me to make some special arrangements?" I felt ashamed for asking for a favor but asked it nevertheless.

"Could you put me and my family, the Mahlendorfs, on the same list as the Dunisch family and Lotte Turnow? And could you put my aunts, Lene and Martha Hennig, on a different list?" I found out several weeks later that she had done as I asked.

A few days later, Frau Dunisch made a request. "I need to sell some of the medical supplies we have that are for hospital use only, because I need some cash for my parents' needs. Would you go to the county hospital and sell them to the administrator, Panje X?" I agreed although I felt uneasy; I did not quite know why. The next morning I picked up several syringes, some surgical instruments, a number of thermometers, and vials of different serums. Since there was a lively black market in all kinds of medical supplies, it was likely that I would not be asked where I had gotten my stock. I went to the hospital, talked to the man, and he indeed paid me the tidy sum I had been told to demand. When I delivered the sum to Frau Dunisch, she wanted to give me a portion of the money. At first I refused, but then on second thought I took the sum and handed it over to Mother. Even as I took the money, I realized that I had lost my respect for Frau Dunisch and that I had undermined my own idealism because of this transaction. My assumption all along had been that we were serving the community for the public good, and that of course our motives were altruistic. Young as I was, I could not comprehend that caring for one's aging parents — her mother had had several strokes — might be part of the public good. I never quite regained my old feelings for Frau Dunisch, nor did I regain trust in my own altruistic motives.

As we stepped up the effort to empty Frau Dunisch's cellar of medical supplies, we must have gotten careless. Early one morning the Polish physician surprised us in the cellar. Loudly and angrily he demanded an explanation from Frau Dunisch. "Whose are these supplies? Your husband and you concealed them?" When she could not satisfy him with her evasions, he threatened in his halting German, "I report to militia. You be sorry!"

Frau Dunisch did not react but motioned me to leave with the usual load in my rucksack as the two of them were still negotiating. I was terrified for the first time, wondering where and when I would be picked up by the militia. Fortunately, the delivery was to a nurse just a few miles from home. I hurried there, left what I had, and practically raced back. Nothing had happened. The next day I had my lessons with Lotte as I did on all free days, did my homework, and waited. Nothing. The following day I went to Krippitz and came home. Still nothing. A few days later, I finally dared to go to see Frau Dunisch. She said that we would stop further deliveries.

"He took the little that was left. We managed to distribute most of it anyway. We'll all be leaving soon in any case."

I never told anyone during the last days we spent in Strehlen how afraid I was that the militia would pick us up and keep us in jail. With my success in delivering the medicines, I had ceased to worry that we might be at risk. For the last months under the Poles, I had known about all kinds of people who had disappeared in militia jails for all kinds of reasons: for being accused of having been a Nazi official, like Bertel's father; or for displeasing this or that official, like Herr S., Mother's Singer sewing machine repairman, who had appeared one day with some militiamen to confiscate our sewing machines and the next day was jailed for no reason we knew of. Sick with worry, I could hardly wait to leave. I now think that there was probably less reason to be afraid than I thought at the time. The Polish physician did not follow up on his threat. For all I know, he was satisfied with getting the rest of the supplies.

During the first week of August, the militia came to our house and called on the first families to be ready within a few hours to leave for the railroad station. Among them were my aunts and several other families from our apartment house. The following morning, it was our turn. We shouldered our knapsacks, took our bedrolls, and, pulling the washtubs on their wheels by a piece of rope, slowly made our way to the station. The militiamen guided us along Promenade Street, past the schools, through the city parks all the way to Post Office Street. I did not look right or left. By the time we reached the post office, many other inhabitants of the town had joined us, carrying similar baggage and pulling similar wheeled contrivances. Looking up, I saw an emaciated white-haired woman with a brown wrinkled face approach at our left. Covered by a shawl, she limped past us. Pausing for breath occasionally, she pulled a small tub with household items behind her and held a bundle of clothes in her other hand. An alley of humanity opened before her as everyone made way. Like a ghost, she progressed unhindered through the chaos of frightened Germans being searched and Poles who cursed them for not moving fast enough.

The militia had erected a barrier at the entrance, which we entered one by one after the phantom of the old woman had passed out of our sight. The militia had put up several tables against a wall bordering Post Office Street on which they searched our baggage. In a few tents on the other side, everyone was patted down for forbidden articles, though none of us knew what they were. At the side of each table mountains of confiscated objects rose up. Aside from my brother's leather football, about which he raised a tearful but fruitless protest, we went through the search without forfeiting anything except for what I thought were worthless papers anyway, some savings books. Together with a crowd of our countrymen who had been searched, we passed the internal revenue building and crossed into Linden Street. Moving from there into the extension of Railroad Station Street, we arrived at the freight yard of the station.

Alongside the tracks in an ever-growing queue, we waited till nightfall, when an empty freight train finally rolled in. While waiting I waved to Lotte and her mother several families behind us in the line; further ahead I spied Frau Dunisch, her parents, and Sister Gisela and joined them to find out if they had any news. Frau Dunisch asked, "Can you help us load several of the old people and the invalids in wheelchairs into the Red Cross compartment when the train gets here? Gisela and I will care for them during the trip."

As the train moved in, the crowd surged into compartments and freight cars. The three of us had trouble emptying a compartment for the invalids after the crowd had filled it. It was difficult and time consuming to lift them in and then to help Frau Dunisch's parents up the steep steps and settle them down. By the time I finished, I had lost sight of Mother and Werner, and the train was about to pull out. I ran alongside the freight cars calling for them. Mother yelled at me and I jumped into a crowded wagon as the train started off. I was glad to have found her, but to my surprise and consternation she was furious.

"Why do you always run off and help other people?" she cried.

"I helped Frau Dunisch. She is in the Red Cross car. There was no one but Gisela and me to help her load the wheelchairs!" I attempted to explain. But her set face told me that she would hear no more.

As the train gathered speed, all the people, in every one of the wagons of the long freight train, suddenly began to sing, "In der Heimat, in der Heimat, da gibt's ein Wiedersehn" (At home, at home, we'll see each other again!). They got louder and louder as they sang.

No, you won't, I thought, blind with tears and anger, stifling my sobs. You are kidding yourselves. This is for good. We will never come back. We have lost our home forever. I knew with amazing clarity: We would never return. Then I felt relieved that the Polish physician had not reported us after all. We were safe! When the crowd started the next song, with its brisk and cheerful beat, "Muss i' denn, muss i ' denn, zum Städtele hinaus" (Must I then, must I then, leave my hometown!), I realized that I was still angry and still crying hard.

The train seemed to hurl itself into the night. The wagons began swaying on the rails, and the baggage that people had stacked up against the walls in front and back threatened to fall. Some of us stood up and leaned against the wall of baggage to hold it up. The singing had stopped a while before; everyone was tense; we did not know in which direction we were going. With the doors closed and locked against the onrushing night, the air in the car grew heavy. It was pitch black. Suddenly a voice started mumbling and got louder. It seemed to be the dark girl whose pale, sensitive face and sad eyes I had spotted earlier. She began to scream, an intense, high-pitched scream. She screamed and screamed. The car felt as if it were going to explode. Several people began screaming and howling. I pushed them aside and bent over the girl, shouting, "Stop it!" She wouldn't. I raised my hand and I smacked her, right across her face. Once, twice. She stopped as suddenly as she had started. One by one, the others quieted down, and with the last fading, drawn-out shriek, the din ceased. Everybody sobered up, sat down, and stared into the darkness as the train roared on.

Gradually, normality asserted itself. I don't know if the train moved more slowly or if we were all tired now and ashamed of our panic. People began to talk quietly, murmuring to each other. "It will be all right. We are on a train being resettled. We will know in the morning where we are going." I don't know where I read what to do if someone becomes hysterical and threatens to cause general panic. But I knew I had done the right thing. I apologized to Agnes—this was her name, I learned—for hitting her. We stopped several times that night on the open tracks. When the train moved, it sped along, racing through the stations. Sometime during the night, we all must have fallen asleep.

The next morning when I woke up, the train was stopped on a side track. The doors were not locked and we could roll them back. We crawled down onto the tracks. We did not know where we were. There was flat country all around, meadows and fields, some woods in the distance. It could be anyplace. Since we could not see the Zopten, we had to be some distance from town. Most of us went into the bushes at the side of the tracks to relieve ourselves. I was thirsty and asked if anyone had thought of bringing along water to drink. No one had, but all were thirsty. I was not hungry, and no one else seemed to be thinking of food. I went up to the car where Frau Dunisch and the invalids were. They seemed to have survived the night better than our car had, but one of the old men breathed heavily and looked very weak. The train stayed on the siding the entire day. The sun beat down on us. It was hot in the cars. Someone discovered a creek, and most of us drank from it, as its water seemed reasonably clean. Sister Gisela and I took some water to the invalids. The whistle of the locomotive at nightfall warned us that the train was about to set out again.

After another night of travel, this time slowly and with many stops, we woke up in the morning when the train stopped in a freight yard. As we opened the doors, we could not see a station sign but heard militiamen talking to men whose uniforms we recognized as those of German railroad workers. The men told us that we had arrived at Görlitz, now the border town between the Russian zone of Germany and the Polish-administered zone. As the train seemed to be stopped for a while, I went to see how the Red Cross car and the invalids had fared. At the door, Frau Dunisch told me that the weak old man had died early that morning. "We will have to stop a while. They will have to take the body off the train."

The old man's family decided to accompany the body and have him buried in Görlitz. They would join another train after the funeral. We waited impatiently for our train to be cleared to move on. Several freight trains full of people passed ours as it stood waiting on the track. Hours passed, the sun growing steadily hotter.

Finally our train left Görlitz and the border of Silesia behind us. We thought that the next station would be Dresden. We did not know then that Dresden had been bombed, but we realized that our train had somehow bypassed it when it roared through the blackened ruins of Halle Station. We did not know until we reached Helmstedt and the western zones late that afternoon that one of the trains that had passed us as we stood waiting at Görlitz had taken our place in the resettlement schedule. Two trains of settlers went to be resettled in the less populated eastern zone of Germany. Every third train went to the densely populated western zones. Our train had originally been scheduled to be resettled in the eastern zone. The old man's timely death assured our train a free ride into the west. Our troubles are over, I thought. We are among our fellow countrymen. Now I will be able to go to high school!

Chapter Eleven

REFUGEE IN THE PROMISED LAND OF THE WEST
Return to School, 1946–1948

THE GERMANY WE CAME TO IN AUGUST 1946 had not yet begun its reconstruction. It lay in ruins. Most cities of more than a hundred thousand inhabitants were destroyed by more than 50 percent by Allied bombing. Available living space in the entire country had been reduced by half, and millions of people had been left homeless by the bombing and sought refuge in neighboring villages and small towns. Four to five million refugees from the Russian invasion, in addition to several million former slave laborers, refugees from Soviet dominion, and concentration camp survivors, had already crowded into the western zones, so when the expellees arrived from the east, a bad situation became worse. Most of the families separated by the war and the bombings were still looking for missing relatives. Most of the German soldiers taken as prisoners of war had not yet returned, and women had assumed the role of head of household. The country's industries had been devastated, and output in raw materials like coal and iron had declined sharply. The production of consumer goods had almost ceased. The food situation for populations of all occupation zones had worsened steadily since the unconditional surrender in May 1945.

The aim of the Allies with regard to Germany as formulated at Tehran, Yalta, and Potsdam had been demilitarization, denazification, decentralization, and reeducation of the population in democracy. But the beginning conflict between the Western powers and the Soviet Union left any hope for a peace settlement with Germany or a resolution of the many problems caused

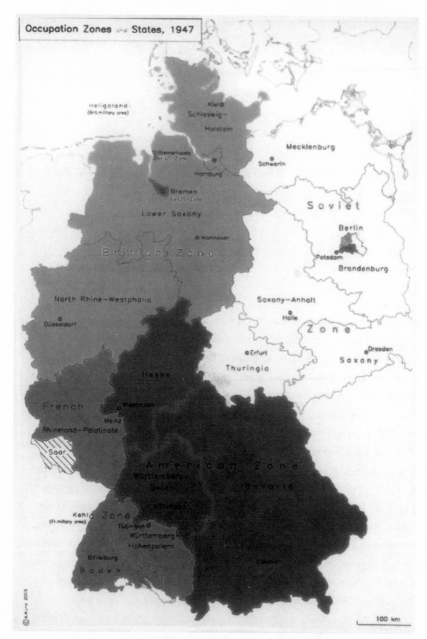

Map of Occupation Zones. IEG Maps. Copyright A. Kunz, 2005

by the war and Nazism in limbo. In 1946–48, when we came to the western part of Germany, the country remained divided into four occupation zones, and the ultimate authority over these zones, the formulation of laws and regulations, and the resolution of conflicts between the Allies rested in the Allied Control Council, headed by the commanders of the four Allied armed forces. The Russian zone included the former eastern German provinces of Mecklenburg, Brandenburg, Saxony, Saxony-Anhalt, and Thuringia; the French zone, the southwest provinces of Baden, Württemberg-Hohenzollern, and the Saarland; the British zone, the former provinces of Lower Saxony, North-Rhein Westphalia, and Schleswig-Holstein; and the American zone, Hessen, Bavaria, part of Baden-Württemberg, and the city-state of Bremen—the last for U.S. access to a harbor. Berlin was likewise divided among the Allies. The occupation authority of each zone governed that zone. By early 1946 the Western occupation authorities had begun to introduce parliamentary democracy by encouraging local self-rule and the formation of political parties so that the responsibilities of civil administration could be assumed by elected officials. In the eastern zone, primarily via the repatriation of German communists and socialists who had fled to the Soviet Union in the mid-1930s, the Soviets encouraged the development of state socialism.

So as to accomplish the transfer of 6.5 to 7 million Germans from the territories east of the Oder-Neisse line to the occupied zones, the Allies had established a combined repatriation executive in late 1945. This newly established agency was to move some twenty-eight thousand expellees daily. Because of the harsh winter of 1945–46, the transfer of the population was halted for a few months, but it had resumed by the spring of 1946. By the summer of 1946, when we were evicted, the transfer was in full swing, and the British zone to which we had been assigned had received 1.2 million exiles by fall, while the American zone had accepted 1.5 million. The Russian zone, by spring of the following year, had taken in 2.4 million "resettlers," as they called expellees. The French had refused to participate in the transfer of people into their zone altogether. The westward movement of more refugees and expellee populations did not cease until East Germany made the Iron Curtain practically impenetrable by building the wall in 1961.

The transfers of the evicted were handled by five huge centers, one of which, Helmstedt, we had come to. From there, after a health examination, delousing, assignment to a refugee category, and issuance of official papers, the evicted were sent to designated localities. The Allies had assumed that

the local populations of "old Germany" would absorb the expellee population within one or two generations. Major concentrations of expellees in
camps were to be prevented so as to avoid the isolation of the new arrivals in
ghettoes. Local German authorities were left with the task of distributing the
evicted in their localities among their populations. None of these authorities
had any choice in the matter of accepting or not accepting expellees. All of
them resisted in various ways, however, and they sometimes had to be forced
by occupation soldiers to accept their contingent of people. Most of the local
authorities thought that the measures they had to take would be temporary
and that the newcomers would leave after a peace treaty was signed. We were
fortunate that we did not know any of this at the time and that we learned of
it only gradually over a period of months.

On a radiant summer day in August 1946, we jumped out of the train that
had brought us from Silesia and joined the line of exiles waiting in front of a
barracks. "Helmstedt," the station sign informed us. A short time earlier, the
train had stopped briefly on the open track. "That must be the border of the
British or the American zone!" someone guessed. It was the British zone. We
had made it into the west! Now what? We hoped for something to drink, or
even to eat. We had been told that our baggage was to stay on the train. As we
waited in line, rumors coursed through the crowd as usual. I paid no attention
but concentrated on controlling my bladder. Finally I left the line and walked
up to a man wearing some kind of a uniform. "Where are the toilets? I cannot
wait much longer!"

"Why don't you go in there?" The man pointed to a barracks. "They'll let
you use their facilities. It might be some time before you get through the delousing." That was the first I had heard of delousing. Did they think we were
coming from Siberia? Obviously, they did. I told the people around us when
I returned from the toilet that we were going to the delousing station.

"First things first," Sister Gisela opined. "Well, if we had any fellow travelers, they'll be wiped out." The process was brief and humiliating. Everybody
was subjected to it. A woman with a pump filled with white powder pushed
the pump into the waistband of my ski pants and gave the pump a push. Next,
she reached into the back of my blouse and gave it another. Then she asked me
to turn around and close my eyes, and put the pump to my hair. That was delousing. I don't know if it worked, but it provided us with a new experience of
equality. We smelled of disinfectant for the next few days. After that we stood
in line to be examined physically. A doctor looked us over several women at

a time, and called me aside. He had noticed the poorly healed scar under my right ear that I had acquired during the bout of typhoid fever. "You'll have to have that looked at when you arrive at your final destination," he said, handing me a piece of paper that said, "Examine for tubercular infection."

After the physical we passed by a table where an official handed us a paper stating our category designation. We learned that we were classified as expellees, as we had not come here of our own free will.

Then, finally, we lined up for food, actual hot food, potato soup and bread, which we ate from the tin bowls we had brought with us. We returned to our freight cars, where we would sleep one more night, stretched out on the floor, using our bedrolls for pillows. But before we turned in we were free to roam about the Helmstedt transit camp, the camp where all trains coming from points east to the British zone arrived with refugees, prisoners of war, and expellees from the east. We went to the registration room to check lists posted on bulletin boards to see if any relatives, neighbors, or friends had come through the camp. Most people read silently; only occasionally would you hear someone exclaim or see a trembling hand, a tear-stained face, note a piece of news. We found nobody and gave up after a while. Werner and I walked around through the warm summer night, happy to be out of the train—free, we felt, for the first time in two years to walk around at our leisure, unafraid, speaking German in open voices. We were cheerful. We had come west. We were in Germany with our countrymen. We would start a new life. I would go to school. Soon.

At the time, I never looked back. All the time I had lived under Russian and Polish occupation, I thought of the west as the Promised Land. We all did. Rumors had reached us even in Silesia that Americans were friendly, that Germans in the western zones lived on sufficient rationing, could go to school, that life was beginning to return to normal. I was happy that we had left the narrow confines of my hometown. Moving to the west, I realized even then, gave me opportunities I would not have had if my family had stayed in our hometown—and the same held true for both my brothers. Mother and her generation of Silesians—at the time in their forties to sixties—were less fortunate. Many of them were never quite acclimated to West Germany. Some of them—like some distant cousins of Mother's—lived in a refurbished chicken coop and remained stuck in refugee poverty until they died in the 1980s.

After the night at Helmstedt camp, our train of expellees pulled out of Helmstedt station just after sunrise. All we knew was that we were scheduled to go north into the British zone. We had no idea where, exactly, but were content to be in the west. We crowded round the opened door of our freight car as the train pulled out. We moved slowly through gently undulating hills, with fields carefully tended; in the distance we saw villages with church steeples untouched by war, meadows with cows and even sheep. The larger towns we rolled through had been bombed, but most of the rubble had been cleared away. For the most part this was a landscape of peace, of order, of prosperity even, compared to where we had come from, where even the village churches had been blown to bits, farms burned down, and the devastated fields overgrown with weeds.

Gradually the architecture of the houses in the villages changed. We passed dwellings with roofs of straw thatching whose cross-beamed gables ended in wooden horse heads. I recognized these as northern German farm dwellings, the horse heads ancient symbols sacred to Wotan, the chief god of Norse mythology. I had heard much about Norse mythology in the Hitler Youth and had admired houses like this then. They looked like something out of a sinister fairy tale to me now, unreal, somehow medieval. At the freight yard of a station called Delmenhorst, our train was switched to a single-track line that passed by the backyards of small brick single-family homes, obviously a suburb. Then the tracks followed a country lane with similar houses on one side, meadows with cows on the other. Every house sported a beautifully tended front lawn bordered by large white hydrangea bushes that led to a wrought-iron front gate.

The warm August day, the cheerful gardens, the white hydrangeas under a pale blue sky seemed to welcome us as we stood in the open doors of the freight cars. People stared at us from their windows and front yards as we rode by and did not return our waved greetings. Yet when the train stopped in the middle of a large, untended field, I leaped down to a small cement platform full of expectation and good feelings. As people climbed down from the cars, stiff from the hours of standing and sitting, some Red Cross nurses and several men in civilian clothes met us. In the distance I saw a row of large two-story buildings that bore huge numbers on their fronts, and behind them I noticed several hangars.

"This is Adelheide Airfield," one of the men told us in greeting. "This will be your new home. It was a Luftwaffe airfield; the buildings housed flight crews and pilots." He seemed to be in charge. "Go look at the rooms in the houses; each family or group of five to six can take one of the rooms. Then come back and unload your baggage."

Before he had even stopped talking, people began to run across the field toward the buildings. We hurried along with them, saw a second row of houses beyond the first, and ran toward them. At the back entrance of the first house I reached, number twelve, we entered a long hallway with doors on each side. Since we got there first, I checked all the rooms. All of them were empty. Two of the rooms in the middle of the hallway held showers and toilets. Showers! Mother and I decided to take the room right at the back entrance to the right. It was a large, empty room, whitewashed but with dirty walls, with two windows looking out across the field to a fir forest beyond. As we were asking Werner to stay and hold the room, Agnes and her sister and their elderly mother arrived at the back entrance.

"Why don't you share the room with us?" Mother asked them. "We will have to share anyway, and at least we know you from the trip." They were happy enough to share and so we left Agnes's mother to hold on to the room while the rest of us got our luggage.

By evening we had obtained sacking and straw from one of the hangars, filled the sacking with straw, and placed the straw mattresses on the floor, three to each side. Our wheeled washtubs, emptied of their contents and turned upside down, served as tables. In another hangar we found empty gasoline canisters and a few buckets that we transformed into seats. As we were busy getting ourselves settled, a siren blast—a conditioned reflex at first made us duck—called us out to another hangar. It was a makeshift mess hall and kitchen. There we were served food twice daily, at noon and at night. After the evening meal we were given bread and jam to take along for breakfast the next morning.

On our first evening at Adelheide, the camp leader who had greeted us spoke for a short while about his plans for the organization of the camp. "You are fortunate because you are the first train to arrive and so can get settled before more expellees get here. We are expecting some five thousand expellees altogether." We looked at each other with consternation because the passengers on our train had already occupied most of the houses. Few people had heeded his first words that five to six people were to share each room.

"The occupation authority," he continued, "has designated Adelheide Airfield as a new civilian settlement. For most of you, this will be your permanent home. After a while, of course, you will be provided more space so that each family can have its own quarters and its own kitchen. But as long as we have no building permits, you will have to make do with six to a room and mess hall food. Before you leave for the night," the camp leader said in conclusion, "each house will take its turn in helping prepare and serve food, and in cleaning up afterward. We will post a rotation tomorrow. If any of you want to apply for positions as cooks and kitchen staff, talk to me now."

That first night, it was enough to know where we would sleep. Aside from that, we all looked forward to a shower and cleaning up after the trip. We had not washed for about a week. The delousing powder still clogged my hair. All of our clothes and bags smelled of it as well, because while we were being given the powder treatment, teams of exterminators had sprayed the train and our baggage. I dug a towel out of my knapsack and raced for the shower; I got there first. It was a large, bare room with showerheads coming out of the walls on both sides, a covered drain in the center of the floor. I turned on the water; it was cold and stayed cold. We found out the next day that the boilers had been stolen after the German airmen were marched off as POWs. No matter! It was August, it was warm, and cold running water was fine by me, an unhoped-for luxury. Back in Strehlen, we had slept in our clothes for a year, afraid that the militia might haul us out of bed in the middle of the night. Without running water, a bathroom, or even a kitchen sink, occasional sponge baths from a bucket had had to suffice. I luxuriated under the cold stream of water.

The next morning I checked all the houses for Mrs. Dunisch and her family and for Lotte. Both were in the next house over, at number nine. Returning to our room, I decided that it looked too dreary with its bare, soiled walls. From home I had brought along several of my favorite books and an illustrated volume of sculptures at German Gothic cathedrals, a volume I had appropriated from the high school library. I sacrificed four of its illustrations for the cause, loosened them carefully out of the binding, held them up to the wall, and then realized that I had no means of fastening them there. As I was deliberating about what to do, a woman who by her dress and demeanor obviously was not an expellee walked past our door. She stopped when she saw what I was about.

"You will need some tags," she remarked, "or some frames and nails."

"Yes, I know, but . . ." I trailed off and stood there awkwardly.

"Frau Behrends," she introduced herself. "I am on the town council of Delmenhorst. The airfield is in our jurisdiction and I thought I would come and check on what is needed here."

"Well, tags, for one," I said and started laughing, and then introduced Mother, Werner, and myself. Frau Behrends was a petite woman with quick gestures, blond graying hair, and gray-green eyes. It took me a moment to get used to her north German accent with its sharp *st* and *sp* sounds, which seemed affected to my Silesian ears. We talked for a while about our trip, where we had come from, and how glad we were to have arrived at a safe haven. She told us about the town, about the neighboring communities, about opportunities for work and, on my inquiry, about local schools.

During the first few days at Adelheide, physicians appeared to check those of us who had been notified in Helmstedt that we might have brought along a disease. I was taken to a town laboratory for blood tests and tubercular tests. A few days later the camp physician, who had arrived just recently, told me to my relief that they were negative. For the rest, we first explored the environs and the town of Delmenhorst. Adelheide was a small dairy farm community; its farmhouses were scattered over several miles without a center. Woods and heath surrounded the airfield camp. The town of Delmenhorst, with some forty-two thousand inhabitants, was a mill town; its factories had produced cotton, carpets, linoleum, and jute sacking. At present, most of the factories had not yet resumed work, as some of the factory buildings had been bombed. The next large city was the Hanseatic League city of Bremen, with some 385,000 inhabitants, as much as 60 percent of it devastated by bombs. Many of the Bremen families who had lost their homes had found shelter in Delmenhorst, which is why the town had been given permission to use the airfield for the arriving expellees. Delmenhorst was about four kilometers from the airfield camp, a hike of about an hour, as bus service had not yet been established. The city of Bremen was some fifteen kilometers away, a half-hour train ride—in normal times. For the time being, though, we confined ourselves to the woods and the heath around the airfield and to the town of Delmenhorst. After a few days, meals from the camp kitchen failed to satisfy and we were hungry all the time. We looked for ways to supplement our rations in the forest and the fields around the camp.

We found blackberries, blueberries, and mushrooms in the forest and the heath. Lotte, knowledgeable about mushrooms, taught us which of the local varieties were safe to eat and which were poisonous. We collected fallen branches and cleared away forest underbrush for kindling. A few stones piled into an outdoor fireplace next to the back entry of our house became our cookstove. On the train, when we did not have sufficient space to lie down, we had sometimes berated ourselves for having taken along the tubs full of household equipment. Now we were glad that we had brought pots and pans in which we could supplement the camp fare with the produce from the forest. At the edge of the potato fields close to the camp, we found, or, as we called it, "organized"—much to the dismay of the local farmers—a few extra potatoes. And behold, with our supplements, the scant and watery camp food became palatable and ample. It did not take a week before small fires all around the airfield betrayed the presence of many gourmets bent on outdoing each other with the flavors of the many varieties of north German mushrooms and berries. Three weeks into our stay, the population of the airfield had risen from fifteen hundred to five thousand. Six or more persons now occupied every room, and we felt lucky that we had boarded with Agnes's family from the start. Frau Behrends, who, I found out, had been a member of the Liberal Party of the Weimar Republic, looked in on us several times over the next few weeks, and I established a good relationship with her. From her second visit on, she supplied me with information on all the cultural events taking place in the town, free events like adult education classes and concerts. Small-town child from a cultural backwater that I was, I had not known that such opportunities as adult education classes existed.

My first visit to town took me to the local high school. I had resumed and intensified lessons with Lotte immediately after arriving at Adelheide. She began to help me catch up in chemistry, physics, and Latin from the elementary textbooks I had brought along. We deliberated about which form in high school I might qualify for. Considering that I had studied mathematics and English without interruption for a year, she put me into the fifth form of an eight-year high school. She trusted that my extensive reading compensated for the lack of study in history, German literature, and geography.

Armed with her instructions, I set off for town. I had dressed in my only summer dress and groomed myself as carefully as possible. Most primary and secondary schools had been running since the previous fall. I arrived at the high school on a Thursday at around ten in the morning, shortly after classes had resumed after the summer vacation. It was break time, and students of all ages, from ten to eighteen, swarmed through the building and the schoolyard.

I looked for the office of the principal, and after a long wait in a line of students and adults outside the office of his secretary, I finally entered. By this time it was shortly after noon, and she motioned me to a chair outside her office to wait while she finished her lunch. At exactly one o'clock she called me in. I requested an interview with the principal of the school. Looking at me quizzically, she said, "I think I can answer your question."

"I would like to register for the fifth form," I proceeded.

"Certainly. Give me your last transcript and birth certificate and we'll notify you if we have space in the form you qualify for," she replied.

I hesitated for a moment, "Well, I am from Silesia. We left my hometown suddenly at the Russian invasion. Therefore I have neither a transcript nor a birth certificate. That is exactly why I wanted to talk to the principal and tell him of my qualifications."

She looked at me disapprovingly, as if I were a lunatic.

"We don't admit students without official records. And aside from that, all of our forms are so overcrowded with refugees that we will not be able to accommodate any newcomers for several years, even if they do have records." She turned to the next person and said, "And what do you want?" before I could even begin to object. I realized for the first time that Mother's unspoken opposition to my quest for an education and my lack of funds for school fees and living expenses might not be my only handicaps.

I had agreed to meet Lotte at the train station waiting room after my visit to the high school. Waiting rooms at train stations were our usual meeting places because there you could sit down without buying something. We were loath to spend on frivolities any of the twenty marks we had been given at Helmstedt camp. The few marks we had had on us when we left home had been confiscated at the checkpoint table before we boarded the train. Lotte saw from my face that my mission had failed, and she tried to console me. "You'll have to be patient." I was furious about my failure to get through to the principal and Lotte's attempt to calm me. Patient? Is that all you can think of! I wanted to shout. But I restrained my anger.

We wandered around town for the rest of the afternoon, looking in on the one bookstore that displayed real books rather than dummies, like all the other stores. Looking at books calmed me down, even though we could not spend any money on them. At 7:30 P.M. we entered the small Protestant church close to the town center for an evening organ concert that Frau Behrends had told me about. We knew neither the organist nor the program, nor did we care, as long as it was music. I have never again in my life been so starved for cultural events as I was then. I also hungered for any information about what the future held for us. I was eager for news about the world outside Silesia, outside Germany, and about the larger picture of the events we had lived through. What had happened to the Nazi leadership? What had the Nazis really done? What about our soldiers? When would they come home? What were the different occupation zones like? What cities were still standing? What was happening with schools and universities? Where had our relatives and my friends settled down? For a time, however, cultural interests held first place for me, and cultural events were the only thing that for a time relieved the pressure of my questions and hunger for news.

The Delmenhorst Evangelical Church, a typically high-windowed Protestant church, lacked all decoration except for a vivid painting of the crucifixion over the altar and several boards with numbers in Gothic script announcing the previous Sunday's hymns. We sat down in the first pew and waited, reading the program announcement an usher had handed us upon entering. The dimly lit church was almost empty but filled up rapidly, and every last seat was taken when the organist finally began his prelude. Even as briefly as I had been in the west, I had noticed with some cynicism that churches in 1946 were doing a thriving business. Many former Nazis found refuge in the church, attempting to forget or make others forget that just months earlier they had proclaimed themselves atheists, faithful only to Hitler. I was very much aware of this as I looked around at the assembled audience. At the time I defined myself as an agnostic, and questions of faith or of God's existence held no interest for me. I was here for the music.

I scarcely heard the introductory Buxtehude prelude, again preoccupied with my anger and thoughts of how to get around the rules that were keeping me out of high school. As the organist started on Bach's Toccata and Fugue in D minor, the simple progressions swept me up. To a more sophisticated ear, the concert probably held few surprises, but, deprived as I was of any background in classical organ music, the organist's playing was a revelation to me. He proceeded from Bach to César Franck, music that transported me into a strange state. When the concert ended with "Jesu, Joy of Man's Desiring," tears ran down my face. Fortunately, except for a few candles, the church was dark and hid them.

Perhaps the music had unfrozen my emotions or the disappointment of the day had been too much, but on the long march back to the camp my anger returned with redoubled strength. As we walked by the lighted windows of the suburban houses with lace curtains and families gathered around late supper tables, I felt like throwing rocks through those windows. I fumed at Lotte, "We should just trample their stupid lawns and hydrangea bushes, knock out their windows." I raged on without restraint, and she, for once, did the wisest thing she could have, and let me rage and never said a word. By the time we got back to the camp, my fury was spent.

A few people left the camp after several weeks, among them the Dunisches and Lotte's mother, Frau Matzinger. Both women could prove that they had not been members of the Nazi Party, and so they found positions quickly. Frau Dunisch got a teaching position at the local trade school, a job that came with an apartment for her and her parents. I visited them a few times but soon found that their lives and mine had nothing in common. Frau Matzinger had applied for and won a position with the Chamber Players in Bremen. Although I knew that Lotte had many conflicts with her mother, and I sympathized with her because of my own quarrels with my mother, I liked Frau Matzinger and was very sorry to see her go.

A minor character actress earlier in life, she became a prompter in her older age. But she had the flamboyance of a theater person and was the wittiest and most outspoken woman I knew. Her ironic flippancy was a welcome relief from her daughter's solemn, doctrinaire pronouncements. There was no issue on which she did not offer a strong, well-formulated opinion; the clarity with which she presented her beliefs drew me to her point of view. In fact, in the matters she discussed with me, I needed little persuasion. She clarified and made legitimate for me what I was beginning to see for myself. Even during our first week at Adelheide Airfield, she cajoled Frau Behrends into bringing us newspapers. At first it was the local Delmenhorst paper, the *Käseblatt* (cheese sheet), as Frau Matzinger called it, and then *Die Zeit*, a major daily out of Hamburg, and several more whose names I have forgotten. The Nuremberg trials had been going on since 1945 but we in Silesia had heard nothing about them—or any other news—before we reached Adelheide. Few people in the camp followed any of the news, let alone the trials. The few who did violently denounced the trials as victor's justice. By contrast, Frau Matzinger was up on the cases of the prosecution as well as on the arguments of the defense. When she first began talking to me about the trials, I could scarcely follow her arguments. Unlike the other expellees, she agreed with the judges and said that she always had known that "the Nazis were a bunch of crooks, thieves, and murderers." She was full of the theater gossip of the late 1920s, 1930s, and early 1940s about Göring's confiscations of artworks and Goebbels's affairs with actresses. Her theater company from Oppeln in Upper Silesia in the early 1940s had even played for the ss at Auschwitz.

"We had some idea what was going on but I did not realize how appalling it really was, that the inmates were deliberately worked to death," she said. "We believed that Gross Rosen was a forced labor camp of Polish inmates for Krupp. We had no idea it was a death camp, that the inmates were gassed. We joked about the terrible smell. We did not know that it was from the ovens."

She spoke like a person who had never liked the Nazi regime and had never held her tongue. "Hitler was a funny little man, a raving lunatic with a ridiculous mustache. Everybody would have noticed it, if somebody had cut it off!" she scoffed. I believed her when she claimed to have known all along who the Nazis really were—all too many of the adults now suddenly claimed to other Germans that they had known. Lotte had told me earlier that she, as a good Nazi, had always objected to her mother's ridiculing "Hitler and his gang." She had worried about her mother's outspokenness. "She only got away with it because she worked for the theater. Most of the theater people talked that way; most of them disliked and joked about the party." I experienced Frau Matzinger's departure for Bremen as a real loss. With her gone, I was cut off for a time from news of the larger world and from a voice and a perspective that brought relief from the stultifying confinement at the airfield camp.

After the disastrous failure of my effort to talk to the principal of the high school, Frau Behrends asked me how I had fared. When I told her, she offered to write to the ministry of education in Hanover on my behalf. Lotte also wrote them a letter. To resolve the issue of the missing birth certificate, Mother and I, like most of the camp inhabitants, applied for identification cards. To receive an identity card, Mother, like many older people, could produce identification papers that had been valid during the Third Reich. I had none, and it seemed absurd to me that she had to swear an affidavit verifying my existence and my date of birth. On another visit to town I had a passport picture taken. We debated briefly whether it might be convenient to make me older by a few years, but we decided to stick with the real date. But time passed, and neither Frau Behrend's letter nor Lotte's produced any results.

Frau Matzinger invited me to visit her in Bremen and promised a theater ticket in the bargain. The play was O'Neill's *Mourning Becomes Electra*. I remember little about the performance except that the small, make-do stage at a

The author at age sixteen, passport photo

Bremen school seemed about to collapse under the shrieks of Electra's lament for her dead father. Since the last train left before the play ended, I stayed overnight on Frau Matzinger's sofa. This would be the first of several such visits.

The next day I went around Bremen in awe at the destruction wrought by high explosive and incendiary bombs. The damage was much worse than what I had seen in Breslau and different from that in Strehlen. Row upon row of houses stood in blackened ruins, interrupted by deep craters surrounded by mountains of bricks, twisted steel beams, and rubble. A profusion of gray-green weeds with brilliant red spikes of blooms that I learned to call fireweeds grew from the rubble and the low walls still standing. Frau Matzinger occupied a furnished room in a long line of turn-of-the-century bourgeois houses at the edge of the inner city in Bremen's West End. As I walked from her house toward the center of town, I saw that every house was only a façade. Street after street was rubble and ruins. After a ten-minute walk I reached the city wall, a wide ditch filled with brackish water that had been part of the town fortifications. Of the former park, of which the ditch had been a part, only a few tree stumps remained. Beyond that lay more blackened ruins, the old city. The cathedral, St. Peter's, stood undamaged, as did the old Rathaus and the statue of Roland across the street. But the bourse and the Renaissance merchant houses around the market were burned-out shells. A Bauhaus hotel, Die Glocke, next to the cathedral, served the Americans stationed in Bremen as an officers' club; the Bremen Opera used its stage for its performances. The bombed-out inner city of Bremen formed the background of my Bremen high school years. I marvel today that I hardly gave the rubble a second thought. It was just the way life was. You lose a war and that is the way your cities are going to look. Some six years later, when I was a student at London University, the neighborhood of St. Paul's reminded me of my years in bombed-out Bremen, cured me of my ignorance about the Battle of Britain, and made me aware once again that my country had started the bombing of civilian cities. In the late 1980s, when Werner and I visited Bremen's reconstructed old town, the houses, with their framework of age-blackened beams, appeared as if the destruction had never happened. At the time I was not sure that such a radical cleanup of its troubled past would protect the country sufficiently against future bouts of national madness.

During this first visit, Frau Matzinger encouraged me to apply to a Bremen high school. "Why don't you try to get into one of the high schools here in

Bremen? Bremen schools are independent of Lower Saxony and its bureaucracy. In fact, the state of Bremen has its own Ministry of Education, and the minister is a woman, Frau Lüders. She is a cousin of my landlady's."

I took her advice, and a few days later went to the girls' high school at the Waller Ring in Bremen. This time I got to talk to the principal. After I had finished my prepared speech, she looked me over critically and began with an artificially sweet voice that boded ill: "Both of our fifth forms are full." After a pause, and looking at the letter from Lotte, she concluded, "And we really could not admit a student without an official transcript." I did not believe that both fifth forms were full, but there was little I could do but turn on my heels and walk out. As I left the building, I had an idea. I went back in and down to the basement, where the school janitor lived in most German schools. I found him in a storeroom full of empty shelves and asked him, "Could you tell me where the Ministry of Education is?" He readily gave me directions in his slow Low German, which I understood just enough to get the name of the street and the house number. He even came to the gate with me and pointed me in the right direction, down through burned-out blocks toward the Weser riverbank.

I followed the houses facing the river and soon arrived at a nineteenth-century villa converted into a provisional office building. I entered the hallway, looking for a sign with the name Lüders. I knocked and, on entering, noted that this was a secretary's room. I guessed that beyond the next door was the minister's office. I did not wait for the secretary to make trouble but simply brushed past her. Before she could hold me back, I opened the door behind her. Frau Lüders faced me with a quizzical look, annoyed at being disturbed.

"Excuse me," I said, "I need *your* help," emphasizing *your* to signal that I did not want to talk to the secretary. I did not leave her time to think it over but blurted out my story, beginning with my futile attempts to be admitted to Delmenhorst high school and my lack of an official transcript or birth certificate. And, as I had started with the truth, I forgot my prepared speech and told her the rest of my true story: that I had not been allowed to go to high school, that I had taken private lessons, studied to make up for my deficiencies, and had just arrived. "I simply have to get into high school. I have lost so much time already."

She looked right at me as I spoke, attentively and thoughtfully, even as she motioned the secretary to leave us and close the door. "Where are you from?" she asked. I had forgotten to say that I was a refugee.

"From Silesia. My family and I now live at the refugee camp at Adelheide Airfield. But I can take the train to Bremen," I concluded, anxious that she might change her mind because I did not live in town. She seemed to come to some conclusion about me as she reached for the phone.

"I will phone Dr. Budde at the Oberschule at Hamburger Street. I think they will have room for you and it is probably the best school for you." After talking for a while to the man who had answered her call, she turned back to me and said, "They are ready for you. Go right over. Miss Müller will give you the directions." Then, as if she felt that something more was called for, she faced me again: "The school I am sending you to is an *Aufbauschule,* a special high school for students who started their academic careers later than usual, not at age ten but at age twelve or even older. They are expected to accomplish the usual eight-year curriculum in six years. Like you, they are somewhat unusual students. Many are commuters to Bremen, as you will be. You'll like it there."

Half an hour later I stood in the principal's office of the high school on Hamburger Street, which also served as the teachers' lounge. An elderly gentleman with a heavily lined face whose large brown eyes scanned me carefully came over, made a small bow, and introduced himself. I did the same. Hearing my name, he noticed his mistake. "I thought you were Frau Becher, the new French teacher the ministry promised to send me. But I see you are Ursula, the student they want us to take into the fifth form. Wait a minute. I'll take you over to the fifth in a second."

I was used to being taken for much older than my sixteen years, yet his mistake flattered me. I waited patiently, and soon he was at my side and knocked at the door opposite his office. "This is the fifth's homeroom. We don't have a homeroom teacher for them yet, but we will all settle in soon. Frau Mittchen is a substitute." As we entered, I was confronted by three rows of desks, most of them filled with boys. Three girls in the background, seemingly much younger, interrupted what they were doing to look at me. Dr. Budde introduced me, and before leaving he turned to me again and said, "This is their fourth hour of instruction. You are done for the day after the fifth, their English lesson; come and see me then."

I sat in the desk the substitute teacher assigned me and listened carefully. It was a geography lesson; the subject, of all things, was Eastern Europe. Frau Mittchen, who had just begun her lesson, repeated what she had told the students. "Today, let's look at the provisional new borders between the Soviet

Union, Poland, Germany, and Czechoslovakia." I was all attention as she pointed at a map of central Europe. "The map shows us the borders of 1938," she continued, as her pointer swept along the Baltic Sea up to East Prussia and down into Polish Upper Silesia. The class sat apathetically, the subject obviously of no interest to them. To get their attention, she dramatically slashed her pointer from Stettin on the Baltic, at the mouth of the Oder River, straight down to Dresden.

"Johannson," she addressed the white-blond boy in the front row, "what are the provinces that this new border leaves outside Germany?"

The boy rose from his seat and stood up, an empty look on his face. "Sit down," she said after a pause, giving up on him, and turned to a boy in the second row whose hand had shot up.

"Meyer?" Meyer jumped up from his seat. "East Prussia, Pomerania, some of Brandenburg, all of Silesia," he blurted out. Meyer, I found out later, always knew the answers, and the others disliked him for it.

Frau Mittchen continued. "These are the borders the occupation forces drew up at the 1945 Potsdam Conference. These provinces now belong to Poland, at least until a final peace settlement is reached."

I was stunned. This was the first time that I understood what had happened to my home province as a result of our losing the war. The lesson confirmed what I apprehended intuitively when our train pulled out of Strehlen station and we left Silesia: that we had lost our home. Nevertheless, the sudden and full comprehension of our situation made my head spin. I sat through the next hour and then the English lesson without hearing a single word. Afterward, Dr. Budde asked me into his office again.

"How did you find the class?"

"It was fine. I'll have a lot to catch up with," I said, referring not to geography but rather to the mathematics, Latin, and English gaps in my background.

"You'll be on probation till next Easter," Dr. Budde told me, concluding the interview. "You will have to make up all deficits by that time. By the way, we have a number of students who commute from Delmenhorst to school. So you won't be alone." We never spoke about probation again. By Easter I had made up most of my deficits and my grades were good enough to warrant a full tuition scholarship from Frau Lüders's ministry.

On the train home, the full realization of what I had accomplished hit me. I refused to give the loss of our home another thought. Instead I worried about how I was going to pay for tuition. And how was I going to get from Adelheide to Bremen daily? When I told Mother, she just shrugged her shoulders with a gesture of helpless perplexity. "I don't know how you'll manage." Lotte was more positive. "You'll just have to get up early, hike the four kilometers to Delmenhorst station, take the train, and walk the rest." I figured two and a half hours to school, two and a half back, conservatively, since the railroad bridges over the Weser were still out and the ferry service to downtown Bremen slow. Once on the downtown side of Bremen, I still had almost an hour's walk to school, unless the streetcars ran and I could pay for them. Lotte lent me money to buy a student monthly train ticket. Frau Behrends promised and delivered help with tuition and tram tickets from the city council.

After several weeks of school, unexpected help arrived with the closing of the airfield camp. With the beginning of the east-west conflict, the airfield, we were told, was needed by the Allies. The occupation authorities forced the town of Delmenhorst to accommodate all five thousand of us during the last weeks of October. The natives reacted to our arrival like it was a barbarian invasion. The mayor and his deputies went from house to house and confiscated, in the name of the Allies, one or two rooms in every house and apartment. Military trucks loaded up our possessions, including our straw mattresses, and deposited us in front of the houses where unwilling families had to take us in. We landed in the apartment of a widower in a three-story apartment house for the families of middle managers in the jute factory. We were assigned a room and told to share the kitchen with our host, who refused even to talk to us. As luck would have it, our new quarters were a two-minute walk from the Delmenhorst railroad station. International tensions benefited me by shortening my way to school by a full hour. I missed only one day of school because of our move.

Not that I enjoyed the benefits for long. Winter set in early. The winter of 1946–47 was the coldest and longest on record. Our school had been fire-bombed and we could use only the classroom wing. The gym, assembly hall, library, laboratories, and science and map collections had burned down. None of the classrooms had proper windows. The heating and electrical systems of the building did not work. For a few weeks we moved in with another school and had lessons in the afternoon, while the other school had theirs in the morning. Then the Weser River froze over and ferry service stopped. For a while it was too dangerous to cross the river by foot. Luckily many of my fellow students were commuters and missed school as well. By January the city had run out of coal, so all the schools were closed.

Throughout my first weeks of high school, I met daily with Lotte. She filled in the gaps in my knowledge, which enabled me to do the homework in mathematics and English. Because I was three years behind my classmates in Latin, she helped me work through a Latin grammar. For the time being, I could get by in all other subjects. With the first in-class German essay exam, I established a track record with Dr. Budde, our German literature teacher. Despite my poor spelling and worse punctuation, I received the best mark in class. Dr. Budde corrected both without deducting points for mistakes. "Some people naturally write well, just like others ride bikes well," Dr. Budde told the class. Turning to me he added, "Learn the rules of punctuation and pay attention to spelling." To my surprise, I actually found this easy to do once I acquired a basic understanding of German grammar by studying Latin and put my mind to it. During these first months in school and through the winter break, I worked harder than I ever had in my life. My mind swarmed with mathematical theorems, grammar rules, English and Latin vocabulary.

For brief breaks from studying, I spent several Sundays in October and November with Frau Matzinger in Bremen. We followed the final judgments at Nuremberg avidly. By this time I had no illusions left about the extent of the crimes the Nazi leaders had committed. Even as an eight-year-old child, I had observed, if not understood, the deportation of the quarry workers, communist opponents, to camps. I had known Polish slave laborers like Wanda, and I had witnessed Kristallnacht. During the last days of the war, when I worked in the hospital, I had heard the ss man and his buddy discuss their treatment of Jews, Russians, and Poles. I had listened to the home guard men complain about the crimes the ss had committed at the eastern front. I had heard about and seen survivors of concentration camps for Jews and political prisoners in Czechoslovakia. I needed no convincing, but I was horrified by the details of the acts of inhumanity in the camps. I despised the many adults I encountered, including my mother, who claimed they had known nothing, or who denied the charges at Nuremberg as enemy propaganda, as victor's justice. It was only during the Vietnam War that I came to understand at least my mother's assertion that she did not remember Kristallnacht. If you feel responsible and keep silent in the face of obvious crimes, it is tempting to erase the memory rather than feel the shame of having failed to protest.

The daily papers made much of Ilse Koch, the wife of the commandant of Buchenwald, and the lampshades she had made from human skin. Frau Matzinger commented dryly that one woman's perversion was distracting the nation's attention from the vast, mostly male network of guards, military police, and ss henchmen who had remained anonymous and disappeared among the population as if they had never existed. I don't remember whether I saw the film *The Murderers Are Among Us* that fall or later, but when I did see it, its melodramatic message seemed less trenchant to me than did Frau Matzinger's matter-of-fact assertion that Nazism survived just fine in the many ordinary perpetrators and bystanders who had simply faded into the woodwork.

"One of my neighbors," she told me, "boasted to me that he had been a party big shot in Berlin. Now he is working for the denazification agency of the Americans and helping local Nazis get their classifications reduced. For a fee, of course."

Denazification had been instituted by the Allied Control Council in 1945 and was still going strong. Its directives specified the organizations and the specific classes of persons affected by denazification and how to deal with them by judicial means. Beyond well-known leaders of Nazi institutions, all those in the general population who wanted to work for a public agency, schools, the press, or cultural institutions and civil administrations were required to fill out a questionnaire on their past political affiliations and the positions they had held during the Third Reich. After submitting the questionnaire, investigations into their background, and an appearance before a committee, they were assigned a category that defined their degree of culpability under the Nazi regime. I do not remember the different categories assigned to applicants by the denazification committees, but within a year the local committee that processed the local population had been totally discredited and became a public joke. The number of adults who claimed membership in the "passive resistance" surprised me. They maintained that they had never participated in any Nazi activities, had withdrawn into the private sphere during the Nazi period, and had deliberately boycotted any public Nazi event. And who could prove otherwise, particularly in the case of nonlocal refugees and expellees?

It was harder to fake membership in the "active resistance," since the few who had been in the resistance were either dead or had a camp tattoo to prove it. Documented members of the parties Hitler had dissolved in 1933, such as Frau Behrends, were able to obtain positions of trust in the newly forming local bureaucracies and school administrations after their denazification. I do not know to what category they were assigned. An acceptable category that did not bar you from lower public offices was that of the "fellow traveler." This meant that the person so assigned could prove that he had become a member of a Nazi organization only during *Gleichschaltung* and had never held an office. The next category, active party member of the NSDAP, included those who had held a minor local leadership function and barred such persons from public positions for a time and occasionally required a brief period of lowly work such as cleaning streets or clearing rubble for the public good. Lotte, who had filled out a questionnaire—"I will not perjure myself as most of them do and hide who I was!" she declared—swept Delmenhorst streets for a few months in 1947 before resuming her teaching career in a middle school, as teachers were badly needed. Young people like myself, and the youth cohorts born in the mid-1920s, fell, I believe, under a general amnesty by late 1946. Yet many members of the SS, former SS judges, and physicians remained in influential official positions in industry, the judiciary, and public health. It was against these old Nazis and their protectors in high places that the students of the 1968 generation rebelled. What kept Nazi publications and the residue of old and of newly formed secret Nazi organizations under control during the late 1940s was their prohibition by the Allies and the discredit they had fallen into with a majority of the population. Most Germans I knew in 1946 and 1947 had had more than enough of them.

Frau Matzinger and I thought of ourselves as sensitive and alert to any Nazi misdeed. Yet I find it curious now that although we lived only about fifty miles from Bergen-Belsen, we did not connect the place, Bergen near Celle, with the actual camp or with the painful, horrifying newsreel the British took of it, part of which I saw at the time. One scene from it remains etched in my mind: stolid-faced German citizens, women in kerchiefs and old men, impassively filing by a ditch filled with emaciated, skeletal, violated naked bodies. The imperturbable blankness on my countrymen's faces makes me burn with shame even now.

That November, 1946, as she had at all former Nazi festive occasions, Lotte asked me to commemorate November 9 with her, the commemoration of Hitler's failed coup in Munich in 1923, when a number of Hitler's faithful had died. She wanted to affirm our loyalty to Hitler and his party, she told me. "No! You still don't understand, do you? Loyalty to them? They were criminals, all of them. Everything they ever taught us was dead wrong," was all I could say. If she refused to teach me after my refusal, I'd just have to manage on my own. She was offended by my rejection but continued our lessons, and I appreciated that she kept strictly to mathematics, English, and Latin from then on. I paid her with the money I began to make from tutoring. Shortly after I had started school, I had asked the families in the neighborhood if their first- to fourth-graders needed any tutoring help. I became a pacifist and an internationalist as a result of my taking stock, that winter, of my experience in HJ, at the field hospital, of the end of the war and the devastation wrought by Nazism, nationalism, and militarism that I saw all around me. But these were intellectual positions. I did not know then that I would struggle for a fuller understanding of my experience for the rest of my life.

It was bitterly cold. Our room in the widower's apartment could not be heated until late that winter, when we finally obtained a small iron stove. But we had only peat, sometimes still wet, to burn in it. For want of kindling and wood we even removed the wooden handles from the cooking utensils and cutlery we had brought along from home. Once we managed to light the stove, the peat fire produced more smoke than warmth. We could not escape the smoke, because our landlord forbade us to use the kitchen after one of us carelessly left a few dirty dishes in the sink. The loss of access to the kitchen also meant that we had to get water for all our needs from a basement tap three flights down. For a while we ate at a public soup kitchen for refugees. Finally Mother managed to get work with several families as a seamstress. She used their sewing machines at their houses and was paid in meals. She usually took Werner along, as his school had closed its doors as well. Sometimes they brought food home for me. I stayed home and studied in bed, covered with all of the featherbeds we had luckily brought from Silesia. Even so, I was cold and hungry, as our rationing cards bought almost nothing.

Werner had made a friend, a carpenter, and soon preferred spending time at his workshop rather than going to customers with Mother. Herr Ammer ("Call me Horst") was stocky, of medium height, and bald, though only in his early thirties, with one arm hanging limp at his side. "No, not at the front," he explained when I asked sympathetically on a visit to his shop to pick up Werner. "I caught my arm in my father's electric saw when I was a kid. It was almost severed, and then reattached. It saved me from having to go into the army." I felt friendly to him because he took care of my brother, and I pitied him for his handicap. At seventeen, I thought of him as an old man.

We still had no furniture except the canisters, some metal bedsteads, and the straw mattresses we had brought along from the airfield. The town council voted to give refugee families five hundred marks to buy furniture as a one-time compensation for losing our homes. Through Werner's negotiations, the carpenter offered to make us a triple-stacked bunk bed, some shelves, a table, and three stools. He delivered them at New Year's and brought along some punch and even goodies from his Christmas meal, so that we could celebrate our new riches. Mother had made soft gray-green curtains for the shelves and the bunk bed, so that we could hide the beds and remove from sight the few pots and pans and dishes we had brought along, as well as the provisions she received from customers. We felt rich and joked around, and we invited the refugee family from downstairs, Frau Schmidt and her daughter Leonie, who was my brother's age, to share in the fun.

After a few days the carpenter came visiting again, but since I had my head in a book, I paid no attention. I had learned to shut out the world around me when I studied back in Silesia when we lived with my aunts. He and Mother talked as I did my homework. I was glad Mother had made a friend. One day, to my surprise, Mother invited him to read his poetry to us, and I finally got the drift.

"He has fallen in love with you," Mother claimed, "and he wants to marry you and provide a home for us all."

Both Mother and Werner saw the proposal as an end to our troubles. I was aghast at the suggestion of marriage. His coming to read his poetry to us seemed ludicrous; I felt embarrassed for him—the poetry was awful—and angry at Mother for encouraging him and putting me into this situation. At the same time, I was hungry, cold, and miserable, and it seemed impossible to catch up in all the subjects I had to during these winter months. Was I tempted to just give up? Yes. Even married, I rationalized, I could still read and think what I wanted to.

"He even told me that he will allow you to finish the next school year and send you to cooking school. You won't need to get married until you are eighteen," Mother said, sensing my hesitation. His "will allow you" stopped me cold. Nobody had "allowed" me anything since I was ten!

"Why don't you marry him yourself, if you want to be taken care of," I told her. From then on I refused to participate in any dealings with the carpenter.

At the end of February there was a thaw, and the extreme cold lessened. Instruction resumed because the city had managed to obtain coal for the schools. Although ferry service across the Weser River had not been restored, the ice was thick enough that we could walk across and get to school. I avoided coming home till late in the evening and did my homework in the station waiting room. One day, by chance, I discovered a better place to study, an oasis of quiet and comfort. Dr. Budde, our German literature teacher, told us about the America House and its reading room, where, with a student pass, we could check out books or read them. That afternoon, on my way to the station after school, I stopped by the America House. Its reading room was well heated, brightly lit, equipped with easy chairs and desks, and open to the reading public till nine o'clock at night. A train from Bremen-Neustadt left after nine, which gave me enough time to use the room to the fullest and still get home by bedtime.

Since I had worked through the English grammar once, I decided to take advantage of the books available at the reading room. Instead of learning English vocabulary, I started to read English novels on my own. I don't know who recommended the Jalna series by Mazo de la Roche. At any rate, I began with the first book of the series, working with a dictionary. For the first twenty pages I had to look up almost every word. But I persisted, and soon I recognized many words and had to check fewer and fewer. About a hundred pages into the novel, I got the drift of the story, read through it, and moved on to the next book. By the fourth volume or so, I was familiar with much of de la Roche's vocabulary and understood the rest from context. By Easter 1947 I had improved my grade in the monthly dictation in English to a B. That left Latin and mathematics to catch up with, but by this time I no longer needed Lotte's tutoring. Fortunately, my fellow students, for lack of laboratories and science teachers, had missed out on several years of biology, physics, and chemistry. From that spring on, with one science room of the burned-out part of our school restored and a new biology and chemistry teacher, we all had to make up our deficiencies in these subjects.

The Bremen America House soon became for me more than a library to study in. A few times a week, late afternoon or early evening public lectures brought together a few Germans—high school students like me, a few teachers, several older citizens who were just curious—and a number of American librarians, officers of the occupation forces, and personnel from various public and private American and British agencies. America Houses at the time were meant to provide Germans with an opportunity to educate themselves in democracy. And most of their lectures, discussions, and other public events concerned issues and problems of democratic governance and policy. Sometimes foreign musicians gave concerts and foreign movies were shown. Discussions followed most of these events. At the time, I derived all my knowledge of the world beyond Germany from these lectures and cultural events. I had been starved for just such fare and since it was free of charge I stayed away only when I had to study for an exam the next day. The naïve idealism that dominated America House events suited my state of mind well, and its positive messages counteracted the gloom and near despair of the world around me.

I remember the details of only a few of the lectures, because they introduced me to points of view that became of particular interest to me. One was a lecture by a British academic who spoke of the Oxford moral rearmament movement. He presented the thesis that the wars of the twentieth century in all Western countries had wrought such demoralization that only through each country's spiritual regeneration, through honesty and taking responsibility, could world peace, reconciliation, and reconstruction be achieved. A heated discussion followed the lecture. One faction, led by a frequent participant in discussions, an American woman, maintained that a more realistic approach toward German youth was needed, a reeducation of German young people in democratic processes. The other faction, led by the speaker, argued that citizens in all the world's countries needed to rally to create a world free of fear, hate, and greed. I was fired up by the Briton's point of view, though I did not agree that religious faith could provide the rallying force for a changed world order. I had observed much too much hypocrisy on the part of our Protestant clergy at home and my fellow citizens after our arrival in the west to believe in regeneration through religious values. Frau Scherzer and Paul had taught me that you did not need to believe in God to act ethically. I did not participate in the discussion, as I was much too shy to speak my mind. But as I was leaving, the American lady spoke to me.

"I have seen you at a number of our events, but you never participate." She was tall, always dressed in black, had a commanding manner, and spoke German with an American accent. I have forgotten her name because I called her, to myself, the Lady in Black.

"I agree with the British gentleman," I replied hesitantly. "But I cannot formulate my ideas as well as he can, and I doubt that the churches here have much else to offer than shelter from having been a Nazi. I believe that we Germans first need to achieve personal regeneration through . . . reflection? Soul-searching? Taking responsibility for what we have done? I am not sure, really," I faltered. "I'll have to run, I'll miss my train," I concluded as I made to go.

"Wait! I'll drive you to the station," she said. We spent another two hours sitting in her car arguing, and she finally drove me home.

From then on, the Lady in Black frequently sat next to me during lectures, and we continued to discuss them afterward. Gradually, through practice with her, I dared to speak up in the public discussions, and I came to enjoy the back-and-forth of intellectual debate.

Another lecture was on women's rights, women and work, and women and the vote. The audience consisted largely of women, as the lecture had been advertised in Bremen's high schools for girls. By this time I had found out that my older friend, the Lady in Black, was the German-born wife of a diplomat who had left Germany in the early 1930s and held a part-time position as an educational officer with the occupation forces. She had been a feminist in the 1920s, one of the women whose studies at Berlin University had been interrupted when she left Germany. This time around, I found myself on her side in the discussion, at least at first. One of the girls from the high school began the debate by saying, "My mother is a feminist. She works as a lawyer. She is not around when my brothers and I need her. I think a woman's first responsibility is to her family and her children." I could sense that my American friend was annoyed. I myself was uncertain what I thought about this subject, but I spoke up anyway.

"My mother works too—as a matter of fact, so do I. And I don't intend to ever stop doing so. I want to have some profession—I am not sure yet which. I cannot imagine ever being dependent on a husband for earning family income. My father died when I was young. It was fortunate that Mother had learned dressmaking. She did not have much time for my brothers and me. But that . . ." and here I faltered, thinking that it might in fact have been good if she had had time for us. My American friend took up where I left off.

"If women want or need to work, child care should be available for them. In the kibbutzim in Israel, women have a choice. Those who want to mother can mind the children of those who don't want to spend all their time doing so." Once again, after the lecture, the American and I argued. I told her about the child care Mother had got for me after Oma died and how miserable I had been in institutional child care. "I doubt whether any impersonal child care is a good solution," I said, while she insisted that I had not listened carefully and that kibbutz child care was not impersonal.

I remained friends with the American woman until I graduated from high school, when I moved away and lost touch with her. I profited much from our conversations and debates. She took me seriously and engaged me on an intellectual level. It never occurred to me then that she was probably Jewish and assumed that I knew this. Had I known, would I have thought to ask her what had happened to her and her family? Or would I have felt too guilty to ask any questions? I don't know. She was as much responsible for my coming to like Americans and everything American as the lectures and my reading were. And she certainly lessened my loneliness, as I failed miserably in making friends with people my own age.

Almost from the beginning, I did not get along with my classmates. I had looked forward to making friends and having peers to talk with who shared my interests. I had not had friends my age at Adelheide or Delmenhorst. About half of my Bremen classmates lived in the city; most of the commuters came from small towns north of Bremen, and only two shared my commute. These kids had been together from the age of twelve. They had spent several vacations since the end of the war clearing rubble. Before that, they had been evacuated as a class to the country to escape the bombs that had destroyed more than half the city. A few had lost their homes. Except for one veteran who soon left, they were all about a year younger than I was. From the outset I had tried to strike up conversations with the commuters, who had a room in the basement where they waited, talked, or did homework before leaving for their trains. Coming down one day, I overheard them talking about me.

"Typical refugee," one of them said derisively, "makes up horror stories about the awful Russians. Brags about her heroics, as they all do."

It was true, refugees told all kinds of fantastic tales about the many times they had been raped, robbed, driven from their homes. About the wealth they had left behind, the estates they had lost. The positions they had held. One of the many refugee jokes satirized their confabulations by way of a shaggy dog story. A St. Bernard and a Dachshund meet. "Back home I was a Great Dane," the Dachshund says.

But how would these boys know the difference between what was reality and what fantasy? How dare they judge! I avoided the commuters from then on. I was so hurt and angered by their rejection that I clammed up and stopped talking to anyone about what I had experienced. In class, I soon sensed that my fellow students resented that I did my homework conscientiously and participated in discussion eagerly. They took my interest in my studies as currying favor with the teachers and teased me about it. I responded to their teasing with intellectual arrogance. Let the stupid juveniles think what they wanted! I rationalized in my arrogance. I need the grades to stay in school. And once I was sure that I could stay in school, I needed good grades for a scholarship. Apart from that, I craved what my teachers had to offer, and took up eagerly any suggestion for extra reading, for attending a lecture or a free concert.

There was only one generational issue about which I agreed with my class-mates: distrust of adults, of the entire older generation. Only a year or so before, they had heard our history teacher, Herr Fridhof (we called him Herr Friedhof, that is, Mr. Cemetery) go on and on about "our beloved Führer." Kritias, a sarcastic wit and mimic, imitated Fridhof's nasal twang to perfection, adding, "Final victory will be ours!" They also made fun of Dr. Budde, whose love of poetry I shared, because his voice broke when reading a poem that moved him. Hiding behind his desk, Kritias would take out a huge hand-kerchief that he kept ready for just that purpose and, with a flourish, wipe his face as the class tittered.

The one teacher they left alone, even giving him a grudging respect, was Herr Beck, the Latin teacher. Herr Beck was relatively new to the school. During the Nazi period he had been dismissed from teaching because he was a socialist. During the bombings, the class knew from Dr. Budde, Herr Beck had not been allowed into an air-raid shelter. A few stories had it that he carried neighbors from burning buildings. And indeed, one side of his face was badly scarred, as were his hands. A man of small stature, he looked like a frail, scraggy gnome at first sight, someone not up to any task. I once saw him stop before opening the door to our classroom and pull himself up straight, as if going into battle. He always entered class with a question on his lips that he shot out. "Friese, first sentence of Cicero's Cataline oration?" At first, I was terrified whenever he entered class. He was the only teacher in that school I came to love.

Lotte and I had taken an adult education class on expressionist painting the first few weeks we were in Adelheide. I had only seen copies of art like Dürer's etchings, and never any art the Nazis designated degenerate, like the expressionists'. I am sure Lotte took the class because she was curious to see what the teacher would do with the subject of degenerate art. Of the first lecture I remember only the illustrations of Franz Marc's and of Karl Schmidt-Rottluff's paintings of the Blue Rider and Brücke schools of paint-ing. They were glorious: blue horses, swirls of red, blue, red, and yellow cows dancing, a crouching tiger made of yellow triangles, blotches of red, green, blue, a dyke break! The remarks of the students about "unnatural" colors and Lotte's derogatory comments about primitivism could not have struck me as more ridiculous or inappropriate. They missed the point. Didn't they see the sinuous lines, the strength of the primary colors? I immediately responded to the teacher's question, "Why did the painter represent the horses as blue?"

Had they not read Novalis's *Heinrich von Ofterdingen*? The blue flower suggests romantic yearning. Abstracted from the flower, blue remains. The essence of romanticism. I felt entranced by the lecture as much as by the illustrations.

"Where are the paintings?" I asked the instructor.

"Sold abroad during the Third Reich," came the answer. "But you can get an idea of what symbolism leading to expressionism was like. Worpswede, a few miles from here, has some of the paintings of Paula Becker-Modersohn. So, by the way, does the Kunsthalle in Bremen."

On a Sunday in the spring of 1947 I talked Lotte into spending the money to go to Worpswede. I had seen a Becker-Modersohn show at the Bremen Kunsthalle late the previous fall and expected I would see marshlands like those Becker-Modersohn had painted, or even observe the evening sky light up with a lurid green as in some of her landscapes. But the sky remained overcast during our visit, and the village of Worpswede, with its thatched farmhouses, was a tourist trap. The Modersohn house, which displayed only a few of Overbeck's, her husband's, pictures, disappointed me even more. Dejectedly we walked back to the Bremen streetcar terminal, and therefore I did not notice that Herr Beck and his family were walking behind us as I loudly expressed my disappointment to Lotte. Suddenly I heard a familiar voice. "I quite agree with you. It's too bad that the Modersohn house shows only Overbeck's paintings." It was Herr Beck. I introduced Lotte and we continued walking and talking together.

From that day on, I was less intimidated by Beck, and he often pointed out to me what shows at the Kunsthalle were worth going to or which architectural points of interest I should look at in Bremen. Learning that I often had to wait for my train home and did my homework at the station waiting room or the America House and skipped supper, he invited me to come and work in their living room. He owned a large collection of art and architecture books and encouraged me to use them. He taught me how to read the floor plans of churches, temples, and public buildings, and how to distinguish and appreciate different styles of architecture. Often the Becks invited me to stay for supper. I accepted their hospitality, although I knew that they, like us, lived only on their ration cards. The acceptance and comfort I experienced at their home made it easier for me to live through the desolation and poverty of our overcrowded room in Delmenhorst.

Most of the time Mother worked as a seamstress for different families for a meal and a few marks. To supplement her income, I tutored a few younger students. Living mostly on ration cards left us hungry much of the time. Unlike natives of the region, we had no possibility of supplementing our diet through a garden, or black market deals, or farming connections. On Sundays in summer and fall, we went out to the Adelheide heath and forest and collected berries and mushrooms. We asked the farmers if we could dig up potatoes left in the ground after they had finished harvesting. When Mother saved some extra material from a dress, she made it into a blouse or a child's dress, and I offered it to farmers in exchange for bread, potatoes, apples, anything edible. But bartering for food supplies only on Sundays was not enough. Soon I spent every Saturday and Sunday going from farm to farm, offering whatever Mother had made during the week or whatever money we had earned. Of course, our bartering was actually begging. We could give the farmers only worthless money or valueless goods. They were accustomed to black market valuables like gold jewelry and oriental carpets. Yet I always came home with something.

As much as I hated going begging for food, my hikes through the countryside that late summer and fall of 1947 at least acquainted me with a different way of farming that I looked at with some interest. I usually took the train to a few stations outside of town—my student pass allowed the free ride. Villages in this part of the country differed from our Silesian villages, in which farmsteads sat close together along a village road or small retainer houses clustered around a big estate. Here, isolated farms lay in the middle of their lands, so that between visiting two houses I had some time to idle by the roadside, sit by a drainage ditch, catch my breath, and refuel my courage for another approach to a forbidding farmer's wife. Rows of trees separated the properties, so I always had shade to rest beneath. To the north and west of town, the huge thatched and gabled farmhouses had stables for cows and horses in addition to the living quarters. Milk and cheese were the main products the farms produced. Meadows stretched to the horizon under what seemed to me a vast and usually gray sky. It seemed a forbidding and somber landscape to me, the houses as hostile as the dogs that barked as I approached. It was a major victory if I could talk an ample, rosy-cheeked woman into selling me a loaf of their dark, heavy bread—it looked like a huge, dark brown brick—which she took from a smokehouse next to the kitchen.

The landscape to the south seemed friendlier to me. Although I longed for the hills of home, the soft undulations of the land here, with fields of ripening grain, rye for the most part, and dry in the late summer heat, at least smelled like home. During one of these visits, just as a farmer's wife had filled my knapsack with apples, I spied a familiar figure. No, that cannot be, I thought. And then I realized that it was indeed one of Mother's farming cousins whose farm we had sometimes visited during my teens. The family had been transplanted to this farm and now worked for the farmer. Though unhappy about having lost their own land and working as common laborers, my relatives gave me a friendly welcome and on later visits introduced me to some local farmers so that my task of getting food supplies became easier.

Finally, I told Dr. Budde that I would not be able to come to school on Saturdays—weekends as we know them today did not exist—explaining that I simply had to get food for the family. As long as I made up the work, the teachers tolerated my absences without comment. My fellow students, not knowing why I was absent, objected. I overheard them complain, "Why can *she* take a long weekend?" and I despised them for their lack of comprehension. I resented their well-fed smugness that could not imagine how a refugee lived. Looking back now, I don't understand why I didn't tell them the reasons for my absence. Was I too ashamed? Did I think they would not believe me? Did I relish my position as the misunderstood, burdened genius? I suppose all of these things, but I never said a word, and I returned their resentment with arrogance and hostility.

Sometime in mid-1947 our constant hunger was mitigated. The American occupation authority in Bremen made a hot noon meal available to all students at all schools. The American armed forces, who had been friendly to all the small children, made even more friends among the student population by what we called *die Schulspeisung* (school meals), when army trucks delivered huge canisters filled with soups that our teachers dished out to us during break. I relished the soups, particularly a sweetened soup made with raisins—a delicacy for a young person starved for sweets. Some of my fellow students did not want their meals, and therefore I often picked up leftovers from the janitor in the basement to take home for our supper.

Clothing and shoes became another problem. My one pair of boots gave out sometime during that first winter. My English teacher noticed the split seams and suggested that I go to an American mission that had its quarters right next to the Ministry of Education. She made an appointment for me, and a friendly elderly lady in heavy makeup and a pink suit took me into a room full of shoes, both new and used. Pointing to the women's section, she selected a pair of high-heeled lady's pumps.

"No, thank you, they would not last me a week," I said as I motioned to the other side of the room. "These are what I need." I chose a pair of men's shoes with heavy rubber soles.

The pink lady looked at me doubtfully. "But you can't wear those. They are men's."

"I walk at least two hours a day to go to school. None of the women's shoes, even those with flat heels, have the kind of soles that can withstand walking in rain and snow," I tried to explain.

"No, these are really not right for you. Why don't you put these rubbers over these loafers," she argued, pointing to a pair of flat-heeled, thin-soled shoes that I later recognized as loafers. I would not budge. I could see her frustration with me, her look even of suspicion at my lack of femininity. I did not want to offend her, but I held on to the men's shoes. They lasted me a year.

By the spring of 1948 I had decided that it was high time for me to catch up with the class in Latin. Having gone through the Latin grammar once, I reckoned that what had served me well in learning English would also help with Latin. I would read Latin texts during summer vacation. In class we had finished reading Cesar and were beginning to dip into Cicero. I knew that Tacitus was too difficult to tackle by myself. But I trusted that I could manage Cicero, all the more so as I knew that Herr Beck valued Cicero's philosophical writings. Equipped with a dictionary, I began. At first the *Somnium scipionis,* Cicero's *Dream,* was hard going, and I managed to translate only some thirty or forty lines an afternoon. But a week into the work, I put the dictionary aside and tried to understand what I was reading and guess the words from context. Six weeks later, by school's start, I could read any Cicero text with some degree of ease and even came to understand some of Beck's enthusiasm for Cicero's style and stoicism. Beck noticed my now eager participation with pleasure but never commented on it.

Between a regular school schedule, tutoring lessons, homework, and expeditions for food, my life had begun to assume some kind of normality. Though the daily trip from Delmenhorst to Bremen was still a chore, it became immeasurably easier once the Weser railroad bridge functioned, streetcars began to run predictably, and I received a free pass for them. Though trains were late and overcrowded, riding on the roof of the cars, as all student commuters did, failed to produce the adrenaline rush of fear and the challenges to my survival skills that the last days of the war, the invasion, and the Polish occupation had provided. At times I experienced almost intolerable spells of boredom; at other times I felt sated and bloated with facts that didn't matter. Who the hell cared if I knew the periodic table or solid geometry? They added nothing to my life. Ultimately, I argued with myself, I needed to know the facts to get my diploma. That was all. I had to persist if I wanted to study at the university.

The only activity during the winter and spring of 1947–48 that satisfied my need for emotional excitement was my encounter, at the America House, with the novels of Thomas Wolfe. I had started with *Look Homeward, Angel* on Dr. Budde's recommendation and soon could not tear myself away from his books. His exuberant love of words, the grandiosity of his vision of America, together with the shabbiness of his boarding houses and their down-and-out inhabitants, matched my experience of the world, even though his was a thoroughly foreign world. I loved Wolfe's evocations of long overnight train rides with train whistles blowing through dense forests that I imagined as primeval. I read every last word Wolfe had written and acquired an intimate familiarity with his fictional world. I did not know at the time that my enthusiasm for his vision would win me a Fulbright Scholarship a few years later.

I visited Delmenhorst and Bremen again in the 1980s. The anger I had felt in the late 1940s struck me forcibly. I again felt the almost blinding fury that dominated my existence as an expellee. Anger at overhearing train conversations about the "good old days under Adolf." Anger at being crowded, hungry, cold, dependent on charity; fury at feeling like an outcast, at our isolation in a West German society that did not want us and looked down on us as homeless beggars and vagrants. I had difficulty understanding why I did not seek relief in violence and criminal activity. Fortunately, my relationship to Oma had taught me to seek alliances that could sustain me emotionally, like those with Frau Scherzer, Frau Behrends, the Lady in Black, and Herr Beck; these helped me persist in my goal to get an education even if the whole world conspired against it. And despite my anger and resentment and loneliness, I saw in retrospect that those first years in West Germany were also hopeful years, filled with idealism about what the country could be. It was not only the America House that provided this moral optimism. Calls for moral regeneration in various guises, as well as expressions of fury at the German military leadership for their abuses of the common soldier, dominated the plays I saw at the time. My teachers, particularly Herr Beck and Dr. Budde, extolled the Kantian idealism of the nineteenth century and the civic virtue of Cicero, that we might apply their ethical norms to the democracy we were to help build. And even Herr Fridhof taught us the political traditions of the Hanseatic League, which he saw as the forerunners of democratic forms of governance on the continent. I identified with the early writings of Borchardt and Böll that I read at the time, because they showed the reaction of the common soldier to the horror of war and of returning to a devastated country. But for the most part, apart from English novels, I read less during my school years than I ever had before.

In reflecting on these early postwar years in West Germany, I am struck by how exclusively all of us focused only on Germany, German misery, German problems, German literature and art. A few blocks from us, displaced persons from the Baltic States and Poland lived in barracks, waiting for permission to emigrate. I passed by their quarters and I heard them talked about. But I never had any curiosity about them beyond an awareness that they would leave Germany. At the time I did not understand how totally we had absorbed the exclusive, aggressive nationalism of our Nazi training, how steeped we were in a self-centeredness that knew no empathy for others. We felt sympathy only for our own kind. When newspapers wrote about the plight and deprivations endured by prisoners of war and refugees, I and everyone I knew thought of German soldiers, German refugees, German victims. Thinking back, I realize how lucky I was to encounter at the America House a positive counterweight to this stultifying insularity, a counterweight that gradually allowed me to gain another, wider, less German-centered point of view. I am convinced that, had I gone to school in Delmenhorst, in the British occupation zone, my insularity would have lasted years longer.

Chapter Twelve

FINDING AN INTELLECTUAL HOME
University, 1949–1954

IN JUNE 1948 THE WESTERN ALLIES INTRODUCED a currency reform for the three western zones, having given up on coming to an agreement with the Soviet Union about a common economic and political future for the four zones of Germany. The old currency, the reichsmark, was devalued against the deutsche mark, the new currency, at an exchange rate of 100 RM for 6.5 DM for savings accounts, a devaluation of the currency by about 93 percent. Everyone could exchange the old currency for the new, including bank savings accounts up to, I believe, ten thousand RM. In addition, every person received 60 DM, on the date set for the reform, in exchange for 60 RM; an additional 20 DM were to be supplied at a later date. The reform brought about a stabilization of the banking and finance system of the western zone and became the economic basis on which the future economic recovery of the Federal Republic of Germany rested.

For my family, the currency reform was a catastrophe. Our savings books, including my mother's documentation of a few investments, had been confiscated by the militia at the checkpoint when we were expelled from Silesia. Not that the amounts were substantial. But rather than having a few extra new DM to help us through the uncertainty about what the reform meant, as many people had, we received only the 60 DM per person. I went with Mother to City Hall to receive our allotment of deutsche marks. Humiliation awaited us as we stood in line: we did not know that we had to produce 180 old reichsmarks to get our share of the new currency. As we approached the counter, we realized that we had only some fifty marks between us and therefore might not even receive our official allotment. A woman behind us overheard us talking.

"How much are you short?" She turned to Mother.

"One hundred and thirty marks," Mother answered. The woman drew forth what seemed to me a huge envelope from her pocketbook and handed Mother two hundred RM.

"Forget about the seventy," the woman said, "it's worthless anyway."

Most of Mother's customers canceled their orders, at least for a time, because no one knew what the future held. The black market stopped operating almost overnight, and people who had been dealing in it had to find legitimate work. For the next month or so no one knew if they could find work. I lost my tutoring students for the same reason.

While stores had been empty and food scarce, except for the little we could buy on ration cards throughout the war and its aftermath to 1948, now every store filled up with valuable merchandise from one day to the next. Tropical fruit that we had not seen since the early 1930s overflowed from the bins. Abundance everywhere! Where had all these goods come from almost overnight? Had store owners hoarded wares for years? We no longer needed ration cards, only money. Fortunately our rent stayed the same, and bread and potatoes remained cheap for the time being. The entire social fabric changed in the blink of an eye. We were astounded by how much people bought. Where did they get the money? Consumption went in waves. At first people bought clothes and shoes and huge quantities of foods that had been rationed, like meat, sausages, butter, and cheeses, or food that had not been available at all, like chocolates and expensive alcoholic beverages; then radios, bicycles, and stuffed furniture; finally, cars. Within a year, the national average weight must have increased by ten kilos from the gorging binge.

To me, the beginnings of West Germany's economic miracle looked like a buying frenzy as hectic as the alcohol frenzy had been during the last year of the war. In West Germany, when the war ended, young and old had turned immediately to the churches and to cultural institutions to nourish their depleted spirits and guilt-ridden souls. This dynamic still dominated public and private life when we arrived in the west. A multitude of cultural institutions— small theaters, cabarets in former air-raid shelters, bookshops with public readings and discussions, concerts in half-bombed-out school rooms, art galleries set up in storefronts—had sprung up all over Bremen. The galleries displayed images of violent and twisted lines against gloomy backgrounds; the plays and readings spoke of guilt, and of a gloomy fate, and of the need for spiritual transformation. Since most of these events were free, I had enjoyed many of them, particularly poetry readings, concerts, museum and gallery exhibits, and America House discussions. But all these calls for spiritual values and moral regeneration faded like ghosts in the glare of the new material consumption.

In the days before the currency reform, I thought that the artists and intellectuals among my countrymen shared my quest for national regeneration through personal moral regeneration—an idealistic position that strengthened my quest for higher education. Democracy, I believed, came only after *individual inner* transformation. I did not see then that our frantic quest for moral atonement and for redemptive art and literature substituted as penance for the vague sense of guilt, unease, and anxiety many people felt about the war and the Nazi years. Only years later did I realize how much self-pity and avoidance of responsibility was reflected in this idealism, which was, after all, enforced by a deprivation none of us had chosen. I slowly came to understand that my clinging to what I then called spiritual values was as much an escape from facing my losses as my countrymen's flight into consumption was. In 1948, however, after the currency reform, I felt the public rejection of cultural and intellectual values as a devastating betrayal of the quest for national transformation. It was fortunate that I had little time to indulge in despair.

Our family participated in none of this material indulgence. For the remaining two years of high school, Mother and I struggled to stay afloat materially. Like several penniless classmates whose families had lived off the black market, I feared that I would have to quit school. But I was more fortunate than they. Immediately after the reform Dr. Budde got me a scholarship from the Ministry of Education that paid for my tuition and transportation and gave me a small stipend for living expenses. Other teachers helped by becoming Mother's customers until her business picked up again. Some of my former students returned for lessons once their families knew what their incomes were.

Stores overflowed with material goods, many of which—chocolate, coffee, coconut—Werner and I knew only from hearsay. I don't know who coined the phrase "prosperity has broken out" (a play on the saying "a plague has broken out"), but this well reflected our experience of the currency reform: its pain, shock, and suddenness, and its immediate plaguelike effect on us. Now that food was available everywhere, the noon meals given to schools by the American occupation ended abruptly. Many days I was hungrier than I had been during the time of food shortages. People ceased dressing in the sackcloth, army cast-off look that had become almost fashionable. Our poverty amid the sudden wealth of the native northern German population now made us true and highly visible pariahs. Many of my classmates appeared in new clothing and acquired new symbols of social status, such as stylish leather book bags and gold jewelry and watches. They participated in a renaissance of teenage bourgeois social activity, like dancing lessons and formal dance events. Excluded by my shabby dress and poverty, I resented them for it.

On a generational level, I shared with my classmates a fundamental distrust of all adults. A few examples of how this distrust manifested itself may suffice. As grateful as I was to Dr. Budde for his help, I often felt as irritated with him as I did with other adults. He liked to have poetry readings in class and occasionally would allow us to read poetry aloud for the entire class period. The boys in class plainly thought these hours a complete waste of time. Sometimes, particularly before an exam in another subject, they did not mind if I suggested a poetry reading to Dr. Budde instead of the usual German lesson. They would then study surreptitiously for the mathematics, Latin, or English exam while a few of us recited aloud. If Dr. Budde noticed that the attention of some of the students was elsewhere, he would interrupt the reading and interrogate students about the poem at hand. It must have been during a Hölderlin reading that he observed our inattention and questioned us about the poem's references to Greek mythology and history. "You won't understand these lines if you don't know who Diotima is, or, for that matter, Marsyas or Artemis. At your age, my generation had had several years of Greek. These names had profound meanings for us, versed as we were in things Greek."

I hated adult lectures that contained the phrase "when I was your age" and somehow expected Dr. Budde to be above that sort of condescension. Degrading us by comparing us to his better-educated generation was the territory of Herr Fridhof, our history teacher. A sudden rage took hold of me, and I blurted out, "Is it our fault that we did not get a classical education? That now we have to cram in so much information that we can hardly catch our breath? Where were you during the Nazi years? During the war? Why didn't you teach us what you expect us to know now?"

By this time I was no longer shouting at him—I was accusing his whole generation. I articulated my generation's feeling of having been shortchanged by our elders and of being berated for what they had failed to teach us. I could tell from the sudden stillness in the classroom that my classmates were surprised, to say the least. For a moment I felt their solidarity with me. For once, I was expressing the anger we all felt at our elders for their evasion of responsibility.

Dr. Budde looked down and said nothing. After a while he turned to Michael, an eager and vocal student. "Why don't you read *Socrates and Alchibiades* now?"

We were keenly aware that most of our teachers, particularly our history teacher, Herr Fridhof, had held opinions different from the "neutrality" they affected now. "The judgment of history is not yet in," he liked to say. "It is impossible to evaluate how World War I or World War II will be seen in the light of history." His insecurity about expressing an "incorrect" view led him to provide us with pages of prepared questions and answers for the eventual *Abitur*—the public comprehensive high school examination. "Precise formulations of historical issues are absolutely mandatory," he explained.

Kritias, the class critic, who had been Fridhof's student since 1942, interrupted under his breath, "Don't we know it! You are not the only one to wish that you had formulated your ideas about Hitler a bit more ambiguously!"

Oblivious to Kritias's rudeness, Fridhof went on. "For your guidance, I have prepared a number of questions and formulated some answers that you might use in the oral exam."

During the next few weeks, he interrupted his usual lectures and dictated his questions and his answers. He expected us to follow the exact wording of his responses to the questions. We felt insulted by the assignment, but directly challenging a teacher's judgment was unimaginable. I memorized a few of the questions and his answers to them, and it was easy for me to imagine his voice and intonation, the precise way in which he would deliver these sentences. But it was Kritias who took the lead. When Fridhof called on him, he started slowly on the passage he also had memorized, enunciating each word deliberately, just as Fridhof did. The others caught on; the boys snickered and the girls began to giggle. Taking their cue, Kritias went faster, bringing out Fridhof's intonation ever more forcefully. By the time he got through one paragraph, the class was laughing openly and applauding without inhibition. Fridhof stopped the practice and never reverted to it again. These episodes illustrate well the unforgiving relationship our generation had with our teachers. We did not rebel openly; that was left to the next generation, the generation of 1968. We wanted, and knew we needed, the knowledge and training our teachers possessed. But we made it as difficult for them as we could, and pounced on their every weakness.

We also agreed in our fundamental rejection of the political parties that had begun to constitute or reconstitute themselves from the days of the Weimar Republic. As far as we were concerned, the parties permitted by the Allies were old boys' clubs and has-beens. To me at that time politics was a dirty word and any form of group association suspect. Politics meant the Nazi Party, Nazi politics. Frau Behrends had attempted to interest me in the FDP (Free Democrats), and the liberal, individualist stance she advocated might have had some appeal if the mere thought of politics had not turned me off. My experience with the Russian occupation had disabused me, as it had most refugees and expellees, of any possible affinity with the Communist Party and, for the time being, also the Social Democratic Party, for communist and socialist meant the same thing to me. Our political slogan as a generation was *Ohne mich* (Without me—that is, count me out!). And since everyone in our class was too young to vote in the local and regional elections of 1948 and 1949, we felt no immediate need to concern ourselves with political issues.

A change in our curriculum introduced by the American occupation authority in Bremen, aimed at familiarizing high school students with the tools we would need to participate in democratic processes, forced us to attend to the subject during our last year of high school. We protested loudly, of course, unwilling to take on another academic subject, even if only for a few hours a week. Skeptical of all authority, as we thought ourselves to be, we would have boycotted the lessons had we dared. The new subject was called *Gemeinschaftskunde* (community / social studies), and Dr. Budde himself, though a teacher of German literature, taught it.

"I am learning the nuts and bolts of democratic governance just as you are," he explained at the first class session.

"What the U.S. liaison officer"—Dr. Budde had become friends with the young Harvard graduate who served our school in this capacity—"wants you to learn is how to become knowledgeable voters. And I need that as much as you do, even though I did vote during the Weimar Republic." And true enough, his instruction had the immediacy and intellectual commitment that comes from a teacher's personal stake in the subject. We began to listen despite ourselves.

Twice weekly until graduation we learned about the programs of the different parties; we studied the German constitutions, from the ill-fated constitutions of 1848–49 to that of Weimar in 1919, and to the basic law of the federal republic-to-be that was being formulated in 1948–49. Maybe because he wanted to demonstrate to us that we had a real stake in political issues, Dr. Budde's lessons centered on the bill of rights, its position within the different constitutions, and its specific provisions. For me, brought up to believe that the individual was nothing and the nation, everything, and taught to believe that citizenship involved only duties and sacrifice, a bill of rights was almost incomprehensible. I think this is why some of its provisions became etched in my mind. The bill of rights' provision of a citizen's "right to free development of the personality" and the "right to refuse to bear arms" won me over to the lessons as well as to the basic law of the emerging Federal Republic.

We compared the German constitutions and the U.S. Constitution, noting the similarities and differences. We learned in which respects the Weimar constitution had failed and how the new basic law addressed these failures so that no authoritarian dictator could ever again seize power. We learned about the division of powers between local, state, and federal agencies. We studied the systems of criminal and civil justice, and the differences in school systems of the different states of the Federal Republic. In most of these subjects Dr. Budde seemed to have consulted with the liaison officer, who appeared a few times to observe the class. A lanky, relaxed young man in civilian clothes, he participated in our instruction on the American public school system. It was less *what* he told us than *how* he discussed issues with us and conducted himself that impressed me. Though we had been hostile to the subject initially, it was his and Dr. Budde's involvement in the teaching that won me over in the end. I see now, in retrospect, that my experience, or rather the positive experience of German youth—particularly with the American occupation forces—pointed the way to how Germany could gradually become a successful democracy. These reeducation efforts laid the foundation on which the 1968 generation could build their rebellion and their later democratic reforms.

During the first years in the west, I had also gone with Mother and Werner to the meetings of the local refugee and expellee organization. At first they served mainly as a social occasion at which we could meet the townspeople we had come west with, reminisce about our hometowns, and exchange information about which agencies in our new home took care—or failed to take care—of our immediate needs. Gradually these meetings devolved into either pointlessly depressing carping or, as frustration with local failures to provide housing or jobs grew, into motivation to run in the local elections as refugee candidates. This might have interested me had the persons who ran for office not allied themselves with the viewpoints of small groups on the extreme right who fantasized about the return of the formerly German territories in the east or even called for revenge. From the very first meeting I realized that, unlike many of our townspeople, I did not yearn to return to Silesia. I remembered all too well how stifling Strehlen had felt to me. Their glorification of our *Heimat* (regional homeland) repelled me, and the idea of *Heimat* never lost its Nazi connotations for me. My school offered intellectual fare more rewarding to me.

As I struggled to adjust to the changes the currency reform had wrought, we received a postcard from the Red Cross, telling us that my older brother, Jochen, was a prisoner of war in Czechoslovakia. I took the card from the postman on a fall day as I returned from school. I raced up the three flights to our room. "Mother, Werner, Jochen is alive!" I shouted as I ran up. Mother and I burst out crying with relief as Werner tore the card from me. "What does it say?" "At X camp, healthy," the printed form read.

That evening we celebrated with our neighbors downstairs, Leonie and Frau Schmidt, who brought along some wine to share with Mother. Throughout the two years since we had come to West Germany, we had envied other families whose men had returned from prison camps. For hours we had listened for a familiar name, as the voice of the impersonal announcer on the public radio station read out name after name of the missing and of those looking for them. Since we heard nothing from either Jochen or Uncle Kurt, we had just about concluded that both must have died during the last days of the fighting. Yet even on that first joyful evening I began to worry, and I saw from Mother's demeanor that she was worried, too. Where would he sleep? In our one room, there was barely enough space for us three. What would he want to do? Go to school? Continue his apprenticeship? Werner and I are both in school, and neither one of us is anywhere near finishing, I thought. Will he want to go to school? Three of us in school at once? What about money? Anticipating his return and hoping that he would want to resume his apprenticeship in farming and schooling at the local agricultural school, I talked to its director and secured Jochen a place once he returned. At least in this way I allayed my anxiety about what his return might mean for us all.

One day early in 1949 I answered the doorbell to encounter a ragged, unshaven stranger. It took me a while to recognize my brother in the emaciated toothless man who greeted me awkwardly and pushed by me into the room. He looked fifty, though he was only twenty. We questioned him eagerly and told him what had happened to us. He listened to our stories but rejected most of our probing about him, except to tell us that a rifle butt had knocked out his front teeth when he was taken prisoner. It was only over many years that I gradually learned what had happened to him. He had looked on his volunteering for the ss as an adventure, a sixteen-year-old boy's fantasy of saving his fatherland. His unit was taken prisoner on their first encounter with the enemy at the Czech border. Lined up for inspection by Russian and Czech officers, the stronger boys were selected to go to Siberia, the weaker to stay in Czechoslovakia. Jochen's boyhood friend Herbert, smaller and younger, who had volunteered with him, was sent to the Czech side of the line, Jochen to the Russian. When Herbert realized that his friend was on the Russian side, he faked a fainting fit, and in the confusion Jochen ran to his aid. No one noticed that he stayed with his friend and the two remained together. For the rest of 1945 the young prisoners of war helped Czech farmers tend the fields and bring in the harvest. They were treated well, and Jochen learned to speak Czech. The following spring he tried to escape, was caught, was sentenced to a labor camp for punishment, and did heavy labor in a brickyard. He was freed three years later by the intervention of the Swiss Red Cross. At this camp, a fatherly older inmate, a Social Democrat whom he respected and trusted, enlightened him about Nazi crimes and educated him about political and ethical issues. His early love for organ music had made him seek out churches even as a boy. During his time in the labor camp, he became religious.

During his first few weeks with us I introduced Jochen to the subjects I was studying and the interests I had acquired. He listened eagerly and welcomed my attempts to fill in information about school, the books I had read, the ideas that occupied me, and particularly the concerts I had heard. Of course, there had been no opportunity at the camp to listen to music. Yet the strain of the four of us living in one room and the uncertainty about Jochen's future became ever more obvious.

Mother had put in an urgent application with the city housing office for new quarters for us, for at least one more room anywhere. More than a dozen times she returned from the housing office discouraged by the red tape. After two months an impersonal official letter notified her of their refusal. "With so many refugees having even greater needs than you, we cannot assign you different living quarters." The housing shortage in the western zones was exacerbated by the fact that individual mobility—though guaranteed as a basic right—was regulated by local authorities; we were truly stuck in the town to which we had been assigned. In the bureaucratic catch-22, you could get living space in a different locality only if you could prove that you had work there; and you could get work only if you could prove you had been assigned living space.

I understood from the remarks of Mother's acquaintances that they expected me to quit school and go to work so that my brother could get the education he had missed. "Surely she won't be so egotistical as to continue high school when her brother cannot go," one of Mother's cousins opined. There was little doubt in my mind that Jochen would have preferred to pursue higher education rather than resume his apprenticeship. But I could not see how my sacrifice could help him get an education. A poorly paid factory job was the only work with immediate income that I qualified for. Jochen resolved the dilemma by resuming his apprenticeship at a nearby farm, which provided him with shelter, food, and fees for agricultural school. Two years later, after he'd completed his apprenticeship, a hometown clergyman who had become his mentor helped him enter a career in the Protestant Church, through which he received the education he had missed out on.

As school and giving lessons became routine, periods of intense boredom made me yearn for some kind of excitement, despite my demanding schedule of school, tutoring, and studying. I yearned for something, anything, to interrupt the tedium of daily life. I understood only years later that many of my contemporaries who had experienced the kind of traumatic events that I had also felt this kind of boredom and looked to escape it by seeking out danger in risky sports, addictions, criminal activity — or police work. My escape from the daily tedium took the academic form typical for me. In our social studies course with Dr. Budde, I chose to produce a final research paper on juvenile crime in the state of Bremen. I identified with delinquents — after all, during the immediate postwar period I, and everyone I knew, had stolen goods in order to survive. The only difference between us and convicted criminals was that we had not been caught.

Of this research paper I remember only the conclusions I reached after much reading and many interviews with personnel of the criminal justice system. The treatment of juvenile offenders was still regulated by the juvenile justice reforms that Nazism had introduced in the mid-1930s. According to the thinking behind these reforms, criminal inclinations were hereditary. Rehabilitation, therefore, consisted in incarceration and other punitive measures intended to keep criminality in check. Based on my reading about American juvenile justice and on my own experience, I proposed in my paper changes in the law and rehabilitation programs that would develop individual talents. Did not the bill of rights of our basic law give every citizen the right to the free development of his talents? Did that not include a right to educational opportunity? Most juvenile offenders, I argued, had access to only the bare minimum of education, and therefore needed the chance to pursue it more deeply. For a time I even wanted to work in a rehabilitation program and give youthful offenders a chance at the education I was getting. One elderly judge at the Bremen palace of justice dampened my enthusiasm. "The law works slowly. Any reform of the legal system will take decades," he said. A hard-nosed, narrow-minded policewoman I interviewed cured me of my desire to work in a juvenile prison. "Delinquents?" she said. "No. *Untermenschen* [sub-humans]." My project did not turn out to be an exciting exploration. But I learned from the statistics on stunted juvenile lives some of the horrendous consequences of the Nazi belief in the power of heredity.

Final exams for high school graduation were a drawn-out affair and a major hurdle on the way to a university education. I had come to think of them as a crucial milestone. During the last year of school, from the late summer of 1949 to March 1950, we spent all our time in preparation for this examination, or *Abitur*. It was a regional exam taken every spring by all high school seniors in the state of Bremen. While our teachers set the themes and problems for the written exams in German literature, English essay, Latin, and mathematics, teachers from other schools evaluated and graded the written examinations. These lasted for a week and were followed by a one-day oral examination in the four main subjects and in secondary subjects like history, geography, chemistry, biology, physics, and social studies. Teachers from other high schools and observers from the Ministry of Education watched as our teachers conducted the oral examination. Every senior and every teacher who had taught the senior class was on trial.

The written exams were less stressful than I had feared. On the overcast early spring morning of the orals, the ministry representative addressed the entire class. After the usual pleasantries of congratulating us on having made it this far on the educational ladder, he read the list of the students who were exempt from the oral exam. Every student coveted this exemption, because it earned extra points for university admission. There were five exemptions; my name was the fifth. I strolled through the damp streets of the neighborhood while my classmates took their orals. When I came home that evening, I felt thoroughly exhausted and deflated; nobody was home. My family had gone to the movies.

Mother was angry with me because I had declined a full scholarship to the Bremen Teachers' Seminary. I had long since stopped wanting to be a grammar school teacher. My resolve to study at the university had only grown stronger over the years of high school, though I was still uncertain about whether I wanted to pursue medicine, law, art history, or literature. By the early 1950s German universities were still overcrowded, as veterans had precedence over recent high school graduates. A waiting period of one, two, or three semesters before admission was common. Additionally, any applicant could be turned down if the subject she had applied for was overenrolled.

On Herr Beck's recommendation, I had sent an application for admission to the humanities division at the University of Tübingen in southern Germany. Herr Beck knew a doctoral candidate at Tübingen who was living in a refugee student hostel, and he believed that I would qualify for rent-free residence there, as well as for a refugee scholarship through *Soforthilfe,* immediate-help grants for refugees and expellees. Dr. Budde and Herr Beck had written me letters of recommendation. I had learned that admission in literature was easier than in medicine or law, but that I could change my major once I was admitted. I had also been told that the faculty in German literature at this southernmost university had an excellent reputation and that the library had not been destroyed, as those at many other German universities had. Most important to me, Tübingen was as far away from my family as I could go within West Germany.

To make some money to go to the university, once admitted, I found a job at the local jute factory and started work the day after our oral exam. I had no idea whether or when I might be admitted to Tübingen. My work as a weaver at the factory involved a two-week period of training on the mechanical loom. I learned quickly how to insert the shuttle, run the machine, stop it, and repair breaks in the thread. The two hundred machines in the hall made a deafening noise as the shuttles with their steel heads raced to and fro. The forty-eight-hour workweek was brutal, starting at 6:00 A.M. and lasting till 4:30 P.M., Monday through Friday. We worked half a day on Saturday. The factory still had no lunchroom, so we munched our sandwiches on our half-hour lunch break sitting on sacking next to our looms. After the two weeks of training, the foreman put me in charge of four machines. By itself, this might not have been too hard a job. But the jute thread broke easily, and the shuttles did not stop when it did. Often the machine had advanced a few inches before I noticed a break. Mending the break by hand after I stopped the machine took several minutes. By the time I set the idle loom in motion again, another one or two, or even three, machines were running ahead with broken threads. I found it impossible to keep up with the other weavers.

During my first week of work, our class speaker, Hans, telephoned me at the factory. The foreman called me to the phone but told me to tell my caller never to call again. With a choking voice—we disliked each other intensely— Hans asked me in the name of the class to be the commencement speaker. I hesitated, suspecting some mischief. But he added, "Nobody else wanted to do it and we thought you would not mind. You write and speak more easily than any of us." I was not exactly enthusiastic, but I agreed, taken in by the backhanded compliment. I composed the speech in my head as I worked on the loom.

The commencement took place on a Saturday afternoon in the auditorium of a neighboring school, as ours still had not been rebuilt. Mother decided not to come because we had only one good dress between us. It was a raw day in late March. Dr. Budde had sent me the program, so I knew I would be the speaker following him. Everybody else's parents seemed to have come. I was extremely nervous, for I had never spoken publicly to a large audience, but my voice steadied as I proceeded. I opened my speech with a quotation from Stefan Zweig's autobiography, *The World of Yesterday*.

"For, if I am to be honest, the entire period of my schooling was nothing other than a constant and wearisome boredom, accompanied year after year by an increased impatience to escape from this treadmill. I cannot recall ever having been either 'joyous' or 'blissful' during that monotonous, heartless, and lifeless schooling which thoroughly spoiled the best and freest period of our existence."

I paused after reading this quotation and looked down at my classmates. They looked up at me, thoroughly shocked and apprehensive about what I would say next. "That is how Stefan Zweig remembers his days at his Vienna Gymnasium at the turn of the last century," I continued. "Our experience was different." I heard sighs of relief. I recognized and praised the teachers who had helped me but was not diplomatic enough even to mention the others.

After the ceremony, my mathematics teacher told me that I had offended several teachers. Serves you right, I thought. The following week I was back at the factory. I never saw any of my classmates again. The few times I came back to my mother's from the universities where I studied and taught, I visited only Herr Beck and Dr. Budde.

Because my days at the factory finished early, I had planned to spend the evenings reading. After a few days, though, I was so depressed that I could not even think of doing anything but sleep. I soon learned that saving money to go to the university was impossible. Weavers received not hourly but piecework wages by the yard of sacking they produced. By the third week, my first on the regular schedule, I made half of the little I made during the two weeks as a trainee. I figured that I might earn an average worker's income by the time I had worked in the factory for a year. Moreover, since my scholarship, as well as my income from lessons, had stopped, the little I made went to Mother for household expenses.

I was appalled at the conditions we worked under. Washrooms and toilets were unspeakably filthy and were never cleaned while I worked there. The stench from the sometimes wet jute yarn clung to our skin and hair. Tiny fibers of the yarn stuck to our clothes and refused to be brushed off. When you left work, everyone could smell where you worked, even if you changed clothes or took a shower. But there were no showers at the factory, and few of us had them at home. Not only were the looms noisy, they were also dangerous, as the shuttles, if not inserted firmly enough, could shoot out at you. With their pointed steel heads they looked like murderous projectiles. "Last month, an errant shuttle sideswiped a new woman's temple and knocked her out," my trainer warned me. "Don't ever be careless!" Six weeks passed, then seven, and still I had not heard from Tübingen. I almost regretted that I had turned down the scholarship to the Teachers' Seminary. Had I put myself through more than four years of strenuous study, only to end up doing what I had wanted to escape in the first place?

My admission letter arrived at the beginning of May, when I had just about given up. A personal note accompanied the letter from the dean of humanities. He said that he himself had been admitted to the university years before with a transcript exactly like mine. Now that I'd been admitted, I did not know what to do. I really had not expected to be admitted right away. I had no money left, not even enough for a train ticket to Tübingen. Coming home from the factory the day after I got my admission letter, I ran into Frau

Behrends and told her of my situation. Once again she came to my rescue with a one-time stipend from the city council to get me launched. Herr Beck gave me the address of the refugee organization that ran the student hostel, and I filled out a form for an immediate-help refugee student grant. I left with ten marks to my name and a one-way overnight rail ticket to Tübingen.

I arrived in Tübingen just as the stores were opening. After depositing my suitcase at the local youth hostel, I went to the dean's house to introduce myself and find out what I was supposed to do. The totally perplexed wife of the dean answered the doorbell, informed me that her husband would not be home till lunchtime, and asked me to wait. That I went straight to the academic dean vividly demonstrates my naïveté and lack of knowledge of German academic protocol. Fortunately, Professor Gamilscheg, a scholar of romance literature, was the picture of graciousness and understood my ignorance completely. He provided some initial guidance on how and where to register. He inquired about my interests in a way that put my visit into the framework of an academic advising call, though I am sure I was the only student that semester who received such an unaccustomed privilege. Once I realized, a few days later, how unusual my visit had been, I was spared undue embarrassment thanks to his kind and gracious reception.

Next I went to the office of the refugee camp administration to gain admittance to the refugee student hostel. "We do not admit first-semester students," the administrator told me sternly. "The hostel is intended for advanced refugee students returning to university who interrupted their studies either because they served in the military, were prisoners of war, or are political refugees from the eastern zone." She looked at me, handed my transcripts and letters of recommendation back to me, and waited for me to get up and leave.

"I don't know where I can live if I don't get admitted to the hostel. I cannot afford a room. I have ten marks on me and that is it," I explained. "I am a refugee from the east just like everybody else. I will get an immediate-help grant, and I don't see what my being a first-semester student has to do with not admitting me." My insistence and my transcript impressed her, and after a while she gave in. She picked up the phone and asked to speak to Herr Heller. "He is the camp director," she told me while she waited. When Herr Heller came to the phone, she explained, "I have an exception here to our admission policy. Do we have a room free for this semester?" I heard a barrage of words from Herr Heller but could not understand what he said. She turned to me and said, "You are lucky; Heller is asking one of the students to leave   .

because of gambling. But remember, only for one semester." In fact, I stayed at Niedernau Refugee Student Hostel until I received a Fulbright grant to study at Brown University in the United States three semesters later.

The refugee camp at Bad Niedernau, of which the student hostel was a small part, was a recently established transit facility run by the civil administration of the Federal Republic of Germany. The camp provided shelter and food to refugees who had fled from the eastern zone of Germany and to expellees from the eastern provinces who had been unable to find satisfactory work and living conditions in the West German locations to which they had been assigned. Members of both groups stayed in the camp only until they had found satisfactory work and living space in the former French zone, which had earlier refused to participate in the resettling of the population expelled from the eastern territories.

This policy of resettlement was part of a wider strategy to integrate expellees and all refugees from East Germany into the Federal Republic. The relatives I had accidentally encountered on one of my jaunts into the countryside to barter for food had come through this camp just a few weeks before I arrived. With an immediate-help grant, they had been able to buy into a small farm in southern Germany and the camp administration helped them relocate. This generous and farsighted government policy largely resolved the postwar expellee and refugee problem, which ultimately involved more than twelve million displaced German nationals. It mitigated a potential cause of social unrest and a serious threat to the fledgling Federal Republic of Germany.

The other part of the wider integrative strategy of the Federal Republic was the *Lastenausgleich*—the balancing out of burdens—a program to equalize the burdens of all who had suffered monetary or property damages or incurred other disadvantages because of the bombings, the war, the division of Germany, and the radical currency reform. The program began as early as 1949 as the so-called *Soforthilfe,* the immediate-help grant program, from which many expellees received small grants to tide them over until a more permanent settlement could be implemented. I received a basic scholarship of about 20 DMS a month through the *Soforthilfe* after I began my studies at Tübingen University. The more permanent equalization program, established by the parliament of the Federal Republic in 1952, compensated refugees and expellees sufficiently to equip their households, start new businesses, and receive loans for purchasing property; or it recompensed them with small pensions, scholarships, or money for retraining. The funds for the *Lastenausgleich* were raised by taxation. Germans who had kept their property, positions, and businesses were taxed to up to 50 percent of their assessed value. Since the payments of these taxes were spread out over thirty years, the actual burden turned out to be less catastrophic than people had feared when the law took effect.

As a consequence of the successful resettlement and burden-balancing programs, the many ultraconservative organizations that had demanded restitution for lost territories and gained representation in the parliament as the BHE (Association of the Displaced and Disenfranchised) never gained broad-based support. Furthermore, the addition of skilled and eager East German expellees and refugees to the West German workforce fueled the speedy and much acclaimed economic recovery of the Federal Republic.

It took several more years before the Federal Republic—under international pressure, to be sure—began to pay reparations to Israel and at least through this financial gesture acknowledged Germany's responsibility for the Holocaust. Individual compensations to survivors for an interrupted education, for businesses and homes lost and careers destroyed, took years longer, and often, because of bureaucratic procedures and officials' insensitivity, traumatized the victims of persecution. I have remained grateful that Germany attempted, if ever so slowly, to acknowledge its *Schuld*—its moral and economic obligation to a people it tried to eradicate. Throughout the 1990s, as former forced laborers were finally beginning to be compensated, I wondered if my Polish friend Wanda was still alive to receive her meager share.

What the administrator in Tübingen had told me about the students at the hostel turned out to be true. All of them were older students who had missed out on years of their lives and study because they had served as soldiers or nurses. Some had had to recover from wounds and were still handicapped—one had lost an arm, another a leg—and others had been prisoners of war and spent time in forced labor camps in Siberia. Their experience had made most of them very serious and some of them cynical.

We were all engrossed in our studies and expected to complete our degrees in two or three semesters. Everyone knew exactly what he or she wanted to accomplish in life. We were about twenty students: several advanced medical students, a few biologists and chemists, half a dozen lawyers, a number of economists, two philosophers, a classicist, and several students of literature—German, English, and Romance languages. All were as poorly dressed as I and lived as make-do an existence as I had accustomed myself to. Here, I was no longer the odd man out. Everyone here had a future goal that required asceticism, seriousness of purpose, and idealism; this forged our common bond. We were always short of money; all of us dressed in castoffs from the various charity shops and lived on the leftover food the refugee transit camp allowed us to pick up once the resident refugees had eaten. All of us held refugee scholarships. Yet at times, with the little money we did have, we celebrated whatever holidays came along and had parties as spirited and entertaining as any I ever went to. No one here was yet preoccupied with the pursuit of consumption, as my high school classmates had been.

From the first day I loved Tübingen, the gentle Swabian landscape and the student hostel at Niedernau, ten miles from Tübingen down on the Neckar River. The camp was located in an old spa hotel complex in the meadows along the river, which flowed swiftly through a narrow valley that filled with wildflowers during summer and spring. One or two of us occupied the smaller rooms of one of the buildings; the refugees, often entire families, had the larger rooms and a few dormitories in the former entertainment and spa facilities in several of the larger buildings. A huge kitchen and dining room served all of us free food. We took the train to Tübingen using our free rail passes. A half-hour ride in a slow, dilapidated local train took us down the river, past several towns and villages that still reflected Swabia's medieval past.

I chose German literature as a major, with English literature and philosophy as minors. Having been confined in my studies at the high school level to making up for deficits, I enjoyed the freedom the German university system allowed students. As a scholarship student I had to take two classes each semester in my subjects and pass them by taking an oral or written exam. For the rest, I could take or audit whatever courses I wanted to. I quickly made friends with the students at the hostel. Since I was the youngest, the hostelers took me under their wings both socially and intellectually. I accepted their academic counseling eagerly. Before the student rebellion of the 1960s, official academic counseling on what courses to take or what subjects to study was unheard of. Because the doctoral candidates at the hostel introduced me to their professors and other advanced students, I was spared the disorientation and alienation most beginning students experienced. The expert advice I received from my new friends led me to the most stimulating professors. Never again during my German studies did I feel as intellectually alive as when I went to lectures on ethics with Professor Spranger or attended Professor Beissner's Hölderlin seminar. Most of my friends saw themselves as future researchers rather than as practitioners of law, medicine, or teaching. They were devoted to study and research for its own sake, an intellectual orientation that I soon shared. The best part of studying literature at Tübingen was the German literature seminary library at the old university, with its view of the Neckar River and the tower in which Swabia's most famous poet, Hölderlin, spent the years of his madness.

Every Saturday night several of us went to dance at a café close to the hostel near the Neckar, ending our evening of dancing by skinny-dipping in the river. Long after midnight we walked back to the hostel through the meadows, still arguing and teasing each other. On many Thursdays, the so-called *dies academicus,* a day intended for lectures of general interest to all students, Karla, an advanced medical student, and I hitchhiked all over Swabia to visit churches, monasteries, and abbeys. While Karla, sitting by a fountain, studied her lecture notes for her next exam, I scouted the buildings and determined their floor plans as Herr Beck had taught me. For a few months I went to class with Karla and deliberated about transferring to medicine after all. But I also audited courses in art history, law, and biology, and attended any lectures my friends were interested in. I was on an almost continuous high induced by the sheer wealth of subjects I was discovering.

As happy as I felt with finally having achieved my goal of studying at the university, occasionally I fell into periods of despair that seemed groundless and unfathomable. During those weeks, thoughts of suicide would suddenly come into my mind and terrify me. As suddenly as these attacks came, they left. Then a discovery made them easier to bear. One evening, as a whole group of us were sitting at the pub, Schmidchen, a law student, began telling suicide jokes. Karla, not to be outdone, interrupted him in a mock macabre voice, "Let me count the ways," and then enumerated the many medical ways she knew of killing herself. Reglaff, a classicist, added lurid Greek and Roman suicide lore. By the time we got through the evening, we counted, laughing hysterically, some twenty ever more grotesque ways of doing ourselves in. It dawned on me that evening that many of my fellow students at the hostel had periods of despair similar to mine and that the black humor of such morbid pastimes as our enumeration was a method of coping with depression, at least for a time.

At carnival time, we danced at the Rothenburg town hall, constantly changing partners till five in the morning. At dawn, walking back along the river meadows to the hostel, we whiled away the time by calling each other by the names of Greek and Roman gods and conducting mock competitions for the highest rank among the Greco-Roman deities. Back at the hostel, Reglaff, whose relatives sent him care packages from the United States, made us a morning coffee with Nescafe. Since none of us had ever had real coffee, his strong brew kept us awake for another two days. Reglaff read to us from Homer's *Odyssey* and we discussed why we liked the *Odyssey* better than the *Iliad,* why we preferred Odysseus to Achilles. It is curious to me now how steeped we all were in classical literature and myth. And even more curious that we had so little understanding of why we preferred the wily Odysseus to heroic Achilles. Like us, the ruthless schemer used his wits to make it home after the war. We did not want to think of ourselves as slaughterers. We recognized the Odysseus in ourselves, while we disowned the Achilles.

I finally realized at my retirement, after some forty-five years of university study and teaching, that all I had ever wanted was to be at a university, to enjoy the stimulation of inquiry wherever it might lead, to engage in the quiet pursuit of intellectual interests, and to share those interests with students and colleagues. The idea of university study became a home for me in Tübingen and stayed a home base for me at whatever university I found myself in. I felt comfortable and at ease as long as I had a library to go to, a group of colleagues to talk with, students to work with. Even when I objected to the institutional realities of the universities where I studied and worked, I would not have exchanged my place in them for another environment. The subjects I studied—German literature, English literature, philosophy, history, historical linguistics, art, sculpture, psychoanalysis—mattered less to me than being part of a university community, free to study whatever held my interest. I could venture forth from this home base into friendship, love, and family, into travel to different countries and associations with artists and all kinds of different people. But I always returned to this home with a deep sense of gratitude.

The first semester break in August brought new worry because my scholarship supported me only during the months classes were in session. For the next two semester breaks I found work in a small factory that produced metal screws. The work itself, lugging heavy metal cases filled with greasy screws, proved so strenuous that I spent the first month of the following semester exhausted. I got relief when one of the hostelers quit her waitressing job at a Tübingen student tavern and restaurant and recommended me to the owner as a replacement. The owner was an eighty-year-old lady called Tante Emilie by the students. A formidable stern-eyed presence, Aunt Emilia was reputed to have been a beauty of loose morals in her younger years. Though kind to some students, she ran her run-down establishment with an iron fist and did not tolerate brawls. Nevertheless, there was always an atmosphere of high good spirits as students and other customers drank their *Moscht* or sipped a lager. Looking me over warily, Aunt Emilia addressed me crossly. "I understand you have never waited on tables. Are you willing to learn?" Noticing my recoil from her bad temper, she added conciliatorily, "What do you say?"

"I'll learn," I blurted out.

"I'll try you out for a few weeks. You start at 5:00 tonight. You'll get off by 9:00 P.M. You get minimum wage, but tips should add a few marks."

A few months after starting my waitressing job, I heard students in the tavern talking about a scholarship to study in the United States for a year. The interviews were to take place in a few days. Since English was my minor, I put my name down for an interview on a list in the English department. When I learned that more than three hundred students had registered for the interviews, I almost decided not to bother with the interview. I did not believe that a second-year student had much of a chance for such an award. But I figured that the experience of an interview might be good for me, and I showed up at the appointed time.

It was late afternoon when I entered the interview room. The interview committee consisted of five members, two professors of English, a labor union representative, a student representative, and an American from the consulate. All of them looked somewhat worse for the wear after hours of interviews. As I entered I overheard the professors apologize to the American for their students' poor command of English. Embarrassed about my own English, I confined my replies to monosyllables, and I could see that they were rapidly losing interest in me. In a final effort to help me out, the student representative asked, "Do you participate in student government?" I simply answered, "No," and rose to leave. Noticing his disapproval, I added, "It's not that I am not interested. I don't have the time. I wait on tables at Tante Emilie's." Everyone but the American started laughing, and then they explained to him who Tante Emilie was and what kind of establishment she ran. The American stopped me from leaving with a question.

"Wait a minute. Let me ask you something else." The laughter had relaxed me and the interviewers suddenly looked less intimidating. "Since you are a literature major," the American began, "you obviously like to read. Who is your favorite English or American author?"

This time I needed no prompting. "Thomas Wolfe. I like *The Web and the Rock* best, his night walks through the city." Once I had broken through my shyness and forgotten about my poor English, I rattled on.

The American interrupted with questions. "What did you think of his Berlin visit during the Olympics?"

"Oh, you mean the fight he got into? Wasn't that at a Munich beer hall? Or do you mean his view of the Nazis?"

Both of us got carried away with reminiscing about our favorite Wolfe passages. I felt good about the interview when I finally left. That evening, when the commission visited Tante Emilie's for a glass of *Moscht*, I knew that I had left a positive impression and that I had a fighting chance of getting a scholarship.

Five weeks later, after a second interview at the Stuttgart consulate, I received the letter granting me a year's study at Pembroke College, the women's college of Brown University. Only two of the more than three hundred students who applied were selected, and I was one of them! I don't think I ever again felt such relief from my constant worry about money. A full year without having to work at a factory or at Tante Emilie's! That was all I could think of.

I knew little about contemporary America aside from what I had read in Faulkner's and Wolfe's novels and from the *Reader's Digest* that our English teacher in high school used to acquaint us with American English. Of course we had studied the Constitution and the Bill of Rights as well as American geography and the American school system. From my years of visiting the America House and my high school in Bremen I had only positive impressions of what it meant to be an American.

A few weeks before our departure, the U.S. State Department invited us for a three-day orientation conference. We were about one hundred German and Austrian students who had been selected as this first year's contingent of State Department Scholars. The program became known as the Fulbright Fellowship Program a year later. We were crammed so full of information that it was hard to remember anything except a sense of what to expect from our stay in the States and how to conduct ourselves in a college environment. Program presenters deemphasized academic study and encouraged us to get to know as many people of different social classes, as many different institutions and places, as we could manage in the space of a year. The State Department paid all our expenses. This included orientations, train tickets, sea passage, books, travel within the United States—as well as tuition, dormitory room and board, and even a generous monthly allowance. I felt almost overwhelmed by so much good fortune. Once again I felt that "prosperity had broken out," as we had said of the turn of fortune of the currency reform. But this time the prosperity included me. I left for Le Havre on August 20 to meet the *Anna Saleen,* a youth hostel ship that transported scholarship students to America.

From the very beginning of the year at Pembroke/Brown, I loved the college system, the comfort of going to small classes rather than large impersonal lectures, the attention the faculty gave to students. I was assigned to a senior dormitory so as to place me among students roughly my age. I was free to sign up for whatever courses I wanted to enroll in, and on the advice of the foreign student advisor I signed up for classes in what was called the American Civilization major, a series of courses and seminars in American literature, history, and philosophy. I found all of them interesting and some, particularly the lectures on the philosophy of New England transcendentalism and the social novel of the 1930s, more challenging than most courses I had taken in my studies in Germany.

More important than the academic program were the friendships I made in my dormitory and the families I met through the talks I gave in surrounding Rhode Island communities. The latter were arranged by the Foreign Student Office and brought me invitations to spend vacations and holidays with American families. Through the mayor of a small town near Providence and his wife, the Larks, I became acquainted with places important to New England colonial history, like Concord, Plymouth, and Boston. And since these friends and I shared a lively interest in history, we took many stimulating trips together. The Larks remained friends and later helped me return to the States.

My friendships with several of my fellow students challenged me in ways that my acquaintance with American families did not. On my very first evening in the dormitory, a dark-haired, dark-complexioned girl with the largest and saddest eyes I had ever seen came into my room. She introduced herself as Rita and addressed me in German. "I grew up in Germany," she told me. "An uncle of mine brought me to the States in 1946. My parents were Polish Jews, my father a professor of mathematics at Warsaw University. They sent me to German friends in Munich as a six-year-old just before the beginning of the war. Both my parents were killed by the ss, I don't know where."

I looked at her, stunned by the straightforward honesty of her introduction. Heartsick about what she had told me, I struggled for a reply. Noticing my difficulty, she said, "Not to worry, I don't hate Germans. The family I grew up with raised me as their child. They were good to me." Through Rita I was directly and personally confronted by what my countrymen had done to European Jewry, how grievously individual people and families had suffered. What had been the abstract ethical problem of collective guilt became an intensely personal issue that I still find difficult to resolve: What if I had been older? What would I have thought? Have done?

As I was talking to Rita, another knock at my door brought in a tall, blond, intensely nervous and high-strung-looking young woman. She turned out to be Jenny, an English major who was curious about what it had been like to grow up in Nazi Germany. Even that first evening she began to question me. She sensitized me—sometimes in a very painful way—to what she called my fascist elitism, arrogance, and the vestiges of racism that she detected in my thinking and behavior. Most important, she acquainted me with the aims of the American socialist movement of the 1930s, so that when I went back to Germany I was willing to look with an open mind at the Social Democratic Party as an option in the upcoming elections, the first I would vote in.

I returned to Germany in the fall of 1952 a very different person from the young woman I had been when I left. I was eager to be involved in the political scene of postwar Germany. I felt it was an obligation I owed the Fulbright Commission to work for peace, for international understanding, for a new and transformed Germany in some leadership capacity. I did not want to go back to the University of Tübingen, much as I had loved its idyllic setting. I chose Bonn University because it was the capital of West Germany and the center of political life in the Federal Republic. I knew I could find part-time work there with the English-speaking embassies while I finished my degree. And work I did need, as my refugee scholarship provided no more than the monthly rent for one room in the working-class part of town. From the start I ran into difficulties with the bureaucracy, which questioned my eligibility for an expellee student grant, difficulties that it took me several months of almost daily visits to settle with the bureaucrat in charge. He finally gave in only because he realized that he was no match for my stubborn insistence on my right. I had hated being a refugee from the time we left Strehlen in January 1945. Nothing with regard to being an unwanted refugee had changed when I came back from the States. But this time around I found it harder to accept being treated like a worthless charity case. In the United States I had had the experience of being a valuable member of society.

It took me even less time to become disillusioned with university life at Bonn. A former housemate at the student hostel in Tübingen had enrolled there the previous year. I thought that by knowing him I at least had an entry into the student community. Interested in a position as high school teacher in the school system, my friend had become a member of a conservative fraternity hardly in tune with my newfound interest in social and political causes. For a while I went to the fraternity dances and socials, but soon the attitudes toward women students there—"is she marriage material?" I overheard them asking—repelled me. Through this same friend and through my eager participation in a seminar on eighteenth-century British literature, I gained admittance to the inner circle of the English department and its research seminar. I had changed to a double major in English and German literature, hoping that a degree in comparative literature might open more opportunities. I soon learned that my chances as a woman for a German university career were poor at best. When one of the older women students who had an excellent reputation as a scholar was passed over in a competition for a lecturer position in favor of a male student, I realized that a university career was probably out of the question. I talked to a number of journalists, thinking that working for the press might be something I'd like. But here, too, chances for a woman were slim. With a friend whose father served in the diplomatic service, I inquired about a career in the Foreign Service. Again I encountered the prevailing gender bias.

What remained for me was to contemplate a career in high school teaching and to take the required courses and exam in pedagogy. After attending a seminar meeting on teaching methodologies, I gave up on this plan. The course, announced as "progressive education," dealt with the educational theories of a nineteenth-century pedagogue in the Pestalozzi tradition. The pedagogue's essays and the first seminar meeting struck me as grotesquely antiquated, and I flatly refused to continue in the course, thus ending any consideration of a career in high school teaching. In light of the climate of deepening conservatism in the Federal Republic in the 1950s, the beginning of parliamentary discussions to reintroduce military service was the last straw for me. Ever since the end of the war, the call among members of my postwar cohort had been "Nie wieder Krieg" (Never again war). It was therefore a matter of course that I, like many of my fellow students in Bonn, took part in a protest march. The march itself passed without incident. But the press and the government denounced the spontaneous protest as inspired by the Communist Party of East Germany. Nothing could have been further from the truth.

My struggle with the bureaucracy and my uncertain position in the university reminded me at every step that I was a refugee with dubious prospects, a woman who at best would be taken for an industrious drone in some office job. As far as political change in the country was concerned, none was in sight. The intellectual and political climate called for the restoration of a conservative bourgeoisie.

My work at the embassies as translator and tutor to various officials from the British, Australian, American, and Canadian trade commissions, while paying me enough to live on without having to resort to factory work, had the added advantage of providing emotional relief. At the embassies I was a young German intellectual valued for her knowledge of German and English, of German history and the current political and even economic situation. Translating at a German-Australian trade conference, I could advise my Australian employer what was produced in what region of Germany. But this work was at best transitory. And since I felt unwanted in Germany, I increasingly began to wonder if I should just emigrate—anywhere.

The issue came to a head after I had completed my research at the British Museum in London for a doctoral thesis on English autobiography and the origins of the British novel. I had to have a degree for some kind of a career— I still had no idea in what exact field. I had been in constant contact through the mail with my American friends of the mayor's family. When I wrote them that I needed time free from the duties at the embassies to complete the writing of my thesis, they invited me to live with them for a year, during which I would get the thesis written. I accepted the invitation without a second thought. At that point all I wanted was to get out of Germany.

I had scarcely arrived at my friends' house near Providence when I received a telephone call from the dean at Pembroke College. "I heard from Mrs. Lark," she explained, "that you are back in the country working on your thesis. I understand that the Brown German department is looking for a teaching assistant to help them teach their elementary German course. They had larger enrollments in German than they expected. Would you be interested in part-time teaching for a small stipend and free tuition?"

I hesitated. "I'll need to ask my hosts," I told her, "whether my taking a job would interfere with their plans." That evening at the dinner table I told the

Larks about the dean's offer, and they, though somewhat reluctantly, agreed that the opportunity to teach and to take a few graduate courses would be good for me. I phoned back the next morning and was told to appear at the German department office at 7:50 A.M. the following day. At 7:30 on a Wednesday morning, Mr. Lark, who had a law office in downtown Providence, delivered me to Marston Hall, then home to the foreign language departments. At the appointed time the awkward, heavyset, perspiring young instructor in charge of the course handed me a textbook in first-year German. Obviously nervous, he gave me the room numbers of the classrooms of the three consecutive sections I was to teach and wished me luck.

I mounted the steps to the first-story cement classroom building, my knees shaking. The instructor's nervousness had shaken me. I found the classroom just as I heard the bell ring. I don't remember how I managed to get to the front desk with its lectern. All I knew was to hold on tight for fear I might faint. I opened the book I had been given to the first text page and said aloud, hoping my voice would not tremble as much as my knees did, "Open your books." Then I waited, listening to the pages turning.

"Say *Guten Morgen*," I managed.

"Kuden moarrgen," came back at me.

I was just about to say the next printed words on the page, when a boyish voice stopped me short and made me look up. Forty threatening eyes confronted me. Then the bright, hesitant voice got through to me.

"Miss, I have used a book like this before in my first-year French class. You are supposed to say the words in German from the German page and we are supposed to have the books open to the page with the English translation. You read a German phrase to us and we repeat it in German, and we know what it means from our English page. We repeat the phrases in German until we almost know them by heart. If we learn from hearing the language rather than from seeing it written," he added almost apologetically, "our pronunciation will be better."

I saw that the young man had stood up to explain. He was obviously trying to be helpful. Suddenly the class lost its threatening look. They were just a bunch of eighteen-year-olds looking at me, most of them even with a friendly and encouraging grin.

"Okay," I said, suddenly calm. "Let us do as you said." And then, as they turned the page, I spoke up again.

"Look, you guys, I just got the book ten minutes ago. I haven't got a clue what I am doing. But I do know German. I am from Germany. By tomorrow I'll have had a look at the book and will know what to do. I'll keep ahead of you. And we'll all learn it together." I knew then that I had them with me.

We started all over again. *Guten Morgen.*

"Okay, let's say it faster. *Guten Morgen.*" I egged them on. "Now, *Wie geht es Ihnen?* How are you?"

"Once again, *Wie geht es Ihnen?*"

I imitated the quavering voice of an old lady, exaggeratedly. *"Wie geht es Ihnen?"* They followed my cue, beginning to laugh.

"Und wie geht es Ihnen?" I assumed a deep bass voice. Again they followed my lead and changed into bass register.

"High voice," I called out. *"Es geht mir gut. I am fine."* We alternated back and forth in high and low register.

"Faster. *Es geht mir gut.*"

"Two of you." I pointed to two students. *"Es geht mir gut."*

"All of you: *Es geht mir gut.*" And so we played with the phrases for the entire hour. We knew it by heart by the time the bell rang. We laughed and had a good time. Their American accents dropped by the wayside as they imitated my exaggerated German. As I worked with them, I lost my shyness. I was totally in the moment, inventing new ways of saying what we had to learn, loudly, swiftly, whispering, in different voices. They were with me all the way, at first, I am sure, because they felt for me and wanted to help, but very soon because they were having a good time. The hour flew by.

When I looked at the empty classroom after the students had left, I knew that this was what I wanted to do: teach students like that. Learn with them, study, draw them along with me. I was exhilarated: I had found out what I wanted to do with my life. I was almost twenty-five years old. This moment was the closest I have ever come to having an epiphany.

Everything fell into place after that class. I finished my Ph.D. at Brown within three years. My friends helped me get a green card. I got a position as a university lecturer and then, after I finished my thesis on the expressionist poet Georg Heym, an assistant professorship. I did not return to Germany till 1969—and then only for a sabbatical leave. By then the German student rebellion had begun, exposing Nazis who had remained in powerful positions and dealing publicly with Germany's Nazi past. I was in full sympathy with that student generation. But by that time I was an American.

EPILOGUE

IN *The Inability to Mourn* (1967), Alexander and Margarete Mitscherlich formulated a theory that Germans needed to mourn Hitler's death and the loss of the ego-ideal he had become for them before they could become a healthy democratic society. As much as I agree with this theory, I do not think that many Germans worked through their attachment to the Nazi ego-ideal or mourned its loss. The change that made democracy in Germany possible came from the children of the Nazis, the generation of 1968. But I believe that the Mitscherlichs' theory, with some modifications, did apply to me and to others of the so-called Hitler Youth generation, the cohort of Germans born between 1925 and 1935 who spent their entire childhood and adolescence under National Socialism.

I reacted to Hitler's death and our abandonment by our HJ leaders as a betrayal that disillusioned me and then made me furiously angry. Anger easily turned on the entire older generation of Germans, whose past I mistrusted and whose motives I questioned long before the 1968 generation came along. Out of my disillusionment and anger grew my wish to survive, to shape my own destiny, and to come to understand what had happened to me, my family, and my country. This challenge never let me go. From the end of the war until I arrived in the United States I was much too preoccupied with mere survival and with study to allow myself to feel much of anything beyond that anger. Full understanding of what my countrymen had done to everyone they defined as "other" came only in the United States, once I met and came to know survivors, and once I became a teacher. Mourning and grief came only gradually, first for long lost family members and friends, and for my child-hood home. Because I had accepted Hitler as a substitute father—distant and demanding, to be sure—mourning for my real father was particularly painful and conflicted. Shame is the one response to my involvement in Hitler's cause that I still feel as keenly as ever.

I was never sorry that I decided to stay in the United States. After com-pleting my Ph.D. in German literature at Brown University, I accepted a posi-tion as instructor of German at the University of California, Santa Barbara. Through many years at UCSB, I gradually advanced to professor of German literature and professor of women's studies. When I started teaching at UCSB, the student body numbered fifteen hundred undergraduates. This number had grown to twenty thousand undergraduate and graduate students by the time I retired in 1993. In a developing institution, I had opportunities that I would not have had at a more established campus. Even as I taught courses in German literature to undergraduates and graduate students, I served the campus community in many functions (as associate director of the UC Educa-tion Abroad Program, department chair, and associate dean of the College of Letters and Science). Most important, however, I was able to help shape the teaching priorities of my departments and of the Humanities Division of the campus. The university's philosophy, which stressed the close interrelationship between teaching and research, suited my temperament, though teaching always remained my first love and priority. It was teaching and my students that got me through whatever personal crises I experienced, and throughout these difficulties I never missed a day of teaching. I was fortunate that my de-partment always allowed me to develop my own courses and to co-teach with faculty from departments as diverse as art history, film studies, history, phi-losophy, and sociology. Together with colleagues and students, I could explore the literary, sociopolitical, psychological, and ethical dimensions of the prob-lems that I lived through in my first twenty years: Nazism, war, trauma, the shame of surviving, the Holocaust, loss of home, country, friends, and loved ones. Teaching, for me, was always about learning together with my students and trying to understand existential dilemmas.

I did not participate in the American political scene until the late 1960s, in part because I felt that as a foreigner I needed to get to know the coun-try and its traditions better before taking political stands, in part because the conservative politics of the 1950s and early 1960s in America alienated me as much as their German equivalent had during the Adenauer era. The Vietnam

War and the student rebellion changed my indifference, and I became a citizen expressly to participate in the struggle to end the war and to end racism and the withholding of civil rights from the nonwhite people of the country. My teaching American students about Nazism, about the ways Germans dealt with their Nazi past, and about the Holocaust was always focused on helping them to understand where militarism and racism in any form could lead.

During the first ten years of my American life, I returned to Germany only twice, for brief visits to my family and work at literary archives. Like many immigrants, I wanted to integrate myself into my new home and to leave old stories behind me. In fact, during both visits to Germany I had nightmares that I had lost my passport and would not be able to return to the United States. My mother joined me for a number of years in the States, as she had failed to establish herself as an independent dressmaker in West Germany and worked as a seamstress in a garment factory. She returned to Germany when she retired and lived in Delmenhorst until her death at age eighty-four.

I did not lose my uneasy relationship to Germany, and except for professional reasons I rarely spoke German. For the next four decades, when I traveled in Germany I limited my time in the country to six weeks or less, explaining to my friends, only half in jest, "I can stand being in Germany for six weeks at best. Then I need to get abroad to England for a break." I am amused when Germans on my short visits compliment me. "You speak excellent German for an American," they say. During the last fifteen years or so, as my brothers, their families, and I have visited each other regularly, I have become more comfortable with the country of my birth.

I went back to Silesia with both my brothers, Jochen and Werner, and Jochen's eighteen-year-old daughter, Annette, in 1983. By that time my brothers had established themselves in their respective careers, were long since married, and had teenage children. We three siblings, then in our late forties and early fifties, had spent no time together since we were separated at ages fourteen, thirteen, and eight. Walking through the ruins of the still destroyed town of Strzelin, we reestablished the exact same—poor—relationship that we had had as children, we older two walking and talking together, with Jochen in the lead, while Werner, five steps behind us, muttered his disagreement with where we were going and what we were doing. It took us a while to relate to each other as the adults we had become. None of us could reconcile the town we saw with the town we remembered. When we drove through the countryside that I had walked and biked through so often, neither I nor they recognized a single one of the villages we passed through. Houses had been torn down; gardens had become fields. New trees had grown up where old ones had fallen; different crops grew in the fields, or fields had become woods. The names of streets, towns, and villages had all been changed to Polish names. Even German business names had been removed with heavy gray paint. We realized with shock how completely our common past had been erased when we could not find Father's or our grandparents' graves in the town cemetery; even the gravestones and family burial vaults, with their German inscriptions, had disappeared. The cemetery had become a park, its chestnut trees a huge forest. On a late afternoon walk, after we gave up looking, we found by chance some gravestones that peeped forth from a heap of garbage half-buried outside the cemetery wall. Gravestones with German names hidden from whose eyes? Vaults dismantled and buried to erase any trace of what once had been a different reality?

It was only then that we realized how afraid the Polish authorities must have been, even as late as the 1980s, that the Germans who had lived here until the end of World War II might want to reclaim Silesia. We did not, of course; that is not why we had come. We had come because we were curious about what the place we had grown up in had been like. We discovered that the place we visited in 1983 was no longer what we had known as home. I realized then that a place, once lost, is gone forever; there is no such thing as the possibility of returning, let alone a right to return. Other generations had grown up in my childhood world. The place we had lost was theirs now. My brothers and I were fortunate that we were young when we were expelled. They and their families in West Germany, and I in California, had grown roots there because young people do grow new roots. My mother's generation fared differently. Although they were compensated for some of their economic losses, many, my mother among them, did not grow roots in their new homes. They lost the war and they lost their home. Even if they did not participate actively in Nazism, the Holocaust, and the war, they tolerated all of it, wittingly or unwittingly. They paid for this with the loss of their homes and their roots. Not that we, the generation of Germans who grew up during the Nazi period, got off scot-free. When we get together, Jochen and I talk about the *what ifs*. Who would I have become if . . . ? Our uneasy questioning, our shame, remorse, and uncertainty is the price we pay, a psychological price.

The fall of the Berlin Wall and the subsequent reunification of Germany in 1989–90 surprised me. I had not thought that it would happen in my lifetime, nor did I think it should. I considered a united and hence more powerful Germany in the heart of Europe too great a threat to peace. Like many intellectuals of the Left, I feared that the democratic tradition in Germany was not strong enough to counteract the authoritarianism, jingoism, and anti-Semitism that, however muted or subliminal, were still alive and well. Since then I have become more optimistic, as the former Democratic Republic, slowly but surely, reintegrates with the former Federal Republic, and as all-German institutions establish a democratic track record.

In these pages I have written repeatedly that even as a teenager I felt at times a leaden depression and a profound alienation from my family. The fear, deprivation, traumatic separations, and disillusionments of the end of the war, the invasion, and the expulsion took their psychic toll. For years my intellectual curiosity and my determination to get an education kept the depression and the fears and alienation at bay. As a university student, Sartre's existentialism had helped: I learned from Sartre that the world is only meaningful as long as we individual humans make it meaningful. In this way I reasoned away my emotional emptiness. It was my task, my ethical imperative, to create meaning for myself and for my community. But all through my twenties I had no understanding of what this intellectualization of ethics entailed. I did not realize that I had no access at all to the feelings that allow you to make something meaningful. Access to emotions like grief and joy lay beyond my conscious deliberations and rationalizations. Except for occasional panic, occasional terrifying nightmares, I did not feel much of anything. In fact, I was proud that I had my emotions under such excellent control. I believed that I had come through the Nazi and war years and the deprivations that followed quite well. The occasional nightmares were the price you pay when you grow up in a country like mine, I told myself.

This façade began to crumble when I achieved material security. I discovered one night that nothing I did, knew, had loved, been curious about, cared for—not even teaching—mattered to me or, I thought, to anyone else. I realized that most days I was living in a world of gray, in perpetual fog, without aim or direction. Nothing and no one mattered to me. It was as if I inhabited Santayana's world of facts that do not matter, that have no relationship to anything or anyone. The world of facts stared back at me emptily. I felt that I was caught in a world of metaphors: encased in steel-hard glass walls, birds falling dead from electric wires. One night, having not slept for a week, I tried to kill myself with sleeping pills. Before going under, I called my physician.

On his advice, after the suicide attempt, I went to a psychiatrist, more to pacify my doctor than from a conviction that anything or anyone could be of help or free me from the walls of glass that imprisoned me. After a few meetings, I quit. I thought that talking about my bouts of panic and my nightmares had helped somewhat. At least for a time, I was no longer as tense as I had become over the years of silence that I had imposed on myself since high school. Since I had talked about some of the experiences that troubled me, I felt that this was all that verbal therapy could do for me.

It took me another eight years to admit to myself that I was bankrupt emotionally. By that time I had had a number of exciting but ultimately humiliating and self-defeating affairs. They provoked physical reactions that I took for emotions. But one day I had to face the fact that they no longer did. I felt dead. I had come to an impasse in my research; I simply could not make myself write or, for that matter, read or think. When I called my former therapist in a panic about having come to an absolute standstill, he saw me immediately. I knew only one thing at the time: that I did not want to kill myself. I did not want to betray my students by this gesture of ultimate despair. But I struggled with suicidal thoughts for many years.

Over a long period I learned to trust my therapist. I moved into a psychiatric halfway house on my therapist's advice to learn to relate to others and to overcome my isolation, to feel safe, to accept that I was understood, to grieve my father's death and my mother's rejections, and to express what I felt clearly and honestly. As I became more comfortable with myself there, in the company of patients much more ill and in need of care than I ever was, I learned to risk becoming engaged with them, to empathize with them, to respect them, and to become their friend. Throughout these years, I used most of my therapy to talk about and analyze my development, my experiences, my motives and goals. My nightmares had stopped rather early in my therapy, but a constant subliminal fear stayed with me. I refused to call it anxiety because it felt like a very specific thing, like a pestilent blob ready to engulf me. I spent most of my time trying to figure out why. Every psychoanalytical theory I read seemed to fit this or that experience or motive. A few times, one insight or another would, for a moment, break through the glass wall that I felt surrounded me, only to evaporate, leaving me as hemmed in as ever.

Gradually I regained my enthusiasm for teaching. Small existential experiences with students, fellow patients, and friends helped me. I began to lose my anxiety about and distrust of others only after I came to realize that I felt better when I was with them on a daily basis. It was not so much the talking that helped as being with, or being at ease in, a group of familiar people. At the time, my therapist spoke a lot of my need to learn *to be*. It seemed an empty phrase to me. But since I felt that I had no other choice, learning became a matter of trusting enough to take the ordinary steps my therapist said would not harm me and might do me some good—like joining the house group for a camping trip. Even deciding to go along on a camping trip was an achievement. At first, I had refused. I had told everyone that, after sleeping on the ground during the Russian invasion, I was never, ever going to go camping. I had had more of camping than anyone was entitled to. Overcoming the arrogance of "been there, done that," which foreclosed further experience, was part of the solution. Understanding that fact, I went on the camping trip with the same attitude that I had gradually adopted about everything in therapy: "I don't want to do it—but I'll do it anyway."

The first night of the trip we were late to arrive at the campsite. It was dark, the campground unlit, and we put our sleeping bags down on a gentle slope. An hour later we discovered that we had bedded down next to a railroad line that was still in use. We were safe enough, but roaring freight trains woke us every hour or so. Trains rattling through my sleep took me back to Silesia, to uneasiness and discomfort. And yet I slept. When I woke up, with friends still asleep on either side of me, I felt cheerful and even looked forward to the day ahead. It was little daily revelations—like waking up in a cheerful mood if I was with friends—that made me realize that my therapist's ordinary prescriptions were on the right track. Yet I continued to resist his suggestions every step of the way. Each resistance taught me something about myself, yet this did not stop me from resisting the next suggestion. Slowly I learned that if I resisted something my therapist suggested would be helpful, then it probably was something I needed to experience.

Yet try as I might—and I conscientiously managed to overcome my resistance—my depression only became more tolerable. It never lifted entirely. I was no longer so tense that my jaw hurt from clenching my teeth, as it had when I began therapy. Most of the time I was sufficiently comfortable in social relationships to no longer feel an overwhelming need to isolate myself. I taught, I worked as an administrator, I did my research, and I wrote again. For all intents and purposes, I was what you would call "cured."

After having had little contact with my family in Germany, I began to take an interest in my brothers' families, particularly in my nieces and nephews.

When one of my nieces asked if she could visit me during summer vacation, I invited her to do so if she could buy her own ticket. A year later she wrote that she had earned the money for her flight by working as an aide in a hospital. We made arrangements for a summer stay.

She was fifteen at the time, the age at which I had to become an adult. I met her, somewhat late, at the Los Angeles airport at two o'clock in the morning. There she was, a pale, slender teenager in a blue frock standing forlornly next to an oversized suitcase and looking for me. Most of the other passengers had already left, I noted, suddenly contrite for being late, and here she was, waiting patiently. She helped me lug the suitcase to my vw Beetle parked some way off. She came with me, so full of trust, as if she had known me all her life. For all I knew she had seen me twice, on short visits when I had seen her as the shyest of my older brother's four children. For the rest of the night we shared a sofa bed in a friend's guestroom. Looking down on her as she slept, I knew with a certainty I had never known before that I would never betray her trust in me. This certainty gave me a sense of direction that I had not experienced since I had worked so desperately to obtain an education as a teenager myself. Over the following years, my bond to her, and then to her son, became the most rewarding I have had in my life.

Even as I was still struggling with a depression that often left me angry and helpless to shake it, and that never allowed me to enjoy the good fortune I had in my work, in my bond with my niece, in my opportunities to travel, or in finding new interests like sculpting, my therapist had an idea that at first left me speechless. He suggested, when I was making plans for a sabbatical leave, "Why don't you just go to the beach? Take a bucket and a shovel. Just play, and see what happens."

I thought he had gone off his rocker. A few days later, he was at it again. "My son is just entering nursery school, at a parent-child workshop. Why don't you volunteer there? Play with the kids, in the sand, you know."

Having nothing to lose and some free time while I was working on my research on child abuse, I took up his suggestion and one morning appeared at the nursery school, located in a neighboring farm community between the railroad and a major highway. I found the school, a temporary barracks and an enclosed play yard with a sandbox and swings at the end of an unpaved road, close to the municipal sewage facility, the local beach, and a eucalyptus grove. I had spoken to the head of the school by phone and explained that I wanted to work with children as a volunteer. After a brief conversation with the head of the school, I was assigned the job of supervising the children in pasting colored tissue paper on forms they had cut out earlier.

"Just prepare the glue, and cut some more tissue paper, and let the children do whatever they want," the head had advised. I had hardly any time to think about what I was doing as the three- and four- and five-year-olds pressed about me. I found myself talking to them in a continuous stream of words as they chattered back to me. I noticed only much later that I chattered with them as if I had done so all my life, spontaneously, without a thought. And that they felt entirely at ease with me. Time passed so quickly that I regretted the morning was over, after we had all sat in a circle and sung a number of songs to the guitar accompaniment of one of the mothers.

As I drove home, I began to cry. I stopped at a quiet park by the roadside and parked my car, sobbing from deep inside my gut. Fortunately, the park was empty. I had no thoughts, I just sat in my car and wept. I did not even try to stop, I just let it happen. I had my therapy appointment an hour later and arrived at the session still crying. It was the first time in many years that I did not say a single word. I just sat on the couch and cried. My therapist sat with me and let me cry. It felt comforting, and at the end of the hour I left lighter, a bit more at ease.

I had agreed with the head of the school that I would come twice weekly. On my next visit the three hours passed as quickly as they had the first time. I was in charge of the sandbox and helped with building a garden there with trees made out of grass and weeds and flowerbeds made out of colored pebbles. Playing with the children I felt as if I were their age, or rather I did not think much at all. I chatted with them, asked questions, did favors, helped where my fingers could tie some blades of grass together more easily than theirs. The moment I got in the car, the tears started. I drove back to the park and sat there and wept. It did not even occur to me to ask myself why I was crying. When I saw my therapist after my third time at the workshop, crying as before, he asked me, "How many times did you go to the school this past week?"

"I said I'd volunteer twice a week," I responded.

"You said! Here, finally, something does you some good, and you schedule it! Go every day!"

I went every morning, and every day, after a few thoughtlessly comfortable hours with the children, I stopped at the park and wept—wept until I had no more tears, usually for an hour. For the rest of the day I did whatever task had to be done and worked on my research more effortlessly than I ever had before. Toward the end of my six-month sabbatical leave, I had to face going back to full-time administrative work and teaching. No more nursery school. It seemed unthinkable. And yet I was ashamed. What should I tell my colleagues? That I wanted to quit my job because I needed to go to nursery school? Unthinkable. And yet, ludicrously enough, that was the truth.

I decided to leave my administrative position for "personal reasons." Fortunately, I was able to arrange my teaching schedule for the afternoons. In the mornings I went to my nursery school. The crying stopped after a year. I gradually felt at ease with myself and gained a sureness about what I felt and what I wanted that I had never had. A number of friends who watched this process questioned me and even teased me about my unwillingness to analyze why I wept. To my surprise, I got very angry.

"Leave me fucking be! I'll cry as much as I want to! I analyzed and analyzed until I was blue in the face and it did me little good. This does. So shut up."

Of course I knew that I had come full circle. Not back to the womb. Just back to kindergarten, before Father's death.

On a clear February day, the activities teacher, a number of mothers, and I took most of the children for a walk to the butterfly grove. On the California coast we have a number of such groves that serve the monarch butterflies as a stopover on their winter peregrinations. On crisp days clusters of butterflies hang down from the eucalyptus trees, and as the sun warms them they begin to swarm and the air fills with fluttering spots of bright yellow and light golden brown against the deep blue sky and silvery-green trees. We followed the meadow along the creek, crossed a small bridge, and ambled along a suburban road, houses on one side, the grove on the other behind a high fence. As I often did on such occasions, I brought up the rear of our procession with a few straggling three-year-olds whose legs had tired from sloshing through fallen leaves by the creek side. At the entrance to the grove, by an open gate, even my stragglers began to run toward the trees. Little dwarves with big heads, flying hair caught by dappled sunlight. Some of the older children had reached the trees and started shaking a few of the trees' lower branches. A swarm of butterflies rose up and moved about, caught now by the rays of the sun. As I looked, almost blinded by the sunlight, the air filled with butterflies as the children jumped up and down, trying to touch them. A dance of children and butterflies on the meadow among the eucalyptus trees. Little arms raised on high into the air to catch an airiness so evanescent, so gleaming.

Small, golden yellow arms stretched toward the blue of the sky and the silver of the trees. Heads bobbing up and down, the melody of their cries sending more butterflies into the air, tumbling up and down and up and down. I stood transfixed, bathed in a cloud of yellow happiness. So this is what joy feels like, I realized. Joy: children and butterflies dancing on sunbeams on a crisp California morning.

I stopped working at the parent-child workshop some five years later, after having gradually reduced my hours when I again became more involved in my work at the university. By this time, though ready for a hip replacement and almost incapable of running after the children, I felt whole. The actual butterfly children of that February morning had long since moved on, and I was ready to live my life.

It was only as I was writing this account of my growing up that I fully realized and understood why I had wept for a year. In writing, the town I lived in as a child arose in my mind as it had been both before and after it was destroyed. To my surprise, I celebrated its streets, its churches, its schools, its businesses, and its parks and trees. As a child living there, I did not know that I had loved these things. In realizing that I loved them, I was able to mourn their loss. And I knew that I wanted to record what of the town fell victim to fire and dynamite during the final days of the war, and what survived.

By writing, my parents came alive again. I could understand what had driven them and attempt to make my peace with them. In my writing, my grandparents came to life. This time around I could express what I felt for them, my love then and my compassion and love now. I could finally mourn them, even as I set them a memorial. I could revive the friends of my childhood and my teen years, and in writing of them, mourn them. I could re-create what I felt for my teachers, for those whom I loved and for those about whom I felt profound ambivalence, a mixture of gratitude and revulsion. Through writing, all of them came alive, and I could mourn their loss. But I do not think that I can ever escape the questioning of my Nazi experience. On the contrary, with age and greater knowledge and insight, with openness to new friends of different national, ethnic, and social backgrounds, my self-questioning has become more demanding and more keenly felt.

BOOKS CONSULTED

Friedlander, Saul. *Memory, History, and the Extermination of the Jews of Europe*. Bloomington: Indiana University Press, 1993.

Harvey, Elizabeth. *Women and the Nazi East: Agents and Witnesses of Germanization*. New Haven: Yale University Press, 2003.

Hoffmeister, Gerhart, and Frederic Tubach. *Germany: 2000 Years*. Vol. 3, *From the Nazi Era to German Unification*. New York: Continuum Books, 1992.

Kater, Michael. *Hitler Youth*. Cambridge: Harvard University Press, 2004.

Klee, Ernst, Willi Dressen, and Volker Ries, eds. *The Good Old Days as Seen by Its Perpetrators and Bystanders*. Translated by Deborah Burnstone. New York: Free Press, 1991.

Koch, H. W. *The Hitler Youth: Origins and Development, 1922–1945*. London: Macdonald and Jane's, 1975.

LaCapra, Dominick. *History and Memory After Auschwitz*. Ithaca: Cornell University Press, 1998.

Levi, Primo. *Moments of Reprieve: A Memoir of Auschwitz*. New York: Penguin Books, 1995.

Moeller, Robert G. *War Stories: The Search for a Usable Past in the Federal Republic of Germany*. Berkeley and Los Angeles: University of California Press, 2001.

Moses, Fritz. *Strehlen: Erinnerungen an eine Kleinstadt und ihre jüdischen Bürger*. Bremen: Edition Temmen, 1995.

Nicholas, Lynn H. *Cruel World: The Children of Europe in the Nazi Web*. New York: Knopf, 2005.

Niven, Bill. *Germans as Victims: Remembering the Past in Contemporary Germany*. New York: Palgrave Macmillan, 2006.

Reese, Dagmar. *Growing Up Female in Nazi Germany*. Translated by William Templer. Ann Arbor: University of Michigan Press, 2006.

Rieber, Alfred J., ed. *Forced Migration in Central and Eastern Europe, 1939–1950*. London: F. Cass, 2000.

Sander, Helke, and Barbara Johr, eds. *Befreier und Befreite: Krieg, Vergewaltigungen, Kinder*. Munich: Antje Kunstmann GmbH, 1992.

Sternheim-Peters, Eva. *Habe ich denn alleine gejubelt: Eine Jugend im Nationalsozialismus*. Cologne: Verlag Wissenschaft und Politik, 2000.

Wolf, Christa. *Patterns of Childhood*. Translated by Ursule Molinaro and Hedwig Rappolt. New York: Farrar, Straus and Giroux, 1984.

A Woman in Berlin: Eight Weeks in the Conquered City, a Diary by Anonymous. Translated by Philip Boehm. New York: Metropolitan Books, 2005.

Zweig, Stefan. *The World of Yesterday*. Lincoln: University of Nebraska Press, 1964.

INDEX

Page numbers in italics refer to photographs and illustrations. The designation "UM" refers to Ursula Mahlendorf.

comradeship, Jungmädel, 95, 105, 107,
109–10, 132, 145–46, 166. *See also*
friends/friendships
concentration camps, 25, 26, 41, 64,
245, 291
survivors of, 69, 217, 269, 289, 321
Confessional Church, 150–51
confirmation, 150–51, 158–59
confiscation, 94, 265
conflict, 93, 269, 288
among Allies, 269, 288
UM's internal, 5, 58, 143, 179
conformity, 2, 134
conservatism, return of, 69, 329, 330, 334
conspiracy, against Hitler, 173, 174, 209
constitution(s), 38, 39, 310–11
consumption, material, 307–8
Cornet (Rilke), 199–200
Crabwalk (Grass), 10
Crimea, invasion of, 151
crying, 341, 342, 343
culture, 63, 64–65, 280, 306–7
curfew, 136, 175, 178, 249, 250
curiosity, 82, 121, 167, 203, 304. *See also*
higher education, UM's striving
for; reading, UM's love of
currency reform, 305–7, 312, 327. *See also*
economic miracle, West German
Czechoslovakia, 42, 235

Daphne blossoms, 262
death(s). *See* Gebel, Grandmother (Oma),
death of; Mahlendorf, Ernst
(father), death of; Mahlendorf,
Grandfather, death of
death camps, 282. *See also* concentration camps
Deeping, George Warrick, 167
defeat
understanding of, 3, 9, 10, 76, 208, 252
World War I, 36
World War II, 10, 185, 221–22
defeatist attitudes, 106, 153, 154, 155

de la Roche, Mazo, 294
delinquents, 178, 314–15
Delmenhorst Evangelical Church, 280
Delmenhorst, living in, 277, 288, 292,
297, 299, 302–4
delousing, 272, 276
democracy. *See also* Weimar Republic
education in, 294, 295, 310–11
establishment of, 10, 271, 303–4, 307,
333, 337
denazification, 290–91
Denmark, invasion of, 82–83, 85
deportation. *See* quarry workers,
deportation of
depression, 133, 318, 323, 337–38, 339, 340
deserters, execution of, 189, 190
despair, 30, 196, 198, 295, 307, 323, 338
destruction, 9, 10, 233, 252, 284. *See also*
bombing(s)
Dinarian racial type, 127
discipline
Hitler Youth, 91, 114, 165
Lotte's, 254
at teacher seminary, 175, 179, 183
disillusionment, 3, 9, 183, 333
with Hitler Youth, 7, 131, 132, 256
displaced persons, 304
distrust, 115, 161, 204, 298, 308–9, 338
Dolchstosslegende, 36, 42
Dönitz, Field Marshall, 208
Dream (Cicero), 302
Dresden, 268
Dunisch, Frau, 139–41, 144, 229
at Adelheide, 276, 281
library of, 140, 150, 175
medical supplies' distribution, 248–
49, 251, 261, 263, 264–65
Red Cross work, 246, 266, 267–68
Dunkirk (France), 84
Dürer, Albrecht, 298
Dutchmen, 127
duty, 114, 170
Dwinger, E. E., 141

Realschule, 77
rebellion. *See also* Hitler Youth (HJ),
    resistance to
    generation of 1968, 291, 309, 311, 322,
        332, 335
    youthful, 90, 107
recycling collections, 95, 103–4, 117
Red Cross
    community nursing, 246–48, 249,
        250, 263
    training course, 193–200
    work at Habelschwerdt hospital,
        201–13
Red School (Strehlen), 30, 228
reeducation, 10–11, 40, 295, 311
refugees. *See also* expellees; resettlement
    assistance for, 11, 187, 188, 292, 320
    denazification of, 290
    distribution of, 271–72, 273
    from eastern provinces, 10, 319–20, 321
    ethnic German, 180
    organizations of, 311–12, 319
    Polish, 130
    from Russian invasion, 269, 310
    scholarships for, 316, 318, 319–20, 328
    stories of, 297
    UM as, 76, 191–92, 213–26, 269–304,
        328–29, 330
regeneration, 295, 303, 307
regimentation, 6, 149
Reglaff (classmate), 323, 324
rehabilitation
    criminals, 314–15
    wounded soldiers, 163, 166
Reich. *See* Third Reich
Reichsjugendführung, 113
Reichskanzler, 22, 38, 39. *See also* Hitler,
    Adolf
Reichskulturkammer, 64
Reichspräsident, 36, 38, 39
Reichstag, 38, 39
Reitsch, Hanna, 95
rejection, 133, 184, 199, 255, 297, 310

religion, 20, 150, 295. *See also* confirma-
    tion; *and individual religions*
reparations
    to Israel, 69, 321
    World War I, 13
repression
    of emotions, 123, 179, 337–38
    of memory, 4–5
research
    background, 3, 5
    on German child abuse, 7, 340
    on juvenile crime, 314–15
    love of, 323, 334, 338
resentment, 257, 261, 301, 303. *See also*
    anger
Reserve Police Battalion 101, 26
resettlement, 10, 262–63, 265–68, 271,
    320–21
resistance
    German, 178, 206, 290
    Protestant, 151
    UM's, 2, 149, 159–60, 254, 339
responsibility, evasion of, 26–27, 289,
    291, 295, 307, 308–9, 336
retreat. *See* German troops, retreat by
Rhineland, reclamation of, 42
Richter, Hans Peter, 4
Riedel, Manfred (friend), 27, 43, 44
    father of, 48, 105–6, 168
rifles, learning to shoot, 196–97
Right, political, 10, 13. *See also* Nazi
    Party
    censorship by, 63
    struggles with the Left, 19, 38–39
    teachers, 161
    women's groups, 96
    youth groups, 91, 93
Rilke, Rainer Maria, 174, 199–200, 260
Rita (Pembroke student), 327–28
role models, 166–67, 169–70, 183–84,
    251, 269
Romans, descendants of, 127
romanticism, 90, 299

Rommel, Field Marshal, 129, 130, 152
Ruhr, reclamation of, 42
ruins, 238–39, 243, 269. *See also* bombing(s); Strehlen, devastation in
rumors
    of Nazi corruption, 144
    Polish occupation, 237, 239, 258
    among refugees, 220–21
    resettlement, 262–63, 272, 273
    Russian invasion, 211, 223
running, 104–5, 109–10, 134
Rushdie, Salman, 1
Russia, German invasion of, 26, 85,
        106–7, 110–11, 129–30, 151–52, 162
Russians
    invasion by, 9–10, 76, 181, 185, *186*,
        188–89, 192–93, 198–99, 211–20,
        225–26, 269, 337
    occupation by, 20, 223, 228, 233, 235,
        236, 242, 244, 273, 310
    persecution of, 289
    prisoners of war, 142, 210
    rapes by, 210, 211, 212, 214, 220, 231,
        252–53, 255–56
Russian zone, 271

Saarland, return of, 42
sacrifice, 93, 101, 105, 111, 132, 192, 311
sagas, 97. *See also* myths
Santayana, George, 337
Sartre, Jean-Paul, 337
Schäfer, Fräulein (teacher), 35, 43, 56
Scherzer, Frau (seminary teacher), 165,
        168, 174, 175–76, 181, 182
    relationship with, 166–67, 169–70,
        183–84, 303
    visits to, 251–53, 256–57
Schirach, Baldur von, 92–93, 94, 96, 103,
        113, 161
Schmagoostern, 51–52
Schmidchen (classmate), 323
Schmidt, Herr (teacher), 128–29, 130
Schmidt-Rotluff, Karl, 298

scholarships
    Fulbright, 303, 320, 325, 326–28
    high school, 78, 79, 287, 297, 307
    refugee, 316, 318, 319–20, 328
    university, 316, 322, 324
school system, 20, 44, 76–77, 96–97, 161.
        See also education
Schulte, Helene and Richard (cousins),
        70–73, 84, 85–89, 115–17, 150
Schultüte, 43
Schutzstaffel (ss), 62
    arrests by, 177–78
    crimes of, 289
    eugenics program, 198
    execution of deserters, 189, 190
    harassment of Jews by, 63, 65–69
    hospital patient, 205–6
    schools run by, 161
    UM's father as member of, 2, 24–25
Schwab, Gustav, 170
sculptures, 9, 21, *54*, *57*, 123, 146, 232
Sebald, W. G., 10
secret weapon, 154, 156, 166, 176, 179,
        181, 190
Selma (farm worker), 71
Senitz, visits to, 141–43, 155–56, 225
sentimentality, 131, 176
settlement. *See* resettlement
sex education, 82, 92, 121, 122, 123–24
shame, 3, 8, 58, 81, 182, 210
    of failing to protest, 289, 291
    over involvement in Hitler's cause,
        27, 334
shoes, 10, 44, 199, 223, 239, 251, 301–2
    shortages of, 137, 145
shortages, 6, 96, 103, 137, 145, 154. *See also*
        rationing/rationing cards
Silence in the Forest (Ganghofer), 155–56
Silesia, 127
    ceded to Poland, 235, 236
    dialects of, 71, 116, 164
    eviction from, 10, 131, 305
    history of, 20, 30, 129, 165